THE ANNOTATED COLLECTED POEMS

EDWARD THOMAS

THE ANNOTATED
Collected Poems

edited by
EDNA LONGLEY

BLOODAXE BOOKS

ISBN: 978 1 85224 746 1

First published 2008 by
Bloodaxe Books Ltd,
Highgreen,
Tarset,
Northumberland NE48 1RP.

Second impression 2008.

www.bloodaxebooks.com
For further information about Bloodaxe titles
please visit our website or write to
the above address for a catalogue.

Bloodaxe Books Ltd acknowledges
the financial assistance of
Arts Council England, North East.

Cover design: Neil Astley & Pamela Robertson-Pearce.

Printed in Great Britain by
Bell & Bain Limited, Glasgow, Scotland.

ACKNOWLEDGEMENTS

The editor and Bloodaxe Books are extremely grateful to the Executors of the Estate of Myfanwy Thomas for permission to quote from manuscripts and typescripts of Edward Thomas's poems; from his letters, diaries and notebooks; and from *The Childhood of Edward Thomas*. They are also indebted to Henry Holt & Co. for permission to quote from *Complete Poems of Robert Frost* (1949) and from (ed.) Lawrance Thompson, *Selected Letters of Robert Frost* (1964); and to Handsel Books, publishers of (ed.) Matthew Spencer, *Elected Friends: Robert Frost & Edward Thomas to one another* (2003).

Further thanks are owed to the following libraries: the Henry W. and Albert A. Berg Collection of English Literature, New York Public Library, Astor, Lenox and Tilden Foundations; the Bodleian Library; the British Library; Cardiff University Library; Dartmouth College Library; the Lockwood Memorial Library; and the National Library of Wales. The editor's personal thanks go to Richard Emeny and the Edward Thomas Fellowship; to Peter Keelan, Head of Special Collections and Archives, Cardiff University Library; to Guy Cuthbertson, Anne Margaret Daniel, Declan Kiely, Andrew Motion, Lucy Newlyn and John Pikoulis; and, above all, to Myfanwy Thomas, to whose memory this edition is dedicated.

CONTENTS

INTRODUCTION

In 1901 Edward Thomas (*b.* 1878) predicted a great future for the lyric poem: 'Increasing complexity of thought and emotion will find no such outlet as the myriad-minded lyric, with its intricacies of form'.[1] Thomas himself would do much to bring that future into being. He is among the half-dozen poets who, in the early twentieth century, remade English poetry. His closest aesthetic ally was Robert Frost, but he shared significant literary, cultural and political contexts with W.B. Yeats and Wilfred Owen. He was also in critical dialogue with emergent "modernism" as represented by Imagism and the first collections of Ezra Pound. While the academy has not always recognised Thomas's centrality to modern poetry, this neglect has been offset by readers' enthusiasm, and by the generations of poets, from W.H. Auden onwards, who have named Thomas as a key influence. Anne Harvey's anthology *Elected Friends: Poems for and about Edward Thomas* (1991) contains seventy-six items. *Branch-Lines: Edward Thomas and Contemporary Poetry* (2007) assembles more recent tributes from poets. The phenomenon of the "Edward Thomas poem" suggests that Thomas's poetry secretes core values, traditions and tricks of the trade.

This annotated *Collected Poems* is another kind of tribute. The Notes include a commentary on the poems. But their main purpose is to indicate, largely in Thomas's own words, the rich hinterland that sustained a uniquely intense poetic journey. In two years, facing towards war, Edward Thomas wrote a lifetime's poetry. Aside from some *juvenilia*, he did not write his first poem 'Up in the Wind' until December 1914. He was then 36. Thomas enlisted in July 1915, and wrote the last of 142 poems on 13 January 1917. Two weeks later, a second lieutenant in the Royal Artillery, he embarked for France. On 9 April, he was killed by shell-blast as the Arras 'Easter Offensive' began. *Poems* (1917) and *Last Poems* (1918) were published after his death. Partly owing to his late poetic start, critics still find Thomas hard to place. His poetry appears in most Great War anthologies, and the war had a crucial role in its genesis. Yet, since he wrote no trench poems, he eludes or disturbs the category "war poet". If he looks rather more like a "Nature poet", his generic range and symbolic reach expose the limits of that category too. Thomas's art also eludes the critical grasp when it is seen as 'quiet', 'understated' or 'diffident'. This is to mistake means for ends.

When Thomas died, he was chiefly known as the author of two kinds of prose: country books, from his precocious *The Woodland Life* (1897) to *In Pursuit of Spring* (1914), and literary criticism. Yet he also wrote meditative

---

1. Review of new verse, *Daily Chronicle*, 27 August 1901. See note, 169.

essays – the title *Horae Solitariae* (1902) speaks for itself – and impressionistic fictions, such as those collected in *Rest and Unrest* (1910) and *Light and Twilight* (1911). He experimented with myth, fantasy and fable. And he could never write about the countryside purely as a naturalist or topographer or folklorist or social historian. All Thomas's mixed-up genres feature in his uncoordinated but atmospheric novel, *The Happy-Go-Lucky Morgans* (1913), based on his London-Welsh childhood. In retrospect, his imaginative prose is always a poet's prose – soul autobiography that bears out Philip Larkin's dictum: 'novels are about other people and poems are about yourself'.[2] Its dispersed modes, images and perceptions aspire to the integration of symbol. As Thomas's prose became more directly autobiographical, with *The Happy-Go-Lucky Morgans* and the memoir published as *The Childhood of Edward Thomas* (1938), he drew closer to poetry.

In 1904 Thomas told his confidant, the poet Gordon Bottomley: 'There is no form that suits me, & I doubt if I can make a new form.'[3] It would be simplistic to say that he kept on missing the obvious. In starting with an unusual form of writer's block, masked by his copious prose, he proved the mysterious chemistry, rather than deliberate decision, from which poems come. When Thomas's poems came, they were poems of 1914, not 1900, although they encoded the years between. Meanwhile his prose was hampered in its original flights by the need to earn money. He had married in 1899, while still studying History at Oxford, because his lover Helen Noble was pregnant. Owing to a venereal infection contracted during celebrations of the Relief of Mafeking, he failed to get the degree that might have made him an academic. Mainly from choice, partly from necessity, and against the wishes of his civil-servant father, Thomas became a freelance writer and literary journalist. His diverse book-commissions included *Oxford* (1903), *Beautiful Wales* (1905), *Maurice Maeterlinck* (1911) and *The Life of the Duke of Marlborough* (1915).

The Thomases rented successive country cottages, principally in or around Steep, Hampshire. By 1910, they had three children. Their most regular source of income was Thomas's reviewing for the *Daily Chronicle* and other newspapers. R. George Thomas calculates that from 1900 to 1914 Thomas wrote 'just over a million words about 1,200 books'.[4] He reviewed new verse, editions of old verse, every kind of rural book, criticism. As living to write became desperately entangled with writing to live, Thomas's sanity and marriage were tested. In February 1905 he told Bottomley: 'My great enemy is physical exhaustion which makes my brain so wild that I am

2. Philip Larkin, *Required Writing* (London: Faber, 1983), 49.
3. *LGB*, 57 [for all abbreviations, see 325].
4. *LGB*, 9.

almost capable of anything & fear I shall one day prove it.' In January 1906 he lamented: 'Oh, I have lost my very last chances of happiness, gusto & leisure now. I am swallowed up. I live for an income of £250 & work all day & often from 9 a.m. until 1 a.m. It takes me so long because I fret & fret... My self criticism or rather my studied self contempt is now nearly a disease.' If such complaints have a theatrical tinge – in December 1912 Thomas described himself as 'advertising my sorrows & decimating my friends' – that, too, was part of the 'disease'.[5] Eleanor Farjeon (who loved him) warned a biographer: 'remember that when his moods weren't on him like a sickness, when his nerves weren't harassed by overwork and anxiety... he was among other things the best talker, the best thinker, the most humorous... His power of friendship was as great as his need of it'.[6]

Yet on the face of it, and despite Helen Thomas's devotion, early marriage was disastrous for a writer who needed creative space. There may have been an underlying mental problem: Thomas refers to 'something wrong at the very centre which nothing deliberate can put right'.[7] But the neurotic symptoms that his letters 'advertise' are bound up with financial worry, domestic claustrophobia, overwork, fear of not getting work, dislike of hustling for work, all compounded by his sense of betraying 'my silly little deformed unpromising bantling of originality'.[8] At certain periods he used opium for relief that may have made things worse: 'I have sent up strange melodies of agony to many a moon'.[9] In January 1908 Thomas found another problematic form of relief in his obsession with a briefly-met young girl who haunts his love poetry. He often brooded on suicide: in November 1908 he took a revolver for a walk; in October 1913 Walter de la Mare had to talk him out of a suicidal 'design'. Thomas told de la Mare afterwards: 'I think I have now changed my mind though I have the Saviour in my pocket.'[10] He also suffered a series of nervous breakdowns. Several doctors tried to treat what he calls 'melancholy' or 'depression'. In 1912 the most effective doctor, Godwin Baynes, introduced him to psychoanalysis. This helped Thomas to understand his symptoms: 'the central evil is self-consciousness carried as far beyond selfishness as selfishness is beyond self denial ... and all I have got to fight it with is the knowledge that in truth I am not the isolated selfconsidering brain which I have come to seem – the

5. *LGB*, 78, 103, 226.
6. *EF* [1997 ed.], xv.
7. *LWD*, 19 November 1911.
8. *LGB*, 85.
9. *Diary*, 22 July 1902, *NLW*.
10. *LWD*, soon after 6 October 1913: the 'Saviour', 'a certain purchase', may have been a drug; for Thomas and suicide see note on *Rain* (268).

knowledge that I am something more, but not the belief that I can reopen the connection between the brain and the rest'.[11]

Although Baynes's own impact dwindled, psychoanalytic principles would influence Thomas's poetic structures. It was poetry that 're-opened the connection' or opened, at least, a series of channels. As therapy, it lacked the downside that Thomas feared when he wondered 'whether for a person like myself whose most intense moments were those of depression a cure that destroys the depression may not destroy the intensity – a *desperate* remedy?'[12] Some of his early poems imply their own emergence from incoherence. 'The Other' begins: 'The forest ended'. Thomas adapts the 'myriad-minded' lyric to dialogue between different voices, different selves, the roles of patient and analyst. His poetry revisits conflicts manifested in his letters and diaries (conflicts that did not, indeed, vanish overnight), but with a new power to objectify them as psychodrama. Like another troubled poet Sylvia Plath, if by different means, he recasts his subjectivity from poem to poem. Yet Thomas's poems are not 'about himself' in a reductive sense. Nor are they 'himself' in the sense that they put a fragmented psyche together again. Autobiography or case-history is only where his poetry starts. When 'The Other' enters the unconscious and dramatises splits within the psyche, it marks the start of a poetic movement that will internalise the perplexities of modern selfhood.

But why did poetry come, or come to the rescue, in December 1914? Eight years before, Thomas had told Bottomley: 'I feel sure that my salvation depends on a person'.[13] The American poet Robert Frost, whom Thomas first met in October 1913, turned out to be a true 'saviour'. Psychological, intellectual and aesthetic affinities explain the rapid advance of their friendship. Frost periodically suffered from depression. He was a sceptical post-Darwinian thinker, with residual mystical inclinations, who had deeply absorbed the Romantic poets and Thomas Hardy. His American precursors, Emerson and Thoreau, had been formative writers for Thomas too. Frost's imagined New Hampshire, like Thomas's old Hampshire, was a tree-landscape with dark vistas and enigmatic inhabitants. And Frost's ideas about speech and poetry, which centred on the 'sentence-sound', were akin to those that Thomas had started to develop in *Walter Pater: A Critical Study* (1914). Aged 39, four years older than Thomas, Frost had yet received little acclaim at home. Thomas, by then an influential poetry critic, largely made Frost's reputation in England and hence in the US. He wrote of Frost's second collection, *North of Boston*:

---

11. *EF*, 13.
12. *LGB*, 163.
13. *LGB*, 129.

This is one of the most revolutionary books of modern times, but one of the quietest and least aggressive. It speaks, and it is poetry... These poems are revolutionary because they lack the exaggeration of rhetoric, and even at first sight appear to lack the poetic intensity of which rhetoric is an imitation. Their language is free from the poetical words and forms that are the chief material of secondary poets. The metre avoids not only the old-fashioned pomp and sweetness, but the later fashion also of discord and fuss. In fact, the medium is common speech and common decasyllables... Many, if not most, of the separate lines and separate sentences are plain and, in themselves, nothing. But they are bound together and made elements of beauty by a calm eagerness of emotion.[14]

A year later and now a poet himself, Thomas produced an impromptu joint manifesto as he set Bottomley straight about Frost's theory:

I think... [Thomas Sturge Moore] had been misled into supposing that Frost wanted poetry to be colloquial. All he insists on is what he believes he finds in all poets – absolute fidelity to the postures which the voice assumes in the most expressive intimate speech. So long as these tones & postures are there he has not the least objection to any vocabulary whatever or any inversion or variation from the customary grammatical forms of talk. In fact I think he would agree that if these tones & postures survive in a complicated & learned or subtle vocabulary & structure the result is likely to be better than if they survive in the easiest form, that is in the very words & structures of common speech, though that is not easy or prose would be better than it is & survive more often.[15]

Robert Frost kick-started Thomas's poetry. In his own words: 'Edward Thomas had about lost patience with the minor poetry it was his business to review. He was suffering from a life of subordination to his inferiors. Right at that moment he was writing as good poetry as anybody alive, but in prose form where it did not declare itself and gain him recognition. I referred him to paragraphs in his book *In Pursuit of Spring* and told him to write it in verse form in exactly the same cadence.'[16] Some critics play down Frost's impact on Thomas. But it was not only his verse-theory or persistent cajoling that counted. More crucially, his practice showed the way. Thomas told Frost on 15 December 1914: 'I will put it down now that you are the only begetter right enough.'[17] He dedicated *Poems* to Frost. But he also called his poems 'quintessences of the best parts of my prose books', and declared aesthetic independence: 'since the first take off they haven't been Frosty very much or so I imagine and I have tried as often as possible to avoid the facilities offered by blank verse and I try not to be long – I even have an ambition to keep under 12 lines (but rarely

14. *Daily News*, 22 July 1914: Thomas wrote two other reviews of *North of Boston*.
15. *LGB*, 250-1.
16. Letter from Frost to Harold Roy Brennan, 1926, quoted *WC*, 184.
17. *RFET*, 39.

succeed).' [18] As Michael Hofmann says: ' "Influence" seems...such a ridiculously, barbarously heavy notion here'.[19] A kind of sibling differentiation led Thomas to eschew Frost's narrative mode, to concentrate primarily on shorter poems. His forms, including his variations on the couplet or quatrain, are more diverse than Frost's, and more specific to each occasion. Further, to apply favourite terms of Thomas's, he found Frost's poetry at once 'familiar' and 'strange': 'It is curious to have such good natural English with just that shade of foreignness in the people and the poet himself.' [20] Frost's 'foreignness' helped to release his own distinctive poetic accent, along with the traditions behind it. All this went beyond personal rapport. England and America met on the ground of the English lyric.

In late 1913 too, after a bad period, Thomas began his memoir of childhood. The task improved both his mental state and creative morale: 'The autobiography has begun by being the briefest quietest carefullest account of virtually everything I can remember up to the age of 8. I don't trust myself to build up the self of which these things were true. I scarcely allow myself any reflection or explanation'; 'My object at present is daily to focus on some period & get in all that relates to it, allowing one thing to follow the other that suggested it. It's very lean but I feel the shape of the sentences & alter continually with some unseen end in view.' [21] Here Thomas identifies therapeutic recall with stylistic breakthrough. And he describes a prose that anticipates his poetic strategies: close focus, little comment, no unitary 'self', sound and image taking the lead. When he lacerates his earlier prose it is for afflatus that imposes on language, for a solipsistic or derivative vision that imposes on life.

Thomas's self-criticism, like his criticism, was always ahead of his literary practice. For instance, he called *The Heart of England* (1906) 'Borrow & Jefferies sans testicles & guts'.[22] But practice and theory fused at this proto-poetic moment. In rebuking Walter Pater (whom he had once imitated) for turning language into static display, for 'using words as bricks', he was again exorcising his own mannerisms. Pater's lifeless style helped him to understand the primacy of rhythm, its physiological and psychological origins: 'Literature ... has to make words of such a spirit, and arrange them in such a manner, that they will do all that a speaker can do by innumerable gestures and their innumerable shades, by tone and pitch of voice, by speed, by pauses, by all that he is and all that he will become.' For Thomas,

---

18. Letter to John Freeman, 8 March 1915, *JM*, 326.
19. Foreword to *RFET*, xxxviii.
20. Letter to John Freeman, 14 August 1914, *ETFN* 38 (January 1998), 7.
21. *EF*, 48, 51.
22. *LGB*, 107.

the 'music of words' also carries 'an enduring echo of we know not what in the past and in the abyss'.[23] Poetic rhythm, thus understood, is latent in prose sketches from which his early poems, 'Up in the Wind' and 'Old Man', emerged.

Believing that salvation must come from outside himself, Thomas sometimes wished for 'a revolution or a catastrophe'.[24] The Great War duly obliged. It changed his daily life, since reviewing and book commisssions dried up. He had time to think, and thinking changed other things. The date of his first poem, 3 December 1914, is to the point. In *Edward Thomas: A Critical Biography* (1970) William Cooke argues that the war was the main 'begetter' of Thomas's poetry. Perhaps, however, 'The sun used to shine', a poem that brings together the war, Frost and English landscape, symbolises his poetic matrix – and the impossibility of separating its various elements. In this edition, the Notes try to track the war's shifting presence as Muse, context, horizon, and shaping force. One starting point might be a letter from Thomas to Walter de la Mare, written during the August 1914 holiday that 'The sun used to shine' commemorates: 'Rupert Brooke I hear has joined the army. The Blast poets I hear have not. If the war goes on I believe I shall find myself a sort of Englishman, though neither poet nor soldier.'[25] A year later, Thomas was all three.

Rivalry with Brooke – as regards Englishness, soldiering, and poetry – may have spurred him on. Thomas explained to Edward Garnett that *Poems* would appear under his pseudonym, 'Edward Eastaway', 'because I should hate the stupid advertisement some papers might give it, though going to France two years late is nothing to advertise a book of verse'.[26] Frost attributes Thomas's enlistment to fear that he had been cowardly when threatened by a belligerent gamekeeper: an event to which Thomas's poem 'An Old Song I' alludes.[27] In June 1915 Thomas saw his immediate future as a choice between enlisting and joining Frost in America, where, with Frost's help, he hoped to find literary work. At that time he wrote to Frost, linking the gamekeeper incident with Brooke's death and his own right to criticise Brooke's poetry: 'I had to spoil the effect of your letter by writing 1000 words about Rupert Brooke's posthumous book – not daring to say that those sonnets about him enlisting are probably not very personal but a nervous attempt to connect with himself the very widespread idea that self

---

23. *WP*, 215, 210, 219.
24. *LGB*, 91.
25. *LWD*, 30 August 1914.
26. *LEG*, 31.
27. See Jay Parini, *Robert Frost: A Life* (New York: Owl Books, 1999), 155; and note, 168.

sacrifice is the highest self indulgence... I daren't say so, not having enlisted or fought the keeper'.[28] Being overage, Thomas did not need to enlist. His motives for doing so were mixed and complex. Interpretations that either stress patriotism by itself, or see his enlistment as a version of his death wish, seem too simple. But certainly, he was setting himself a test: a test that fused war and poetry. Thomas later tested himself to the uttermost by joining the Royal Artillery, volunteering for service overseas, and, once in France, seeking front-line action. For a family man, even though some financial help was secured,[29] all this might seem highly irresponsible. Or we might reflect on Frost's epitaph: 'I have heard Edward doubt if he was as brave as the bravest. But who was ever so completely himself right up to the verge of destruction, so sure of his thought, so sure of his word?'[30]

Thomas's poetry can be read as the metaphysical counterpart of his enlistment. If at one level it is psychodrama, at another it is cultural defence; while being at odds with the self-sacrificial Brooke-cult, with propagandist verse, and with the co-option of poetry for bombast about "heritage". The war mobilised his historical as well as contemporary sense of English poetry. The literariness that had blighted his prose suddenly became a creative asset: an intertextual stimulus that works on many levels. In terms of form alone, Thomas runs through the lyric gamut. There are parallels with Wilfred Owen saying: 'what would hold me together on a battlefield [is the] sense that I was perpetuating the language in which Keats and the rest of them wrote'.[31] Thomas's deep allusiveness tests the best-read reader (he and Frost were sardonic about Pound wearing his erudition on his poetic sleeve). Yet he did not take continuity for granted. He realised that English poetic "tradition", its language, forms, structures and genres, had been pitched into the war's vortex. This is partly what Frost means when he says that Thomas's poetry 'ought to be called Roads to France'.[32] Similarly, France haunts the poetic landscapes that distil Thomas's experience of the English and Welsh countryside, including its literary incarnations and his own past writings. If his poetry can be called "Home Front" poetry, it exposes the contradiction in those terms.

The founding narratives of "modern poetry" marginalise Edward Thomas. This is odd, given his transatlantic alliance with Frost and call-up of English poetry – obsession with tradition being a mark of the modern movement.

---

28. *RFET*, 61.

29. He applied for a commission in June 1916 after receiving a £300 government grant.

30. Letter to Helen Thomas, 27 April 1917, *SLRF*, 216.

31. (Ed.) John Bell, *Wilfred Owen: Selected Letters* (Oxford: OUP, 1998), 130.

32. Letter to Edward Garnett, 29 April 1917, *SLRF*, 217.

Again, the fact that he never met Owen does not mean that they belong to different poetic universes. But American appropriation of the "modern", licensed by English cultural cringe, demotes "Nature poetry". Neither Thomas nor Frost got into Michael Roberts's epoch-defining *Faber Book of Modern Verse* (1936). To treat Thomas as an isolated figure is also to ignore his criticism, his transition from art for art's sake to speech rhythms, and his argument with Ezra Pound (see below). His aesthetic, which retains a *fin-de-siècle* interest in 'beauty', is closely meshed with developments since the 1890s. That includes his relation to so-called "Georgian" poetry. Thomas knew, and had often reviewed, most of the poets chosen by Edward Marsh for his five *Georgian* anthologies (1912-1922). In *Edward Thomas's Poets* (2007) Judy Kendall sets poems and letters by Thomas alongside texts by English poet-friends as well as by Frost. The arrangement shows how Thomas's 'struggles and experiments in composition' intersect with his critical response to contemporaries like Bottomley, de la Mare and W.H. Davies.[33] But, apart from de la Mare (his most significant poet-friend before Frost), who in-fluenced his handling of childhood, folk sources, and 'strangeness', this group is more or less covered by Frost's remark about Thomas 'losing patience' with minor poets. Thomas assimilated French Symbolism, English aesth-eticism and the Irish Revival, and he reviewed Hardy, Yeats, Pound and Lawrence with remarkable insight. His poetry criticism stresses the ear, as if – long before Frost turned up – he were listening for the sounds of the new century. Thus in 1904 he praised the 'infinitely varied measure' of Yeats's blank verse.[34] Conversely, he could be merciless to the old century, as when dismissing Swinburne's 'musical jargon that includes human snatches, but is not and never could be speech'.[35]

Thomas's mature criticism desires poetry to balance speech and music so that words 'support one another', and each word 'lives its intensest life'. He invokes this ideal to question the esoteric tendencies of French Sym-bolism, as when a poem by Maeterlinck is 'hardly more than a catalogue of symbols that have no more literary value than words in a dictionary'.[36] He praises Yeats's more holistic symbols for being 'natural, ancient, instinctive, not invented'.[37] Thomas and Yeats conceive symbolism as appealing to widely intelligible archetypes, and as applying to every aspect of a poem's structure. This, like other parallels between the poets, marks their common origins in Romanticism. Both poets dramatise the self by manipulating 'tone

---

33. *JK*, xiv.
34. Review of W.B. Yeats, *Plays for an Irish Theatre*, *Week's Survey*, 18 June 1904.
35. *ACS*, 171.
36. *MM*, 27.
37. Review of W.B. Yeats, *Collected Works*, *Morning Post*, 17 December 1908.

and pitch of voice'. Both associate poetic rhythm with the body. Both invest in the mystique of nomadic 'life that loves the wild' ('Up in the Wind'). Both activate the folk ghost by drawing on country speech and traditional songs. Attracted to the Irish Revival's local, national and mythic frameworks, Thomas said that Yeats was 'to be envied, like a man with a fine house'.[38] Yeats's "Ireland" influenced Thomas's "England". And, while never seeking a surrogate religion, Thomas shared Yeats's objections to the triumph of scientific modernity: 'Myths have been destroyed which helped to maintain a true and vivid acknowledgment of the mystery of the past.'[39]

Thomas's doubts about Pound and Imagism are continuous with his attitudes to Pater and to shallow symbolism. This quarrel still affects how we think about poetry today. Thomas was initially stirred by Pound's 'revolt against the crepuscular spirit in modern poetry', which may have remained a provocative stimulus. But he condemned Pound's *Exultations* (1909) for being 'dappled with French, Provençal, Spanish, Italian, Latin, and old English, with proper names that we shirk pronouncing, with crudity, violence and obscurity, with stiff rhythms and no rhythms at all', and shrewdly warned: 'If he is not careful he will take to meaning what he says instead of saying what he means.'[40] Reviewing the anthology *Des Imagistes* (1914), Thomas finds that Pound 'has seldom done better than... under the restraint imposed by Chinese originals or models'. But he calls the anthology itself 'a tall marble monument', and compares its prevailing style to 'the ordinary prose translation of the classics – in short, the crib'.[41] For Frost and Thomas, Imagist mimicry of the visual arts fails to understand that the ear, not the eye, is primary in poetry: 'The ear is the only true writer and the only true reader'.[42] Thus they turn Imagism's painterly and sculptural self-image against it: Frost attacks 'kiln-dried tabule poetry'.[43] Their resistance to Imagism also covers the spatial effects introduced by free verse layout.

Today it is clear that varieties of free verse have not taken over English-language poetry, which moves between poles of "freedom" and "traditional form". Not that traditional form has stood still (if it ever did). A century ago, Yeats, Frost and Thomas found new ways to exploit the counterpoint between syntax and line or stanza. It is also now clear that disjunctive poetry has no monopoly on modernity. Like Yeats and Frost, Thomas adapts lyrical

---

38. Review of W.B. Yeats, *The Celtic Twilight*, new ed., *Daily Chronicle*, 12 July 1902.
39. *TC*, 2.
40. Review of Ezra Pound, *Personae*, *Daily Chronicle*, 7 June 1909; review of Pound, *Exultations*, *Daily Chronicle*, 23 November 1909.
41. Review of *Des Imagistes: An Anthology*, *New Weekly*, 9 May 1914.
42. *SLRF*, 113.
43. *SLRF*, 217.

syntax to relativistic metaphysics. His poems destabilise perception, split or decentre the lyric "I", ponder slippages between 'word' and 'thing'. But Thomas's dark forests and nihilistic prospects are in dialogue with other symbols and perspectives, and his questing imagination never rests on any pole. His poetry is radically dialectical.

Since first editing Thomas's poetry thirty-five years ago,[44] I have come to realise how fully he worked out his *ars poetica*, and how often the poems themselves "reflexively" encode aesthetic principles. Meanwhile, critics such as Andrew Motion, Stan Smith and Michael Kirkham have illuminated the poetry, partly by expanding our sense of its literary and historical contexts. Smith, for instance, reads it in close relation to the socio-political tensions of Edwardian England. These and other critics are quoted in the Notes. On the textual and biographical front, the invaluable scholarship of R. George Thomas climaxed in his edition of the *Collected Poems* (1978), *Edward Thomas: A Portrait* (1985), and *Edward Thomas: Selected Letters* (1995). Yet many other letters remain unpublished; the mass of archival documents warrants another biography; and an edition of Thomas's 'Essential Prose' (Oxford University Press) has only now been mooted. Small presses, such as the Cyder Press, have valiantly kept the prose in print. It seems that we are still catching up with Edward Thomas: perhaps because his poetry is so far ahead. I had to write a wholly different commentary this time round, and it too will date in due course. And if Thomas's poetry still escapes the "modernist" narrative predicated on Eliot and Pound (rather than on Yeats), that narrative is showing its own age. Yet newer critical vocabularies – I will mention three – may not so much open up his poems as *vice versa*, since the poems got there first.

As already noted, Thomas's poetry was psychoanalytical before psychoanalytical criticism. Second, on a more public front, it both explores and complicates "identity politics". Thomas thought that imperialism had hollowed out England's inner life: a highly topical theme today. Thus he praises Irish poets for 'singing of Ireland ... with an intimate reality often missing from English patriotic poetry, where Britannia is a frigid personification'.[45] Hence his creation of 'Lob' and refusal to aim his wartime anthology *This England* at 'what a committee from Great Britain and Ireland might call complete'. But in representing "England" with an inwardness partly learned from Irish, Welsh and American sources, in devolving it to Hampshire or Wiltshire, in breaking up "Britain", Thomas does not fix new boundaries, just as he does not ring-fence a national canon. His Welsh horizons, which make "home" itself ever unstable, prompt many kinds of poetic border-

---

44. (Ed.) Longley, *Edward Thomas: Poems and Last Poems* (London: Collins, 1973).
45. Review of *The Dublin Book of Irish Verse*, *Morning Post*, 6 January 1910.

crossing. He calls himself both 'mainly Welsh' and one of 'those modern people who belong nowhere'.[46] Thomas allows a poem's structures to define its affiliations. He unpredictably shrinks or enlarges a mental landscape or knowable community. This explains why his own 'intimate realities' have fed back into poetry from the rest of these islands, as has his historical sense of place and landscape.

In 'History and the Parish', an important chapter in *The South Country* (1909), Thomas writes:

> The eye that sees the things of today, and the ear that hears, the mind that contemplates or dreams, is itself an instrument of an antiquity equal to whatever it is called upon to apprehend. We are not merely twentieth-century Londoners or Kentish men or Welshmen...And of these many folds in our nature the face of the earth reminds us, and perhaps, even where there are no more marks visible upon the land than there were in Eden, we are aware of the passing of time in ways too difficult and strange for the explanation of historian and zoologist and philosopher.[47]

Few poets can match Thomas's historical imagination. In fact, his post-Darwinian approach to 'the mystery of the past' is ultimately "eco-historical": to introduce a term that will recur in the Notes. Of all the ways in which Thomas's poetry anticipates ideas that help us to read it, his ecological vision may be the most inclusive. Taken together, his poetry and prose pioneer "ecocriticism". His earliest influence was the Wiltshire writer Richard Jefferies (1848-87), of whom he wrote a fine biography (1909). Reading Jefferies sent Thomas out into the fields, inspired him to make field notes, and gave him a credo: 'Let us get out of these indoor narrow modern days, whose twelve hours somehow have become shortened, into the sunlight and the pure wind.'[48] Jefferies also set Thomas on the track of English rural writing from Gilbert White to W.H. Hudson – another tradition that his poetry condenses. With his equally deep absorption of the Romantic poets, no poet was better equipped to take what Jonathan Bate calls 'Romantic ecology' into new dimensions and into the new century.

Thomas's ideal Nature study would reveal 'in animals, in plants...what life is, how our own is related to theirs', and show us 'our position, responsibilities and debts among the other inhabitants of the earth'.[49] His self-perception as 'an inhabitant of the earth' is fundamental to the ecocentric, rather than anthropocentric, structures of his poetry. Thus he exposes the lyric "I" to the uncertainties of 'our position', as well as to inner divisions,

---

46. *SC*, 7.
47. *SC*, 151-2.
48. From the last paragraph of Jefferies's *The Amateur Poacher* (1879), see *CET*, 134.
49. *SC*, 144.

and (in 'The Combe' and 'The Gallows') correlates the Great War with human violence towards other species. Asked in 1908 to define Nature, he attacked man's 'belief that Nature is only a house, furniture etc round about him. It is not my belief, and I don't oppose Nature to Man. Quite the contrary. Man seems to me a very little part of Nature and the part I enjoy least. But civilisation has estranged us superficially from Nature, and towns make it possible for a man to live as if a millionaire could really produce all the necessities of life – food, drink, clothes, vehicles etc and then a tombstone.'[50] Thomas's prophetic environmentalism was conditioned by his London up-bringing and by rural England 'dying' as London grew.[51] Since the 1870s, when the government refused to protect English wheat against American imports, the agricultural economy (particularly of south-east England) had been in decline. Thomas sardonically observes that the countryman is 'sink-ing before the *Daily Mail* like a savage before pox or whisky', and that 'brewers, bankers, and journalists... are taking the place of hops in Kent'.[52] From all this, he intuited a deeper crisis. In some ways, the war only inten-sified the elegiac tilt of Thomas's eco-history. While he may not always enjoy 'man', and recognises 'nature's independence of humanity',[53] his poetry invites us to remember what man in Nature, and Nature in man, have created.

'Old Man', in which humanity and Nature puzzlingly entangle, is among Thomas's best-known poems. Here he spells out the concern with memory – personal, cultural, ecological – that constitutes, as much as occupies, his poetry:

> I, too, often shrivel the grey shreds,
> Sniff them and think and sniff again and try
> Once more to think what it is I am remembering...

Other poems, too, represent themselves as acts of memory or as failure to remember. The words 'memory' and 'remember' recur. We also find 'recall', 'call back', 'call to mind', 'came back again', 'hung in my mind', 'forget'. The importance of memory, as it comes or calls or hangs or hangs back suggests why Thomas so fully exploits poetry's licence to play with syn-tactical order. The relation of syntax to line (and both to rhyme) is notable for inversion, reversion and other quirks of sequence. 'The past hovering as it revisits the light' ('It rains') shapes the metaphysics of Thomas's forms and language. For Thomas, 'word' and 'thing' are neither identical nor distinct but marked by their association through time. Further, in attending

---

50. *SL*, 51.
51. See Alun Howkins, *The Death of Rural England* (London: Routledge, 2003).
52. *TC*, 21-2; review of new verse, *Daily Chronicle*, 30 August 1905.
53. *RJ*, 144.

to the folk-ghost, as to tradition in all its guises, he reaches for poetry's mnemonic roots. A memorable poem lets the past hover longer. Perhaps his own poems should be called 'Roads *from* France'.

It seems, then, that Mnemosyne (Memory) was the mother of Thomas's late-starter Muse in a special sense. Certainly, he trawled all the resources of his own past. The Notes to this edition quote passages from his published writings, and from his notebooks, letters and diaries. Others might have been quoted or await discovery. These passages, in one way or another, contain seeds of poems. They also cast light on any poem's origins in a synaptic spark between long-term and short-term term memory: between materials that a poet has consciously or unconsciously accumulated and some new factor that switches on a process of selection and transformation. I believe that Thomas's intensive odyssey from poem to poem, with its formal and thematic twists, tells us a lot about poetry itself as well as about his own work. We may learn, for instance, that poetry's sources remain mysterious; that we now expect too little from poetry; or that the academy has distorted readings of modern poetry by favouring surface difficulty. Admittedly, Thomas's poems have superseded the textual mountain on which they perch, as the butterfly supersedes the caterpillar. So perhaps (to quote 'I never saw that land before') 'what was hid should still be hid'. Yet all that Edward Thomas compressed into his poems can be too well hidden.

NOTE ON TEXT OF THIS EDITION

Anyone who edits Edward Thomas's poems is greatly indebted to the late R. George Thomas. Among his other contributions to Thomas studies, he edited *The Collected Poems of Edward Thomas* (Oxford: Clarendon Press, 1978) [henceforth *CP1978*], which has a virtually comprehensive textual apparatus. If I have arrived at some different textual decisions – all differences are indicated in the Notes – it is largely R. George Thomas who marshalled the materials on which such decisions must be based. He also created the invaluable Edward Thomas Collection (Cardiff University Library), where many relevant documents are assembled. In the present edition, the textual note on each poem records its main manuscript source(s) and its initial publication(s) in book-form (including pamphlets and anthologies). Other sources and printings are cited where necessary. Details of manuscripts, typescripts and publications of poems are given in Abbreviations (325).

In 1917, shortly before Thomas's death, he published eighteen poems in *An Annual of New Poetry* [*AANP*] under his pseudonym 'Edward Eastaway' (Eastaway was a family name). *Poems* by Edward Eastaway [*P*] appeared posthumously in the same year. *P* contains sixty-four poems, none repeated from *AANP*. *Last Poems* by Edward Thomas [*LP*] was published in 1918. *LP* contains all but seven of Thomas's remaining poems. The first *Collected Poems* by Edward Thomas [*CP1920*] added 'Up in the Wind'. The second *Collected Poems* [*CP1928*] added four more poems. Transferred to Faber and Faber in 1936, the *Collected Poems* later appeared in a new edition [*CP1944*], which remained the significant text for many years. Its fifth impression [*CP1949*] added one more poem, as did *CP1978*. The current Faber *Collected Poems* [*CP2004*] takes its text from *CP1978*, but treats the titles of poems differently (see below). *CP2004* does not reprint any textual apparatus, although, rather confusingly, it retains the textual aspect of R. George Thomas's Introduction to *CP1978*.

Thomas oversaw the publication of his poems in *AANP* and *P*. This edition thus regards these texts as authoritative, except for a few instances discussed in the Notes. *CP1978* departs more frequently from *P*, mainly owing to 'doubts' about how its text was assembled (see *CP1978*, 38). Such doubts would have been dispelled by the printer's typescript of *P* [*PTP*], which clearly passed through Thomas's hands. But *PTP* did not become known to R. George Thomas until the paperback edition of *CP1978* (without its apparatus) had gone to press in 1981. Among other textual consequences, since no changes were subsequently made, this affects the titles of certain poems in *CP1978*, and still in *CP2004*.

Often when Thomas wrote a poem, he did not immediately give it a title.

That can be gauged from the manuscript notebooks, now in the British Library [*BL*] and the Bodleian [*B*], in which he made fair (more or less) copies of nearly all his poems. In *PTP* twenty-three titles in Thomas's handwriting are added to typescript poems (Eleanor Farjeon was his principal typist). Apart from 'The Trumpet' and 'The Gallows', these are first-line titles, e.g., 'Bright Clouds', 'Women he liked', 'How at once', and 'Gone, gone again'. Thus R. George Thomas should not have named those poems and 'Like the touch of rain' (where the title is typed) from references in Thomas's letters. His new titles are: 'The Pond', 'Bob's Lane', 'The Swifts', 'Blenheim Oranges', and '"Go now"'. Such references are, surely, a form of shorthand. Similarly, he turns Thomas's mention of 'the household poems' into an overarching title for the sequence beginning 'If I should ever by chance'. In *PTP* Thomas gives these four poems first-line titles. R. George Thomas also attaches the generic title 'Song' to the poems named by Thomas in *PTP* as 'The clouds that are so light' and 'Early one morning'. Finally, in addition to the evidence of *PTP*, a letter from Thomas to his wife (20 October 1916) shows him to be up to speed with 'the set [of verses] Ingpen has' (*SL*, 133). Roger Ingpen, then at Selwyn & Blount, saw *P* through the press.

As regards *LP* (apart from the poems already printed in *AANP*) and six of the poems later added to *Collected Poems*, titles and other textual issues become more difficult. It appears that the *LP* editors, presumably literary friends of Thomas's, adopted two procedures with formerly un-named poems. First, they gave them first-line titles ('She dotes', 'I built myself a house of glass', 'This is no case of petty right or wrong', 'Those things that poets said', 'I never saw that land before', 'No one cares less than I', 'There was a time', 'That girl's clear eyes', 'What will they do?', 'Out in the dark'). Second, they named poems for a central image or motif ('Over the Hills', 'Man and Dog', 'The Gypsy', 'Ambition', 'The Wasp Trap', 'Digging' ['Today I think'], 'Health', 'A Cat', 'The Dark Forest', 'The Child in the Orchard'). At the same time, as with other aspects of the *LP* text, it should be remembered that the editors may have consulted papers, or had information, no longer extant. In *CP1978* R. George Thomas brackets all the above titles as questionable. I have indicated where he does so, and also where *CP2004* (on no clear basis) has either dropped the titles completely or, in five instances, dropped the brackets instead. This edition retains the *LP* titles, together with the titles first given as 'The Lane' and 'The Watchers' in *Two Poems* (1927) [*TP*], and as 'No one so much as you' and 'The Wind's Song' in *CP1928*. The poem for Thomas's father, included in *CP1949* as 'P.H.T.', has here been named for its first line ('I may come near loving you'); as has his last poem, 'The sorrow of true love', first printed in *CP1978*.

There are several arguments for retaining titles that cannot confidently be traced to Thomas. First: nearly half (eleven) are first-line titles. The ms. titles added to *PTP*, like some titles already in place, show that the first-line title was his default-setting. (Hence 'I may come near loving you' and 'The sorrow of true love' in this edition.) Second: *P*, *AANP*, and the few poems printed elsewhere during his lifetime prove that Thomas came up with titles when publication loomed. Thus, even if 'To name a thing beloved man sometimes fails' ('Women he liked'), he was no purist who feared that a title might limit a poem's suggestiveness. Third: both established usage and convenience of reference should count for something. Certain poems by Thomas have been long known and discussed under particular titles. Such familiarity was controversially upset by *CP1978*; more so by *CP2004*, where poems are identified by their first lines in the Contents list, but only have a number on the page. This is awkward both for reading and for reference. The most problematic cases, then, are established titles which are not first-line titles, and whose provenance is uncertain (see previous paragraph). If editors bestowed those titles, perhaps they felt either that a first-line title would not work (as in the case of 'Man and Dog'), or that an obvious title beckoned. Some of their apparent choices may be slightly more open to question than others. But, with the possible exception of 'Over the Hills', none obtrudes as inappropriate.

Like other poets killed in the First World War, Edward Thomas bequeathed a degree of textual uncertainty to his editors. Editors of the *Collected Poems* before *CP1978* occasionally make changes from *P* and *LP* (changes that usually reflect *BL* or *B*), but without indicating their authority for doing so. Here and there they also standardise punctuation, adding exclamation-marks, for instance. This edition follows *CP1978* in altering 'to-day' to 'today' etc. A difficulty for all editors is that at times Thomas revised poems, and then (as in the case of 'Sedge-Warblers') seemingly rejected the revision. In the absence of clear evidence as to his final preferences, the ear must play a part in weighing the balance of probability. Since some issues will always remain undecidable, the Notes provide a basis for readers to make up their own minds. A conspicuous way in which this edition (like *CP1978*, *CP2004*, and my own earlier edition of *P* and *LP* [1973]) departs from Thomas's own schemes is by ordering his poems chronologically. Evidently, he could never have conceived such a *Collected Poems*, any more than a collection called *Last Poems*. One drawback is that chronological editions must sacrifice the sequencing of poems in *P*, although Thomas had to omit the *AANP* poems from *P* itself. But, given the tight time-frame of Thomas's poetry – as if he set out to write his collected poems in one go – it may be well served by a chronological arrangement.

COLLECTED POEMS

Up in the Wind

'I could wring the old thing's neck that put it here!
A public-house! It may be public for birds,
Squirrels and such-like, ghosts of charcoal-burners
And highwaymen.' The wild girl laughed. 'But I
Hate it since I came back from Kennington.   5
I gave up a good place.' Her Cockney accent
Made her and the house seem wilder by calling up –
Only to be subdued at once by wildness –
The idea of London, there in that forest parlour,
Low and small among the towering beeches   10
And the one bulging butt that's like a font.

Her eyes flashed up; she shook her hair away
From eyes and mouth, as if to shriek again;
Then sighed back to her scrubbing. While I drank
I might have mused of coaches and highwaymen,   15
Charcoal-burners and life that loves the wild.
For who now used these roads except myself,
A market waggon every other Wednesday,
A solitary tramp, some very fresh one
Ignorant of these eleven houseless miles,   20
A motorist from a distance slowing down
To taste whatever luxury he can
In having North Downs clear behind, South clear before,
And being midway between two railway lines
Far out of sight or sound of them? There are   25
Some houses – down the by-lanes; and a few
Are visible – when their damsons are in bloom.
But the land is wild, and there's a spirit of wildness
Much older, crying when the stone-curlew yodels
His sea and mountain cry, high up in Spring.   30
He nests in fields where still the gorse is free as
When all was open and common. Common 'tis named
And calls itself, because the bracken and gorse
Still hold the hedge where plough and scythe have chased them.
Once on a time 'tis plain that 'The White Horse'   35
Stood merely on the border of a waste
Where horse or cart picked its own course afresh.
On all sides then, as now, paths ran to the inn;
And now a farm-track takes you from a gate.

Two roads cross, and not a house in sight   40
Except 'The White Horse' in this clump of beeches.
It hides from either road, a field's breadth back;
And it's the trees you see, and not the house,
Both near and far, when the clump's the highest thing
And homely, too, upon a far horizon   45
To one that knows there is an inn within.

''Twould have been different' the wild girl shrieked, 'suppose
That widow had married another blacksmith and
Kept on the business. This parlour was the smithy.
If she had done, there might never have been an inn;   50
And I, in that case, might never have been born.
Years ago, when this was all a wood
And the smith had charcoal-burners for company,
A man from a beech-country in the shires
Came with an engine and a little boy   55
(To feed the engine) to cut up timber here.
It all happened years ago. The smith
Had died, his widow had set up an alehouse –
I could wring the old thing's neck for thinking of it.
Well, I suppose they fell in love, the widow   60
And my great-uncle that sawed up the timber:
Leastways they married. The little boy stayed on.
He was my father.' She thought she'd scrub again –
'I draw the ale and he grows fat' she muttered –
But only studied the hollows in the bricks   65
And chose among her thoughts in stirring silence.
The clock ticked, and the big saucepan lid
Heaved as the cabbage bubbled, and the girl
Questioned the fire and spoke: 'My father, he
Took to the land. A mile of it is worth   70
A guinea; for by that time all the trees
Except these few about the house were gone:
That's all that's left of the forest unless you count
The bottoms of the charcoal-burners' fires –
We plough one up at times. Did you ever see   75
Our signboard?' No. The post and empty frame
I knew. Without them I should not have guessed
The low grey house and its one stack under trees
Was a public-house and not a hermitage.
'But can that empty frame be any use?   80
Now I should like to see a good white horse

Swing there, a really beautiful white horse,
Galloping one side, being painted on the other.'
'But would you like to hear it swing all night
And all day? All I ever had to thank   85
The wind for was for blowing the sign down.
Time after time it blew down and I could sleep.
At last they fixed it, and it took a thief
To move it, and we've never had another:
It's lying at the bottom of the pond.   90
But no one's moved the wood from off the hill
There at the back, although it makes a noise
When the wind blows, as if a train were running
The other side, a train that never stops
Or ends. And the linen crackles on the line   95
Like a wood fire rising.' 'But if you had the sign
You might draw company. What about Kennington?'
She bent down to her scrubbing with 'Not me:
Not back to Kennington. Here I was born,
And I've a notion on these windy nights   100
Here I shall die. Perhaps I want to die here.
I reckon I shall stay. But I do wish
The road was nearer and the wind farther off,
Or once now and then quite still, though when I die
I'd have it blowing that I might go with it   105
Somewhere distant, where there are trees no more
And I could wake and not know where I was
Nor even wonder if they would roar again.
Look at those calves.'

              Between the open door
And the trees two calves were wading in the pond,   110
Grazing the water here and there and thinking,
Sipping and thinking, both happily, neither long.
The water wrinkled, but they sipped and thought,
As careless of the wind as it of us.
'Look at those calves. Hark at the trees again.'   115

November

November's days are thirty:
November's earth is dirty,
Those thirty days, from first to last;
And the prettiest things on ground are the paths
With morning and evening hobnails dinted,   5
With foot and wing-tip overprinted
Or separately charactered,
Of little beast and little bird.
The fields are mashed by sheep, the roads
Make the worst going, the best the woods   10
Where dead leaves upward and downward scatter.
Few care for the mixture of earth and water,
Twig, leaf, flint, thorn,
Straw, feather, all that men scorn,
Pounded up and sodden by flood,   15
Condemned as mud.

But of all the months when earth is greener
Not one has clean skies that are cleaner.
Clean and clear and sweet and cold,
They shine above the earth so old,   20
While the after-tempest cloud
Sails over in silence though winds are loud,
Till the full moon in the east
Looks at the planet in the west
And earth is silent as it is black,   25
Yet not unhappy for its lack.
Up from the dirty earth men stare:
One imagines a refuge there
Above the mud, in the pure bright
Of the cloudless heavenly light: 30
Another loves earth and November more dearly
Because without them, he sees clearly,
The sky would be nothing more to his eye
Than he, in any case, is to the sky;
He loves even the mud whose dyes   35
Renounce all brightness to the skies.

March

Now I know that Spring will come again,
Perhaps tomorrow: however late I've patience
After this night following on such a day.

While still my temples ached from the cold burning
Of hail and wind, and still the primroses   5
Torn by the hail were covered up in it,
The sun filled earth and heaven with a great light
And a tenderness, almost warmth, where the hail dripped,
As if the mighty sun wept tears of joy.
But 'twas too late for warmth. The sunset piled   10
Mountains on mountains of snow and ice in the west:
Somewhere among their folds the wind was lost,
And yet 'twas cold, and though I knew that Spring
Would come again, I knew it had not come,
That it was lost too in those mountains chill.   15

What did the thrushes know? Rain, snow, sleet, hail,
Had kept them quiet as the primroses.
They had but an hour to sing. On boughs they sang,
On gates, on ground; they sang while they changed perches
And while they fought, if they remembered to fight: 20
So earnest were they to pack into that hour
Their unwilling hoard of song before the moon
Grew brighter than the clouds. Then 'twas no time
For singing merely. So they could keep off silence
And night, they cared not what they sang or screamed;   25
Whether 'twas hoarse or sweet or fierce or soft;
And to me all was sweet: they could do no wrong.
Something they knew – I also, while they sang
And after. Not till night had half its stars
And never a cloud, was I aware of silence   30
Stained with all that hour's songs, a silence
Saying that Spring returns, perhaps tomorrow.

Old Man

Old Man, or Lad's-love, – in the name there's nothing
To one that knows not Lad's-love, or Old Man,
The hoar-green feathery herb, almost a tree,
Growing with rosemary and lavender.
Even to one that knows it well, the names   5
Half decorate, half perplex, the thing it is:
At least, what that is clings not to the names
In spite of time. And yet I like the names.

The herb itself I like not, but for certain
I love it, as some day the child will love it   10
Who plucks a feather from the door-side bush
Whenever she goes in or out of the house.
Often she waits there, snipping the tips and shrivelling
The shreds at last on to the path, perhaps
Thinking, perhaps of nothing, till she sniffs   15
Her fingers and runs off. The bush is still
But half as tall as she, though it is as old;
So well she clips it. Not a word she says;
And I can only wonder how much hereafter
She will remember, with that bitter scent,   20
Of garden rows, and ancient damson-trees
Topping a hedge, a bent path to a door,
A low thick bush beside the door, and me
Forbidding her to pick.

                As for myself,
Where first I met the bitter scent is lost.   25
I, too, often shrivel the grey shreds,
Sniff them and think and sniff again and try
Once more to think what it is I am remembering,
Always in vain. I cannot like the scent,
Yet I would rather give up others more sweet,   30
With no meaning, than this bitter one.

I have mislaid the key. I sniff the spray
And think of nothing; I see and I hear nothing;
Yet seem, too, to be listening, lying in wait
For what I should, yet never can, remember: 35

No garden appears, no path, no hoar-green bush
Of Lad's-love, or Old Man, no child beside,
Neither father nor mother, nor any playmate;
Only an avenue, dark, nameless, without end.

The Signpost

The dim sea glints chill. The white sun is shy,
And the skeleton weeds and the never-dry,
Rough, long grasses keep white with frost
At the hilltop by the finger-post;
The smoke of the traveller's-joy is puffed   5
Over hawthorn berry and hazel tuft.

I read the sign. Which way shall I go?
A voice says: You would not have doubted so
At twenty. Another voice gentle with scorn
Says: At twenty you wished you had never been born.   10

One hazel lost a leaf of gold
From a tuft at the tip, when the first voice told
The other he wished to know what 'twould be
To be sixty by this same post. 'You shall see,'
He laughed – and I had to join his laughter –   15
'You shall see; but either before or after,
Whatever happens, it must befall,
A mouthful of earth to remedy all
Regrets and wishes shall freely be given;
And if there be a flaw in that heaven   20
'Twill be freedom to wish, and your wish may be
To be here or anywhere talking to me,
No matter what the weather, on earth,
At any age between death and birth, –
To see what day or night can be,   25
The sun and the frost, the land and the sea,
Summer, Autumn, Winter, Spring, –
With a poor man of any sort, down to a king,
Standing upright out in the air
Wondering where he shall journey, O where?'   30

After Rain

The rain of a night and a day and a night
Stops at the light
Of this pale choked day. The peering sun
Sees what has been done.
The road under the trees has a border new   5
Of purple hue
Inside the border of bright thin grass:
For all that has
Been left by November of leaves is torn
From hazel and thorn   10
And the greater trees. Throughout the copse
No dead leaf drops
On grey grass, green moss, burnt-orange fern,
At the wind's return:
The leaflets out of the ash-tree shed   15
Are thinly spread
In the road, like little black fish, inlaid,
As if they played.
What hangs from the myriad branches down there
So hard and bare   20
Is twelve yellow apples lovely to see
On one crab-tree,
And on each twig of every tree in the dell
Uncountable
Crystals both dark and bright of the rain   25
That begins again.

Interval

Gone the wild day:
A wilder night
Coming makes way
For brief twilight.

Where the firm soaked road 5
Mounts and is lost
In the high beech-wood
It shines almost.

The beeches keep
A stormy rest, 10
Breathing deep
Of wind from the west.

The wood is black,
With a misty steam.
Above, the cloud pack 15
Breaks for one gleam.

But the woodman's cot
By the ivied trees
Awakens not
To light or breeze. 20

It smokes aloft
Unwavering:
It hunches soft
Under storm's wing.

It has no care 25
For gleam or gloom:
It stays there
While I shall roam,

Die, and forget
The hill of trees, 30
The gleam, the wet,
This roaring peace.

The Other

The forest ended. Glad I was
To feel the light, and hear the hum
Of bees, and smell the drying grass
And the sweet mint, because I had come
To an end of forest, and because   5
Here was both road and inn, the sum
Of what's not forest. But 'twas here
They asked me if I did not pass
Yesterday this way? 'Not you? Queer.'
'Who then? and slept here?' I felt fear.   10

I learnt his road and, ere they were
Sure I was I, left the dark wood
Behind, kestrel and woodpecker,
The inn in the sun, the happy mood
When first I tasted sunlight there.   15
I travelled fast, in hopes I should
Outrun that other. What to do
When caught, I planned not. I pursued
To prove the likeness, and, if true,
To watch until myself I knew.   20

I tried the inns that evening
Of a long gabled high-street grey,
Of courts and outskirts, travelling
An eager but a weary way,
In vain. He was not there. Nothing   25
Told me that ever till that day
Had one like me entered those doors,
Save once. That time I dared: 'You may
Recall' – but never-foamless shores
Make better friends than those dull boors.   30

Many and many a day like this
Aimed at the unseen moving goal
And nothing found but remedies
For all desire. These made not whole;
They sowed a new desire, to kiss   35
Desire's self beyond control,

Desire of desire. And yet
Life stayed on within my soul.
One night in sheltering from the wet
I quite forgot I could forget.   40

A customer, then the landlady
Stared at me. With a kind of smile
They hesitated awkwardly:
Their silence gave me time for guile.
Had anyone called there like me,   45
I asked. It was quite plain the wile
Succeeded. For they poured out all.
And that was naught. Less than a mile
Beyond the inn, I could recall
He was like me in general.   50

He had pleased them, but I less.
I was more eager than before
To find him out and to confess,
To bore him and to let him bore.
I could not wait: children might guess   55
I had a purpose, something more
That made an answer indiscreet.
One girl's caution made me sore,
Too indignant even to greet
That other had we chanced to meet.   60

I sought then in solitude.
The wind had fallen with the night; as still
The roads lay as the ploughland rude,
Dark and naked, on the hill.
Had there been ever any feud   65
'Twixt earth and sky, a mighty will
Closed it: the crocketed dark trees,
A dark house, dark impossible
Cloud-towers, one star, one lamp, one peace
Held on an everlasting lease: 70

And all was earth's, or all was sky's;
No difference endured between
The two. A dog barked on a hidden rise;
A marshbird whistled high unseen;

The latest waking blackbird's cries 75
Perished upon the silence keen.
The last light filled a narrow firth
Among the clouds. I stood serene,
And with a solemn quiet mirth,
An old inhabitant of earth. 80

Once the name I gave to hours
Like this was melancholy, when
It was not happiness and powers
Coming like exiles home again,
And weaknesses quitting their bowers, 85
Smiled and enjoyed, far off from men,
Moments of everlastingness.
And fortunate my search was then
While what I sought, nevertheless,
That I was seeking, I did not guess. 90

That time was brief: once more at inn
And upon road I sought my man
Till once amid a tap-room's din
Loudly he asked for me, began
To speak, as if it had been a sin, 95
Of how I thought and dreamed and ran
After him thus, day after day:
He lived as one under a ban
For this: what had I got to say?
I said nothing. I slipped away. 100

And now I dare not follow after
Too close. I try to keep in sight,
Dreading his frown and worse his laughter.
I steal out of the wood to light;
I see the swift shoot from the rafter 105
By the inn door: ere I alight
I wait and hear the starlings wheeze
And nibble like ducks: I wait his flight.
He goes: I follow: no release
Until he ceases. Then I also shall cease. 110

Birds' Nests

The summer nests uncovered by autumn wind,
Some torn, others dislodged, all dark,
Everyone sees them: low or high in tree,
Or hedge, or single bush, they hang like a mark.

Since there's no need of eyes to see them with   5
I cannot help a little shame
That I missed most, even at eye's level, till
The leaves blew off and made the seeing no game.

'Tis a light pang. I like to see the nests
Still in their places, now first known,   10
At home and by far roads. Boys knew them not,
Whatever jays and squirrels may have done.

And most I like the winter nest deep-hid
That leaves and berries fell into:
Once a dormouse dined there on hazel-nuts,   15
And grass and goose-grass seeds found soil and grew.

The Mountain Chapel

Chapel and gravestones, old and few,
Are shrouded by a mountain fold
From sound and view
Of life. The loss of the brook's voice
Falls like a shadow. All they hear is   5
The eternal noise
Of wind whistling in grass more shrill
Than aught as human as a sword,
And saying still:
''Tis but a moment since man's birth   10
And in another moment more
Man lies in earth

For ever; but I am the same
Now, and shall be, even as I was
Before he came;   15
Till there is nothing I shall be.'
Yet there the sun shines after noon
So cheerfully
The place almost seems peopled, nor
Lacks cottage chimney, cottage hearth: 20
It is not more
In size than is a cottage, less
Than any other empty home
In homeliness.
It has a garden of wild flowers   25
And finest grass and gravestones warm
In sunshine hours
The year through. Men behind the glass
Stand once a week, singing, and drown
The whistling grass   30
Their ponies munch. And yet somewhere,
Near or far off, there's a man could
Be happy here,
Or one of the gods perhaps, were they
Not of inhuman stature dire,   35
As poets say
Who have not seen them clearly; if
At sound of any wind of the world
In grass–blades stiff
They would not startle and shudder cold   40
Under the sun. When gods were young
This wind was old.

The Manor Farm

The rock-like mud unfroze a little and rills
Ran and sparkled down each side of the road
Under the catkins wagging in the hedge.
But earth would have her sleep out, spite of the sun;
Nor did I value that thin gilding beam   5
More than a pretty February thing
Till I came down to the old Manor Farm,
And church and yew-tree opposite, in age
Its equals and in size. The church and yew
And farmhouse slept in a Sunday silentness.   10
The air raised not a straw. The steep farm roof,
With tiles duskily glowing, entertained
The midday sun; and up and down the roof
White pigeons nestled. There was no sound but one.
Three cart-horses were looking over a gate   15
Drowsily through their forelocks, swishing their tails
Against a fly, a solitary fly.

The Winter's cheek flushed as if he had drained
Spring, Summer, and Autumn at a draught
And smiled quietly. But 'twas not Winter –   20
Rather a season of bliss unchangeable
Awakened from farm and church where it had lain
Safe under tile and thatch for ages since
This England, Old already, was called Merry.

An Old Song I

I was not apprenticed nor ever dwelt in famous Lincolnshire;
I've served one master ill and well much more than seven year;
And never took up to poaching as you shall quickly find;
    But 'tis my delight of a shiny night in the season of the year.

I roamed where nobody had a right but keepers and squires, and there   5
I sought for nests, wild flowers, oak sticks, and moles, both far and near,
And had to run from farmers, and learnt the Lincolnshire song:
    'Oh, 'tis my delight of a shiny night in the season of the year.'

I took those walks years after, talking with friend or dear,
Or solitary musing; but when the moon shone clear   10
I had no joy or sorrow that could not be expressed
    By ''Tis my delight of a shiny night in the season of the year.'

Since then I've thrown away a chance to fight a gamekeeper;
And I less often trespass, and what I see or hear
Is mostly from the road or path by day: yet still I sing: 15
    'Oh, 'tis my delight of a shiny night in the season of the year.'

For if I am contented, at home or anywhere,
Or if I sigh for I know not what, or my heart beats with some fear,
It is a strange kind of delight to sing or whistle just:
    'Oh, 'tis my delight of a shiny night in the season of the year.'   20

And with this melody on my lips and no one by to care,
Indoors, or out on shiny nights or dark in open air,
I am for a moment made a man that sings out of his heart:
    'Oh, 'tis my delight of a shiny night in the season of the year.'

An Old Song II

The sun set, the wind fell, the sea
Was like a mirror shaking:
The one small wave that clapped the land
A mile-long snake of foam was making
Where tide had smoothed and wind had dried   5
The vacant sand.

A light divided the swollen clouds
And lay most perfectly
Like a straight narrow footbridge bright
That crossed over the sea to me;   10
And no one else in the whole world
Saw that same sight.

I walked elate, my bridge always
Just one step from my feet:
A robin sang, a shade in shade: 15
And all I did was to repeat:
   'I'll go no more a-roving
   With you, fair maid.'

The sailors' song of merry loving
With dusk and sea-gull's mewing   20
Mixed sweet, the lewdness far outweighed
By the wild charm the chorus played:
   'I'll go no more a-roving
   With you, fair maid:
   A-roving, a-roving, since roving's been my ruin,   25
   I'll go no more a-roving with you, fair maid.'

In Amsterdam there dwelt a maid –
Mark well what I do say –
In Amsterdam there dwelt a maid
And she was a mistress of her trade: 30
I'll go no more a-roving
With you, fair maid:
A-roving, a-roving, since roving's been my ruin,
I'll go no more a-roving with you, fair maid.

The Combe

The Combe was ever dark, ancient and dark.
Its mouth is stopped with bramble, thorn, and briar;
And no one scrambles over the sliding chalk
By beech and yew and perishing juniper
Down the half precipices of its sides, with roots   5
And rabbit holes for steps. The sun of Winter,
The moon of Summer, and all the singing birds
Except the missel-thrush that loves juniper,
Are quite shut out. But far more ancient and dark
The Combe looks since they killed the badger there,   10
Dug him out and gave him to the hounds,
That most ancient Briton of English beasts.

The Hollow Wood

Out in the sun the goldfinch flits
Along the thistle-tops, flits and twits
Above the hollow wood
Where birds swim like fish –
Fish that laugh and shriek –   5
To and fro, far below
In the pale hollow wood.

Lichen, ivy, and moss
Keep evergreen the trees
That stand half-flayed and dying,   10
And the dead trees on their knees
In dog's-mercury and moss:
And the bright twit of the goldfinch drops
Down there as he flits on thistle-tops.

The New Year

He was the one man I met up in the woods
That stormy New Year's morning; and at first sight,
Fifty yards off, I could not tell how much
Of the strange tripod was a man. His body,
Bowed horizontal, was supported equally   5
By legs at one end, by a rake at the other:
Thus he rested, far less like a man than
His wheel-barrow in profile was like a pig.
But when I saw it was an old man bent,
At the same moment came into my mind   10
The games at which boys bend thus, *High-cockolorum*,
Or *Fly-the-garter*, and *Leap-frog*. At the sound
Of footsteps he began to straighten himself;
His head rolled under his cape like a tortoise's;
He took an unlit pipe out of his mouth   15
Politely ere I wished him 'A Happy New Year',
And with his head cast upward sideways muttered –
So far as I could hear through the trees' roar –
'Happy New Year, and may it come fastish, too,'
While I strode by and he turned to raking leaves.   20

The Source

All day the air triumphs with its two voices
Of wind and rain:
As loud as if in anger it rejoices,
Drowning the sound of earth
That gulps and gulps in choked endeavour vain   5
To swallow the rain.

Half the night, too, only the wild air speaks
With wind and rain,
Till forth the dumb source of the river breaks
And drowns the rain and wind,   10
Bellows like a giant bathing in mighty mirth
The triumph of earth.

The Penny Whistle

The new moon hangs like an ivory bugle
In the naked frosty blue;
And the ghylls of the forest, already blackened
By Winter, are blackened anew.

The brooks that cut up and increase the forest,   5
As if they had never known
The sun, are roaring with black hollow voices
Betwixt rage and a moan.

But still the caravan-hut by the hollies
Like a kingfisher gleams between: 10
Round the mossed old hearths of the charcoal-burners
First primroses ask to be seen.

The charcoal-burners are black, but their linen
Blows white on the line;
And white the letter the girl is reading   15
Under that crescent fine;

And her brother who hides apart in a thicket,
Slowly and surely playing
On a whistle an olden nursery melody,
Says far more than I am saying.   20

A Private

This ploughman dead in battle slept out of doors
Many a frosty night, and merrily
Answered staid drinkers, good bedmen, and all bores:
'At Mrs Greenland's Hawthorn Bush,' said he,
'I slept.' None knew which bush. Above the town,   5
Beyond 'The Drover', a hundred spot the down
In Wiltshire. And where now at last he sleeps
More sound in France – that, too, he secret keeps.

Snow

In the gloom of whiteness,
In the great silence of snow,
A child was sighing
And bitterly saying: 'Oh,
They have killed a white bird up there on her nest,   5
The down is fluttering from her breast.'
And still it fell through that dusky brightness
On the child crying for the bird of the snow.

Adlestrop

Yes. I remember Adlestrop –
The name, because one afternoon
Of heat the express-train drew up there
Unwontedly. It was late June.

The steam hissed. Someone cleared his throat.   5
No one left and no one came
On the bare platform. What I saw
Was Adlestrop – only the name

And willows, willow-herb, and grass,
And meadowsweet, and haycocks dry,   10
No whit less still and lonely fair
Than the high cloudlets in the sky.

And for that minute a blackbird sang
Close by, and round him, mistier,
Farther and farther, all the birds   15
Of Oxfordshire and Gloucestershire.

Tears

It seems I have no tears left. They should have fallen –
Their ghosts, if tears have ghosts, did fall – that day
When twenty hounds streamed by me, not yet combed out
But still all equals in their rage of gladness
Upon the scent, made one, like a great dragon   5
In Blooming Meadow that bends towards the sun
And once bore hops: and on that other day
When I stepped out from the double-shadowed Tower
Into an April morning, stirring and sweet
And warm. Strange solitude was there and silence.   10
A mightier charm than any in the Tower
Possessed the courtyard. They were changing guard,
Soldiers in line, young English countrymen,
Fair-haired and ruddy, in white tunics. Drums
And fifes were playing 'The British Grenadiers'.   15
The men, the music piercing that solitude
And silence, told me truths I had not dreamed,
And have forgotten since their beauty passed.

Over the Hills

Often and often it came back again
To mind, the day I passed the horizon ridge
To a new country, the path I had to find
By half-gaps that were stiles once in the hedge,
The pack of scarlet clouds running across   5
The harvest evening that seemed endless then
And after, and the inn where all were kind,
All were strangers. I did not know my loss
Till one day twelve months later suddenly
I leaned upon my spade and saw it all,   10
Though far beyond the sky-line. It became
Almost a habit through the year for me
To lean and see it and think to do the same
Again for two days and a night. Recall
Was vain: no more could the restless brook   15
Ever turn back and climb the waterfall

To the lake that rests and stirs not in its nook,
As in the hollow of the collar-bone
Under the mountain's head of rush and stone.

The Lofty Sky

Today I want the sky,
The tops of the high hills,
Above the last man's house,
His hedges, and his cows,
Where, if I will, I look   5
Down even on sheep and rook,
And of all things that move
See buzzards only above: –
Past all trees, past furze
And thorn, where naught deters   10
The desire of the eye
For sky, nothing but sky.
I sicken of the woods
And all the multitudes
Of hedge-trees. They are no more   15
Than weeds upon this floor
Of the river of air
Leagues deep, leagues wide, where
I am like a fish that lives
In weeds and mud and gives   20
What's above him no thought.
I might be a tench for aught
That I can do today
Down on the wealden clay.
Even the tench has days   25
When he floats up and plays
Among the lily leaves
And sees the sky, or grieves
Not if he nothing sees:
While I, I know that trees   30
Under that lofty sky
Are weeds, fields mud, and I
Would arise and go far
To where the lilies are.

The Cuckoo

That's the cuckoo, you say. I cannot hear it.
When last I heard it I cannot recall; but I know
Too well the year when first I failed to hear it –
It was drowned by my man groaning out to his sheep 'Ho! Ho!'

Ten times with an angry voice he shouted   5
'Ho! Ho!' but not in anger, for that was his way.
He died that Summer, and that is how I remember
The cuckoo calling, the children listening, and me saying, 'Nay.'

And now, as you said, 'There it is!' I was hearing
Not the cuckoo at all, but my man's 'Ho! Ho!' instead.   10
And I think that even if I could lose my deafness
The cuckoo's note would be drowned by the voice of my dead.

Swedes

They have taken the gable from the roof of clay
On the long swede pile. They have let in the sun
To the white and gold and purple of curled fronds
Unsunned. It is a sight more tender-gorgeous
At the wood-corner where Winter moans and drips   5
Than when, in the Valley of the Tombs of Kings,
A boy crawls down into a Pharaoh's tomb
And, first of Christian men, beholds the mummy,
God and monkey, chariot and throne and vase,
Blue pottery, alabaster, and gold.   10

But dreamless long-dead Amen-hotep lies.
This is a dream of Winter, sweet as Spring.

The Unknown Bird

Three lovely notes he whistled, too soft to be heard
If others sang; but others never sang
In the great beech-wood all that May and June.
No one saw him: I alone could hear him
Though many listened. Was it but four years   5
Ago? or five? He never came again.

Oftenest when I heard him I was alone,
Nor could I ever make another hear.
La-la-la! he called, seeming far-off –
As if a cock crowed past the edge of the world,   10
As if the bird or I were in a dream.
Yet that he travelled through the trees and sometimes
Neared me, was plain, though somehow distant still
He sounded. All the proof is – I told men
What I had heard.

               I never knew a voice,   15
Man, beast, or bird, better than this. I told
The naturalists; but neither had they heard
Anything like the notes that did so haunt me,
I had them clear by heart and have them still.
Four years, or five, have made no difference. Then   20
As now that La-la-la! was bodiless sweet:
Sad more than joyful it was, if I must say
That it was one or other, but if sad
'Twas sad only with joy too, too far off
For me to taste it. But I cannot tell   25
If truly never anything but fair
The days were when he sang, as now they seem.
This surely I know, that I who listened then,
Happy sometimes, sometimes suffering
A heavy body and a heavy heart,   30
Now straightway, if I think of it, become
Light as that bird wandering beyond my shore.

The Mill-Pond

The sun blazed while the thunder yet
Added a boom:
A wagtail flickered bright over
The mill-pond's gloom:

Less than the cooing in the alder   5
Isles of the pool
Sounded the thunder through that plunge
Of waters cool.

Scared starlings on the aspen tip
Past the black mill   10
Outchattered the stream and the next roar
Far on the hill.

As my feet dangling teased the foam
That slid below
A girl came out. 'Take care!' she said –   15
Ages ago.

She startled me, standing quite close
Dressed all in white:
Ages ago I was angry till
She passed from sight.   20

Then the storm burst, and as I crouched
To shelter, how
Beautiful and kind, too, she seemed,
As she does now!

Man and Dog

''Twill take some getting.' 'Sir, I think 'twill so.'
The old man stared up at the mistletoe
That hung too high in the poplar's crest for plunder
Of any climber, though not for kissing under:
Then he went on against the north-east wind –   5

56

Straight but lame, leaning on a staff new-skinned,
Carrying a brolly, flag-basket, and old coat, –
Towards Alton, ten miles off. And he had not
Done less from Chilgrove where he pulled up docks.
'Twere best, if he had had 'a money-box',   10
To have waited there till the sheep cleared a field
For what a half-week's flint-picking would yield.
His mind was running on the work he had done
Since he left Christchurch in the New Forest, one
Spring in the 'seventies, – navvying on dock and line   15
From Southampton to Newcastle-on-Tyne, –
In 'seventy-four a year of soldiering
With the Berkshires, – hoeing and harvesting
In half the shires where corn and couch will grow.
His sons, three sons, were fighting, but the hoe   20
And reap-hook he liked, or anything to do with trees.
He fell once from a poplar tall as these:
The Flying Man they called him in hospital.
'If I flew now, to another world I'd fall.'
He laughed and whistled to the small brown bitch   25
With spots of blue that hunted in the ditch.
Her foxy Welsh grandfather must have paired
Beneath him. He kept sheep in Wales and scared
Strangers, I will warrant, with his pearl eye
And trick of shrinking off as he were shy,   30
Then following close in silence for – for what?
'No rabbit, never fear, she ever got,
Yet always hunts. Today she nearly had one:
She would and she wouldn't. 'Twas like that. The bad one!
She's not much use, but still she's company,   35
Though I'm not. She goes everywhere with me.
So Alton I must reach tonight somehow:
I'll get no shakedown with that bedfellow
From farmers. Many a man sleeps worse tonight
Than I shall.' 'In the trenches.' 'Yes, that's right.   40
But they'll be out of that – I hope they be –
This weather, marching after the enemy.'
'And so I hope. Good luck.' And there I nodded
'Good-night. You keep straight on.' Stiffly he plodded;
And at his heels the crisp leaves scurried fast,   45
And the leaf-coloured robin watched. They passed,
The robin till next day, the man for good,
Together in the twilight of the wood.

57

Beauty

What does it mean? Tired, angry, and ill at ease,
No man, woman, or child alive could please
Me now. And yet I almost dare to laugh
Because I sit and frame an epitaph –
'Here lies all that no one loved of him   5
And that loved no one.' Then in a trice that whim
Has wearied. But, though I am like a river
At fall of evening while it seems that never
Has the sun lighted it or warmed it, while
Cross breezes cut the surface to a file,   10
This heart, some fraction of me, happily
Floats through the window even now to a tree
Down in the misting, dim-lit, quiet vale,
Not like a pewit that returns to wail
For something it has lost, but like a dove   15
That slants unswerving to its home and love.
There I find my rest, and through the dusk air
Flies what yet lives in me. Beauty is there.

The Gypsy

A fortnight before Christmas Gypsies were everywhere:
Vans were drawn up on wastes, women trailed to the fair.
'My gentleman,' said one, 'You've got a lucky face.'
'And you've a luckier,' I thought, 'if such a grace
And impudence in rags are lucky.' 'Give a penny   5
For the poor baby's sake.' 'Indeed I have not any
Unless you can give change for a sovereign, my dear.'
'Then just half a pipeful of tobacco can you spare?'
I gave it. With that much victory she laughed content.
I should have given more, but off and away she went   10
With her baby and her pink sham flowers to rejoin
The rest before I could translate to its proper coin
Gratitude for her grace. And I paid nothing then,
As I pay nothing now with the dipping of my pen
For her brother's music when he drummed the tambourine   15
And stamped his feet, which made the workmen passing grin,
While his mouth-organ changed to a rascally Bacchanal dance

'Over the hills and far away'. This and his glance
Outlasted all the fair, farmer and auctioneer,
Cheap-jack, balloon-man, drover with crooked stick, and steer,   20
Pig, turkey, goose, and duck, Christmas corpses to be.
Not even the kneeling ox had eyes like the Romany.
That night he peopled for me the hollow wooded land,
More dark and wild than stormiest heavens, that I searched and scanned
Like a ghost new-arrived. The gradations of the dark   25
Were like an underworld of death, but for the spark
In the Gypsy boy's black eyes as he played and stamped his tune,
'Over the hills and far away', and a crescent moon.

Ambition

Unless it was that day I never knew
Ambition. After a night of frost, before
The March sun brightened and the South-west blew,
Jackdaws began to shout and float and soar
Already, and one was racing straight and high   5
Alone, shouting like a black warrior
Challenges and menaces to the wide sky.
With loud long laughter then a woodpecker
Ridiculed the sadness of the owl's last cry.
And through the valley where all the folk astir   10
Made only plumes of pearly smoke to tower
Over dark trees and white meadows happier
Than was Elysium in that happy hour,
A train that roared along raised after it
And carried with it a motionless white bower   15
Of purest cloud, from end to end close-knit,
So fair it touched the roar with silence. Time
Was powerless while that lasted. I could sit
And think I had made the loveliness of prime,
Breathed its life into it and were its lord,   20
And no mind lived save this 'twixt clouds and rime.
Omnipotent I was, nor even deplored
That I did nothing. But the end fell like a bell:
The bower was scattered; far off the train roared.
But if this was ambition I cannot tell.   25
What 'twas ambition for I know not well.

House and Man

One hour: as dim he and his house now look
As a reflection in a rippling brook,
While I remember him; but first, his house.
Empty it sounded. It was dark with forest boughs
That brushed the walls and made the mossy tiles   5
Part of the squirrels' track. In all those miles
Of forest silence and forest murmur, only
One house – 'Lonely!' he said, 'I wish it were lonely' –
Which the trees looked upon from every side,
And that was his.

              He waved good-bye to hide   10
A sigh that he converted to a laugh.
He seemed to hang rather than stand there, half
Ghost-like, half like a beggar's rag, clean wrung
And useless on the briar where it has hung
Long years a-washing by sun and wind and rain.   15

But why I call back man and house again
Is that now on a beech-tree's tip I see
As then I saw – I at the gate, and he
In the house darkness, – a magpie veering about,
A magpie like a weathercock in doubt.   20

Parting

The Past is a strange land, most strange.
Wind blows not there, nor does rain fall:
If they do, they cannot hurt at all.
Men of all kinds as equals range

The soundless fields and streets of it.   5
Pleasure and pain there have no sting,
The perished self not suffering
That lacks all blood and nerve and wit,

And is in shadow-land a shade.
Remembered joy and misery   10
Bring joy to the joyous equally;
Both sadden the sad. So memory made

Parting today a double pain:
First because it was parting; next
Because the ill it ended vexed   15
And mocked me from the Past again,

Not as what had been remedied
Had I gone on, – not that, oh no!
But as itself no longer woe;
Sighs, angry word and look and deed   20

Being faded: rather a kind of bliss,
For there spiritualised it lay
In the perpetual yesterday
That naught can stir or stain like this.

First known when lost

I never had noticed it until
'Twas gone, – the narrow copse
Where now the woodman lops
The last of the willows with his bill.

It was not more than a hedge overgrown.   5
One meadow's breadth away
I passed it day by day.
Now the soil is bare as a bone,

And black betwixt two meadows green,
Though fresh-cut faggot ends   10
Of hazel make some amends
With a gleam as if flowers they had been.

Strange it could have hidden so near!
And now I see as I look
That the small winding brook,   15
A tributary's tributary, rises there.

May 23

There never was a finer day,
And never will be while May is May, –
The third, and not the last of its kind;
But though fair and clear the two behind
Seemed pursued by tempests overpast;   5
And the morrow with fear that it could not last
Was spoiled. Today ere the stones were warm
Five minutes of thunderstorm
Dashed it with rain, as if to secure,
By one tear, its beauty the luck to endure.   10

At midday then along the lane
Old Jack Noman appeared again,
Jaunty and old, crooked and tall,
And stopped and grinned at me over the wall,
With a cowslip bunch in his button-hole   15
And one in his cap. Who could say if his roll
Came from flints in the road, the weather, or ale?
He was welcome as the nightingale.
Not an hour of the sun had been wasted on Jack.
'I've got my Indian complexion back'   20
Said he. He was tanned like a harvester,
Like his short clay pipe, like the leaf and bur
That clung to his coat from last night's bed,
Like the ploughland crumbling red.
Fairer flowers were none on the earth   25
Than his cowslips wet with the dew of their birth,
Or fresher leaves than the cress in his basket.
'Where did they come from, Jack?' 'Don't ask it,
And you'll be told no lies.' 'Very well:
Then I can't buy.' 'I don't want to sell.   30
Take them and these flowers, too, free.
Perhaps you have something to give me?
Wait till next time. The better the day...
The Lord couldn't make a better, I say;
If he could, he never has done.'   35
So off went Jack with his roll-walk-run,
Leaving his cresses from Oakshott rill
And his cowslips from Wheatham hill.

'Twas the first day that the midges bit;
But though they bit me, I was glad of it: 40
Of the dust in my face, too, I was glad.
Spring could do nothing to make me sad.
Bluebells hid all the ruts in the copse,
The elm seeds lay in the road like hops,
That fine day, May the twenty-third,   45
The day Jack Noman disappeared.

The Barn

They should never have built a barn there, at all –
Drip, drip, drip! – under that elm tree,
Though then it was young. Now it is old
But good, not like the barn and me.

Tomorrow they cut it down. They will leave   5
The barn, as I shall be left, maybe.
What holds it up? 'Twould not pay to pull down.
Well, this place has no other antiquity.

No abbey or castle looks so old
As this that Job Knight built in '54,   10
Built to keep corn for rats and men.
Now there's fowls in the roof, pigs on the floor.

What thatch survives is dung for the grass,
The best grass on the farm. A pity the roof
Will not bear a mower to mow it. But   15
Only fowls have foothold enough.

Starlings used to sit there with bubbling throats
Making a spiky beard as they chattered
And whistled and kissed, with heads in air,
Till they thought of something else that mattered.   20

But now they cannot find a place,
Among all those holes, for a nest any more.
It's the turn of lesser things, I suppose.
Once I fancied 'twas starlings they built it for.

Home

Not the end: but there's nothing more.
Sweet Summer and Winter rude
I have loved, and friendship and love,
The crowd and solitude:

But I know them: I weary not; 5
But all that they mean I know.
I would go back again home
Now. Yet how should I go?

This is my grief. That land,
My home, I have never seen; 10
No traveller tells of it,
However far he has been.

And could I discover it,
I fear my happiness there,
Or my pain, might be dreams of return 15
Here, to these things that were.

Remembering ills, though slight
Yet irremediable,
Brings a worse, an impurer pang
Than remembering what was well. 20

No: I cannot go back,
And would not if I could.
Until blindness come, I must wait
And blink at what is not good.

The Owl

Downhill I came, hungry, and yet not starved;
Cold, yet had heat within me that was proof
Against the North wind; tired, yet so that rest
Had seemed the sweetest thing under a roof.

Then at the inn I had food, fire, and rest,   5
Knowing how hungry, cold, and tired was I.
All of the night was quite barred out except
An owl's cry, a most melancholy cry

Shaken out long and clear upon the hill,
No merry note, nor cause of merriment,   10
But one telling me plain what I escaped
And others could not, that night, as in I went.

And salted was my food, and my repose,
Salted and sobered, too, by the bird's voice
Speaking for all who lay under the stars,   15
Soldiers and poor, unable to rejoice.

The Child on the Cliffs

Mother, the root of this little yellow flower
Among the stones has the taste of quinine.
Things are strange today on the cliff. The sun shines so bright,
And the grasshopper works at his sewing-machine
So hard. Here's one on my hand, mother, look;   5
I lie so still. There's one on your book.

But I have something to tell more strange. So leave
Your book to the grasshopper, mother dear, –
Like a green knight in a dazzling market-place, –
And listen now. Can you hear what I hear   10
Far out? Now and then the foam there curls
And stretches a white arm out like a girl's.

Fishes and gulls ring no bells. There cannot be
A chapel or church between here and Devon,
With fishes or gulls ringing its bell, – hark! –   15
Somewhere under the sea or up in heaven.
'It's the bell, my son, out in the bay
On the buoy. It does sound sweet today.'

Sweeter I never heard, mother, no, not in all Wales.
I should like to be lying under that foam,   20
Dead, but able to hear the sound of the bell,
And certain that you would often come
And rest, listening happily.
I should be happy if that could be.

The Bridge

I have come a long way today:
On a strange bridge alone,
Remembering friends, old friends,
I rest, without smile or moan,
As they remember me without smile or moan.   5

All are behind, the kind
And the unkind too, no more
Tonight than a dream. The stream
Runs softly yet drowns the Past,
The dark-lit stream has drowned the Future and the Past.   10

No traveller has rest more blest
Than this moment brief between
Two lives, when the Night's first lights
And shades hide what has never been,
Things goodlier, lovelier, dearer, than will be or have been.   15

Good-night

The skylarks are far behind that sang over the down;
I can hear no more those suburb nightingales;
Thrushes and blackbirds sing in the gardens of the town
In vain: the noise of man, beast, and machine prevails.

But the call of children in the unfamiliar streets   5
That echo with a familiar twilight echoing,
Sweet as the voice of nightingale or lark, completes
A magic of strange welcome, so that I seem a king

Among man, beast, machine, bird, child, and the ghost
That in the echo lives and with the echo dies.   10
The friendless town is friendly; homeless, I am not lost;
Though I know none of these doors, and meet but strangers' eyes.

Never again, perhaps, after tomorrow, shall
I see these homely streets, these church windows alight,
Not a man or woman or child among them all: 15
But it is All Friends' Night, a traveller's good-night.

But these things also

But these things also are Spring's —
On banks by the roadside the grass
Long-dead that is greyer now
Than all the Winter it was;

The shell of a little snail bleached   5
In the grass; chip of flint, and mite
Of chalk; and the small birds' dung
In splashes of purest white:

All the white things a man mistakes
For earliest violets   10
Who seeks through Winter's ruins
Something to pay Winter's debts,

While the North blows, and starling flocks
By chattering on and on
Keep their spirits up in the mist,   15
And Spring's here, Winter's not gone.

The New House

Now first, as I shut the door,
I was alone
In the new house; and the wind
Began to moan.

Old at once was the house,   5
And I was old;
My ears were teased with the dread
Of what was foretold,

Nights of storm, days of mist, without end;
Sad days when the sun   10
Shone in vain: old griefs, and griefs
Not yet begun.

All was foretold me; naught
Could I foresee;
But I learnt how the wind would sound   15
After these things should be.

The Barn and the Down

It stood in the sunset sky
Like the straight-backed down,
Many a time – the barn
At the edge of the town,

So huge and dark that it seemed   5
It was the hill
Till the gable's precipice proved
It impossible.

Then the great down in the west
Grew into sight,   10
A barn stored full to the ridge
With black of night;

And the barn fell to a barn
Or even less
Before critical eyes and its own   15
Late mightiness.

But far down and near barn and I
Since then have smiled,
Having seen my new cautiousness
By itself beguiled   20

To disdain what seemed the barn
Till a few steps changed
It past all doubt to the down;
So the barn was avenged.

Sowing

It was a perfect day
For sowing; just
As sweet and dry was the ground
As tobacco-dust.

I tasted deep the hour   5
Between the far
Owl's chuckling first soft cry
And the first star.

A long stretched hour it was;
Nothing undone   10
Remained; the early seeds
All safely sown.

And now, hark at the rain,
Windless and light,
Half a kiss, half a tear,   15
Saying good-night.

March the Third

Here again (she said) is March the third
And twelve hours singing for the bird
'Twixt dawn and dusk, from half-past six
To half-past six, never unheard.

'Tis Sunday, and the church-bells end   5
When the birds do. I think they blend
Now better than they will when passed
Is this unnamed, unmarked godsend.

Or do all mark, and none dares say,
How it may shift and long delay,   10
Somewhere before the first of Spring,
But never fails, this singing day?

And when it falls on Sunday, bells
Are a wild natural voice that dwells
On hillsides; but the birds' songs have   15
The holiness gone from the bells.

This day unpromised is more dear
Than all the named days of the year
When seasonable sweets come in,
Because we know how lucky we are.   20

Two Pewits

Under the after-sunset sky
Two pewits sport and cry,
More white than is the moon on high
Riding the dark surge silently;
More black than earth. Their cry   5
Is the one sound under the sky.
They alone move, now low, now high,
And merrily they cry
To the mischievous Spring sky,
Plunging earthward, tossing high,   10
Over the ghost who wonders why

So merrily they cry and fly,
Nor choose 'twixt earth and sky,
While the moon's quarter silently
Rides, and earth rests as silently.   15

Will you come?

Will you come?
Will you come?
Will you ride
So late
At my side?   5
O, will you come?

Will you come?
Will you come
If the night
Has a moon,   10
Full and bright?
O, will you come?

Would you come?
Would you come
If the noon   15
Gave light,
Not the moon?
Beautiful, would you come?

Would you have come?
Would you have come   20
Without scorning,
Had it been
Still morning?
Beloved, would you have come?

If you come,   25
Haste and come.
Owls have cried;
It grows dark
To ride.
Beloved, beautiful, come.   30

The Path

Running along a bank, a parapet
That saves from the precipitous wood below
The level road, there is a path. It serves
Children for looking down the long smooth steep,
Between the legs of beech and yew, to where   5
A fallen tree checks the sight: while men and women
Content themselves with the road and what they see
Over the bank, and what the children tell.
The path, winding like silver, trickles on,
Bordered and even invaded by thinnest moss   10
That tries to cover roots and crumbling chalk
With gold, olive, and emerald, but in vain.
The children wear it. They have flattened the bank
On top, and silvered it between the moss
With the current of their feet, year after year.   15
But the road is houseless, and leads not to school.
To see a child is rare there, and the eye
Has but the road, the wood that overhangs
And underyawns it, and the path that looks
As if it led on to some legendary   20
Or fancied place where men have wished to go
And stay; till, sudden, it ends where the wood ends.

The Wasp Trap

This moonlight makes
The lovely lovelier
Than ever before lakes
And meadows were.

And yet they are not,   5
Though this their hour is, more
Lovely than things that were not
Lovely before.

Nothing on earth,
And in the heavens no star,   10
For pure brightness is worth
More than that jar,

For wasps meant, now
A star – long may it swing
From the dead apple-bough,   15
So glistening.

A Tale

There once the walls
Of the ruined cottage stood.
The periwinkle crawls
With flowers in its hair into the wood.

In flowerless hours   5
Never will the bank fail,
With everlasting flowers
On fragments of blue plates, to tell the tale.

Wind and Mist

They met inside the gateway that gives the view,
A hollow land as vast as heaven. 'It is
A pleasant day, sir.' 'A very pleasant day.'
'And what a view here. If you like angled fields
Of grass and grain bounded by oak and thorn,   5
Here is a league. Had we with Germany
To play upon this board it could not be
More dear than April has made it with a smile.
The fields beyond that league close in together
And merge, even as our days into the past,   10
Into one wood that has a shining pane
Of water. Then the hills of the horizon –

That is how I should make hills had I to show
One who would never see them what hills were like.'
'Yes. Sixty miles of South Downs at one glance.   15
Sometimes a man feels proud of them, as if
He had just created them with one mighty thought.'
'That house, though modern, could not be better planned
For its position. I never liked a new
House better. Could you tell me who lives in it?'   20
'No one.' 'Ah – and I was peopling all
Those windows on the south with happy eyes,
The terrace under them with happy feet;
Girls – ' 'Sir, I know. I know. I have seen that house
Through mist look lovely as a castle in Spain,   25
And airier. I have thought: "'Twere happy there
To live." And I have laughed at that
Because I lived there then.' 'Extraordinary.'
'Yes, with my furniture and family
Still in it, I, knowing every nook of it   30
And loving none, and in fact hating it.'
'Dear me! How could that be? But pardon me.'
'No offence. Doubtless the house was not to blame,
But the eye watching from those windows saw,
Many a day, day after day, mist – mist   35
Like chaos surging back – and felt itself
Alone in all the world, marooned alone.
We lived in clouds, on a cliff's edge almost
(You see), and if clouds went, the visible earth
Lay too far off beneath and like a cloud.   40
I did not know it was the earth I loved
Until I tried to live there in the clouds
And the earth turned to cloud.' 'You had a garden
Of flint and clay, too.' 'True; that was real enough.
The flint was the one crop that never failed.   45
The clay first broke my heart, and then my back;
And the back heals not. There were other things
Real, too. In that room at the gable a child
Was born while the wind chilled a summer dawn:
Never looked grey mind on a greyer one   50
Than when the child's cry broke above the groans.'
'I hope they were both spared.' 'They were. Oh yes.
But flint and clay and childbirth were too real
For this cloud castle. I had forgot the wind.
Pray do not let me get on to the wind.   55

74

You would not understand about the wind.
It is my subject, and compared with me
Those who have always lived on the firm ground
Are quite unreal in this matter of the wind.
There were whole days and nights when the wind and I   60
Between us shared the world, and the wind ruled
And I obeyed it and forgot the mist.
My past and the past of the world were in the wind.
Now you will say that though you understand
And feel for me, and so on, you yourself   65
Would find it different. You are all like that
If once you stand here free from wind and mist:
I might as well be talking to wind and mist.
You would believe the house-agent's young man
Who gives no heed to anything I say.   70
Good morning. But one word. I want to admit
That I would try the house once more, if I could;
As I should like to try being young again.'

A Gentleman

'He has robbed two clubs. The judge at Salisbury
Can't give him more than he undoubtedly
Deserves. The scoundrel! Look at his photograph!
A lady-killer! Hanging's too good by half
For such as he.' So said the stranger, one   5
With crimes yet undiscovered or undone.
But at the inn the Gypsy dame began:
'Now he was what I call a gentleman.
He went along with Carrie, and when she
Had a baby he paid up so readily   10
His half a crown. Just like him. A crown'd have been
More like him. For I never knew him mean.
Oh! but he was such a nice gentleman. Oh!
Last time we met he said if me and Joe
Was anywhere near we must be sure and call.   15
He put his arms around our Amos all
As if he were his own son. I pray God
Save him from justice! Nicer man never trod.'

75

Lob

At hawthorn-time in Wiltshire travelling
In search of something chance would never bring,
An old man's face, by life and weather cut
And coloured, – rough, brown, sweet as any nut, –
A land face, sea-blue-eyed, – hung in my mind   5
When I had left him many a mile behind.
All he said was: 'Nobody can't stop 'ee. It's
A footpath, right enough. You see those bits
Of mounds – that's where they opened up the barrows
Sixty years since, while I was scaring sparrows.   10
They thought as there was something to find there,
But couldn't find it, by digging, anywhere.'

To turn back then and seek him, where was the use?
There were three Manningfords, – Abbots, Bohun, and Bruce:
And whether Alton, not Manningford, it was,   15
My memory could not decide, because
There was both Alton Barnes and Alton Priors.
All had their churches, graveyards, farms, and byres,
Lurking to one side up the paths and lanes,
Seldom well seen except by aeroplanes;   20
And when bells rang, or pigs squealed, or cocks crowed,
Then only heard. Ages ago the road
Approached. The people stood and looked and turned,
Nor asked it to come nearer, nor yet learned
To move out there and dwell in all men's dust.   25
And yet withal they shot the weathercock, just
Because 'twas he crowed out of tune, they said:
So now the copper weathercock is dead.
If they had reaped their dandelions and sold
Them fairly, they could have afforded gold.   30

Many years passed, and I went back again
Among those villages, and looked for men
Who might have known my ancient. He himself
Had long been dead or laid upon the shelf,
I thought. One man I asked about him roared   35
At my description: ''Tis old Bottlesford
He means, Bill.' But another said: 'Of course,

It was Jack Button up at the White Horse.
He's dead, sir, these three years.' This lasted till
A girl proposed Walker of Walker's Hill,   40
'Old Adam Walker. Adam's Point you'll see
Marked on the maps.'

     'That was her roguery,'
The next man said. He was a squire's son
Who loved wild bird and beast, and dog and gun
For killing them. He had loved them from his birth,   45
One with another, as he loved the earth.
'The man may be like Button, or Walker, or
Like Bottlesford, that you want, but far more
He sounds like one I saw when I was a child.
I could almost swear to him. The man was wild   50
And wandered. His home was where he was free.
Everybody has met one such man as he.
Does he keep clear old paths that no one uses
But once a life-time when he loves or muses?
He is English as this gate, these flowers, this mire.   55
And when at eight years old Lob-lie-by-the-fire
Came in my books, this was the man I saw.
He has been in England as long as dove and daw,
Calling the wild cherry tree the merry tree,
The rose campion Bridget-in-her-bravery;   60
And in a tender mood he, as I guess,
Christened one flower Love-in-idleness,
And while he walked from Exeter to Leeds
One April called all cuckoo-flowers Milkmaids.
From him old herbal Gerard learnt, as a boy,   65
To name wild clematis the Traveller's-joy.
Our blackbirds sang no English till his ear
Told him they called his Jan Toy "Pretty dear".
(She was Jan Toy the Lucky, who, having lost
A shilling, and found a penny loaf, rejoiced.)   70
For reasons of his own to him the wren
Is Jenny Pooter. Before all other men
'Twas he first called the Hog's Back the Hog's Back.
That Mother Dunch's Buttocks should not lack
Their name was his care. He too could explain   75
Totteridge and Totterdown and Juggler's Lane:
He knows, if anyone. Why Tumbling Bay,
Inland in Kent, is called so, he might say.

'But little he says compared with what he does.
If ever a sage troubles him he will buzz   80
Like a beehive to conclude the tedious fray:
And the sage, who knows all languages, runs away.
Yet Lob has thirteen hundred names for a fool,
And though he never could spare time for school
To unteach what the fox so well expressed,   85
On biting the cock's head off, – Quietness is best, –
He can talk quite as well as anyone
After his thinking is forgot and done.
He first of all told someone else's wife,
For a farthing she'd skin a flint and spoil a knife   90
Worth sixpence skinning it. She heard him speak:
"She had a face as long as a wet week"
Said he, telling the tale in after years.
With blue smock and with gold rings in his ears,
Sometimes he is a pedlar, not too poor   95
To keep his wit. This is tall Tom that bore
The logs in, and with Shakespeare in the hall
Once talked, when icicles hung by the wall.
As Herne the Hunter he has known hard times.
On sleepless nights he made up weather rhymes   100
Which others spoilt. And, Hob being then his name,
He kept the hog that thought the butcher came
To bring his breakfast. "You thought wrong," said Hob.
When there were kings in Kent this very Lob,
Whose sheep grew fat and he himself grew merry,   105
Wedded the king's daughter of Canterbury;
For he alone, unlike squire, lord, and king,
Watched a night by her without slumbering;
He kept both waking. When he was but a lad
He won a rich man's heiress, deaf, dumb, and sad,   110
By rousing her to laugh at him. He carried
His donkey on his back. So they were married.
And while he was a little cobbler's boy
He tricked the giant coming to destroy
Shrewsbury by flood. "And how far is it yet?"   115
The giant asked in passing. "I forget;
But see these shoes I've worn out on the road
And we're not there yet." He emptied out his load
Of shoes for mending. The giant let fall from his spade
The earth for damming Severn, and thus made   120
The Wrekin hill; and little Ercall hill

Rose where the giant scraped his boots. While still
So young, our Jack was chief of Gotham's sages.
But long before he could have been wise, ages
Earlier than this, while he grew thick and strong   125
And ate his bacon, or, at times, sang a song
And merely smelt it, as Jack the giant-killer
He made a name. He too ground up the miller,
The Yorkshireman who ground men's bones for flour.

'Do you believe Jack dead before his hour?   130
Or that his name is Walker, or Bottlesford,
Or Button, a mere clown, or squire, or lord?
The man you saw, – Lob-lie-by-the-fire, Jack Cade,
Jack Smith, Jack Moon, poor Jack of every trade,
Young Jack, or old Jack, or Jack What-d'ye-call,   135
Jack-in-the-hedge, or Robin-run-by-the-wall,
Robin Hood, Ragged Robin, lazy Bob,
One of the lords of No Man's Land, good Lob, –
Although he was seen dying at Waterloo,
Hastings, Agincourt, and Sedgemoor too, –   140
Lives yet. He never will admit he is dead
Till millers cease to grind men's bones for bread,
Not till our weathercock crows once again
And I remove my house out of the lane
On to the road.' With this he disappeared   145
In hazel and thorn tangled with old-man's-beard.
But one glimpse of his back, as there he stood,
Choosing his way, proved him of old Jack's blood,
Young Jack perhaps, and now a Wiltshireman
As he has oft been since his days began.   150

Digging

Today I think
Only with scents, – scents dead leaves yield,
And bracken, and wild carrot's seed,
And the square mustard field;

Odours that rise   5
When the spade wounds the root of tree,
Rose, currant, raspberry, or goutweed,
Rhubarb or celery;

The smoke's smell, too,
Flowing from where a bonfire burns   10
The dead, the waste, the dangerous,
And all to sweetness turns.

It is enough
To smell, to crumble the dark earth,
While the robin sings over again   15
Sad songs of Autumn mirth.

Lovers

The two men in the road were taken aback.
The lovers came out shading their eyes from the sun,
And never was white so white, or black so black,
As her cheeks and hair. 'There are more things than one
A man might turn into a wood for, Jack,'   5
Said George; Jack whispered: 'He has not got a gun.
It's a bit too much of a good thing, I say.
They are going the other road, look. And see her run.' –
She ran – 'What a thing it is, this picking may.'

In Memoriam (Easter, 1915)

The flowers left thick at nightfall in the wood
This Eastertide call into mind the men,
Now far from home, who, with their sweethearts, should
Have gathered them and will do never again.

Head and Bottle

The downs will lose the sun, white alyssum
Lose the bees' hum;
But head and bottle tilted back in the cart
Will never part
Till I am cold as midnight and all my hours   5
Are beeless flowers.
He neither sees, nor hears, nor smells, nor thinks,
But only drinks,
Quiet in the yard where tree trunks do not lie
More quietly.   10

Home

Often I had gone this way before:
But now it seemed I never could be
And never had been anywhere else;
'Twas home; one nationality
We had, I and the birds that sang,   5
One memory.

They welcomed me. I had come back
That eve somehow from somewhere far:
The April mist, the chill, the calm,
Meant the same thing familiar   10
And pleasant to us, and strange too,
Yet with no bar.

The thrush on the oaktop in the lane
Sang his last song, or last but one;
And as he ended, on the elm   15
Another had but just begun
His last; they knew no more than I
The day was done.

Then past his dark white cottage front
A labourer went along, his tread   20
Slow, half with weariness, half with ease;
And, through the silence, from his shed
The sound of sawing rounded all
That silence said.

Health

Four miles at a leap, over the dark hollow land,
To the frosted steep of the down and its junipers black,
Travels my eye with equal ease and delight:
And scarce could my body leap four yards.

This is the best and the worst of it –   5
Never to know,
Yet to imagine gloriously, pure health.

Today, had I suddenly health,
I could not satisfy the desire of my heart
Unless health abated it,   10
So beautiful is the air in its softness and clearness, while Spring
Promises all and fails in nothing as yet;
And what blue and what white is I never knew
Before I saw this sky blessing the land.

For had I health I could not ride or run or fly   15
So far or so rapidly over the land
As I desire: I should reach Wiltshire tired;
I should have changed my mind before I could be in Wales.
I could not love; I could not command love.
Beauty would still be far off   20
However many hills I climbed over;
Peace would still be farther.
Maybe I should not count it anything
To leap these four miles with the eye;
And either I should not be filled almost to bursting with desire,   25
Or with my power desire would still keep pace.

Yet I am not satisfied
Even with knowing I never could be satisfied.
With health and all the power that lies
In maiden beauty, poet and warrior,   30
In Caesar, Shakespeare, Alcibiades,
Mazeppa, Leonardo, Michelangelo,
In any maiden whose smile is lovelier
Than sunlight upon dew,
I could not be as the wagtail running up and down   35
The warm tiles of the roof slope, twittering
Happily and sweetly as if the sun itself
Extracted the song
As the hand makes sparks from the fur of a cat:

I could not be as the sun.   40
Nor should I be content to be
As little as the bird or as mighty as the sun.
For the bird knows not of the sun,
And the sun regards not the bird.
But I am almost proud to love both bird and sun,   45
Though scarce this Spring could my body leap four yards.

The Huxter

He has a hump like an ape on his back;
He has of money a plentiful lack;
And but for a gay coat of double his girth
There is not a plainer thing on the earth
    This fine May morning.   5

But the huxter has a bottle of beer;
He drives a cart and his wife sits near
Who does not heed his lack or his hump;
And they laugh as down the lane they bump
    This fine May morning.   10

She dotes

She dotes on what the wild birds say
Or hint or mock at, night and day, –
Thrush, blackbird, all that sing in May,
    And songless plover,
Hawk, heron, owl, and woodpecker.   5
They never say a word to her
    About her lover.

She laughs at them for childishness,
She cries at them for carelessness
Who see her going loverless   10
    Yet sing and chatter
Just as when he was not a ghost,
Nor ever ask her what she has lost
    Or what is the matter.

Yet she has fancied blackbirds hide   15
A secret, and that thrushes chide
Because she thinks death can divide
    Her from her lover;
And she has slept, trying to translate
The word the cuckoo cries to his mate   20
    Over and over.

Song

At poet's tears,
Sweeter than any smiles but hers,
She laughs; I sigh;
And yet I could not live if she should die.

And when in June   5
Once more the cuckoo spoils his tune,
She laughs at sighs;
And yet she says she loves me till she dies.

A Cat

She had a name among the children;
But no one loved though someone owned
Her, locked her out of doors at bedtime
And had her kittens duly drowned.

In Spring, nevertheless, this cat   5
Ate blackbirds, thrushes, nightingales,
And birds of bright voice and plume and flight,
As well as scraps from neighbours' pails.

I loathed and hated her for this;
One speckle on a thrush's breast   10
Was worth a million such; and yet
She lived long, till God gave her rest.

Melancholy

The rain and wind, the rain and wind, raved endlessly.
On me the Summer storm, and fever, and melancholy
Wrought magic, so that if I feared the solitude
Far more I feared all company: too sharp, too rude,
Had been the wisest or the dearest human voice.   5
What I desired I knew not, but whate'er my choice
Vain it must be, I knew. Yet naught did my despair
But sweeten the strange sweetness, while through the wild air
All day long I heard a distant cuckoo calling
And, soft as dulcimers, sounds of near water falling,   10
And, softer, and remote as if in history,
Rumours of what had touched my friends, my foes, or me.

Tonight

Harry, you know at night
The larks in Castle Alley
Sing from the attic's height
As if the electric light
Were the true sun above a summer valley: 5
Whistle, don't knock, tonight.

I shall come early, Kate:
And we in Castle Alley
Will sit close out of sight
Alone, and ask no light   10
Of lamp or sun above a summer valley:
Tonight I can stay late.

April

The sweetest thing, I thought
At one time, between earth and heaven
Was the first smile
When mist has been forgiven
And the sun has stolen out,   5
Peered, and resolved to shine at seven
On dabbled lengthening grasses,
Thick primroses and early leaves uneven,
When earth's breath, warm and humid, far surpasses
The richest oven's, and loudly rings 'cuckoo'   10
And sharply the nightingale's 'tsoo, troo, troo, troo':
To say 'God bless it' was all that I could do.

But now I know one sweeter
By far since the day Emily
Turned weeping back   15
To me, still happy me,
To ask forgiveness, –
Yet smiled with half a certainty

To be forgiven, – for what
She had never done; I knew not what it might be,   20
Nor could she tell me, having now forgot,
By rapture carried with me past all care
As to an isle in April lovelier
Than April's self. 'God bless you' I said to her.

The Glory

The glory of the beauty of the morning, –
The cuckoo crying over the untouched dew;
The blackbird that has found it, and the dove
That tempts me on to something sweeter than love;
White clouds ranged even and fair as new-mown hay;   5
The heat, the stir, the sublime vacancy
Of sky and meadow and forest and my own heart: –
The glory invites me, yet it leaves me scorning
All I can ever do, all I can be,
Beside the lovely of motion, shape, and hue,   10
The happiness I fancy fit to dwell
In beauty's presence. Shall I now this day
Begin to seek as far as heaven, as hell,
Wisdom or strength to match this beauty, start
And tread the pale dust pitted with small dark drops,   15
In hope to find whatever it is I seek,
Hearkening to short-lived happy-seeming things
That we know naught of, in the hazel copse?
Or must I be content with discontent
As larks and swallows are perhaps with wings?   20
And shall I ask at the day's end once more
What beauty is, and what I can have meant
By happiness? And shall I let all go,
Glad, weary, or both? Or shall I perhaps know
That I was happy oft and oft before,   25
Awhile forgetting how I am fast pent,
How dreary-swift, with naught to travel to,
Is Time? I cannot bite the day to the core.

July

Naught moves but clouds, and in the glassy lake
Their doubles and the shadow of my boat.
The boat itself stirs only when I break
This drowse of heat and solitude afloat
To prove if what I see be bird or mote,   5
Or learn if yet the shore woods be awake.

Long hours since dawn grew, – spread, – and passed on high
And deep below, – I have watched the cool reeds hung
Over images more cool in imaged sky:
Nothing there was worth thinking of so long;   10
All that the ring-doves say, far leaves among,
Brims my mind with content thus still to lie.

The Chalk-Pit

'Is this the road that climbs above and bends
Round what was once a chalk-pit: now it is
By accident an amphitheatre.
Some ash trees standing ankle-deep in briar
And bramble act the parts, and neither speak   5
Nor stir.' 'But see: they have fallen, every one,
And briar and bramble have grown over them.'
'That is the place. As usual no one is here.
Hardly can I imagine the drop of the axe,
And the smack that is like an echo, sounding here.'   10
'I do not understand.' 'Why, what I mean is
That I have seen the place two or three times
At most, and that its emptiness and silence
And stillness haunt me, as if just before
It was not empty, silent, still, but full   15
Of life of some kind, perhaps tragical.
Has anything unusual happened here?'
'Not that I know of. It is called the Dell.

They have not dug chalk here for a century.
That was the ash trees' age. But I will ask.'   20
'No. Do not. I prefer to make a tale,
Or better leave it like the end of a play,
Actors and audience and lights all gone;
For so it looks now. In my memory
Again and again I see it, strangely dark,   25
And vacant of a life but just withdrawn.
We have not seen the woodman with the axe.
Some ghost has left it now as we two came.'
'And yet you doubted if this were the road?'
'Well, sometimes I have thought of it and failed   30
To place it. No. And I am not quite sure,
Even now, this is it. For another place,
Real or painted, may have combined with it.
Or I myself a long way back in time...'
'Why, as to that, I used to meet a man –   35
I had forgotten, – searching for birds' nests
Along the road and in the chalk-pit too.
The wren's hole was an eye that looked at him
For recognition. Every nest he knew.
He got a stiff neck, by looking this side or that,   40
Spring after spring, he told me, with his laugh, –
A sort of laugh. He was a visitor,
A man of forty, – smoked and strolled about.
At orts and crosses Pleasure and Pain had played
On his brown features; – I think both had lost; –   45
Mild and yet wild too. You may know the kind.
And once or twice a woman shared his walks,
A girl of twenty with a brown boy's face,
And hair brown as a thrush or as a nut,
Thick eyebrows, glinting eyes – ' 'You have said enough.   50
A pair, – free thought, free love, – I know the breed:
I shall not mix my fancies up with them.'
'You please yourself. I should prefer the truth
Or nothing. Here, in fact, is nothing at all
Except a silent place that once rang loud,   55
And trees and us – imperfect friends, we men
And trees since time began; and nevertheless
Between us still we breed a mystery.'

Fifty Faggots

There they stand, on their ends, the fifty faggots
That once were underwood of hazel and ash
In Jenny Pinks's Copse. Now, by the hedge
Close packed, they make a thicket fancy alone
Can creep through with the mouse and wren. Next Spring   5
A blackbird or a robin will nest there,
Accustomed to them, thinking they will remain
Whatever is for ever to a bird:
This Spring it is too late; the swift has come.
'Twas a hot day for carrying them up: 10
Better they will never warm me, though they must
Light several Winters' fires. Before they are done
The war will have ended, many other things
Have ended, maybe, that I can no more
Foresee or more control than robin and wren.   15

Sedge-Warblers

This beauty made me dream there was a time
Long past and irrecoverable, a clime
Where any brook so radiant racing clear
Through buttercup and kingcup bright as brass
But gentle, nourishing the meadow grass   5
That leans and scurries in the wind, would bear
Another beauty, divine and feminine,
Child to the sun, a nymph whose soul unstained
Could love all day, and never hate or tire,
A lover of mortal or immortal kin.   10

And yet, rid of this dream, ere I had drained
Its poison, quieted was my desire
So that I only looked into the water,
Clearer than any goddess or man's daughter,
And hearkened while it combed the dark green hair   15
And shook the millions of the blossoms white

Of water-crowfoot, and curdled to one sheet
The flowers fallen from the chestnuts in the park
Far off. And sedge-warblers, clinging so light
To willow twigs, sang longer than the lark, 20
Quick, shrill, or grating, a song to match the heat
Of the strong sun, nor less the water's cool,
Gushing through narrows, swirling in the pool.
Their song that lacks all words, all melody,
All sweetness almost, was dearer then to me 25
Than sweetest voice that sings in tune sweet words.
This was the best of May – the small brown birds
Wisely reiterating endlessly
What no man learnt yet, in or out of school.

I built myself a house of glass

I built myself a house of glass:
It took me years to make it:
And I was proud. But now, alas,
Would God someone would break it.

But it looks too magnificent. 5
No neighbour casts a stone
From where he dwells, in tenement
Or palace of glass, alone.

Words

Out of us all
That make rhymes,
Will you choose
Sometimes –
As the winds use 5
A crack in a wall
Or a drain,

Their joy or their pain
To whistle through –
Choose me,   10
You English words?

I know you:
You are light as dreams,
Tough as oak,
Precious as gold,   15
As poppies and corn,
Or an old cloak:
Sweet as our birds
To the ear,
As the burnet rose   20
In the heat
Of Midsummer:
Strange as the races
Of dead and unborn:
Strange and sweet   25
Equally,
And familiar,
To the eye,
As the dearest faces
That a man knows,   30
And as lost homes are:
But though older far
Than oldest yew, –
As our hills are, old, –
Worn new   35
Again and again:
Young as our streams
After rain:
And as dear
As the earth which you prove   40
That we love.

Make me content
With some sweetness
From Wales
Whose nightingales   45
Have no wings, –
From Wiltshire and Kent
And Herefordshire,

And the villages there, −
From the names, and the things   50
No less.

Let me sometimes dance
With you,
Or climb
Or stand perchance   55
In ecstasy,
Fixed and free
In a rhyme,
As poets do.

The Word

There are so many things I have forgot,
That once were much to me, or that were not,
All lost, as is a childless woman's child
And its child's children, in the undefiled
Abyss of what can never be again.   5
I have forgot, too, names of the mighty men
That fought and lost or won in the old wars,
Of kings and fiends and gods, and most of the stars.
Some things I have forgot that I forget.
But lesser things there are, remembered yet,   10
Than all the others. One name that I have not −
Though 'tis an empty thingless name − forgot
Never can die because Spring after Spring
Some thrushes learn to say it as they sing.
There is always one at midday saying it clear   15
And tart − the name, only the name I hear.
While perhaps I am thinking of the elder scent
That is like food, or while I am content
With the wild rose scent that is like memory,
This name suddenly is cried out to me   20
From somewhere in the bushes by a bird
Over and over again, a pure thrush word.

Under the Woods

When these old woods were young
The thrushes' ancestors
As sweetly sung
In the old years.

There was no garden here,   5
Apples nor mistletoe;
No children dear
Ran to and fro.

New then was this thatched cot,
But the keeper was old,   10
And he had not
Much lead or gold.

Most silent beech and yew:
As he went round about
The woods to view   15
Seldom he shot.

But now that he is gone
Out of most memories,
Still lingers on
A stoat of his,   20

But one, shrivelled and green,
And with no scent at all,
And barely seen
On this shed wall.

Haymaking

After night's thunder far away had rolled
The fiery day had a kernel sweet of cold,
And in the perfect blue the clouds uncurled,

Like the first gods before they made the world
And misery, swimming the stormless sea   5
In beauty and in divine gaiety.
The smooth white empty road was lightly strewn
With leaves – the holly's Autumn falls in June –
And fir cones standing stiff up in the heat.
The mill-foot water tumbled white and lit   10
With tossing crystals, happier than any crowd
Of children pouring out of school aloud.
And in the little thickets where a sleeper
For ever might lie lost, the nettle-creeper
And garden warbler sang unceasingly;   15
While over them shrill shrieked in his fierce glee
The swift with wings and tail as sharp and narrow
As if the bow had flown off with the arrow.
Only the scent of woodbine and hay new-mown
Travelled the road. In the field sloping down,   20
Park-like, to where its willows showed the brook,
Haymakers rested. The tosser lay forsook
Out in the sun; and the long waggon stood
Without its team, it seemed it never would
Move from the shadow of that single yew.   25
The team, as still, until their task was due,
Beside the labourers enjoyed the shade
That three squat oaks mid-field together made
Upon a circle of grass and weed uncut,
And on the hollow, once a chalk-pit, but   30
Now brimmed with nut and elder-flower so clean.
The men leaned on their rakes, about to begin,
But still. And all were silent. All was old,
This morning time, with a great age untold,
Older than Clare and Cobbett, Morland and Crome,   35
Than, at the field's far edge, the farmer's home,
A white house crouched at the foot of a great tree.
Under the heavens that know not what years be
The men, the beasts, the trees, the implements
Uttered even what they will in times far hence –   40
All of us gone out of the reach of change –
Immortal in a picture of an old grange.

A Dream

Over known fields with an old friend in dream
I walked, but came sudden to a strange stream.
Its dark waters were bursting out most bright
From a great mountain's heart into the light.
They ran a short course under the sun, then back   5
Into a pit they plunged, once more as black
As at their birth; and I stood thinking there
How white, had the day shone on them, they were,
Heaving and coiling. So by the roar and hiss
And by the mighty motion of the abyss   10
I was bemused, that I forgot my friend
And neither saw nor sought him till the end,
When I awoke from waters unto men
Saying: 'I shall be here some day again.'

The Brook

Seated once by a brook, watching a child
Chiefly that paddled, I was thus beguiled.
Mellow the blackbird sang and sharp the thrush
Not far off in the oak and hazel brush,
Unseen. There was a scent like honeycomb   5
From mugwort dull. And down upon the dome
Of the stone the cart-horse kicks against so oft
A butterfly alighted. From aloft
He took the heat of the sun, and from below.
On the hot stone he perched contented so,   10
As if never a cart would pass again
That way; as if I were the last of men
And he the first of insects to have earth
And sun together and to know their worth.
I was divided between him and the gleam,   15
The motion, and the voices, of the stream,
The waters running frizzled over gravel,
That never vanish and for ever travel.
A grey flycatcher silent on a fence
And I sat as if we had been there since   20

96

The horseman and the horse lying beneath
The fir-tree-covered barrow on the heath,
The horseman and the horse with silver shoes,
Galloped the downs last. All that I could lose
I lost. And then the child's voice raised the dead.   25
'No one's been here before' was what she said
And what I felt, yet never should have found
A word for, while I gathered sight and sound.

Aspens

All day and night, save winter, every weather,
Above the inn, the smithy, and the shop,
The aspens at the cross-roads talk together
Of rain, until their last leaves fall from the top.

Out of the blacksmith's cavern comes the ringing   5
Of hammer, shoe, and anvil; out of the inn
The clink, the hum, the roar, the random singing –
The sounds that for these fifty years have been.

The whisper of the aspens is not drowned,
And over lightless pane and footless road,   10
Empty as sky, with every other sound
Not ceasing, calls their ghosts from their abode,

A silent smithy, a silent inn, nor fails
In the bare moonlight or the thick-furred gloom,
In tempest or the night of nightingales,   15
To turn the cross-roads to a ghostly room.

And it would be the same were no house near.
Over all sorts of weather, men, and times,
Aspens must shake their leaves and men may hear
But need not listen, more than to my rhymes.   20

Whatever wind blows, while they and I have leaves
We cannot other than an aspen be
That ceaselessly, unreasonably grieves,
Or so men think who like a different tree.

The Mill-Water

Only the sound remains
Of the old mill;
Gone is the wheel;
On the prone roof and walls the nettle reigns.

Water that toils no more   5
Dangles white locks
And, falling, mocks
The music of the mill-wheel's busy roar.

Pretty to see, by day
Its sound is naught   10
Compared with thought
And talk and noise of labour and of play.

Night makes the difference.
In calm moonlight,
Gloom infinite,   15
The sound comes surging in upon the sense:

Solitude, company, –
When it is night, –
Grief or delight
By it must haunted or concluded be.   20

Often the silentness
Has but this one
Companion;
Wherever one creeps in the other is:

Sometimes a thought is drowned   25
By it, sometimes
Out of it climbs;
All thoughts begin or end upon this sound,

Only the idle foam
Of water falling   30
Changelessly calling,
Where once men had a work-place and a home.

For These

An acre of land between the shore and the hills,
Upon a ledge that shows my kingdoms three,
The lovely visible earth and sky and sea,
Where what the curlew needs not, the farmer tills:

A house that shall love me as I love it,　　　　　　　　5
Well-hedged, and honoured by a few ash-trees
That linnets, greenfinches, and goldfinches
Shall often visit and make love in and flit:

A garden I need never go beyond,
Broken but neat, whose sunflowers every one　　　　10
Are fit to be the sign of the Rising Sun:
A spring, a brook's bend, or at least a pond:

For these I ask not, but, neither too late
Nor yet too early, for what men call content,
And also that something may be sent　　　　　　　　15
To be contented with, I ask of fate.

Digging

What matter makes my spade for tears or mirth,
Letting down two clay pipes into the earth?
The one I smoked, the other a soldier
Of Blenheim, Ramillies, and Malplaquet
Perhaps. The dead man's immortality　　　　　　　　5
Lies represented lightly with my own,
A yard or two nearer the living air
Than bones of ancients who, amazed to see
Almighty God erect the mastodon,
Once laughed, or wept, in this same light of day.　　10

Two Houses

Between a sunny bank and the sun
The farmhouse smiles
On the riverside plat:
No other one
So pleasant to look at   5
And remember, for many miles,
So velvet-hushed and cool under the warm tiles.

Not far from the road it lies, yet caught
Far out of reach
Of the road's dust   10
And the dusty thought
Of passers-by, though each
Stops, and turns, and must
Look down at it like a wasp at the muslined peach.

But another house stood there long before: 15
And as if above graves
Still the turf heaves
Above its stones:
Dark hangs the sycamore,
Shadowing kennel and bones   20
And the black dog that shakes his chain and moans.

And when he barks, over the river
Flashing fast,
Dark echoes reply,
And the hollow past   25
Half yields the dead that never
More than half hidden lie:
And out they creep and back again for ever.

Cock-Crow

Out of the wood of thoughts that grows by night
To be cut down by the sharp axe of light, –
Out of the night, two cocks together crow,
Cleaving the darkness with a silver blow:
And bright before my eyes twin trumpeters stand,   5
Heralds of splendour, one at either hand,
Each facing each as in a coat of arms:
The milkers lace their boots up at the farms.

October

The green elm with the one great bough of gold
Lets leaves into the grass slip, one by one, –
The short hill grass, the mushrooms small milk-white,
Harebell and scabious and tormentil,
That blackberry and gorse, in dew and sun,   5
Bow down to; and the wind travels too light
To shake the fallen birch leaves from the fern;
The gossamers wander at their own will.
At heavier steps than birds' the squirrels scold.

The rich scene has grown fresh again and new   10
As Spring and to the touch is not more cool
Than it is warm to the gaze; and now I might
As happy be as earth is beautiful,
Were I some other or with earth could turn
In alternation of violet and rose,   15
Harebell and snowdrop, at their season due,
And gorse that has no time not to be gay.
But if this be not happiness, – who knows?
Some day I shall think this a happy day,
And this mood by the name of melancholy   20
Shall no more blackened and obscured be.

There's nothing like the sun

There's nothing like the sun as the year dies,
Kind as it can be, this world being made so,
To stones and men and beasts and birds and flies,
To all things that it touches except snow,
Whether on mountain side or street of town.   5
The south wall warms me: November has begun,
Yet never shone the sun as fair as now
While the sweet last-left damsons from the bough
With spangles of the morning's storm drop down
Because the starling shakes it, whistling what   10
Once swallows sang. But I have not forgot
That there is nothing, too, like March's sun,
Like April's, or July's, or June's, or May's,
Or January's, or February's, great days:
And August, September, October, and December   15
Have equal days, all different from November.
No day of any month but I have said –
Or, if I could live long enough, should say –
'There's nothing like the sun that shines today.'
There's nothing like the sun till we are dead.   20

The Thrush

When Winter's ahead,
What can you read in November
That you read in April
When Winter's dead?

I hear the thrush, and I see   5
Him alone at the end of the lane
Near the bare poplar's tip,
Singing continuously.

Is it more that you know
Than that, even as in April,   10
So in November,
Winter is gone that must go?

Or is all your lore
Not to call November November,
And April April,   15
And Winter Winter – no more?

But I know the months all,
And their sweet names, April,
May and June and October,
As you call and call   20

I must remember
What died in April
And consider what will be born
Of a fair November;

And April I love for what   25
It was born of, and November
For what it will die in,
What they are and what they are not,

While you love what is kind,
What you can sing in   30
And love and forget in
All that's ahead and behind.

Liberty

The last light has gone out of the world, except
This moonlight lying on the grass like frost
Beyond the brink of the tall elm's shadow.
It is as if everything else had slept
Many an age, unforgotten and lost   5
The men that were, the things done, long ago,
All I have thought; and but the moon and I
Live yet and here stand idle over the grave
Where all is buried. Both have liberty
To dream what we could do if we were free   10
To do some thing we had desired long,
The moon and I. There's none less free than who
Does nothing and has nothing else to do,

Being free only for what is not to his mind,
And nothing is to his mind. If every hour   15
Like this one passing that I have spent among
The wiser others when I have forgot
To wonder whether I was free or not,
Were piled before me, and not lost behind,
And I could take and carry them away   20
I should be rich; or if I had the power
To wipe out every one and not again
Regret, I should be rich to be so poor.
And yet I still am half in love with pain,
With what is imperfect, with both tears and mirth,   25
With things that have an end, with life and earth,
And this moon that leaves me dark within the door.

This is no case of petty right or wrong

This is no case of petty right or wrong
That politicians or philosophers
Can judge. I hate not Germans, nor grow hot
With love of Englishmen, to please newspapers.
Beside my hate for one fat patriot   5
My hatred of the Kaiser is love true: –
A kind of god he is, banging a gong.
But I have not to choose between the two,
Or between justice and injustice. Dinned
With war and argument I read no more   10
Than in the storm smoking along the wind
Athwart the wood. Two witches' cauldrons roar.
From one the weather shall rise clear and gay;
Out of the other an England beautiful
And like her mother that died yesterday.   15
Little I know or care if, being dull,
I shall miss something that historians
Can rake out of the ashes when perchance
The phoenix broods serene above their ken.
But with the best and meanest Englishmen   20
I am one in crying, God save England, lest
We lose what never slaves and cattle blessed.

The ages made her that made us from the dust:
She is all we know and live by, and we trust
She is good and must endure, loving her so: 25
And as we love ourselves we hate her foe.

Rain

Rain, midnight rain, nothing but the wild rain
On this bleak hut, and solitude, and me
Remembering again that I shall die
And neither hear the rain nor give it thanks
For washing me cleaner than I have been 5
Since I was born into this solitude.
Blessed are the dead that the rain rains upon:
But here I pray that none whom once I loved
Is dying tonight or lying still awake
Solitary, listening to the rain, 10
Either in pain or thus in sympathy
Helpless among the living and the dead,
Like a cold water among broken reeds,
Myriads of broken reeds all still and stiff,
Like me who have no love which this wild rain 15
Has not dissolved except the love of death,
If love it be towards what is perfect and
Cannot, the tempest tells me, disappoint.

The clouds that are so light

The clouds that are so light,
Beautiful, swift and bright,
Cast shadows on field and park
Of the earth that is so dark,

And even so now, light one! 5
Beautiful, swift and bright one!
You let fall on a heart that was dark,
Unillumined, a deeper mark.

But clouds would have, without earth
To shadow, far less worth: 10
Away from your shadow on me
Your beauty less would be,

And if it still be treasured
An age hence, it shall be measured
By this small dark spot   15
Without which it were not.

Roads

I love roads:
The goddesses that dwell
Far along invisible
Are my favourite gods.

Roads go on   5
While we forget, and are
Forgotten like a star
That shoots and is gone.

On this earth 'tis sure
We men have not made   10
Anything that doth fade
So soon, so long endure:

The hill road wet with rain
In the sun would not gleam
Like a winding stream   15
If we trod it not again.

They are lonely
While we sleep, lonelier
For lack of the traveller
Who is now a dream only.   20

From dawn's twilight
And all the clouds like sheep
On the mountains of sleep
They wind into the night.

The next turn may reveal   25
Heaven: upon the crest
The close pine clump, at rest
And black, may Hell conceal.

Often footsore, never
Yet of the road I weary,   30
Though long and steep and dreary
As it winds on for ever.

Helen of the roads,
The mountain ways of Wales
And the Mabinogion tales,   35
Is one of the true gods,

Abiding in the trees,
The threes and fours so wise,
The larger companies,
That by the roadside be,   40

And beneath the rafter
Else uninhabited
Excepting by the dead;
And it is her laughter

At morn and night I hear   45
When the thrush cock sings
Bright irrelevant things,
And when the chanticleer

Calls back to their own night
Troops that make loneliness   50
With their light footsteps' press,
As Helen's own are light.

Now all roads lead to France
And heavy is the tread
Of the living; but the dead   55
Returning lightly dance:

Whatever the road bring
To me or take from me,
They keep me company
With their pattering, 60

Crowding the solitude
Of the loops over the downs,
Hushing the roar of towns
And their brief multitude.

The Ash Grove

Half of the grove stood dead, and those that yet lived made
Little more than the dead ones made of shade.
If they led to a house, long before they had seen its fall:
But they welcomed me; I was glad without cause and delayed.

Scarce a hundred paces under the trees was the interval – 5
Paces each sweeter than sweetest miles – but nothing at all,
Not even the spirits of memory and fear with restless wing,
Could climb down in to molest me over the wall

That I passed through at either end without noticing.
And now an ash grove far from those hills can bring 10
The same tranquillity in which I wander a ghost
With a ghostly gladness, as if I heard a girl sing

The song of the Ash Grove soft as love uncrossed,
And then in a crowd or in distance it were lost,
But the moment unveiled something unwilling to die 15
And I had what most I desired, without search or desert or cost.

February Afternoon

Men heard this roar of parleying starlings, saw,
A thousand years ago even as now,
Black rooks with white gulls following the plough
So that the first are last until a caw
Commands that last are first again, – a law   5
Which was of old when one, like me, dreamed how
A thousand years might dust lie on his brow
Yet thus would birds do between hedge and shaw.

Time swims before me, making as a day
A thousand years, while the broad ploughland oak   10
Roars mill-like and men strike and bear the stroke
Of war as ever, audacious or resigned,
And God still sits aloft in the array
That we have wrought him, stone-deaf and stone-blind.

I may come near loving you

I may come near loving you
When you are dead
And there is nothing to do
And much to be said.

To repent that day will be   5
Impossible
For you and vain for me
The truth to tell.

I shall be sorry for
Your impotence: 10
You can do and undo no more
When you go hence,

Cannot even forgive
The funeral.
But not so long as you live   15
Can I love you at all.

Those things that poets said

Those things that poets said
Of love seemed true to me
When I loved and I fed
On love and poetry equally.

But now I wish I knew   5
If theirs were love indeed,
Or if mine were the true
And theirs some other lovely weed:

For certainly not thus,
Then or thereafter, I   10
Loved ever. Between us
Decide, good Love, before I die.

Only, that once I loved
By this one argument
Is very plainly proved: 15
I, loving not, am different.

No one so much as you

No one so much as you
Loves this my clay,
Or would lament as you
Its dying day.

You know me through and through   5
Though I have not told,
And though with what you know
You are not bold.

None ever was so fair
As I thought you: 10
Not a word can I bear
Spoken against you.

All that I ever did
For you seemed coarse
Compared with what I hid   15
Nor put in force.

My eyes scarce dare meet you
Lest they should prove
I but respond to you
And do not love.   20

We look and understand,
We cannot speak
Except in trifles and
Words the most weak.

For I at most accept   25
Your love, regretting
That is all: I have kept
Only a fretting

That I could not return
All that you gave   30
And could not ever burn
With the love you have,

Till sometimes it did seem
Better it were
Never to see you more   35
Than linger here

With only gratitude
Instead of love –
A pine in solitude
Cradling a dove.   40

The Unknown

She is most fair,
And when they see her pass
The poets' ladies
Look no more in the glass
But after her.   5

On a bleak moor
Running under the moon
She lures a poet,
Once proud or happy, soon
Far from his door.   10

Beside a train,
Because they saw her go,
Or failed to see her,
Travellers and watchers know
Another pain.   15

The simple lack
Of her is more to me
Than others' presence,
Whether life splendid be
Or utter black.   20

I have not seen,
I have no news of her;
I can tell only
She is not here, but there
She might have been.   25

She is to be kissed
Only perhaps by me;
She may be seeking
Me and no other: she
May not exist.   30

Celandine

Thinking of her had saddened me at first,
Until I saw the sun on the celandines lie
Redoubled, and she stood up like a flame,
A living thing, not what before I nursed,
The shadow I was growing to love almost,   5
The phantom, not the creature with bright eye
That I had thought never to see, once lost.

She found the celandines of February
Always before us all. Her nature and name
Were like those flowers, and now immediately   10
For a short swift eternity back she came,
Beautiful, happy, simply as when she wore
Her brightest bloom among the winter hues
Of all the world; and I was happy too,
Seeing the blossoms and the maiden who   15
Had seen them with me Februarys before,
Bending to them as in and out she trod
And laughed, with locks sweeping the mossy sod.

But this was a dream: the flowers were not true,
Until I stooped to pluck from the grass there   20
One of five petals and I smelt its juice
Which made me sigh, remembering she was no more,
Gone like a never perfectly recalled air.

'Home'

Fair was the morning, fair our tempers, and
We had seen nothing fairer than that land,
Though strange, and the untrodden snow that made
Wild of the tame, casting out all that was
Not wild and rustic and old; and we were glad.   5

Fair, too, was afternoon, and first to pass
Were we that league of snow, next the north wind.

There was nothing to return for, except need,
And yet we sang nor ever stopped for speed,
As we did often with the start behind.   10
Faster still strode we when we came in sight
Of the cold roofs where we must spend the night.
Happy we had not been there, nor could be,
Though we had tasted sleep and food and fellowship
Together long.
               'How quick' to someone's lip   15
The words came, 'will the beaten horse run home.'

The word 'home' raised a smile in us all three,
And one repeated it, smiling just so
That all knew what he meant and none would say.
Between three counties far apart that lay   20
We were divided and looked strangely each
At the other, and we knew we were not friends
But fellows in a union that ends
With the necessity for it, as it ought.

Never a word was spoken, not a thought   25
Was thought, of what the look meant with the word
'Home' as we walked and watched the sunset blurred.
And then to me the word, only the word,
'Homesick', as it were playfully occurred:
No more.

         If I should ever more admit   30
Than the mere word I could not endure it
For a day longer: this captivity
Must somehow come to an end, else I should be
Another man, as often now I seem,
Or this life be only an evil dream.   35

Thaw

Over the land freckled with snow half-thawed
The speculating rooks at their nests cawed
And saw from elm-tops, delicate as flower of grass,
What we below could not see, Winter pass.

If I should ever by chance

If I should ever by chance grow rich
I'll buy Codham, Cockridden, and Childerditch,
Roses, Pyrgo, and Lapwater,
And let them all to my elder daughter.
The rent I shall ask of her will be only   5
Each year's first violets, white and lonely,
The first primroses and orchises –
She must find them before I do, that is.
But if she finds a blossom on furze
Without rent they shall all for ever be hers,   10
Whenever I am sufficiently rich:
Codham, Cockridden, and Childerditch,
Roses, Pyrgo and Lapwater, –
I shall give them all to my elder daughter.

If I were to own

If I were to own this countryside
As far as a man in a day could ride,
And the Tyes were mine for giving or letting, –
Wingle Tye and Margaretting
Tye, – and Skreens, Gooshays, and Cockerells,   5
Shellow, Rochetts, Bandish, and Pickerells,
Martins, Lambkins, and Lillyputs,
Their copses, ponds, roads, and ruts,
Fields where plough-horses steam and plovers
Fling and whimper, hedges that lovers   10
Love, and orchards, shrubberies, walls
Where the sun untroubled by north wind falls,
And single trees where the thrush sings well
His proverbs untranslatable,
I would give them all to my son   15
If he would let me any one
For a song, a blackbird's song, at dawn.
He should have no more, till on my lawn

Never a one was left, because I
Had shot them to put them into a pie, –   20
His Essex blackbirds, every one,
And I was left old and alone.

Then unless I could pay, for rent, a song
As sweet as a blackbird's, and as long –
No more – he should have the house, not I: 25
Margaretting or Wingle Tye,
Or it might be Skreens, Gooshays, or Cockerells,
Shellow, Rochetts, Bandish, or Pickerells,
Martins, Lambkins, or Lillyputs,
Should be his till the cart tracks had no ruts.   30

What shall I give?

What shall I give my daughter the younger
More than will keep her from cold and hunger?
I shall not give her anything.
If she shared South Weald and Havering,
Their acres, the two brooks running between,   5
Paine's Brook and Weald Brook,
With pewit, woodpecker, swan, and rook,
She would be no richer than the queen
Who once on a time sat in Havering Bower
Alone, with the shadows, pleasure and power.   10
She could do no more with Samarcand,
Or the mountains of a mountain land
And its far white house above cottages
Like Venus above the Pleiades.
Her small hands I would not cumber   15
With so many acres and their lumber,
But leave her Steep and her own world
And her spectacled self with hair uncurled,
Wanting a thousand little things
That time without contentment brings.   20

And you, Helen

And you, Helen, what should I give you?
So many things I would give you
Had I an infinite great store
Offered me and I stood before
To choose. I would give you youth,   5
All kinds of loveliness and truth,
A clear eye as good as mine,
Lands, waters, flowers, wine,
As many children as your heart
Might wish for, a far better art   10
Than mine can be, all you have lost
Upon the travelling waters tossed,
Or given to me. If I could choose
Freely in that great treasure-house
Anything from any shelf,   15
I would give you back yourself,
And power to discriminate
What you want and want it not too late,
Many fair days free from care
And heart to enjoy both foul and fair,   20
And myself, too, if I could find
Where it lay hidden and it proved kind.

The Wind's Song

Dull-thoughted, walking among the nunneries
Of many a myriad anemones
In the close copses, I grew weary of Spring
Till I emerged and in my wandering
I climbed the down up to a lone pine clump   5
Of six, the tallest dead, one a mere stump.
On one long stem, branchless and flayed and prone,
I sat in the sun listening to the wind alone,
Thinking there could be no old song so sad
As the wind's song; but later none so glad   10

Could I remember as that same wind's song
All the time blowing the pine boughs among.
My heart that had been still as the dead tree
Awakened by the West wind was made free.

Like the touch of rain

Like the touch of rain she was
On a man's flesh and hair and eyes
When the joy of walking thus
Has taken him by surprise:

With the love of the storm he burns,   5
He sings, he laughs, well I know how,
But forgets when he returns
As I shall not forget her 'Go now'.

Those two words shut a door
Between me and the blessed rain   10
That was never shut before
And will not open again.

When we two walked

When we two walked in Lent
We imagined that happiness
Was something different
And this was something less.

But happy were we to hide   5
Our happiness, not as they were
Who acted in their pride
Juno and Jupiter:

For the Gods in their jealousy
Murdered that wife and man,   10
And we that were wise live free
To recall our happiness then.

Tall Nettles

Tall nettles cover up, as they have done
These many springs, the rusty harrow, the plough
Long worn out, and the roller made of stone:
Only the elm butt tops the nettles now.

This corner of the farmyard I like most: 5
As well as any bloom upon a flower
I like the dust on the nettles, never lost
Except to prove the sweetness of a shower.

The Watchers

By the ford at the town's edge
Horse and carter rest:
The carter smokes on the bridge
Watching the water press in swathes about his horse's chest.

From the inn one watches, too,   5
In the room for visitors
That has no fire, but a view
And many cases of stuffed fish, vermin, and kingfishers.

I never saw that land before

I never saw that land before,
And now can never see it again;
Yet, as if by acquaintance hoar
Endeared, by gladness and by pain,
Great was the affection that I bore   5

To the valley and the river small,
The cattle, the grass, the bare ash trees,
The chickens from the farmsteads, all
Elm-hidden, and the tributaries
Descending at equal interval;   10

The blackthorns down along the brook
With wounds yellow as crocuses
Where yesterday the labourer's hook
Had sliced them cleanly; and the breeze
That hinted all and nothing spoke.   15

I neither expected anything
Nor yet remembered: but some goal
I touched then; and if I could sing
What would not even whisper my soul
As I went on my journeying,   20

I should use, as the trees and birds did,
A language not to be betrayed;
And what was hid should still be hid
Excepting from those like me made
Who answer when such whispers bid.   25

The Cherry Trees

The cherry trees bend over and are shedding
On the old road where all that passed are dead,
Their petals, strewing the grass as for a wedding
This early May morn when there is none to wed.

It rains

It rains, and nothing stirs within the fence
Anywhere through the orchard's untrodden, dense
Forest of parsley. The great diamonds
Of rain on the grassblades there is none to break,
Or the fallen petals further down to shake.   5

And I am nearly as happy as possible
To search the wilderness in vain though well,
To think of two walking, kissing there,
Drenched, yet forgetting the kisses of the rain:
Sad, too, to think that never, never again,   10

Unless alone, so happy shall I walk
In the rain. When I turn away, on its fine stalk
Twilight has fined to naught, the parsley flower
Figures, suspended still and ghostly white,
The past hovering as it revisits the light.   15

Some eyes condemn

Some eyes condemn the earth they gaze upon:
Some wait patiently till they know far more
Than earth can tell them: some laugh at the whole
As folly of another's making: one
I knew that laughed because he saw, from core   5
To rind, not one thing worth the laugh his soul
Had ready at waking: some eyes have begun
With laughing; some stand startled at the door.

Others, too, I have seen rest, question, roll,
Dance, shoot. And many I have loved watching. Some   10
I could not take my eyes from till they turned
And loving died. I had not found my goal.
But thinking of your eyes, dear, I become
Dumb: for they flamed, and it was me they burned.

The sun used to shine

The sun used to shine while we two walked
Slowly together, paused and started
Again, and sometimes mused, sometimes talked
As either pleased, and cheerfully parted

Each night. We never disagreed   5
Which gate to rest on. The to be
And the late past we gave small heed.
We turned from men or poetry

To rumours of the war remote
Only till both stood disinclined   10
For aught but the yellow flavorous coat
Of an apple wasps had undermined;

Or a sentry of dark betonies,
The stateliest of small flowers on earth,
At the forest verge; or crocuses   15
Pale purple as if they had their birth

In sunless Hades fields. The war
Came back to mind with the moonrise
Which soldiers in the east afar
Beheld then. Nevertheless, our eyes   20

Could as well imagine the Crusades
Or Caesar's battles. Everything
To faintness like those rumours fades –
Like the brook's water glittering

Under the moonlight – like those walks   25
Now – like us two that took them, and
The fallen apples, all the talks
And silences – like memory's sand

When the tide covers it late or soon,
And other men through other flowers   30
In those fields under the same moon
Go talking and have easy hours.

No one cares less than I

'No one cares less than I,
Nobody knows but God,
Whether I am destined to lie
Under a foreign clod,'
Were the words I made to the bugle call in the morning.   5

But laughing, storming, scorning,
Only the bugles know
What the bugles say in the morning,
And they do not care, when they blow
The call that I heard and made words to early this morning.   10

As the team's head-brass

As the team's head-brass flashed out on the turn
The lovers disappeared into the wood.
I sat among the boughs of the fallen elm
That strewed an angle of the fallow, and
Watched the plough narrowing a yellow square   5
Of charlock. Every time the horses turned
Instead of treading me down, the ploughman leaned
Upon the handles to say or ask a word,
About the weather, next about the war.
Scraping the share he faced towards the wood,   10
And screwed along the furrow till the brass flashed
Once more.
            The blizzard felled the elm whose crest
I sat in, by a woodpecker's round hole,
The ploughman said. 'When will they take it away?'
'When the war's over.' So the talk began –   15
One minute and an interval of ten,
A minute more and the same interval.
'Have you been out?' 'No.' 'And don't want to, perhaps?'
'If I could only come back again, I should.

I could spare an arm. I shouldn't want to lose   20
A leg. If I should lose my head, why, so,
I should want nothing more.... Have many gone
From here?' 'Yes.' 'Many lost?' 'Yes: a good few.
Only two teams work on the farm this year.
One of my mates is dead. The second day   25
In France they killed him. It was back in March,
The very night of the blizzard, too. Now if
He had stayed here we should have moved the tree.'
'And I should not have sat here. Everything
Would have been different. For it would have been   30
Another world.' 'Ay, and a better, though
If we could see all all might seem good.' Then
The lovers came out of the wood again:
The horses started and for the last time
I watched the clods crumble and topple over   35
After the ploughshare and the stumbling team.

After you speak

After you speak
And what you meant
Is plain,
My eyes
Meet yours that mean –   5
With your cheeks and hair –
Something more wise,
More dark,
And far different.
Even so the lark   10
Loves dust
And nestles in it
The minute
Before he must
Soar in lone flight   15
So far,
Like a black star

He seems –
A mote
Of singing dust   20
Afloat
Above,
That dreams
And sheds no light.
I know your lust   25
Is love.

Bright Clouds

Bright clouds of may
Shade half the pond.
Beyond,
All but one bay
Of emerald   5
Tall reeds
Like criss-cross bayonets
Where a bird once called,
Lies bright as the sun.
No one heeds.   10
The light wind frets
And drifts the scum
Of may-blossom.
Till the moorhen calls
Again   15
Naught's to be done
By birds or men.
Still the may falls.

Early one morning

Early one morning in May I set out,
And nobody I knew was about.
    I'm bound away for ever,
    Away somewhere, away for ever.

There was no wind to trouble the weathercocks. 5
I had burnt my letters and darned my socks.

No one knew I was going away,
I thought myself I should come back some day.

I heard the brook through the town gardens run.
O sweet was the mud turned to dust by the sun. 10

A gate banged in a fence and banged in my head.
'A fine morning, sir,' a shepherd said.

I could not return from my liberty,
To my youth and my love and my misery.

The past is the only dead thing that smells sweet, 15
The only sweet thing that is not also fleet.
    I'm bound away for ever,
    Away somewhere, away for ever.

It was upon

It was upon a July evening.
At a stile I stood, looking along a path
Over the country by a second Spring
Drenched perfect green again. 'The lattermath
Will be a fine one.' So the stranger said, 5
A wandering man. Albeit I stood at rest,
Flushed with desire I was. The earth outspread,
Like meadows of the future, I possessed.

And as an unaccomplished prophecy
The stranger's words, after the interval 10
Of a score years, when those fields are by me
Never to be recrossed, now I recall,
This July eve, and question, wondering,
What of the lattermath to this hoar Spring?

Women he liked

Women he liked, did shovel-bearded Bob,
Old Farmer Hayward of the Heath, but he
Loved horses. He himself was like a cob,
And leather-coloured. Also he loved a tree.

For the life in them he loved most living things, 5
But a tree chiefly. All along the lane
He planted elms where now the stormcock sings
That travellers hear from the slow-climbing train.

Till then the track had never had a name
For all its thicket and the nightingales 10
That should have earned it. No one was to blame.
To name a thing beloved man sometimes fails.

Many years since, Bob Hayward died, and now
None passes there because the mist and the rain
Out of the elms have turned the lane to slough 15
And gloom, the name alone survives, Bob's Lane.

There was a time

There was a time when this poor frame was whole
And I had youth and never another care,
Or none that should have troubled a strong soul.
Yet, except sometimes in a frosty air
When my heels hammered out a melody 5
From pavements of a city left behind,
I never would acknowledge my own glee
Because it was less mighty than my mind
Had dreamed of. Since I could not boast of strength
Great as I wished, weakness was all my boast. 10
I sought yet hated pity till at length
I earned it. Oh, too heavy was the cost.
But now that there is something I could use
My youth and strength for, I deny the age,
The care and weakness that I know – refuse 15
To admit I am unworthy of the wage
Paid to a man who gives up eyes and breath
For what would neither ask nor heed his death.

The Green Roads

The green roads that end in the forest
Are strewn with white goose feathers this June,

Like marks left behind by someone gone to the forest
To show his track. But he has never come back.

Down each green road a cottage looks at the forest. 5
Round one the nettle towers; two are bathed in flowers.

An old man along the green road to the forest
Strays from one, from another a child alone.

In the thicket bordering the forest,
All day long a thrush twiddles his song. 10

It is old, but the trees are young in the forest,
All but one like a castle keep, in the middle deep.

That oak saw the ages pass in the forest:
They were a host, but their memories are lost,

For the tree is dead: all things forget the forest   15
Excepting perhaps me, when now I see

The old man, the child, the goose feathers at the edge of the forest,
And hear all day long the thrush repeat his song.

The Gallows

There was a weasel lived in the sun
With all his family,
Till a keeper shot him with his gun
And hung him up on a tree,
Where he swings in the wind and rain,   5
In the sun and in the snow,
Without pleasure, without pain,
On the dead oak tree bough.

There was a crow who was no sleeper,
But a thief and a murderer   10
Till a very late hour; and this keeper
Made him one of the things that were,
To hang and flap in rain and wind,
In the sun and in the snow.
There are no more sins to be sinned   15
On the dead oak tree bough.

There was a magpie, too,
Had a long tongue and a long tail;
He could both talk and do –
But what did that avail?   20
He, too, flaps in the wind and rain
Alongside weasel and crow,
Without pleasure, without pain,
On the dead oak tree bough.

And many other beasts   25
And birds, skin, bone and feather,
Have been taken from their feasts
And hung up there together,
To swing and have endless leisure
In the sun and in the snow,   30
Without pain, without pleasure,
On the dead oak tree bough.

The Dark Forest

Dark is the forest and deep, and overhead
Hang stars like seeds of light
In vain, though not since they were sown was bred
Anything more bright.

And evermore mighty multitudes ride   5
About, nor enter in;
Of the other multitudes that dwell inside
Never yet was one seen.

The forest foxglove is purple, the marguerite
Outside is gold and white,   10
Nor can those that pluck either blossom greet
The others, day or night.

When he should laugh

When he should laugh the wise man knows full well:
For he knows what is truly laughable.
But wiser is the man who laughs also,
Or holds his laughter, when the foolish do.

How at once

How at once should I know,
When stretched in the harvest blue
I saw the swift's black bow,
That I would not have that view
Another day   5
Until next May
Again it is due?

The same year after year –
But with the swift alone.
With other things I but fear   10
That they will be over and done
Suddenly
And I only see
Them to know them gone.

Gone, gone again

Gone, gone again,
May, June, July,
And August gone,
Again gone by,

Not memorable   5
Save that I saw them go,
As past the empty quays
The rivers flow.

And now again,
In the harvest rain,   10
The Blenheim oranges
Fall grubby from the trees,

As when I was young –
And when the lost one was here –
And when the war began   15
To turn young men to dung.

Look at the old house,
Outmoded, dignified,
Dark and untenanted,
With grass growing instead   20

Of the footsteps of life,
The friendliness, the strife;
In its beds have lain
Youth, love, age and pain:

I am something like that;   25
Only I am not dead,
Still breathing and interested
In the house that is not dark: –

I am something like that:
Not one pane to reflect the sun,   30
For the schoolboys to throw at –
They have broken every one.

That girl's clear eyes

That girl's clear eyes utterly concealed all
Except that there was something to reveal.
And what did mine say in the interval?
No more: no less. They are but as a seal
Not to be broken till after I am dead;   5
And then vainly. Every one of us
This morning at our tasks left nothing said,
In spite of many words. We were sealed thus,
Like tombs. Nor until now could I admit
That all I cared for was the pleasure and pain   10
I tasted in the stony square sunlit,
Or the dark cloisters, or shade of airy plane,
While music blazed and children, line after line,
Marched past, hiding the 'Seventeen Thirty-Nine'.

132

What will they do?

What will they do when I am gone? It is plain
That they will do without me as the rain
Can do without the flowers and the grass
That profit by it and must perish without.
I have but seen them in the loud street pass;   5
And I was naught to them. I turned about
To see them disappearing carelessly.
But what if I in them as they in me
Nourished what has great value and no price?
Almost I thought that rain thirsts for a draught   10
Which only in the blossom's chalice lies,
Until that one turned back and lightly laughed.

The Trumpet

Rise up, rise up,
And, as the trumpet blowing
Chases the dreams of men,
As the dawn glowing
The stars that left unlit   5
The land and water,
Rise up and scatter
The dew that covers
The print of last night's lovers –
Scatter it, scatter it!   10

While you are listening
To the clear horn,
Forget, men, everything
On this earth newborn,
Except that it is lovelier   15
Than any mysteries.
Open your eyes to the air
That has washed the eyes of the stars

Through all the dewy night:
Up with the light,   20
To the old wars;
Arise, arise!

When first

When first I came here I had hope,
Hope for I knew not what. Fast beat
My heart at sight of the tall slope
Of grass and yews, as if my feet

Only by scaling its steps of chalk   5
Would see something no other hill
Ever disclosed. And now I walk
Down it the last time. Never will

My heart beat so again at sight
Of any hill although as fair   10
And loftier. For infinite
The change, late unperceived, this year,

The twelfth, suddenly, shows me plain.
Hope now, – not health, nor cheerfulness,
Since they can come and go again,   15
As often one brief hour witnesses, –

Just hope has gone for ever. Perhaps
I may love other hills yet more
Than this: the future and the maps
Hide something I was waiting for.   20

One thing I know, that love with chance
And use and time and necessity
Will grow, and louder the heart's dance
At parting than at meeting be.

The Child in the Orchard

'He rolls in the orchard: he is stained with moss
And with earth, the solitary old white horse.
Where is his father and where is his mother
Among all the brown horses? Has he a brother?
I know the swallow, the hawk, and the hern;   5
But there are two million things for me to learn.

'Who was the lady that rode the white horse
With rings and bells to Banbury Cross?
Was there no other lady in England beside
That a nursery rhyme could take for a ride?   10
The swift, the swallow, the hawk, and the hern.
There are two million things for me to learn.

'Was there a man once who straddled across
The back of the Westbury White Horse
Over there on Salisbury Plain's green wall?   15
Was he bound for Westbury, or had he a fall?
The swift, the swallow, the hawk, and the hern.
There are two million things for me to learn.

'Out of all the white horses I know three,
At the age of six; and it seems to me   20
There is so much to learn, for men,
That I dare not go to bed again.
The swift, the swallow, the hawk, and the hern.
There are millions of things for me to learn.'

Lights Out

I have come to the borders of sleep,
The unfathomable deep
Forest where all must lose
Their way, however straight,
Or winding, soon or late;   5
They cannot choose.

135

Many a road and track
That, since the dawn's first crack,
Up to the forest brink,
Deceived the travellers   10
Suddenly now blurs,
And in they sink.

Here love ends,
Despair, ambition ends,
All pleasure and all trouble,   15
Although most sweet or bitter,
Here ends in sleep that is sweeter
Than tasks most noble.

There is not any book
Or face of dearest look   20
That I would not turn from now
To go into the unknown
I must enter and leave alone,
I know not how.

The tall forest towers;   25
Its cloudy foliage lowers
Ahead, shelf above shelf;
Its silence I hear and obey
That I may lose my way
And myself.   30

The long small room

The long small room that showed willows in the west
Narrowed up to the end the fireplace filled,
Although not wide. I liked it. No one guessed
What need or accident made them so build.

Only the moon, the mouse and the sparrow peeped   5
In from the ivy round the casement thick.
Of all they saw and heard there they shall keep
The tale for the old ivy and older brick.

When I look back I am like moon, sparrow and mouse
That witnessed what they could never understand   10
Or alter or prevent in the dark house.
One thing remains the same – this my right hand

Crawling crab-like over the clean white page,
Resting awhile each morning on the pillow,
Then once more starting to crawl on towards age.   15
The hundred last leaves stream upon the willow.

The Sheiling

It stands alone
Up in a land of stone
All worn like ancient stairs,
A land of rocks and trees
Nourished on wind and stone.   5

And all within
Long delicate has been;
By arts and kindliness
Coloured, sweetened, and warmed
For many years has been.   10

Safe resting there
Men hear in the travelling air
But music, pictures see
In the same daily land
Painted by the wild air.   15

One maker's mind
Made both, and the house is kind
To the land that gave it peace,
And the stone has taken the house
To its cold heart and is kind.   20

The Lane

Some day, I think, there will be people enough
In Froxfield to pick all the blackberries
Out of the hedges of Green Lane, the straight
Broad lane where now September hides herself
In bracken and blackberry, harebell and dwarf gorse.   5
Today, where yesterday a hundred sheep
Were nibbling, halcyon bells shake to the sway
Of waters that no vessel ever sailed...
It is a kind of spring: the chaffinch tries
His song. For heat it is like summer too.   10
This might be winter's quiet. While the glint
Of hollies dark in the swollen hedges lasts –
One mile – and those bells ring, little I know
Or heed if time be still the same, until
The lane ends and once more all is the same.   15

Out in the dark

Out in the dark over the snow
The fallow fawns invisible go
With the fallow doe;
And the winds blow
Fast as the stars are slow.   5

Stealthily the dark haunts round
And, when a lamp goes, without sound
At a swifter bound
Than the swiftest hound,
Arrives, and all else is drowned;   10

And star and I and wind and deer
Are in the dark together, – near,
Yet far, – and fear
Drums on my ear
In that sage company drear.   15

How weak and little is the light,
All the universe of sight,
Love and delight,
Before the might,
If you love it not, of night.   20

The sorrow of true love

The sorrow of true love is a great sorrow
And true love parting blackens a bright morrow.
Yet almost they equal joys, since their despair
Is but hope blinded by its tears, and clear
Above the storm the heavens wait to be seen.   5
But greater sorrow from less love has been
That can mistake lack of despair for hope
And knows not tempest nor the perfect scope
Of summer, but a frozen drizzle perpetual
Of drops that from remorse and pity fall   10
And cannot ever shine in the sun or thaw,
Removed eternally from the sun's law.

NOTES

Up in the Wind (31)

3 December 1914

Edward Thomas's field notebook for October-December 1914 (*FNB79*) contains jottings that enter his first poems. Here anticipations of *Up in the Wind* are set out like poetry: 'I could wring the old girl's neck / That put it here / A public house! (Charcoal burner) / But she's dead long ago / by bringing up and quite outdoing / The idea of London / Two woods around and never a road in sight / Trees roaring like a train without an end / Only a motorist from far away / Or marketers in carts once a fortnight / Or a few fresh tramps ignorant / of the houselessness'. On 27 November Thomas noted: 'Clothes on the line violently blowing in wind crackle like a rising woodfire'. *Up in the Wind*, like *Old Man*, also began as a prose sketch: 'The White Horse' (*LML*, 16 November). In each case, comparison between the two versions suggests what it means to move from one medium to the other. The setting of *Up in the Wind* and 'The White Horse' is a pub on the Froxfield plateau, above Steep, in the parish of Prior's Dean.

The White Horse

Tall beeches overhang the inn, dwarfing and half hiding it, for it lies back a field's breadth from the byroad. The field is divided from the road by a hedge and only a path from one corner and a cart track from the other which meet under the beeches connect the inn with the road. But for a sign board or rather the post and empty iron frame of a signboard close to the road behind the hedge, a traveller could not guess it an inn. The low dirty-white building looks like a farmhouse, with a lean-to, a rick and a shed of black boarding at one side; and in fact the landlord is more than half farmer. Except from the cottages which are scattered far around, only one of them visible from the inn, customers are few. And yet it is almost at a crossing of roads. One field away from the field with the signpost the byroad crosses a main road at a high point on the table land: the inn itself stands so high that its beeches mark it for those who know and form a station for the eyes of strangers, many miles away on 3 sides. But both roads lack houses and travellers, especially on the main road, are motorists from the ends of the earth and farmers going to market from remote villages. The main road runs for one length of 4 miles without a house of any sort. Once the land was all common. Many acres of it are still possessed by gorse and inhabited chiefly by linnets and a pair of stone curlews. The name of Common clings to it though it is hedged. Gorse and bracken mingle with the hedgerow hawthorns and keep memories of the old waste alive. Few trees of any age stand alongside the road, and as the hedges are low and broken, and everywhere gorse is visible, even the [~~traveller~~] stranger has whiffs of the past and tastes something like the olden sensation of journeying over wide common, high and unpopulated, higher than anything except Butser Hill far behind him and Inkpen far before him northward.

The farmhouses naturally then are placed far back behind the gorse or the fields once belonging to it and are reached by lanes of various lengths out of the main road. Once, I think, the roads crossed in the midst of a tract of common which perhaps ended where now the inn is. But as things are it might well seem to have been hidden there out of someone's perversity. 'I should like to wring the old [~~thing's~~] girl's neck for coming away here.' So said the [~~girl~~] woman who [~~served me~~] fetched my beer when I found myself at the inn first. She was a daughter of the house, fresh from a long absence in service in London, a bright [~~active~~] wildish slattern with a cockney accent and her hair half down. She spoke angrily. If she did not get away before long, she said, she would go mad with the loneliness. She looked out sharply: [~~there was nothing for her to see but~~] all she could see was the beeches and the tiny pond beneath them and the calves standing in it drinking, alternately grazing the water here and there and thinking, and at last going out and standing still on the bank thinking. Who the 'old girl' was, whether she had built the house here, or what, I did not inquire. It was just the loneliness of the high placed little inn isolated under those tall beeches that pleased me. Every year I used to go there once or twice, never so often as to overcome the original feeling it had given me. I was always on the verge of turning that feeling or having it turned by a natural process, into a story. Whoever the characters would have been I do not think they would have included either the 'old girl' or the landlord's [~~mysterious~~] indignant cockney daughter. The story that was to [~~explain~~] interpret the look that the house had as you came up to it under the trees never took shape. The daughter stayed on several years, bearing it so well that her wildish looks and cockney accent seemed to fit the scene, and I used to look forward to meeting her again. She would come in with her hair half down as at first or I would find her scrubbing the bricks or getting dinner ready in the taproom which was kitchen also. But before I had learnt anything from her she went. [~~I can only trust~~] I have to be content with what the landlord told me years afterwards, when he left his wheelbarrow standing in profile like a pig and came in to his taproom out of his farmyard for a glass and stood drinking outside the door.

Originally or as far back as he knew of, the house was a blacksmith's, the lean-to taproom was the smithy as you can tell by the height of it, and the man was remembered and still spoken of for his skill. The landlord spoke of him yet had never seen him. The smith died and left a widow and as she could not use hammer and tongs and as no 2nd smith arrived to marry her, she turned the smithy into a [~~taproom~~] shop and had an off-licence to sell beer. Presently a man came along from the Chiltern beech country with a two-cylinder engine for sawing timber. At that day the land here carried far more woodland. The beech trunks were cut up to make chairs. The branches were burnt for charcoal, and the circular black floors of the charcoal-burners' fires are still now and then cut into by the farmer's plough. The man from the Chilterns came here to saw beech planks and brought with him a little boy, his nephew, who had to pick up chips to feed the fire of the engine. 'My uncle' said the landlord 'fell in love, I suppose, with the widow, and married her.'

144

He continued to go about the country with his engine sawing timber. But the beeches overhanging the house were spared. The boy stayed on and farmed. The shop was turned into a taproom with a full licence and the widow sold ale until she died. The man grew old and gave up sawing and then he died. Now the nephew farms the land. It is worth a guinea a mile he says, but he has grown fat on the beer which his daughters draw. On the wall of the taproom is a list of the officers of a slate club and also coloured diagrams illustrating certain diseases of the cow. The room smells as much of bacon and boiled vegetables as of ale and shag, and it is often silent and empty except for a painted wooden clock ticking loudly above the fire. Yet it is one of the pleasantest rooms in Hampshire, well deserving the footpaths which lead men to it from all directions over ploughland and meadow, and deserving as good a story as a man could write. [*Not every erasure has been transcribed.*]

Up in the Wind is Thomas's closest approximation to the Robert Frost "eclogue" in which rural speakers tell or act out their story. In Frost's dramatic monologue 'A Servant to Servants' a disturbed woman talks to strangers about her hard life in a lonely place. Yet, despite Frostian echoes, and the poets' shared symbolism of houses and trees, Thomas establishes distinctive poetic co-ordinates. He sets London against 'wild' land, society ('public-house') against solitude ('hermitage'). And he shows his power to imagine the English countryside historically. The poem traces shifting relations between family history and socio-economic history, between landscape and rural work. In Stan Smith's words: 'It compacts into a brief space an individual narrative which has the generations behind it' (*SS*, 159).

1. '*I could wring the old thing's neck that put it here!* In the poem, the woman's voice becomes the main narrative voice. By giving primacy to speech-rhythms, Thomas lays down an aesthetic marker. A sixth of the poem's blank-verse lines are monosyllabic (the proportion is high in Frost's eclogues) and many have eleven or more syllables.

9. *forest parlour.* By replacing 'taproom' with 'parlour', Thomas brings 'wild' and 'homely' (l.45) into tension.

12-13. *flashed up...shriek.* These verbs ('shriek' recurs) might seem to exaggerate the girl's 'wildness', but they signal its later inward turn. Her brooding on 'wind' prepares for the more purely psychological scenario of *Wind and Mist*.

15. *I might have mused of coaches and highwaymen.* William Cooke comments: 'If Thomas had forced the "story" in 1911 it might have appeared as one of the romantic tales in *Light and Twilight*' (*WC*, 166). He quotes from a passage in *The Isle of Wight* which also fertilised *The Chalk-Pit* (see 237): 'there are other places which immediately strike us as fit scenes for some tragic or comic episode out of the common. I know a little white inn standing far back from the road, behind a double row of noble elms – an extraordinary combination, this house no bigger than a haystack, and these trees fit to lead up to a manor house where Sidney or Falkland was once a guest. You approach the inn from the road by crossing a stile and following a path among a tangle of gorse which is much overgrown by honeysuckle. Well, I never see this place, the gorse, the

great trees, the house at their feet, without a story haunting my mind but never quite defining itself. To others more ready of fancy it is no doubt already a scene of some highway robbery, with blunderbusses, masks, pretty ladies, and foaming horses' (*IOW*, 29). Yet the passage as a whole prefigures the poetic strategy whereby Thomas splits perspectives between different voices. Another speaker says: 'I don't know why you should want to fit a story to a scene like that. I am quite willing to wait until the tragedy or comedy arrives' (*IOW*, 30).

20. *houseless*: a word, and construction, that Thomas repeats – perhaps because it combines presence and absence. Cf. 'nameless', 'flowerless', 'beeless', 'lightless', 'footless', 'sunless', 'branchless'. 'Windless' (*Sowing*) and 'stormless' (*Haymaking*) are more positive instances.

32. *When all was open and common*: an allusion to the time before the major phase of land enclosure, initiated by the government in 1760, sealed the transition from feudal to modern tenure. Even before the industrial revolution, this shift accelerated emigration from country to city. The girl's story points to more recent rural depopulation (see Introduction, 23). The inn's apparently odd position is due to the fact that 'before the common of Froxfield, called the Barnet, was enclosed [in 1805] and farmed, an old road from Alton to Petersfield...came across the plateau past the inn, where a smithy and a pond met some other needs of eighteenth century travellers' (*WW*, 32). The White Horse, known as 'the pub with no name' (because of the absent sign), also as 'the highest pub in Hampshire', currently flourishes amid further socio-economic and gastronomic shifts.

   Ms: *LML*. **Published text**: *CP1920*. **Differences from *CP1978***: 1 here! *there!* 3 such-like *suchlike* 9 London, *London* 10 the *those* 35/41 'The White Horse' *the 'White Horse'* 45 homely, too, *homely too* 46 that knows *who knows* 50 inn; *inn:* 63 again – *again, /* – 64 ale *ale,* 72 these...gone: *those...gone.* 77 should *could* 79 a public-house and not a hermitage *not a hermitage but a public-house* 90 the pond *our pond* 93 were *was* 96 wood fire *woodfire* 98 me: *me.* 106 distant *far off* **Note**: *CP1978* follows a typescript [*JT*], which seems earlier than the typescript [*MET*] followed here as, except for minor discrepancies, in *CP1920*. *CP1920*, *CP1928* and *CP1944* omit 'a' before 'waste' in l.36.

November (34)

4 December 1914

FNB79 indicates Thomas's obsession with weather: 'After yesterday's rain and a dull showery morning a glorious high blue winter [?sky]', 'up and down in deep muddy lanes among hopgardens' (1 November 1914); 'lovely cold bright pale blue cloudless day, almost windless after heavy rime frost' (24 November); 'a fine bright morning then sunny drops slanting a <u>few</u> in a sprinkle, then heavy rain and a blue and black sky where wind comes from. Then at 12-3 bright sun, clear sweet cold sky with a few white clouds low – the sky so bright and clear and clean, the roads all muddy with mashed leaves and twigs, and bare hedges and sodden fields. Clear till moon rise (big full white moon towards East and sun going crimson cloudless in West – When Jupiter was visible at 4.45 there was some wet sandcoloured cloud in West – a big rag of it. Beautiful hobnail pattern on path over reddish light ploughland' (1 December); on opposite page:

'fields stamped over by sheep – mud and mangolds'.

On 15 December Thomas accepted Frost's criticisms of *November* and rejoiced in his first poetic riff: 'I am glad you spotted "wing's light word". I knew it was wrong & also that many would like it; also "odd men" – a touch nearing facetiousness in it. I've got rid of both now. But I am in it & no mistake...I find myself engrossed & conscious of a possible perfection as I never was in prose' (*RFET*, 38-9). The typescript sent to Frost has 'And in amongst them clearly printed / The foot's seal and the wing's light word' (lines 6-7) and 'Only odd men (who do not matter) / Care' etc (lines 11-12).

1. *November's days are thirty*. Thomas liked 'weather rhymes' (see *Lob*, 100-1), which his own poems often are.

5-7. *dinted...overprinted...charactered*. These verbs imply a penetrating poetic 'eye' (l.33) that reads landscape like a text or palimpsest. The poem proceeds to a microscopic analysis of 'mud'.

16. *Condemned as mud*: cf. 'Few care for' (l.12) and 'all that men scorn' (l.14). This sequence of phrases asserts an aesthetic that notices what other poets miss: 'it is characteristic of modern poetry, as a criticism of life by livers, that it has left the praise of rain to hop farmers and of mud to shoe-blacks' (*RAP*, 42).

21. *after-tempest cloud*: a favourite adjectival construction, cf. *Two Pewits* ('after-sunset sky'), and in prose: 'The moon was mounting the clear east, and Venus stood with Orion in the west above a low, horizontal ledge of darkest after-sunset cloud' (*IPS*, 74). 'After-tempest' appears in a passage that parallels the trajectory of lines 28-36: 'Just before night the sky clears. It is littered with small dark clouds upon rose, like rocks on a wild and solitary coast of after-tempest calm, and it is infinitely remote and infinitely alluring. Those clouds are the Islands of the Blest. Even so alluring might be this life itself, this world, if I were out of it' (*SC*, 216).

28-36. *One imagines...skies*. The 'one' who 'imagines a refuge', and fails to grasp the interdependence of 'earth' and 'sky', may represent Thomas's former literary self. Romantically vague language ('in the pure bright') parodies the writer who could ask of sunset clouds in 'Recollections of November' (*HS*, 86-102): 'To what weird banquet, to what mysterious shrine, were they advancing?' 'Another' (l.31), whose 'clear' sight seems endorsed by the poem, knows how to value 'earth and November'. Despite the second stanza's skyward movement, 'earth' occurs five times, exerting a gravitational rhythmic pull. The dialectic here resembles that at the end of *The Signpost* (see note, 153).

Ms: *LML*. **Published text:** *P*. **Differences from** *CP1978*: title: November [*P*] *November Sky* **Note on title:** *CP1978* follows a typescript [*JT*]. 'Sky' is cancelled in *PTP*.

March (35)

5 December 1914

March complements *November*. Together they initiate the seasonal movement that occurs between, and within, many of Thomas's poems. They also promise that his diurnal time-settings (a day's seasons) will be precise. *March* may be a direct result of Frost's telling Thomas to turn passages from *In Pursuit of Spring* into poetry (see Introduction, 15). Reciprocally, *March* may have influenced

Frost's 'Our Singing Strength', in which a snowstorm prompts massed birds to 'sing the wildflowers up from root and seed'. The first chapter of *In Pursuit of Spring* records volatile March weather:

> Snow succeeded, darkening the air, whitening the sky, on the wings of a strong wind from the north of north-west, for a minute only, but again and again, until by five o'clock the sky was all blue except at the horizon, where stood a cluster of white mountains, massive and almost motionless, in the south above the Downs, and round about them some dusty fragments not fit to be used in the composition of such mountains. They looked as if they were going to last for ever. Yet by six o'clock the horizon was dim, and the clouds all but passed away, the Downs clear and extended; the blackbird singing as if the world were his nest, the wind cold and light, but dying utterly to make way for a beautiful evening of one star and many owls hooting.
>
> The next day was the missel-thrush's and the north-west wind's. The missel-thrush sat well up in a beech at the wood edge and hailed the rain with his rolling, brief song; so rapidly and oft was it repeated that it was almost one long, continuous song But as the wind snatched away the notes again and again, or the bird changed his perch, or another answered him or took his place, the music was roving like a hunter's...
>
> ... [days] of cloudy brightness, brightened cloudiness, rounded off between half-past five and half-past six by blackbirds singing. The nights were strange children for such days, nights of frantic wind and rain, threatening to undo all the sweet work in a swift, howling revolution. Trees were thrown down, branches broken, but the buds remained... With the day came snow, hail, and rain, each impotent to silence the larks for one minute after it had ceased. (*IPS*, 26-7)

Thomas writes of another March evening: 'All the thrushes of England sang at that hour, and against that background of myriads I heard two or three singing their frank, clear notes in a mad eagerness to have all done before dark; for already the blackbirds were chinking and shifting places along the hedgerows' (*IPS*, 178).

March blends several March days and Thomas's perennial 'pursuit of Spring' into a quintessential symbol. He identified with an English Spring's halting progress: *In Pursuit of Spring* takes three hundred pages to find 'Winter's grave'. A favourite poem was William Morris's 'The Message of the March Wind': 'Fair now is the springtide, now earth lies beholding / With the eyes of a lover, the face of the sun...' Given the radical thrust of Morris's 'message', *March* may have Romantic-visionary as well as psychological resonances. At one level, the irrepressible birdsong, and the way in which it energises the rhythm, affirm Thomas' paradoxical 'hoar Spring' (*It was upon*) as man and poet. In celebrating Spring's moral victory here, he celebrates his own. He, too, would 'pack into that hour / [His] unwilling hoard of song'.

7-9. *The sun...tears of joy.* Cooke finds these lines 'unsatisfactory' (*WC*, 130), because they approach too nearly the inflated style of a prose equivalent: 'Day after day the sun poured out a great light and heat and joy over the earth and

148

the delicately clouded sky...So mighty was the sun that the miles of pale new foliage shimmered mistily like snow' (*LAT*, 1). Thomas is usually at his weakest where he personifies natural phenomena.

30-1. *silence / Stained with all that hour's songs.* When Thomas took opium in his early twenties, it intensified his hearing: 'I experienced for 1st time since I was about 10 my early wild <u>sensations</u> of silence...It was to ordinary silence what shouting is to speech' (*Diary*, 8 March 1901, *NLW*). H. Coombes says: 'we feel the silence not only as something enjoyed and as perhaps heralding a near spring but also as the silence which always comes back and which exists at the back of every sound; we note too that for the poet the silence was stained, equivocally but not deprecatingly – stain may beautify or mar, or beautify while it mars' (*HC*, 197-8). That Thomas packs so much into 'silence / Stained', with its hint of stained glass, its synaesthesia of ear and eye, is one reason for regarding this version of the line as his improvement on that cited below.

Ms: *LML*. **Published text:** *LP*. **Differences from** *CP1978*: 15 lost too... chill *lost, too,...cold* 25 screamed; *screamed,* 26 soft; *soft,* 31 Stained with all that hour's songs *Rich with all that riot of songs* **Note:** *CP1978* follows a typescript [*JT*] rather than *LP*, mainly cognate with another typescript [*MET*] which [see above] seems preferable on aesthetic grounds.

Old Man (36)
6 December 1914

Appropriately, many experiential and textual strata underlie this poem (for Thomas and memory, see Introduction, 23). Like *Up in the Wind*, *Old Man* was first written as prose: 'Old Man's Beard' (*LML*, 17 November 1914). But, in contrast to the narrative expansiveness of 'The White Horse', 'Old Man's Beard' sounds like a prose poem or prose from which poetry is trying to get out. Similarly, the blank verse of *Old Man* is braced by assonance and refrain, by the ghost of stanzaic structure. In combining blank-verse freedoms (including lines that run to twelve or thirteen syllables) with lyrical intensity, the poem pioneers one of Thomas's distinctive forms.

Old Man's Beard

Just as she is turning in to the house or leaving it, the baby plucks a feather of old man's beard. The bush grows just across the path from the door. Sometimes she stands by it squeezing off tip after tip from the branches and shrivelling them between her fingers on to the path in grey-green shreds. So the bush is still only half as tall as she is, though it is the same age. She never talks of it, but I wonder how much of the garden she will remember, the hedge with the old damson trees topping it, the vegetable rows, the path bending round the house corner, the old man's beard opposite the door, and me sometimes forbidding her to touch it, if she lives to my years. As for myself I cannot remember when I first smelt that green bitterness. I, too, often gather a sprig from the bush and sniff it and roll it between my fingers and sniff again and think, trying to [~~remember~~] discover what it is that I am remembering. [~~but in vain.~~] I do not wholly like the smell, yet would rather lose many meaningless

149

sweeter ones than this bitter [~~unintelligible~~] one of which I have mislaid the key. As I hold the sprig to my nose and slowly withdraw it, I think of nothing, I see, I hear, nothing; yet I seem too to be listening [~~as I hold the sprig to my nose and withdraw it~~], lying in wait for whatever it is I ought to remember but never do. No garden comes back to me, no hedge or path, no grey-green bush called old man's beard or lad's love, no figure of mother or father or [~~chil~~] playmate, only [~~an endless~~] a dark avenue without an end. [*Not every erasure has been transcribed.*]

On 11 November Thomas had noted: '<u>Old Man</u> scent, I smell again and again not really liking it but venerating it because it holds the secret of something very long ago which I feel it may someday recall, but I have yet no idea what' (*FNB79*). The plant's names appear in a list of 'Associations' in a 1908 notebook (*FNB19*); and R. George Thomas quotes from an unpublished story 'The Old House' (1909) in which 'Mr Banks' sniffs 'a feathery sprig of grey green' and tries 'to think and smell at the same time, closing his eyes, as if he were diving through some new medium into a strange land, – but in vain' (*CP1978*, 380).

Memory and childhood gardens come together in Thomas's prose: 'I confess to remembering little joy, but to much drowsy pleasure in the mere act of memory. I watch the past as I have seen workless, homeless men leaning over a bridge to watch the labours of a titanic crane and strange workers below in the ship running to and fro and feeding the crane...I recall many scenes: a church and churchyard and black pigs running down from them towards me in a rocky lane – ladslove and tall, crimson, bitter dahlias in a garden – the sweetness of large, moist, yellow apples eaten out of doors – children: I do not recall happiness in them, yet the moment that I return to them in fancy I am happy' (*SC*, 127). 'I once saw a girl of seven or eight years walking alone down a long grassy path in an old garden...For the child there was no end to the path. She walked slowly, at first picking a narcissus or two, or stooping to smell a flower and letting her hair fall over it to the ground; but soon she was content only to brush the tips of the flowers with her outstretched hands, or, rising on tiptoe, to force her head up amongst the lowest branches of cherry-bloom. Then she did nothing at all but gravely walk on into the shadow and into Eternity, dimly foreknowing her life's days' (*SC*, 139-40). '[In a friend's] back garden I first saw dark crimson dahlias and smelt bitter crushed stalks in plucking them. As I stood with my back to the house among the tall blossoming bushes I had no sense of any end to the garden between its brown fences: there remains in my mind a greenness, at once lowly and endless' (*CET*, 15-16). See, too, 'The Perfume of an Evening Primrose', W.H. Hudson, *Idle Days in Patagonia* (1893).

1. *Old Man, or Lad's-love*: folk-names of the long-cultivated plant 'southernwood' or *artemisia abrotanum*, which played a continuing part in Thomas's life and now grows on his grave in Agny. A mundane explanation for the plant's contradictory names is that the former derives from its silvery-'feathery' foliage ('old man's beard' as a name for 'traveller's joy' derives from that plant's seedheads); the latter from its use in lovers' bouquets – hence another folk-name: 'maiden's ruin'. Old Man, with its bitter taste as well as scent, has many traditional uses in herbal medicine, and is combined 'with rosemary and lavender'

for drawer sachets etc. Writing from Wick Green in April 1910, Thomas told Gordon Bottomley: 'The Old Man or Lad's Love you gave me is now a beautiful great bush at my study door' (*LGB*, 201). A cutting from this bush was planted in the Thomases' garden at Yew Tree Cottage: the poem's immediate setting. 'I hope you have a dooryard as neat as ours is, with all the old man & rosemary & lavender strong & the vegetable rows fairly continuous & parallel & the may thick in the hedge' (*RFET*, 57).

6-8. *Half decorate, half perplex…And yet I like the names.* Stuart Sillars argues that Thomas's approach to language anticipates the poststructuralist stress on the non-identity of word and thing: 'dissolution of self and dissolution of language in relation to objects' (*Structure and Dissolution in English Writing* [Basingstoke: Palgrave Macmillan, 1999], 178). Besides pondering contradictory names, *Old Man* variously terms its central image 'herb', 'bush', 'almost a tree'. Yet, rather than an insuperable gulf between the human mind and the world it aspires to name, such variants may mark their fluid intercourse in time and space. Thus Thomas brings the different faces of 'Old Man' closer together in the freshly coined oxymoron 'hoar-green'. Cf. the metamorphoses traced in *Fifty Faggots* (see note, 240). Thomas recoiled from Walter Pater's style precisely because 'We are forced to regard the words as words, and only in part able to think of the objects denoted by them' (*WP*, 125). At one level, *Old Man* reflects on poetry-as-language. The poem begins with (or from) the allure of words ('decorate'); then probes their failure to pin down 'the thing it is' ('perplex'). But this discrepancy or mystery, perhaps the founding impulse of poetry, neither invalidates the poet-speaker's 'liking' for words, nor cancels their associations with the phenomenal world, even if 'the things are forgotten, and it is an aspect of them, a recreation of them, a finer development of them, which endures in the written words' (*RJ*, 298). Poetry, like memory, functions at a remove: further mysteries are latent in the conundrum of 'how much' the child 'will remember'.

10. *the child:* Myfanwy Thomas, on whom (as in *Snow* and *The Brook*) Thomas usually bases his generic 'child'. In the Romantic tradition, he situates children close to the threshold of vision. The speaker's own consciousness moves between adult and childhood selves.

14-15. *perhaps / Thinking, perhaps of nothing:* a rhetorically cunning line-break. The verb 'think' is as central to the poem as the verb 'remember'. The tension between them suggests that memory, and certain kinds of 'meaning', operate in zones unreachable by the conscious mind or zones that only poetry might reach: 'try /…to think what it is I am remembering' (lines 27-8). In l.33, where 'thinking of nothing' becomes scarier, 'nothing' carries its full weight as 'no thing'.

19-24. *And I can only…Forbidding her to pick.* As with the speculative movement of the opening lines, Thomas plays syntax against metre. This rhythmical crescendo, like its darker counterpart (lines 36-9), emerges from 'Old Man's Beard'. 'Forbidding her to pick' evokes the Garden of Eden. Its wording and placing make the prohibition more forbidding than in the prose.

39. *Only an avenue, dark, nameless, without end.* Here Thomas presents a prospect of 'dissolution' (see note on lines 6-8). But this pole of his dialectic may have less to do with the arbitrariness of language than with a psychic split in the speaker, or a cognitive breach between humanity and earth, or both. Yet, at all

its removes from various origins, the poem itself serves as transposed memory. More disturbingly, it may 'remember the future'.

Ms: *LML*. **Published text:** *AANP, LP*.

The Signpost (37)

7 December 1914

The Signpost may be in subtextual dialogue with Frost's 'The Road Not Taken':

> Two roads diverged in a yellow wood,
> And sorry I could not travel both
> And be one traveller, long I stood
> And looked down one as far as I could
> To where it bent in the undergrowth...
>
> I shall be telling this with a sigh
> Somewhere ages and ages hence:
> Two roads diverged in a wood, and I –
> I took the one less travelled by,
> And that has made all the difference.

Frost conceived 'The Road Not Taken' as a parody of Thomas, consciously assuming his friend's more hesitant personality: 'While living in Gloucestershire in 1914, Frost frequently took long walks with Thomas through the country-side. Repeatedly Thomas would choose a route which might enable him to show his American friend a rare plant or a special vista; but it often happened that before the end of such a walk Thomas would regret the choice he had made and would sigh over what he might have shown Frost if they had taken a "better" direction' (*SLRF*, xiv). But Cooke questions Frost's story as an 'attempt to veil ...secret places of his mind from the over-curious' (*WC*, 206). Certainly, Frost objected to readers taking the 'sigh' of his last line straight, rather than as an ironical implication that no real 'difference' is at stake. On 26 June 1915 he wrote to Thomas: 'I wonder if it was because you were trying too much out of regard for me that you failed to see that the sigh was a mock sigh, hypo–critical for the fun of the thing. I dont suppose I was ever sorry for anything I ever did except by assumption to see how it would feel. I may have been sorry for having given a certain kind of people a chance at me: I have passionately regret-ting exposing myself' (*RFET*, 70). Here Frost is replying to a letter in which Thomas had both accepted the 'sigh' at face value, and represented 'choice' as illusory: 'It is all very well for you poets in a wood to say you choose, but you don't. If you do, ergo I am no poet. I didn't choose my sex yet I was simpler then. And so I can't "leave off" going in after myself tho some day I may' (*RFET*, 63-4). Frost's wariness of being seen to sigh and Thomas's compulsion to 'go in after myself' cast light on their aesthetic 'divergences'.

Even if he did not altogether know himself, Frost knew Thomas. That this poem's 'I' (pursuing a kind of static quest) never leaves the signpost reflects patterns elsewhere: 'I could not decide. If I went on foot, I could do as I liked on the Plain. There are green roads leading from everywhere to everywhere. But, on the other hand, it might be necessary at that time of year to keep walking all day, which would mean at least thirty miles a day, which was more than I was inclined for' (*IPS*, 16). 'I looked at my maps. Should I go through Swindon, or Andover, or Winchester, or Southampton? I had a mind to compass all four; but the objection was that the kinks thus to be made would destroy any feeling of advance in the journey' (*IPS*, 26-7). The moral map (above all, the choice between enlisting and going to America) also exacted obsessive deliberation or retrospection. Thomas would 'spend hours, when I ought to be reading or enjoying the interlacing flight of 3 kestrels, in thinking out my motives for this or that act or word in the past until I long for sleep' (*LGB*, 129). With its echo of folk-tales in which travellers fatefully choose their road, *The Signpost* gives Thomas's poetic journey 'in after' himself an archetypal starting-point. If his poems are stages in a quest or question, it stands as question mark.

8-10. *A voice says...never been born.* The first 'voice' speaks for (what should have been) zestfully confident youth. In fact, the gloom-quotient in Thomas's early letters and diaries supports the second voice's point that self-doubt is not age-specific. Seemingly older and wiser, like 'another' in *November*, this voice speaks for earthly existence with all its necessities and contradictions. Notes for the poem include: 'When – / ~~Will~~ there come a day / When I could wish to be alive / Somehow 20 or 40 or not' (*FNB79*).

11. *One hazel lost a leaf of gold.* This shorter line and a flattening out of stress in its first three syllables intensify 'loss'. The contrasting anapaestic beat of l.12 epitomises a larger counterpoint between lyrical and folk-verse rhythms in Thomas's couplets: tradition and the individual talent also meet at the signpost. Delicate variations of stress enhance the eerie setting: 'chill' sea, 'shy' sun, 'skeleton weeds'. These images are among the 'signs' that the poem 'reads'. But when the second voice takes over, stressed and unstressed syllables become more sharply distinguished, rhymes and line-endings more emphatic. 'Be', significantly, is rhymed three times.

13, 21. *'twould... 'Twill.* Such dialect contractions, most frequently ''twas', recur in Thomas's poems, not only where (as in *Man and Dog*) country people are speaking or spoken with. Depending on context and tone, Thomas also switches between them and Standard English in first-person lyrics. Indexed to the poem's urgency, ''twas' occurs four times in *March*. It appears in the last line of *Ambition* (an ironical usage); in l.39 of *May 23* (a celebratory usage); and in l.4 of *Home* (81, an affirmative usage). But he slowed down ''Twas June' in *Adlestrop* (l.4) to 'It was late June'. According to his brother Julian, Thomas wished to make his later prose 'as near akin as possible to the talk of a Surrey peasant' (quoted, *CET*, Preface, 6). In *The Signpost* such talk adds to the archetypal aura, as do phrases like 'it must befall' and 'between death and birth'. For Thomas's interest in proverbial speech, see general note to *Lob* (215).

21-9. *and your wish may be...out in the air.* After reading 'poems abounding in references to a future life', Thomas reflected: 'If we survived – "we" in any real sense – what joy could it be if from our thoughts this life were blotted?...And how "heavenly"? if we know not the lives beneath us, as poets and scientists know' (*Diary*, 22 November 1901, *NLW*). 'The life of Tirnanoge was all beautiful, being of a kind that men have always refused to think possible, because it was active and full of variety yet never brought death or decay, weariness or regret. This cannot easily be imagined by earthly men. They say that perfect happiness would be dull if it were possible. If they could imagine it, they would not love it so utterly when they possessed it like Ossian; many would refuse it because it wipes out the desire and the conscious memory of earth' (*CS*, 78). Thomas often quotes or misquotes Wordsworth's affirmation that 'the very world' ('earth' in Thomas's versions) is 'the place where in the end / We find our happiness, or not at all' (1804 poem on the French Revolution). Even 'a mouthful of earth' is not a wholly ironical 'gift'. Homesickness for earth, as predicted in these lines, also amounts to an *ars poetica*. Thomas lays out the conditions and materials of his poetry; sets its diurnal/seasonal coordinates; and attaches his underlying artistic 'voice' to someone 'Standing upright out in the air / Wondering...'.

30. *Wondering where he shall journey, O where?'* In coming full circle, the poem confirms a preference for earthly doubts over heavenly answers. To be is a question.

Ms: *LML*. **Published text:** *P*. **Differences from** *CP1978*: 5 the traveller's-joy *traveller's-joy* 14 see, *see* 24 birth, – *birth*, 27 Spring, – *Spring*, **Note:** *CP1978* follows a typescript [*MET*] where it diverges from *P*.

After Rain (38)

14 December 1914

After Rain is the first poem in Thomas's working notebook *M₁*. No manuscript of the four poems printed next in this edition (*Interval, The Other, Birds' Nests, The Mountain Chapel*) survives. Nor can any of these poems be precisely dated (some may antedate *After Rain*), although they were written before *The Manor Farm* (24 December). All five poems have been placed in a sequence chosen by the editor.

'Each autumn a dozen little red apples hung on one of [the apple-tree's] branches like a line of poetry in a foreign language, quoted in a book' (*HGLM*, 145). '[?]Dripping clear (wind light) after days of rain and about 12 yellow apples are scattered smooth bright all over big crab in leafless dark copse...all boughs and berries plastered with raindrops...Rain shines on boughs and drops on dead leaves Stone has a green edge of grass but also under that a purple narrowed edge of dead moist leaves thick together' (14 December, *FNB79*). As Coombes says, an 'interesting "rain" anthology could be compiled from Thomas's writings' (*HC*, 89):

> At all times I love rain, the early momentous thunder-drops, the per-pendicular cataract shining, or at night the little showers, the spongy mists, the tempestuous mountain rain. I like to see it possessing the whole earth at evening, smothering civilisation, taking away from me myself everything except the power to walk under the dark trees and to enjoy as humbly as the hissing grass, while some twinkling house-light or song sung by a lonely man gives a foil to the immense dark force. I like to see the rain making the streets, the railway station, a pure desert, whether bright with lamps or not. It foams off the roofs and trees and bubbles into the water-butts. It gives the grey rivers a daemonic majesty. It scours the roads, sets the flints moving, and exposes the glossy chalk

in the tracks through the woods. It does work that will last as long as the earth. It is about eternal business. In its noise and myriad aspects I feel the mortal beauty of immortal things. (*SC*, 274-5)

The 'myriad aspects' of rain are central to Thomas's symbolism. It can suggest an alien or alienated 'immense dark force' (*Rain*) or softer qualities and a more sympathetic universe: 'Half a kiss, half a tear' (*Sowing*). In *After Rain* it is 'both dark and bright': a destroyer that has ravaged the scene (perhaps also interior) and a creator, an artist, adding new beauties.

17-18. *like little black fish, inlaid, / As if they played.* In Thomas's fantasy 'The Castle of Leaves' children watch, when the castle falls, 'the dead leaves swim by like fishes, crimson and emerald and gold' (*HGLM*, 214). Thomas maintained a polite argument with Eleanor Farjeon over these lines: '"As if they played" I was anxious to have in. It describes the patterns of the fish but it comes in awkwardly perhaps after inlaid.' Six days later: 'I wonder whether I can do anything with "inlaid" and "played". The inlaid, too, is at any rate perfectly precise as I saw the black leaves 2 years ago up at the top of the hill, so that neither is a rhyme word only' (*EF*, 110-11). 'Inlaid' is an inlaid word.

24. *Uncountable.* This one-word, off-rhymed, run-on line breaks the poem's formal mould just as it and the rainless lull end. Also placed in a sequence of liquid sounds, the line brims with the subliminally therapeutic return of rain. Thomas employs the same 'limping' couplet form to different effect in *Head and Bottle*.

Ms: *M₁*. **Published text:** *AANP*, *LP*.

Interval (39)
December 1914

For date, see general note to *After Rain* (154). While *After Rain* and *Interval* seem closely linked by December weather and moods, the latter's aural rather than visual emphasis echoes a passage in *The South Country*: 'The wind reigns …in the surging trees…yet in the open there is a strange silence because the roar in my ears as I walk deafens me to all sound…And yet once more the road pierces the dense woodland roar, form and colour buried as it were in sound' (*SC*, 217-18).

3. *makes way.* 'I mean in "Interval" that the night did postpone her coming a bit for the twilight. Night might have been expected to come down on the end of day and didn't. "Held off" would have been stricter' (*EF*, 110). 'Makes way', which suggests that night relinquishes a position already gained, aligns 'brief twilight' with unexpected remission in some psychic 'storm'. Cf. *The Ash Grove* (1.5), where the word 'interval' also has temporal, spatial and psychological aspects.

22. *Unwavering.* The contrast with 'Uncountable' (*After Rain*, 1.24) stakes out the poems' shared poles of stability and flux.

24. '…"under storm's wing" was not just for the metre' (*EF*, 110).

32. *This roaring peace.* Cf. 'stormy rest'. The oxymorons of *Interval*, set off by the poem's strong beat and short line, complement the tessellated effects of *After Rain*. For Vernon Scannell: 'all Edward Thomas's poems show a deliberate and

fruitful opposing of contrasting moods and attitudes and a counterpoising and reconciling of the language in which these attitudes are embodied. They reflect the ceaseless inner conflict and the struggle for peace which never seemed to give him respite. [*Interval*] shows clearly the way in which Thomas used opposites to create associative tensions which move gradually towards the final reconciliation of "This roaring peace", the calm which is actually a suspended violence' (*VS*, 17-18).

Ms: none. Published text: *P*. **Differences from** *CP1978*: 1 day: *day*. 6-8 Mounts and is lost / In the high beech-wood / It shines almost. *Mounts beneath pines / To the high beech wood / It almost shines.* 15 Above, the cloud pack *Above it the rack* 29 Die, *Die* **Note:** *CP1978* follows a typescript [*MET*] rather than *P*. At the points of difference, *MET* seems rhythmically cruder.

The Other (40)
December 1914

For date, see general note to *After Rain* (154). *The Other* reads like a prophetic microcosm of Thomas's brief poetic career. Its allegorical landscape – in part, a transposed Wiltshire – spans his poetic habitats, and contains the seeds of later poems. As in *The Signpost*, but more elaborately, he adapts folk motifs (forest, haunted quest, helpers and frustrators of the questing hero, the *Doppelgänger* legend, signs and omens) to modern psychodrama. His symbolism of the journey taps into its archetypal sources. The result is what Louis MacNeice, in *Varieties of Parable* (London: Faber, 1965), calls 'parable' or 'double-level writing'. Thomas's chosen stanza, tightly rhymed ABABABCB [A in the first stanza] CC, seems well suited to parable. Its octosyllabic line and echo of the ballad–quatrain lend narrative impetus, while the clinching couplet helps to make each stanza a distinct stage in the quest. Yet, at the poem's meditative climax, the stanza allows 'Moments of everlastingness' their necessary syntactical scope.

German Romanticism endowed the notion of a person's double (*Doppelgänger*) 'with tragic and fatal overtones... It may sometimes be our complement but is more often the foe with whom we are lured to fight... In some ancient traditions, meeting one's double is an unlucky occurrence, and is sometimes even a presage of death' (*Penguin Dictionary of Symbols* [1996], 306). For Karl Miller, 'The double stands at the start of that cultivation of uncertainty by which the literature of the modern world has come to be distinguished' (Miller, *Doubles* [Oxford: Oxford University Press, 1985], vi). "Doubles" intensified as a literary theme in the nineteenth century, with James Hogg's *Confessions of a Justified Sinner* (1824), Dostoevsky's *The Double* (1846), Robert Louis Stevenson's *Dr Jekyll and Mr Hyde* (1886), Oscar Wilde's *Picture of Dorian Gray* (1891). Like Henry James in *The Turn of the Screw* (1898) and Joseph Conrad in *The Secret Sharer* (1910), Thomas moves beyond quasi-Gothic scenarios towards the concern with the unconscious self that they prefigure. In 1912, he underwent analysis with Godwin Baynes: a charismatic doctor interested in Freud and psychological medicine, later Carl Jung's chief British disciple. Yet here, as throughout his poetry, Thomas creates his own language for the workings of the psyche. Parable, which can transmute dream and nightmare, is among the structural strategies that enable him to objectify and universalise his problems.

Thomas's originality as poetic psychoanalyst makes parallels with the ideas of Freud and Jung all the more interesting. In '*Das Unheimliche*' ['The Uncanny'] (1919), Freud sees the "double" both as self-critical 'conscience' and as 'incorporating...all the unfulfilled but possible futures to which we like to cling in fantasy, all the strivings of the ego which adverse external circumstances have crushed, and all our suppressed acts of volition which nourish in us the illusion of free will' (Sigmund Freud, *Art and Literature*, Penguin Freud Library 14 [1985], 357-8). Hélène Cixous writes of Freud's essay in terms that might equally fit Thomas's poem: 'this search whose movement constitutes the labyrinth which instigates it; the sense of strangeness imposes its secret necessity everywhere' (quoted in Nicholas Royle, *The Uncanny* [Manchester: Manchester University Press, 2003], 16). Thomas's 'Other' also has parallels with Jung's 'Shadow', thus glossed by Jung in 1951: 'The shadow is a moral problem that challenges the whole ego-personality, for no one can become conscious of the shadow without considerable moral effort. To become conscious of it involves recognising the dark aspects of the personality as present and real. This act is the essential condition for any kind of self-knowledge, and it therefore, as a rule, meets with considerable resistance.' Anthony Storr notes: 'The shadow behaves compensatorily to consciousness; hence its effects can be positive as well as negative' (ed., Anthony Storr, *Jung: Selected Writings* [London: Fontana, 1983], 91, 422). Thomas himself writes: 'Probably every man has more or less clearly and more or less constantly before his mind's eye an ideal self which the real seldom more than approaches. This ideal self may be morally or in other ways inferior, but it remains the standard by which the man judges his acts. Some men prove the existence of this ideal self by announcing now and then that they are misunderstood. Or they do things which they afterwards condemn as irrelevant or uncharacteristic and out of harmony' (*GB*, 13-14).

Thomas's use of opium during his twenties (the initials PO: Persian Opium appear in his diaries) may have precipitated experiences of duality. In autumn 1911 he wrote: 'I hope it [vegetarianism] will cure my head, which is almost always wrong now – a sort of conspiracy going on in it which leaves me only a joint tenancy and a perpetual scare of the other tenant and wonder what he will do' (*JM*, 172). His prose contains many thinly masked self-portraits and *alter egos*, their conception impelled by the need to understand his neurotic symptoms. Thus the depressive prose origin of *Rain* is voiced by 'a ghostly double' (*IW*, 280). The most explicit instance is the 'Other Man' in *In Pursuit of Spring*, a book that also fertilised *The Other* in subsidiary details. Thomas had noted in *FNB*62 (June 1913): 'Other Man – wraith – when seen at Salterley I was not sure he had existed before – he avoids a Difficulty in telling truth'. First sighted freeing a caged chaffinch, then sketching a weather-vane, the Other Man surfaces at an inn:

At first I did not grasp the connection between this dripping, indubitably real man and the wraith of the day before. But he was absurdly pleased to recognise me, bowing with a sort of uncomfortable graciousness and a trace of a cockney accent. His expression changed in those few moments from a melancholy and too yielding smile to a pale, thin-lipped rigidity. I did not know whether to be pleased or not with the reincarnation, when he departed to change his clothes. (*IPS*, 119)

'I suppose you write books,' said I. 'I do,' said he. 'What sort of books do you write?' 'I wrote one all about this valley of the Frome...But no one knows that it was the Frome I meant. You look surprised. Nevertheless, I got fifty pounds for it.' 'That is a lot of money for such a book!' 'So my publisher thought.' 'And you are lucky to get money for doing what you like.' 'What I like!' he muttered, pushing his bicycle back uphill, past the goats by the ruin, and up the steps between walls that were lovely with humid moneywort, and saxifrage like filigree, and ivy-leaved toadflax. Apparently the effort loosened his tongue. He rambled on and on about himself, his past, his writing, his digestion; his main point being that he did not like writing. He had been attempting the impossible task of reducing undigested notes about all sorts of details to a grammatical, continuous narrative. He abused notebooks violently. He said that they blinded him to nearly everything that would not go into the form of notes; or, at any rate, he could never afterwards reproduce the great effects of Nature and fill in the interstices merely – which was all they were good for – from the notes. The notes – often of things which he would otherwise have forgotten – had to fill the whole canvas. Whereas, if he had taken none, then only the important, what he truly cared for, would have survived in his memory, arranged not perhaps as they were in Nature, but at least according to the tendencies of his own spirit. (*IPS*, 219-20)

The portrait of the Other Man involves self-irony and self-parody. It satirises Thomas's literary problems (with a reflexive swipe at *In Pursuit of Spring*), his love of Nature and traditional things, his diet-fads and clay-pipe smoking, his 'melancholy' introversion. The poem reverses the roles of narrator-protagonist and double – insofar as they are distinct. The 'eager' narrator becomes the stalker, the greater 'bore', while the Other – up to a point – represents a better or better-adjusted Self. Thus his shadower may be the Shadow. At the same time, if psychic health can only be attained through acknowledging the Shadow, the Other is also the defensive 'ego-personality'. Since the poem's action takes place inside one head or psyche, Self and Other keep crossing over. See Andrew Motion's analysis (*AM*, 37-51).

2-4. *To feel the light...the sweet mint.* The poem begins with a burst of sense-impressions. The synaesthesia 'feel the light' will be picked up by 'tasted sunlight' (l.15). Motion notes that 'clear sight is crucially absent' (*AM*, 38). But this blind sensing of the world suggests birth or youth as well as (recurrent) emergence from a dark place in the psyche. It is characteristic of parable to encompass the human life cycle.

17-20. *What to do...until myself I knew.* Cooke comments: 'Even the syntax makes him the pursuer of himself' (*WC*, 204). Cf. the syntactical mystery tour of lines 89-90. 'When caught' cuts both ways, like 'keep in sight' (l.102).

21. *I tried the inns.* 'An impulse as sick and as profound as the *fatigue du nord*, or as that which drove Richard Jefferies from inland meadows to the sea, goads

some of us to the life of inns. Something, we may think, that overpowers the delicious sense of home, bids us exchange that for an abode that is a truer symbol of our inconstant lodging on the earth' (*HS*, 39). Besides 'inconstant lodging', inns (as in *Aspens*) may represent society: Thomas compares an 'inn door' to 'the entrance to a bright cave in the middle of the darkness: the illumination had a kind of blessedness...not without foreignness; and a half-seen man within it belonged to a world, blessed indeed, but far different from this one of mine, dark, soft, and tranquil. I felt that I could walk on thus, sipping the evening silence and solitude, endlessly' (*IPS*, 214). Motion detects a contrast between the (rural) 'inn in the sun', linked with a 'happy mood', and the narrator's reception in this 'urban context [where] social harmony has been replaced by isolation' (*AM*, 40). But the poem draws on Thomas's touchiness about all inhospitable inns, as well as his sense of all society as 'foreign'. He recalls his anger at being churlishly refused a bed in a country village: 'To be elbowed out at nightfall after a day's walking by an unconscious conspiracy of a whole village was enough either to produce either a hate of Chiseldon or a belief that the devil or a distinguished relative was organising the opposition' (*IW*, 307).

22. *a long gabled high-street grey*: a trace of Wiltshire (see note on lines 61-80): 'Marlborough town, with its dormered and gabled High Street, long, wide and discreet, and, though genial, obviously an entity which the visitor can know little of...The downs and Savernake Forest dominate the town. It is but a place at the edge of the forest' (*RJ*, 5).

24. *weary way*: perhaps an echo of Gray's 'Elegy' ('The ploughman homeward plods his weary way'), but see note on l.87.

29-30. *never-foamless shores / Make better friends than those dull boors*. A similar declaration to that about 'man's ingratitude' in 'Blow, blow, thou winter wind' (*As You Like It*, II, vii). Thomas may also allude to 'the foam / Of perilous seas' in Keats's 'Ode to a Nightingale', thereby countering social alienation with poetic vocation. Yet 'dull boors', a phrase that covers his sensitivity to perceived neglect by 'friends', strikes a paranoid note that prepares for the next stanza.

32. *Aimed at the unseen moving goal*. In its reflexive aspect, this line sums up the empiricist and agnostic metaphysics that make the quest / journey the defining trope of Thomas's poetry. Cf. 'some goal / I touched then' (*I never saw that land before*); 'I had not found my goal' (*Some eyes condemn*).

37. *Desire of desire*. 'Desire' (like 'beauty') is a word that survives from Thomas's formative exposure to Romantic poetry and his baptism in *fin-de-siècle* aesthetics. It tends to carry a feverish, erotic charge. Although 'desire' also denotes other kinds of lack, including frustrated creativity, at one level the poem has moved from friendship to love ('kiss'), thus prefiguring themes of Thomas's love poetry. 'Remedies / For all desire' may be any alleviation that entails self-suppression, as when Thomas wonders 'whether for a person like myself whose most intense moments were those of depression a cure that destroys the depression may not destroy the intensity – a *desperate* remedy?' (*LGB*, 163). Such 'cures' aggravate neurosis by inducing 'Desire of desire'. This vicious spiral takes the narrator 'beyond control', and prevents 'wholeness'.

40. *I quite forgot I could forget.* Here difficult memory is no longer being evaded or sedated or sublimated.

53-4. *To find him out...bore.* 'I don't like...to meet continually some respectable acquaintance with whom I must stop to bore or be bored' (*SL*, 23). 'Find him out' rather than 'find him' makes 'confession', like boredom, a two-way traffic.

61-80. *I sought then in solitude...An old inhabitant of earth.* On 18 December 1913, when staying with Vivian Locke Ellis at Selsfield House, East Grinstead, Thomas recorded in *FNB67*: 'East Grinstead. 4.30 one of those eternal evenings – the wind gone, no one upon the road. I grasp the stile by the holly and look over the ploughland to the near ridge, the crocketed spruces, the dark house mass, and behind them a soft dulling flame-coloured sky where large shapeless soft dull-dark clouds in roughly horizontal lines are massing with one bright star in an interstice – and far behind me an owl calls again and again and somewhere far to one side in a hid hollow a dog barks and nearer, one or two blackbirds chink as they fly along hedges. What does it mean? I feel an old inhabitant of earth at such times. How many hundred times have I seen the same since I was 15'. The note continues: 'at 5.30 wind moaning and over the west is a mass of cloud like a great hand with a star eastward'. The composite landscape of these stanzas also recalls climactic images of Salisbury Plain in *In Pursuit of Spring*. As in *Lob*, Wiltshire provides conditions for revelation: 'I emerged into the glory and peace of the Plain, of the unbounded Plain and the unbounded sky, and the marriage of sun and wind that was being celebrated upon them'; 'over the wall [of the Plain] rounded clouds, pure white and sunlit, were heaving up ...The late afternoon grew more and more quiet and still, and in the warmth I mistook a distant dog's bark, and again a cock's crowing, for the call of a cuckoo, mixed with the blackbird's singing...already the blackbirds were chinking and shifting places along the hedgerows. And presently it was dark, but for a lamp at an open door, and silent, but for a chained dog barking' (*IPS*, 172, 177-8). After the disappointments of social intercourse, 'solitude' becomes intrinsic to self-discovery and to the integration projected onto harmony with, and within, Nature. 'Naked' implies return to a primal state. The narrator communes with 'hidden' and 'unseen' things. The 'Other' (along with 'difference') vanishes from these stanzas, in which the two merge under the sign of 'one star, one lamp, one peace'.

67. *crocketed dark trees.* Crockets are Gothic architectural ornaments in the form of buds or curled leaves: this phrase returns them to their natural origins. Thomas describes Steeple Ashton church as 'bristling with coarse crockets all over, and knobby with coarse gargoyles' (*IPS*, 176).

79. *solemn quiet mirth.* This echoes a phrase in 'A Nocturnal Reverie' by Anne Finch, Countess of Winchilsea (1661-1720), a poem that Thomas quotes in *Feminine Influence on the Poets*: 'When a sedate Content the Spirit feels, / And no fierce Light disturbs, whilst it reveals; /...Till the free Soul to a compos'dness charm'd, / Finding the Elements of Rage disarm'd, / O'er all below, a solemn Quiet grown, / Joys in th'inferiour World, and thinks it like her Own'. Thomas comments: '[the poem] makes us feel that she has had the magical experience which has only been perfectly expressed by much later poets' (*FIP*, 60). 'A Nocturnal Reverie' may have influenced lines 61-80 more generally, also *Liberty* (see note, 261).

80. *An old inhabitant of earth.* See Thomas's use of this key formulation in the passage from *FNB67* quoted above. His praise of George Meredith links it with his favourite Wordsworth quotation (see note, 154): 'From first to last he wrote as an inhabitant of this earth, where, as Wordsworth says, "we have our happiness or not at all", just or unjust' (*IPS*, 60). In 'The First Cuckoo' Thomas analyses our pleasure in recurrent seasonal events: 'I am not forgetting how much of the thrill may be due to the feeling of a fresh start, combined with that of being an old inhabitant of the earth' (*LS*, 60). 'An old inhabitant of earth' situates the speaker, healingly, not in the contemporary social world ('far off from men', 1.86), but in a community defined by an ecological sense of history: '[Salisbury Plain] makes us feel the age of the earth, the greatness of Time, Space, and Nature; the littleness of man even in an aeroplane, the fact that the earth does not belong to man, but man to the earth' (*IPS*, 150). 'The Stile', based on a harmonious walk with a friend, ends at sunset with the narrator – now solitary – saying: 'Somewhere…I was gathered up with an immortal company, where I and poet and lover and flower and cloud and star were equals, as all the little leaves were equal…And in that company I learned that I am something which no fortune can touch, whether I be soon to die, or long years away…I shall go on, something that is here and there like the wind, something unconquerable, something not to be separated from the dark earth and the light sky, a strong citizen of infinity and eternity' (*LAT*, 50-1).

81-7. *Once the name…everlastingness.* Thomas's concern with the interpenetration of 'melancholy' and 'happiness' will reappear in *Melancholy* and *October* (see notes, 231, 259). 'Melancholy' is indeed the name he gives to his depression in early letters and diaries: 'I cannot relieve my melancholy today; it is so oppressive that I long to have some physical ill which would swallow it' (*Diary*, 4 January 1902, *NLW*). At that time, he was devoted to Burton's *Anatomy of Melancholy* and identifying with De Quincey's *Opium-Eater*. 'When…bowers' seems to be a self-contained clause that proposes alternative versions of the narrator's condition: another doubleness. If an understood 'I' is the subject of 'Smiled and enjoyed', this suppression of the first-person singular and the odd syntax situate him in a psychic orbit where his symptoms change their aspect, perhaps where they are translated into poetry. 'Powers' implies resurgent creativity.

87. *Moments of everlastingness*: an oxymoron, like 'everlasting lease' in 1.70. Both phrases may allude to the writing of poems. Thomas included Henry Vaughan's 'The Retreat' in his *Pocket Book of Poems and Songs for the Open Air*: 'But felt through all this fleshly dress / Bright shoots of everlastingness'. Another seventeenth-century religious poet may also hover over what is almost a declaration of faith. Coombes notes that *The Other* 'curiously recalls in one or two places' George Herbert's 'The Pilgrimage': e.g., 1.24 parallels Herbert's line, 'A long it was and weary way' (*HC*, 217). Like Thomas's 'goal', Herbert's 'gladsome hill' is always 'further'. In his introduction to Herbert's *The Temple* and *A Priest to the Temple* (1908) Thomas appreciates the Englishness of Herbert's Anglicanism, but clearly prefers more visionary religious poetry: 'he seems most himself when he is most an Anglican…and he rarely soars out of that gracious and well-ordered park' (xi). Yet Herbert's 'afflicted' mode (as in 'The Pilgrimage') is not remote from Thomas's own sensibility. *In Pursuit of Spring* visits Bemerton,

once Herbert's parish: 'The bells, the sunshine after storm, the elm trees, and the memory of that pious poet, put me into what was perhaps an unconscious imitation of a religious humour. And in that humour, repeating [Herbert's 'Sunday'] with a not wholly sham unction, I rode away from Bemerton. The Other Man, however, overtook me, and upset the humour.' He does so by 'repeating in his turn, with unction exaggerated to an incredibly ridiculous degree, [Herbert's] sonnet on Sin' (*IPS*, 140).

89-90. See note on lines 17-20.

98. *under a ban*. A 'ban' is a curse or interdict that carries supernatural sanction. Coombes says: 'when the other in the taproom complains that he lives "under a ban" because of the pursuer's relentlessness, he is stating a condition which is precisely central to the pursuer himself' (*HC*, 219).

100. *I slipped away*. The impulse on each side to evade the Other has its counterpart in how Thomas depicts his reaction to being overtaken in a walking race by 'the boy who notoriously ran': 'I hated being pursued...I began to believe that the running boy was gaining on me. I could not stand it. Turning off the track I threw myself down on the grass on the pretext that I had a stitch' (*CET*, 115). The Other's abuse of the narrator may denote 'resistance' (Jung's word for 'ban') to acknowledging one's Shadow.

101-10. *And now...cease*. 'I awoke to hear ducklings squeaking, and a starling in the pine tree imitating the curlew and the owl hunting' (*IPS*, 216). This stanza brings the poem full circle and repeats its course in miniaturised form. However, in keeping with overtones of death rather than birth, the repeated elements have become 'uncanny', *unheimlich*. Freud defines the uncanny as a 'frightening' effect produced by 'something repressed which *recurs*'; also as 'nothing new or alien, but something which is familiar and old-established in the mind and which has become alienated from it only through the process of repression' (363-4). The disturbingly imitative starlings contrast with the earlier 'kestrel and woodpecker', 'marshbird' and 'blackbird'. The effect resembles the exchange of attributes between birds, fish and human beings in *The Hollow Wood* (see note, 171). Yet, if this distortion in Nature mirrors the blocked meeting between narrator and Other, further cycles of the journey are anticipated. Perhaps a 'fortunate' search, integration or remission, can only be 'brief' (lines 88, 91).

104. *I steal*. Miller glosses 'steal' as 'a furtiveness which courts or desires disclosure...[The narrator] steals towards rather than away – which would have been the more familiar move of the two' (Miller, *Doubles*, 27).

Ms: none. **Published text**: *LP*. **Differences from *CP1978***: 85 weaknesses *weakness* [misprint] **Note**: *LP* is identical with the only surviving typescript, sent by Thomas to Robert Frost.

Birds' Nests (43)

December 1914

For date, see general note to *After Rain* (154). 'In the dense green coverts of the summer hedgerows nests were difficult to find, but now they show at every turn. The cunning basket-work of the lesser whitethroat, so frail as to seem incapable of holding the smallest egg, is filled with rotting black leaves and haws that have dropped thus early' (*TWL*, 91). Chapter 7 of *The Happy-*

Go-Lucky Morgans recalls Thomas's birds-nesting as a boy. W.H. Davies's elegy for Thomas, 'Killed in Action', alludes to later 'days...When you and I, with thoughtful mind, / Would help a bird to hide her nest, / For fear of other hands less kind'.

5. *no need of eyes to see them with*: a paradox that implies Thomas's high standards for 'seeing' natural phenomena, and hence for other forms of perception. Cf. 'And now I see as I look' in *First known when lost*, which has other links with *Birds' Nests*.

13. *winter nest*. *P* and *PTP* have 'winter nests'. Like *CP1978*, this edition prefers the singular, to which 'nests' is altered in several typescripts, and which seems warranted by the specificity of 'Once' and 'there', and by the following entry in *FNB79* among scattered notes for the poem: 'one – grass and goosegrass and a squirrel's dined there often'. Thomas's Wiltshire mentor 'Dad' Uzzell showed him a pet dormouse's 'empty kernels...bored with a round hole as neatly as if it had been drilled' (*ETFN* 46 [January 2002], 8).

Ms: none. **Published text**: *P*. **Differences from** *CP1978*: 11 knew them not *never found them* 12 and squirrels *or squirrels* 14 into: *into;* 15 hazel-nuts, *hazel nuts;* **Note**: In *P* lines 1 and 2 end with full stops: probably a misprint since *PTP* has commas. For this edition's other departure from *P*, see note on l.13 above. *CP1978* throughout follows a typescript [*MET*] rather than *P*.

The Mountain Chapel (43)

December 1914

For date, see general note to *After Rain* (154). Thomas's prose contains several representations of Welsh chapels:

> [Siloh stands] bravely, – at night, it often seems perilously, – at the end of a road, beyond which rise immense mountains and impassable... But Siloh stands firm, and ventures once a week to send up a thin music that avails nothing against the wind; although close to it, threatening it, laughing at it, able to overwhelm it, should the laugh become cruel, is a company of elder trees, which, seen at twilight, are sentinels embossed upon the sky – sentinels of the invisible, patient, unconquerable powers: or (if one is lighter-hearted) they seem the empty homes of what the mines and chapels think they have routed; and at midnight they are not empty, and they love the mountain rain, and at times they summon it and talk with it, while the preacher thunders and the windows of the chapel gleam. (*BW*, 25-6)

> ...a little desolate white church and white-walled graveyard, which on December evenings will shine and seem to be the only things at one with the foamy water and the dim sky, before the storm; and when the storm comes the church is gathered up into its breast and is a part of it, so that he who walks in the churchyard is certain that the gods – the gods that grow old and feeble and die – are there still, and with them all those phantoms following phantoms in a phantom land...which make Welsh history, so that to read it is like walking in that place among December leaves...while an ancient wind is ceaselessly remembering ancient things. (*BW*, 199)

The church, a plain building of harsh stone on the highest ground, was locked, but the grave digger was still at work filling up with bits of limestone the grave of a Morgan or Jones or Jenkins or Evans...The grass grew among the tombs thick and long...when I crossed the brook the rustle of an overhanging aspen deceived me into thinking I heard water run. Between that sound and the rush of water there is not more difference than between the meaning of Penderyn to me and its meaning to an inhabitant. ('Penderyn', *COE*, 26-7)

The poem, like the prose, is tinged by the mystique of desolation and dereliction in which "Celticism" has 'shrouded' western landscapes since the publication of James Macpherson's *Ossian* in the 1760s. In *Beautiful Wales* Thomas attacks 'lovers of the Celt' as aesthetes and poseurs: 'Their aim and ideal is to go about the world in a state of self-satisfied dejection, interrupted, and perhaps sustained, by days when they consume strange mixed liquors to the tune of all the fine old Celtic songs which are fashionable...I cannot avoid the opinion that to boast of the Celtic spirit is to confess you have it not' (see *BW*, 10-13). Yet his own 'early feeling for Wales' had been partly formed by Celticism: '[it] culminated in my singing of Moore's "Minstrel Boy"...I knew only of Welsh harps. I...trembled with a kind of gloomy pleasure in being about to die for Wales' (Addenda to *CET*, *BC*). And, despite now mocking the Ossianic cult of lost battles and lost civilisation (the 'reader feels that it is a baseness to exist'), Thomas can still write of a Welsh mountain: 'it is clear, as it is not in a city or in an exuberant English county, that the world is old and troubled...Sometimes comes a thought that it is a huge gravestone...It belongs to the past, to the dead; and the dead, as they are more numerous, so here they are greater than we' (*BW*, 149). Similarly, Cornwall's 'deserted mines are frozen cries of despair as if they had perished in conflict with the waste' (*SC*, 158-9). But if *The Mountain Chapel* and *The Manor Farm* appear antithetical as earthly abodes, autobiographical loci or psychic states, the chapel has 'homely' aspects, and 'empty homes' haunt Thomas's Hampshire landscapes too. Indeed, Celticism may have influenced the prophetic thrust of his eco-historical vision. *The Mountain Chapel* prefigures *The Mill-Water* in being reflexively occupied with natural sounds that overpower the 'human'.

4-5. *The loss of the brook's voice / Falls like a shadow*. This negative synaesthesia reinforces the sense that life has receded.

9-16. *saying still...I shall be'*. The wind's speech echoes, although more bleakly, the philosophy that Richard Jefferies puts into the mouth of the wind in *Wood Magic*: 'this [prehistoric] man, and all his people...were all buried on the tops of the hills...There I come to them still, and sing through the long dry grass... The sun comes, too, and the rain, but I am here most...I am always here' (quoted, *RJ*, 148).

16. *Till there is nothing*. Possibly an allusion to W.B. Yeats's play *Where There is Nothing*, from which Thomas took his epigraph for *The South Country*. See note on *Roads* (269).

32-42. *a man...This wind was old*. The scene may constitute the only chapel where 'a man' like Thomas – a post-Darwinian agnostic with an ecocentric vision –

can worship (see note on the end of *February Afternoon*, 274). The speaker looks beyond a Welsh chapel, beyond the pagan (Celtic) gods that its setting conjures up, beyond poetic pantheons, to invoke the wind as the proper object of awe.

Ms: none. **Published text:** *LP*. **Differences from** *CP1978*: 10 birth *birth*, 15 came; *came:* 16/17 no stanza-break *stanza break* 31 somewhere, *somewhere* 32-3 off, there's a man could / Be *off there's some man could / Live* 35 dire, *dire* 37 clearly; *clearly,* 41 gods *Gods* **Note:** *CP1978* follows a typescript [*JT*] [in which 'Be' is cancelled for 'Live'], rather than *LP*. The basis of the *LP* text is unknown, but the repetition 'somewhere...some man' seems awkward, as does 'Live happy'.

The Manor Farm (45)
24 December 1914

Thomas included *Haymaking* and *The Manor Farm* in his anthology *This England* (*TE*, see general note to *Lob*, 214) under his pseudonym 'Edward Eastaway'. Preceded by Coleridge's 'Fears in Solitude' (see note, 263), and numbered I and II, the poems end the section 'Her Sweet Three Corners'. Like the anthology itself, they seem designed to suggest 'some of the echoes called up by the name of England' (*TE*, 'Note'), and to counter wartime rhetoric that took England's name in vain. Thomas's Summer and Winter scenes, set in long perspectives, aim at a deeper form of cultural resistance. Yet, while *Haymaking*, written just before Thomas enlisted, ends ambiguously, the climax of *The Manor Farm* strikes an unusually hyperbolic note, perhaps because it enacts the discovery of an 'English' Muse. A process of internal as well as external thaw culminates in epiphany. Years earlier, Thomas had evoked a similar oasis in winter: 'almost at a farmhouse door, a great yew-tree leans over...On the ancient bricks so dull and brown the yellow blossoms of the jasmine are studded thick, and they creep on to the tiled roof, weather-stained to browns and dingy reds... pied pigeons fluttering among the horses feet' (*TWL*, 114-15). 'Winter Music', timed at 'the end of the first warm day in February', features a house 'glow[ing] with tiles of olive and ochre and orange' and 'the huge, quiet, all-sustaining earth mutely communing with the sun' (*LAT*, 69-73). More immediately, the poem is set near Steep: 'at Prior's Dean, where the Elizabethan house looks across at the primitive little Norman church and its aged yew' (*WW*, 34). In moving from locality to 'This England', *The Manor Farm* overtly follows the structure for thinking about nationality – and for writing poetry – at which Thomas arrives in his essay 'England': 'I believe...that all ideas of England are developed, spun out, from such a centre into something large or infinite, solid or aëry...that England is a system of vast circumferences circling round the minute neighbouring points of home' (*LS*, 111).

1-2. *The rock-like mud unfroze...road.* Hard, stressed consonants unfreeze in 'unfroze', giving way to more liquid sounds. Thomas had attempted a similar effect in prose: 'Down each side of every white road runs a stream that sings and glitters in ripples like innumerable crystal flowers. Water drips and trickles and leaps and gushes and oozes everywhere, and extracts the fragrance of earth and green and flowers under the heat that hastens to undo the work of the snow' (*SC*, 41).

8. *yew-tree opposite.* 'From historical records and analysis of ring growth and evidence in the landscape it now seems certain that large numbers of church-yard yews are not so much "coeval" with the church as vastly older than it, often pre-dating Christianity itself. Most probably they were the lode-stones round which early, possibly pagan, religious sites grew, which in their turn formed the basis for sites of Christian worship' (Richard Mabey, *Nature Cure* [London: Chatto & Windus, 2005], 168).

18. *The Winter's cheek flushed*: a risky personification. Elsewhere Thomas inter-mingles seasons more subtly (see note on *But these things also*, 203).

22. *lain*: 'lurked' and 'waited' are alternatives rejected in *BL*.

24. *This England, Old already, was called Merry.* 'This England' ('England' in *BL*) quotes John of Gaunt's speech in *Richard II* (II, i); 'Merry' quotes Robert of Gloucester: 'Already, before Langland, a Gloucester man, Robert of Gloucester, had called England "merry" in his chronicle: – "England is a right merry land, of all on earth it is best, / Set in the end of the world as here, all in the west." It was the Merry England of the English people, "full of mirth and of game, and men oft-times able to mirth and game, free men of heart and with tongue"' ('England', *LS*, 101-2). Despite this pedigree and Hazlitt's essay 'Merry England', excerpted in the 'Merry England' section of *This England*, the line takes another stylistic risk. Thomas defended it to W.H. Hudson: 'But about "Merry" in "The Manor Farm", I rather think I will stick to it. If one can feel what one has written, and not what one *meant*. I feel here as if the *merry* England asleep at Prior's Dean added to the sleepiness and enriched it some-how' (*SL*, 108).

Ms: *BL*. **Published text:** *TE, P*. **Differences from *CP1978*:** 9 The church and yew *Small church, great yew*, **Note:** *CP1978* follows *TE* rather than *P*, which is validated by *PTP*.

An Old Song I (46)

25 December 1914

Thomas's earliest memories were inseparable from song: 'The songs, first of my mother, then of her younger sister, I can hear not only afar off behind the veil but on this side of it also. I was, I should think, a very still listener whom the music flowed through and filled to the exclusion of all thought and of all sensation except of blissful easy fullness, so that too early or too sudden ceasing would have meant pangs of expectant emptiness' (*CET*, 13). '[Edward] loved singing – old songs, racy songs, songs that had won the acceptance of a robust democracy as a permanent possession, songs of Tudor fragility and daintiness – but he limited his audience to a family circle... He would perch a small child on his knee, and clasp his clay pipe...and the music that was in him would come forth, wistfully or jauntily' (*LJB*, 88). 'I prefer any country church or chapel to Winchester or Chichester or Canterbury Cathedral, just as I prefer "All round my hat", or "Somer is icumen in", to Beethoven' (*SC*, 4).

With reference to Thomas's anthology *The Pocket Book of Poems and Songs for the Open Air* (1907), R. George Thomas comments: '[his] informed interest in folk-music...has almost passed unnoticed by critics of his poetry' (*LGB*, 127n.). Jonathan Barker's essay 'Edward Thomas and the Folk Tradition' makes up some of the deficit (*JB*, 133-46). When compiling the *Pocket Book*, he sought out the most authentic words and airs from song-collectors like Cecil Sharp, and supplied musical notation, especially for lesser-known songs. Thomas's division of the *Pocket Book* into sections (The Invitation, The Start in the Morning, Wayside Rest, Village and Inn, The Footpath, Evening) makes it an embryonic *This England* constructed as a journey. All this associates him with a movement of indigenous cultural retrieval that had begun in the eighteenth century, with Burns and Wordsworth, and was then renewing itself. Reviewing Sharp's *English Folk-Songs* and Francis B. Gummere's *The Popular Ballad*, he hoped that folk-melodies might be 'the foundation of a truly English school of music that may equal those other schools which have grown up where folk-song is not only indigenous but alive, beloved and national' (*Daily Chronicle*, 23 January 1908). The folksong movement influenced Ralph Vaughan Williams's music, Thomas's poetry, Ivor Gurney's music and poetry. Vaughan Williams and Gurney would later set poems by Thomas.

[O]f all music, the old ballads and folk songs and their airs are richest in the plain, immortal symbols. The best of them seem to be written in a language that should be universal, if only simplicity were truly simple to mankind. Their alphabet is small; their combinations are as the sunlight or the storm, and their words also are symbols. Seldom have they any direct relation to life as the realist believes it to be. They are poor in such detail as reveals a past age or a country not our own. They are in themselves epitomes of whole generations, of a whole countryside. They are the quintessence of many lives and passions made into a sweet cup for posterity...The words, in league with a fair melody, lend themselves to infinite interpretations, according to the listener's heart. What great literature by known authors enables us to interpret thus by virtue of its subtlety, ballads and their music force us to do by their simplicity. The melody and the story or the song move us suddenly and launch us into an unknown. They are not art, they come to us imploring a new lease of life on the sweet earth, and so we come to give them something which the dull eye sees not in the words and notes themselves, out of our own hearts, as we do when we find a black hearthstone among the nettles... (*HE*, 226-7)

Perhaps folksong takes Thomas deeper into England than does the 'Manor Farm'. But, as the Welsh, Scottish and Irish songs in the *Pocket Book* indicate, he was not only interested in English songs or in songs for England's sake. By mixing poems with songs he was contributing to the more strictly literary revival that W.B. Yeats highlights in his *Oxford Book of Modern Verse* (London: Oxford University Press, 1936): 'Folk-song...must, because never declamatory or eloquent, fill the scene. If anybody will turn these pages attending to poets born in the 'fifties, 'sixties, and 'seventies, he will find how successful are their folk-songs and their imitations' (xiii). In dismissing 'realists', Thomas (like Yeats) attaches folksong to symbolist aesthetics. Yet 'plain, immortal symbols' obliquely rebukes the privatised obscurity into which symbolist poems can fall (see Introduction, 19). Thomas speculates: 'I cannot help wondering whether the great work done in the last century and a half towards the recovery of old ballads in their integrity will have any effect beyond the entertainment of a few scientific men and lovers of what is ancient, now that the first effects upon Wordsworth and his contemporaries have died away. Can it possibly give a vigorous impulse to a new school of poetry that shall treat the life of our time and what in past times has most meaning for us as freshly as those ballads did the life of their time?' (*SC*, 241).

Evidently Thomas himself received such an 'impulse'. His two 'old songs' signal its pervasive workings in his poetry – as varieties of refrain, for instance – and in January 1915 he wrote *The Penny Whistle* and *The Gypsy*: Muse-poems that invoke folk-music's archetypal sources. Barker maintains that 'over one third of [his] poems show evidence of the influence of the ballad tradition in adapting the four line ballad stanza pattern' (*JB*, 139). For Smith, Thomas's concern with folksong expresses his attraction to utterance that is social, communal, collective; while, at the same time: 'What interests [him]...is the moment of separation between individual voice and community' (see *SS*, 159-67). Yet Thomas also felt that the historical 'separation' between folksong and poetry had both distorted and gendered poetic tradition: 'Could English poetry have been founded earlier upon the native ballad instead of upon conceited ceremonious and exotic work, it would not have spent two centuries in an almost exclusively masculine world' (*FIP*, 14). In *An Old Song I* and *II*, as in *The Signpost*, tradition and the individual talent visibly cross-fertilise. Each 'old song' turns into a celebration of Thomas's new song.

'The Lincolnshire Poacher' appears in both the *Pocket Book* and *This England*. Its imagery of a subversive night-life must have appealed: Richard Jefferies's *The Amateur Poacher*, with its 'spice of illegality and daring', was a formative book (*CET*, 134). Thomas easily adapts the song to autobiography, including the 'moment' when the speaker is 'made a man that sings out of his heart' – 'made a poet', perhaps. But if he translates the extraverted tale of 'me and my companions' into soliloquy, he also translates psychic tensions into folk-idiom. His main formal deviation from the original is the unrhymed third line of each stanza. After the first stanza, this line sets up the refrain to express reflexive 'delight' in 'singing' as much as 'roaming'. The refrain becomes a song – to song – within a song.

13. *Since then I've thrown away a chance to fight a gamekeeper*. Walking in the countryside near Dymock, Gloucestershire, in October 1914, Thomas and Robert Frost met Lord Beauchamp's gamekeeper who threatened them with a shotgun. The Frosts were then living in The Gallows, a house at Ryton owned by Lord Beauchamp. One reason for the gamekeeper's behaviour was wartime suspicion of strangers. Frost reacted angrily, and wanted to 'fight' the gamekeeper. But when the poets sought him out, he threatened them again. Although Lord Beauchamp reprimanded the gamekeeper, Thomas felt that he had been cowardly; and, as this line may imply, the belief entered his thoughts about enlisting. See Introduction (17) and Sean Street, *The Dymock Poets* (Bridgend, Mid Glamorgan: Seren Books, 1994), 114-16.

19. *to sing or whistle just*. 'As to "sing and whistle first" [*sic*], I don't think "to whistle and to sing" which is formally correct is as good. If I am consciously

doing anything I am trying to get rid of the last rags of rhetoric and formality which left my prose so often with a dead rhythm only. If I can be honest and am still bad in rhythm it will be because I am bad in rhythm' (*EF*, 110).

Ms: *BL*. **Published text**: *LP*. **Note on title**: The next poem was numbered *II* in a typescript sent to Frost. In *PTP* its title appears as *An Old Song H*. Where these successively composed poems are printed together, it seems justifiable to number them.

An Old Song II (47)
26 December 1914

See notes on previous poem. '[Edward] delighted in sea-songs or shanties' (*LJB*, 88). The *Pocket Book* (see above) contains several. In 1912 he learned others from a neighbour who had been on the *Nimrod* with Shackleton's polar expedition (*HT*, 252). Here he draws on the shanty, perhaps dating from the sixteenth century, usually called 'A-rovin'' but also known as 'Amsterdam' or 'The Maid of Amsterdam'. Shortly before writing his first poems, Thomas walked 'to the Mumbles up to Oystermouth Castle and back chiefly by the sands', and sang during the walk: 'I liked walking thus, humming tunes and combining or improvising tunes. I remember how I did it when I was most cheerful at Minsmere – often ribald tunes. I was going to write an essay to be called "In Amsterdam there dwelt a maid"' (letter to Helen from Swansea, 10 October 1914, *NLW*). A *BL* draft includes the lines: 'the chorus made / The song the best song of the sea'. Stanza five gives the first verse and full chorus. In moving from individual vision to tradition, this *Old Song* reverses its predecessor's course. But the same aesthetic logic applies: folksong, as much as a unique 'light', can be a 'bridge' to poetry. Poem and song themselves are seamlessly bridged by the latter's gradual infiltration of rhyme scheme and rhythm. This rare seascape (*The Child on the Cliffs* is Thomas's only other sea-poem) contains images that figure inspiration in Romantic poetry: sea and mirror, perceptual strangeness ('shaking'), twilight, a shore or liminal zone, a 'vacant' space awaiting inscription, birdsong, the 'wild charm' of folksong itself. 'Wild charm' also covers the erotic intimations ('snake of foam', 'swollen clouds') that the song brings to the surface, although Thomas omits its 'lewder' verses.

7-12. *A light divided...that same sight*. This image appears in an early review in which Thomas reflects on the 'supremacy' of lyric poetry since the Romantics, and distinguishes between the lyric as 'homeopathy' and the lyric as 'intricacies of form':

> At that...time the lyric was asserting a supremacy which it has never lost... Coleridge, Wordsworth, Shelley and their great contemporaries revealed its adaptability to every mode of thought and emotion...Today at least the place of the lyric seems assured...And its place in poetry is almost equalled by its place in homeopathy. Thousands of the sad people in the streets write lyrics, following Goethe, no doubt, to get rid of their dreams, their debts, and the effect of reading other men's verse...But we venture to think that for this, and for still nobler reasons, the lyric will prosper, at least so long as individualism makes way in literature. Increasing

complexity of thought and emotion will find no such outlet as the myriad-minded lyric, with its intricacies of form as numerous and as exquisite as those of a birch-tree in the wind...The lyric may claim other points of superiority. Contrasted with the drama in couplets or blank verse, how much more truthful it is. As an ejaculation, a volume of laughter or lament, the best lyrics seem to be the poet's natural speech... The lyric then is self-expression, whether by necessity or by mere malice afore-thought. Those that practise the art include men who have spent a labo-rious life in sounding their own stops, like Shelley or Sidney, and also the men (and women) who mistake the lowest form of vanity for the highest form of art. Everyone must have noticed, standing on the shore, when the sun or moon is over the sea, how the highway of light on the water comes right to his feet, and how those on the right and on the left seem not to be sharing his pleasure, but to be in darkness. In some such way the former class views life. (*Daily Chronicle*, 27 August 1901)

Ms: *BL.* **Published text:** *P.* **Note on title:** See textual note on *An Old Song I.*

The Combe (48)
30 December 1914

The poem's 'combe' may be the gorge of Ashford Stream, below Thomas's study on the Shoulder of Mutton Hill, but it also represents 'the beechen coombes which are characteristic of Hampshire. They are steep-sided bays, run-ning and narrowing far into and up the sides of the chalk hills, and especially of those hills with which the high flinty plateau breaks down to the greensand and the plain. These steep sides are clothed with beeches, thousands of beeches interrupted by the black yews that resemble caverns among the paler trees... emerging from the coombe, whose sides shut out half the heavens' (*SC*, 28, 31). *The Combe* has links with *The Chalk-Pit* and with Thomas's essay 'Chalk Pits': 'The old chalk pits, being too steep and rough to be cultivated, soon grow into places as wild as ancient Britain...Once I met a small bear in one of the tangled dells in this neighbourhood. He was curled up in the sun between bushes of gorse, and his master's head was buried in his fur. If the bear had been alone it might have been a scene in Britain before Caesar's time, but though it was 1904 the bear looked indigenous. This dell is one of those which may be natural or artificial, or perhaps partly both, a small natural coombe having been convenient for excavation in the chalk...The sides of [the dell] are worn by the rabbits and support little but gaunt elder bushes' (*LS*, 33-7). 'One [dell] is so broken up by the uneven diggings, the roots of trees, and the riot of brambles that a badger is safe in it with a whole pack of children' (*LS*, 32). Thomas was drawn to such overgrown hollows with their entanglements of living and dead matter, their human and non-human resonances, their mixed messages of presence and absence: 'The coombes breed whole families, long genealogical trees, of echoes' (*SC*, 29).
3-6. *And no one...rabbit holes for steps.* Mimetic rhythms underscore the point that the poem, at least, can enter the combe. The internal rhyme 'bramble' /

'scramble' sparks off a downhill momentum *via* 'steps' of nouns reinforced by alliteration and assonance.

8. *Except the missel-thrush*. For Smith, the missel-thrush represents 'the loving and persistent seeker' who alone can penetrate 'meanings preserved, out of easy access', and 'the bird's name subtly links it with the Celtic druids who also valued mistletoe' (*SS*, 22).

12. *That most ancient Briton of English beasts*. Here the repeated 'ancient' comes to a brilliantly specific climax. In compressing historical layers and labels, this line echoes but subverts the last line of *The Manor Farm*. It also clinches other oppositions between the poems: the combe's 'stopped' 'mouth' denies access to the past; the 'sun of Winter' is 'shut out'; no sleeping English beauty is 'awakened'. Rather, this scene magnetises an indigenous darkness lately inten-sified – presumably by war. The badger's death violates covenants with Nature. It manifests a savagery whose sources go very far back or in very deep. 'Ancient' shifts in nuance between 'primeval' and 'primitive'; 'dark', between 'obscure' and 'evil'. 'Ancient Briton' at once attaches a 'beast' to human history and questions that history. By invoking Celtic or pre-Roman Britain, Thomas may also rebuke imperial "Britain". He calls the Welsh bard Iolo Morganwg, 'Ned of Glamorgan': 'an Ancient Briton, and not the last one: he said once that he always possessed the freedom of his thoughts and the independence of his mind "with an Ancient Briton's warm pride"' (*HGLM*, 188).

Ms: *BL*. **Published text:** *P*.

The Hollow Wood (48)

31 December 1914

Besides a wood in a hollow, which the sun cannot penetrate, 'hollow wood' suggests a wood consisting of hollow or dead trees, a ghost-wood emptied of life. *The Hollow Wood* echoes the *unheimlich* finale of *The Other*, and may revisit that poem's psychic splits. Its imagery has sources in the same prose passages as *The Combe*, with similar added violence. Cecil Day-Lewis writes: 'if we venture nearer the heart of this hollow wood, we find it a very disquieting place: the contrast between the goldfinch in the sun outside and the goings-on within is sinister: there is something wrong with a wood "Where birds swim like fish – Fish that laugh and shriek", and where dead or dying trees are kept evergreen by lichen, ivy, and moss – the hosts given a semblance, a mockery of life, by their parasites. The way he talks about them – "*half-flayed* and dying", "the dead trees *on their knees*" – they might almost be people. What makes this little poem so disturbing is that, from its description of natural processes, there arises a sense of something *against* nature' (*Essays by Divers Hands*, XXVIII, 87-8). In rhyme-scheme and line-length, the stanzas, like other sound-effects in the poem, are almost mirror-images. Doubleness, otherness, shapes the entire structure.

1. *the goldfinch flits*. The poem's one 'bright' spot is prefigured in 'Chalk Pits': 'Others [dells] are full of all that a goldfinch loves – teasel, musk, thistle and sunshine'; 'little bands [of green-finches] flitting and twittering' (*LS*, 32, 36).

8-9. *Lichen, ivy, and moss...trees*. 'Never was ivy more luxuriant under the beeches, nor moss so powerful as where it arrays them from crown to pedestal. The lichens, fine grey-green bushy lichens on the thorns, are as dense as if a tide of them had swept through the coombe' (*SC*, 30).

12. *dog's-mercury*: 'the foliage of dog's mercury, everywhere of equal height, gloomy and cool and tinged with a lemon hue, almost closed over the narrow grassless ribbons of brown earth and dead leaves...the many dead and mossy stems of trees already decayed' ('The Maiden's Wood', *RU*, 146-7). Geoffrey Grigson terms dog's-mercury 'a gloomy crop-plant of damp woods and leaf mould and dead twigs'. Other names for this poisonous plant are 'boggart-flower' and 'snakeweed'. (See Grigson, *The Englishman's Flora* [London: Phoenix House, 1958], 226).

Ms: *BL*. **Published text:** *LP*. **Differences from** *CP1978*: 12 dog's-mercury and moss *dog's-mercury, ivy, and moss* **Note:** *CP1978* follows *BL* and a type-script [*MET*] rather than *LP*. The repetition of 'ivy' as well as 'moss' in l.12 seems a less subtle cadence: one that Thomas might well have revised.

The New Year (49)

1 January 1915

Several of Thomas's early poems reinvent Wordsworth's narratives of meeting solitary old men in lonely places. The dialogue between the poet-speaker and such figures becomes more egalitarian and more suggestively compressed. Smith cites the man's parting comment as an example of how often scraps of conversation in Thomas's poems are 'abrupt and perfunctory, and yet suggesting a whole world of unspoken meanings' (*SS*, 168). One subtextual element here may be the war.

3-14. *I could not tell...like a tortoise's*. Wordsworth's 'leech-gatherer' in 'Resolution and Independence' is similarly linked with animals and inanimate objects. He is said to resemble 'a huge stone', itself 'like a sea-beast', while 'His body was bent double, feet and head / Coming together in life's pilgrimage'. Here 'strange tripod', along with the triad of ages to which the poem alludes, brings the image still closer to the Sphinx's riddle.

8. *wheel-barrow...like a pig*. This simile, which first appears in the prose version of *Up in the Wind* (see 144), compounds the perceptual confusion amid 'stormy' conditions. Later 'the trees' roar' causes auditory confusion too. The whole riddling effect continues the ominous imagery in the last stanza of *The Other*, in *The Combe* and *The Hollow Wood*.

12. *Fly-the-garter*. A memory from the time when Thomas was 'sent to a day school...in Battersea' (presumably *High-cockolorum* is another name for the same game):

> The playground was asphalt; again there were no organised games, but a dozen groups playing leap frog, fly the garter, or tops, or chasing one another, or simply messing about. 'Fly the garter' – if that is its right name – was a grand game to see played by a dozen of the biggest boys. I forget how it came about, but by degrees at length there were four or five boys bent double, forming a continuous line of backs. Each grasped the one in front of him and the first of them had his head, protected by his hands, against the playground wall. From half-way across the playground a big boy ran at a gallop, his ironshod heels pounding the asphalt, towards

this line of boys who could see him approaching between their legs. Reaching the line and putting his hands upon the first back to help him leap he leaped forward into the air. A brilliant leaper would use only one hand for the take off: the other gave a sonorous smack on the right place in passing. With legs outspread he flew along the line of backs, and alighted upon the fourth or fifth of them. The lighter his weight, the more fortunate was the steed thus accidentally mounted: the heavier, the greater was the chance that both together crashed to the ground. Then, I think, the leaper added another to the line of backs and set the next leaper an impossible task. The last stayer had a good double row of admirers, silent during the run and the leap, uproarious at the alighting. (*CET*, 79-80)

19. In *BL* the poem ends here.
Ms: *BL*. **Published text:** *LP*.

The Source (49)
4 January 1915
The *BL* title is 'The Source of the Ouse at Selsfield'. Thomas's friend Vivian Locke Ellis lived at Selsfield House, East Grinstead. In Autumn 1912, and occasionally later on, Thomas stayed there as a paying guest. 'Next day the north-east wind began to prevail, making a noise as if the earth were hollow and rumbling all through the bright night, and all day a rhythmless and steady roar. The earth was being scoured like a pot' (*IPS*, 23). With its strong aural dimension, the poem's symbolism combines powerful natural forces, psychological turbulence, and utterance ('voices', 'speaks'). This may identify personal integration with (poetic) articulation. When 'forth the dumb source of the river breaks', 'two voices' become one. Here the splitting and inversion of 'breaks forth' helps to suggest a dam bursting. But if poetry overcomes or mediates inner 'rain and wind', these also partly constitute its 'source'. The conflict between 'wild air' and 'earth' resembles the psychic storm in *Wind and Mist*.
7. *wild air*: a phrase that also occurs in *Melancholy* and *The Sheiling*.
Ms: *BL*. **Published text:** *AANP, LP*.

The Penny Whistle (50)
5 January 1915
See general note to *An Old Song I* (166). On 5 December 1913 Thomas noted ('blue' provides a context for 'kingfisher', 1.10): '3.30 pm charcoal burner by blue hut piping slowly a bright old country tune and making it melancholy and birdlike in the hollow deep valley' (*FNB67*). Like *The Source*, this poem derives from observations at East Grinstead.
1. *hangs like an ivory bugle*. Thomas quotes Richard Jefferies: 'The curved moon hung on the sky as the hunter's horn on the wall' (*RJ*, 200).
3. *ghylls*: deep rocky clefts, usually wooded, and following the course of a stream. The word was 'gill' until Wordsworth romanticised its spelling. Thomas originally wrote 'gullies' (*BL*).
5-8. *The brooks...are roaring with black hollow voices / Betwixt rage and a moan.* This effect condenses words and images from previous poems. Thomas again

blends the natural with the psychological: 'rage' and 'moan' define manic-depressive poles. After the death of the deranged visionary David Morgan, in *The Happy-Go-Lucky Morgans*, the narrator can 'hear the dark hills convulsed with a hollow roaring as of an endless explosion' (*HGLM*, 108). 'Roar' recurs obsessively in Thomas's poetry. Its mostly negative connotations derive both from windy tree-country and from 'the roar of towns' (*Roads*). 'This roaring peace' (*Interval*) is a positive exception.

9-11. *caravan-hut...charcoal-burners.* See *Up in the Wind* (lines 53, 73-5) and a sentence in 'The White Horse' (144). For a description of English charcoal-burners, see Arthur Ransome, *Swallows and Amazons* (1930), Chapter 13. Charcoal-burning, the oldest chemical process, made metal-smelting (and Bronze Age Europe) possible. Wood and other organic materials were slowly burned under an earth-clamp to produce pure carbon. Charcoal-burners constructed makeshift cabins in woodland clearings so that they could watch their fires. By 1900, metal kilns had made traditional charcoal-burning a vanishing way of life. 'Mossed old hearths' implies the antiquity of the practice.

16. *that crescent fine.* This phrase, along with the folk music, relates the climax of *The Penny Whistle* to that of *The Gypsy*. The 'old' and 'new' images, the conjunction of moon, 'melody' and text (the girl's letter), suggest that Thomas is again tapping creative sources which might transmute 'black...voices' into art: 'Says far more than I am saying'.

Ms: *BL.* **Published text:** *P.* **Note:** In *CP1928* and *CP1944* 'olden' [*P*], l.19, is altered to 'old', perhaps because of its risky – if deliberate – archaism.

A Private (50)
6, 7 January 1915 and later

BL contains two drafts:

> A labouring man lies hid in that bright coffin
> Who slept out many a frosty night and kept
> Good drinkers and bedmen tickled with his scoffing:
> 'At Mrs Greenland's Hawthorn Bush I slept.'

> The labouring man here lying slept out of doors
> Many a frosty night, and merrily
> Answered good drinkers and bedmen and all bores:
> 'At Mrs Greenland's Hawthorn Bush' said he,
> 'I slept.' None knew which bush. Above the town,
> Beyond 'The Drover' a hundred spot the down.

Thomas probably alludes to these drafts, and to the poem's original inspiration, in a letter to Eleanor Farjeon (24 January): 'I haven't thrown away anything, even the worse version of "Old Dick"' (*EF*, 114). The rhyme 'coffin' / 'scoffing' may make the first draft the 'worse'.

A Private evidently took time to acquire its Great War dimension. In August 1915, when Gordon Bottomley wanted the poem for *AANP*, Thomas mentions 'The Mrs Greenland's Hawthorn Bush lines', but this could still refer to a draft (*LGB*, 254-5). The final version first appeared in *SP* (1916). When R. George

Thomas rules out *A Private* as 'Old Dick' (*CP1978*, xxx), he ignores the possibility that its evolution – from an elegy for an *old* man – reflects Thomas's developing sense of the war's impact on rural England. The outcome strangely echoes 'Providence', a poem he wrote in 1901, presumably for a Boer-war casualty *(Diary,* 18 August 1901, *NLW)*:

(i)
The veteran smoked in the twilight tender,
And life to him was an old, old jest;
So old, so good, he would not surrender
(Except for Heaven) his place of rest –

(ii)
A trumpet on the sea was blown;
The veteran sailed to a strange country;
The foes were driven and beaten and strown;
(~~But~~) He rests for ever far over the sea.

Like *In Memoriam (Easter, 1915)*, *A Private* is a suitably elusive memorial to the missing. Just as the 'ploughman' pretends that 'Mrs Greenland's Hawthorn Bush' is an inn like 'The Drover', so the poem works as an ironical catch or riddle: 'sleeps more sound' is not consolatory; the ploughman's new 'privacy' is not his old 'secrecy'.

4. *Mrs Greenland*: a personification that prefigures "Gaia". Thomas may also elegise the ploughman's easy connection with the earth, in all its weathers, which war has severed and travestied.

Ms: *BL.* **Published text:** *SP, AANP, LP.* **Note:** In l.2 *LP, CP1920* etc print 'frozen' rather than 'frosty': the text in *AANP* and other extant sources. The lilt 'many' / 'frosty' / 'merrily' seems to fit the ploughman's character.

Snow (51)

7 January 1915

'If snow fell, there was no more of it in the valleys than if a white bird had been plucked by a sparrow-hawk' (*IPS*, 23). The idea is traditional, as in the riddle of the snow and the sun, which begins: 'White bird featherless / Flew from Paradise'. The 'December: Christmass' section of John Clare's *Shepherds' Calendar* contains this picture of children:

And some to view the winter weathers
Climb up the window seat wi glee
Likening the snow to falling feathers
In fancy's infant extacy
Laughing wi superstitious love
Oer visions wild that youth supplyes
Of people pulling geese above
And keeping christmass in the skyes

In *Snow* oxymorons ('gloom of whiteness', 'dusky brightness') and elegiac cadences darken the metaphor.

3. *A child.* See note on *Old Man*, l.10 (151).

8. *the bird of the snow.* A version of this in *BL* is 'the dying of the snow'.

Ms: *BL*. **Published text**: *AANP, LP*.

Adlestrop (51)

8 January 1915

Adlestrop is a village in Gloucestershire, near the River Evenlode, a few miles east of Stow-on-the-Wold and west of Chipping Norton (Oxfordshire). Adlestrop station was on the main Great Western Railway line from London to Oxford, Worcester and Malvern. A victim of Dr Beeching's cuts, the station was finally closed to passengers on 3 January 1966. But, as Anne Harvey shows in *Adlestrop Revisited* (Stroud, Gloucestershire: Henry Sutton, 1999), the poem had already superseded its occasion, and made the Adlestrop poem a sub-genre of the "Edward Thomas poem" (see Introduction, 11). John Loveday's 'The Imaginative Franchise' begins: 'Does it matter, whether Yeats really stood / Among schoolchildren?' and ends: 'Does it have to be true? Suppose the train did not pull / Up at Adlestrop at all…' In fact, *FNB75* proves that it did; but also indicates that Thomas conflated details from different stops:

> 24th [June 1914] a glorious day from 4.20 a.m. and at 10 tiers above tiers of white cloud with dirtied grey bars above the sea of slate and dull brick by Battersea Park – then at Oxford tiers of pure white with loose large masses above and gaps of dark clear blue above haymaking and elms
>
> Then we stopped at Adlestrop, through the willows could be heard a chain of blackbirds songs at 12.45 and one thrush and no man seen, only a hiss of engine letting off steam.
>
> Stopping outside Campden by banks of long grass willowherb and meadowsweet, extraordinary silence between the two periods of travel – looking out on grey dry stones between metals and the shining metals and over it all the elms willows and long grass – one man clears his throat – a greater than rustic silence. No house in view Stop only for a minute till signal is up.
>
> Another stop like this outside Colwell on 27th with thrush singing on hillside above on road.

On 23 June Edward and Helen Thomas attended the Russian ballet in London. They set off next day to visit the Frosts in Ledbury, Herefordshire, and seek summer holiday lodgings there (see general note to *The sun used to shine*, 296). Around the time of the poem's composition, as if memory had surfaced and sent him to his earlier notes, Thomas wrote in *FNB80*: 'Train stopping outside station at Adlestrop June 1914'.

Thomas's prose sketch 'A Third-Class Carriage' pivots on a moment when 'the train stopped at the edge of a wood where a thrush was singing, calling out very loud, clear things in his language over and over again', and ends: 'The train whistled, frightening the thrush, and moved on again' (*LS*, 49-50). In 'Death by Misadventure', a train kills a man: 'There was not a sound except the hissing of the steam, until the guilty train began to grunt forward again…' (*CC*, 115). The poem more indirectly sets the 'express' train's modernity against

176

the perspective, and aesthetic, opened up by what Thomas's note calls 'extra-ordinary silence'. *Adlestrop* has inspired homages, imitations and parodies. It remains a model not only for the "train-window" poem, such as Philip Larkin's 'I Remember, I Remember', but also for the translation of memory into poetic epiphany – including the negative epiphany of 'I Remember, I Remember': 'Nothing, like something, happens anywhere'. A model, too, for art that conceals art, *Adlestrop* knows exactly what it is doing. The remembered scene alludes to the lyric it will engender: 'Someone cleared his throat'; 'And for that minute a blackbird sang'.

4. *Unwontedly*. *BL* drafts have 'drew up / There unexpectedly', then 'drew up there / Against its custom'. 'Unwontedly' suggests a train juddering to a halt. Its first two syllables link 'one' and 'June'; its last two syllables belong to a sequence of sounds that embed 'Adlestrop' in a complex assonantal texture: late / left / platform / whit less / and lonely / cloudlets. The adverb's stresses and texture contrast with the four monosyllables that follow – perhaps one reason for the change from ''Twas June' in Thomas's first *BL* draft (see note, 153).

8-16. *only the name…Gloucestershire*. See note on Thomas and place names (285). 'Adlestrop' is most often pronounced so that its first two syllables rhyme with 'paddle' rather than 'ladle'. It has been spelled 'Addlestrop', and other variants over the centuries are Titlestrop, Tattlest(h)rop, Attlesthorpe, and Adelsthrope: 'there can be little doubt that the original form of the name was Tat(e)les-thorp; the…form Attle, Adle-, etc. arises from wrong analysis of phrases like "at Tatlesthrop"…i.e. Taetel's dependent farmstead' (Harvey, *Adlestrop Revisited*, 28). Yet 'only the name' invokes neither etymology nor the cognitive anxieties of *Old Man* (contrast 'Only an avenue…nameless'). The poem obliquely affirms the associative nexus between word and thing, and its constant reweaving by life and poetry. 'Adlestrop' serves as conduit to the recovery or creation of a unique moment. Strategically placed, 'only the name' launches the spiralling syntax and rhythm of the last two stanzas, and the little cosmos they encompass. More strictly and subtly than in *The Manor Farm*, the structure corresponds to Thomas's conception of England as 'a system of vast circumferences circling round…minute neighbouring points' (see note, 165). The double off-rhyme 'mistier' / 'Gloucestershire', the repeated 'farther' and 'shire', make the poem's echoes linger beyond its last words.

9. *willow-herb*: not Rosebay willow herb, common today, but 'Great willow-herb, nicknamed Codlins-and-Cream' (Harvey, *Adlestrop Revisited*, 12).

12. *high cloudlets*. In *BL* this replaces 'high cloud tiers' (see extracts above from *FNB75*).

Ms: BL. Published text: P. Differences from *CP1978*: 1 Yes. *Yes,* **Note:** *CP1978* follows *BL* rather than *P*. A full-stop appears in *PTP*. **Note on title:** Title is given in *BL*.

Tears (52)
8 January 1915

Like *Adlestrop*, *Tears* represents itself as translating memory into epiphany. Once again, sun, silence and solitude are intrinsic to the process. Yet these juxtaposed "English" scenes sit less peacefully in the speaker's consciousness.

Neither 'still' nor stills, they force him to probe the meaning of their traces in memory and now poetry. History, absent from *Adlestrop*, has returned. Cooke and Smith comment on disturbingly unresolved effects: 'despite their superficial splendour, both hounds and soldiers also suggest a less attractive reality. The hounds are out to kill ("Upon the scent") and merge into one menacing animal – "a great dragon"; the troops have lost some of their individuality by being "in line" and "in white tunics", while it is a martial air that "pierces" the silence. The profound ambiguity of the poem's basic emotion is caught in that astonishing paradox "rage of gladness"' (*WC*, 222). 'The gulf opened up between "English countrymen" and 'British Grenadiers" is like that…in "The Combe". The former are innocent in their pastoral pathos; the latter carries the burden of an imperial ideology and the exultant violence which sustains it. The two concepts define the gap in Englishness where allegiance founders…The charm, it may be, is that of a hypnotic ideological magic, seducing both young men and poet to an unnecessary and pointless death. Allegiance to such images may be misplaced…If [the speaker] is emotionally bankrupt, unable any more to respond spontaneously to the traditional symbols, the fault, though he refuses to admit it, may lie with those symbols, not with the self' (*SS*, 118).

3-4. *twenty hounds…rage of gladness.* It was the human element in foxhunting that Thomas disliked: 'Run hard hounds, and drown the jackdaws' calling with your concerted voices. It is good to see your long swift train across the meadow …Run hard, fox, and may you escape, for it would not be well to die on such a day unless you could perchance first set your fair teeth in the throats of the foolish ones who now break through the hedge on great horses and pursue you' (*HE*, 155-6). 'I like to see fine horses running at full speed. To see this sight, or hounds running on a good scent, or children dancing, is to me the same as music, and therefore, I suppose, as full of mortality and beauty' (*IW*, 104). 'Backwards and forwards galloped the scarlet before the right crossing of the railway was taken. The fox died in obscurity two miles away. How warm and sweet the sun was can be imagined when I say that it made one music of the horn-blowing, the lambs' bleating, the larks' singing' (*IPS*, 92).

6. *Blooming Meadow.* From May 1904 to late 1906 the Thomases lived at Elses Farm in the Weald of Kent. Helen Thomas recalls: 'hay-making on the lovely slope of Blooming meadow was a festival for us all at the farm' (*HT*, 104). The name both attracts and irradiates all the poem's effects of vigour, fertility, and colour.

8. *double-shadowed Tower*: the Tower of London. 'Double-shadowed', which throws the 'stirring' images into relief, may also imply the speaker's interior state, and interpret his susceptibility to 'charm'.

15. *'The British Grenadiers'.* 'I don't think I could alter "Tears" to make it marketable. I feel that the correction you want made is only essential if the whole point is in the British Grenadiers as might be expected in these times' (*LEG*, 25). 'White tunics' marks the soldiers' pre-war ceremonial role as custodians of the Tower, but another role seems latent in the image. Guy Cuthbertson calls attention to a passage that Thomas quotes from Richard Jefferies's *The Story of My Heart*: 'So subtle is the chord of life that sometimes to watch troops marching in rhythmic order, undulating along the column as the feet

are lifted, brings tears in my eyes' (*RJ*, 182; *GC*, 159).

18. *And have forgotten since their beauty passed.* *Tears* poses questions about the proximity of violence to 'beauty', about the need for violence to defend beauty, about their conjoined power to kick-start feeling. Each scene is 'pierced' by an emotion (ironically deprecated as the 'ghosts' of tears) alien to previous sunlit epiphanies. A homoerotic charge runs between 'stirring', 'charm', the soldiers' physicality, and 'piercing'. As Smith points out, enlistment seems to be a sub-text. In saying he has 'forgotten' what the poem makes so vividly present, the speaker parallels Thomas's self-reproach for lack of true patriotism in his essay 'This England' (see notes on *The sun used to shine* and *This is no case of petty right or wrong*): 'it seemed to me that either I had never loved England, or I had loved it foolishly, aesthetically, like a slave' (*LS*, 221). To enjoy English 'beauty' (as in *Adlestrop*, perhaps) without regard to underlying 'truths' – truths that attach the individual to community – is to behave like Thomas's dreaded *alter ego* the aesthetic spectator (see note, 290). The interplay of 'dreamed', 'truths' and 'beauty' implicates Keats and Romantic poetry in this scenario where responsibilities are being obliquely deliberated. Thomas placed *Tears* early in *P*, close to four other poems associated with the war: *The Trumpet*, *The Manor Farm*, *The Owl* and *As the team's head-brass*.

Ms: *BL*. **Published text:** *P*. **Note:** *P* omits the comma after 'guard' [l.12], present in *PTP*.

Over the Hills (52)

9 January 1915

Although the title given to this poem in *LP* has been retained, it is the most questionable of the instances listed in the Note on Text. As John Pikoulis observes: 'the poem mentions no hills, only a single "horizon ridge"' (*JP*, 54). Yet 'over the hills' occurs in a passage (about 'August') from *Beautiful Wales*, which is possibly linked with the poem: '[A] mountain stream, which many stones tore to ribbons, was with me for miles, and to the left and to the right many paths over the hills ran with alluring courses for half a mile, like happy thoughts or lively fancies, and ended suddenly. The mountains increased in height as the sun sank… And in the end of the afternoon I came to a village I knew… From the inn I could see the whole village… Six bells that rang three miles off and some white downs of cloud on the horizon were in harmony. It was a time when the whole universe strove to speak a universal speech… But, as it seemed, owing to my fault, the effort was unsuccessful' (*BW*, 176-7). If the poem echoes that passage, this does not necessarily make its landscape "Welsh". Alun John points out that Thomas's depictions of 'romantic North Wales' (not then known to him) 'were culled almost entirely from the notes he had previously made of the countryside of England' (quoted, Sally Roberts Jones, 'Edward Thomas and Wales', *JB*, 79).

Over the Hills is another poem that represents itself as a process of remembering – or of remembering remembering. But here epiphany proves elusive. While the 'path' can be retraced, it figures a psychic loop-tape rather than thera-peutic retrieval. As if again puncturing the unities of *Adlestrop*, Thomas sets 'saw it all' against 'Recall / Was vain'. Another line breaks on the adversative asyndeton: 'all were kind, / All were strangers'. Some hinted problem, whether in the original experience or in the speaker, makes 'loss' the poem's pivotal word. *BL* has 'I forgot my loss': the change to 'I did not know my loss' deepens the interior drama.

5. *pack of scarlet clouds*: a strange echo of the hunting image in *Tears*.

15-19. *no more...rush and stone*. An image from the mountain scene serves as a bridge back to it. The rhythmical dynamic, which culminates in this intricately rhymed poem's only couplet, runs counter to the impossibility that the lines assert. As often in Thomas, the poem gets further than the speaker. Like Jungian therapy, it pushes back towards a source. Metaphors of the body sustain the analogy between the brook and a 'restless' spirit seeking repose. *Over the Hills* has parallels with Frost's 'The Mountain', which similarly circles around a point of origin: 'There's a brook / That starts up on it somewhere – I've heard say / Right on the top'.

Ms: *BL*. **Published text:** *LP*. **Note on title:** See general note above. *CP1978* brackets the title; *CP2004* removes the brackets. See Note on Text.

The Lofty Sky (53)
10 January 1915

The Lofty Sky begins where *Over the Hills* leaves off. Here psychic obstacles are symbolically overcome by rhythms that make 'The desire of the eye' kinetic. Reviewing a book on punctuation, Thomas writes: 'We know the beauty...of a complex sentence in which the stops are as valuable as the division of a stanza of verse into lines, or as the hedges and littered crags and out-cropping rock by which the eye travels up a mountain to the clouds' (*Academy*, 23 September 1905). 'Sky' rarely prevails over 'earth' in Thomas's poetry. Yet the transcendental urge instilled by his youthful passion for Shelley is never wholly exorcised, and may here be affirmed. In l.1 he changed 'hills' (*BL*) to 'sky'. 'They are no more / Than weeds upon this floor / Of the river of air', like 'dark surge' in *Two Pewits*, echoes Shelley's 'Ode to the West Wind'. *The Lofty Sky* also echoes Walter de la Mare's 'Nobody Knows' (*Peacock Pie*, 1913), which contrasts the wind's freedom ('Just a great wave of the air') with earthly conditions: 'And so we live under deep water, / All of us, beasts and men'.

19-34. *I am like a fish...where the lilies are*. Another Romantic poet may be on the poem's mind. Thomas describes looking out of the window after reading Keats: 'outside, the trees and barns and shed were quiet and dim, and as much submerged and hidden from the air in which I had been living as the green streets of motionless lily and weed at the bottom of some lonely pool where carp and tench go slowly' (*HE*, 161). Also in *The Heart of England*, Thomas compares a rare moment to the 'old tale' in which people see 'an anchor let out of the clouds and rooted in the ground' and then a man climbing down a rope to free the anchor and 'dying at last, as if he had been drowned in the air which they breathed easily' (*HE*, 112-13). 'Where the lilies are' is a wonderful image for the direction of Romantic desire. Michael Kirkham reads lines 32-4, with their echo of Yeats's 'Lake Isle of Innisfree', as 'self-parody' (*MK*, 41). But perhaps the whole conceit consciously dramatises the human and artistic need to press beyond limits.

Ms: *BL*. **Published text:** *LP*. **Note on title:** Apart from *LP*, title's only surviving source is *RB* 2, 2 [December 1917].

The Cuckoo (54)

15 January 1915

In 'An Old Farm' Thomas refers to 'the palpitating, groaning shout of the shepherd, Ho! ho! ho! ho! ho!' (*HE*, 72). The same passage fed *Haymaking* and *Cock-Crow* (see notes, 248, 256). This is unique among Thomas's poems in being a dramatic monologue spoken by a woman. He lays out a mnemonic paradox: the widow's inability to hear the cuckoo brings a human voice into elegiac presence.

Ms: *BL*. **Published text:** *AANP, LP*. **Differences from** *CP1978*: 9 'There it is!' [*BL*] '*There it is*' [*AANP*] **Note:** To match 'Ho! Ho!', and to sharpen this miniature drama, an exclamation-mark seems to be required. **Note on title:** Title is given in *BL*.

Swedes (54)

15 January 1915

'I wonder if I can touch "Swedes". It is one of the least like myself I fancy' (*LGB*, 247). But actual and verbal colour is more common in Thomas's poems than it might appear. *The Path* surprises us with tints of moss ('gold, olive, and emerald'), *Health* with a Yeatsian litany of proper names. Thomas's deceptively muted style masks its rhetorical depth-charges – like fine tweed, which in close-up reveals brilliant flecks. *Swedes* itself certainly achieves Wordsworth's objective in *Lyrical Ballads*: 'to choose incidents from common life…and…to throw over them a certain colouring of imagination, whereby ordinary things should be presented to the mind in an unusual way'. In 'The Mangel-Bury' Ivor Gurney, for whom Thomas was both model and muse, continues the process by using *Swedes* to bring the Great War home to rural England:

> It was after war; Edward Thomas had fallen at Arras –
> I was walking by Gloucester musing on such things
> As fill his verse with goodness; it was February; the long house
> Straw-thatched of the mangels stretched two wide wings;
> And looked as part of the earth heaped up by dead soldiers
> In the most fitting place – along the hedge's yet-bare lines.
> West spring breathed there early…

1-4. *They have taken the gable…Unsunned.* Clamping is a traditional way of storing root-vegetables during Winter. A pyramid of vegetables, which extends above ground, is built in a straw-strewn trench. This is covered with more straw and then earth. 'A cart goes by all a-gleam with a load of crimson-sprouting swedes and yellow-sprouting mangolds that seem to be burning through the net of snow above them' (*SC*, 40-1).

4. *more tender-gorgeous.* This oxymoronic compound initiates the switch from vibrantly familiar to coldly exotic. It also makes 'sight' empathetic rather than spectatorial. In *The Icknield Way* Thomas less happily calls rain-soaked

primrose petals 'tender-blubbering' (*IW*, 12).

7-10. *A boy crawls down...Blue pottery, alabaster, and gold.* The items in l.10 refer back to the colours in l.3. At the end of 'Leaving Town' (*HE*, 1-18) Thomas compares entering a 'shadowed wood' at dawn to finding an Egyptian tomb:

> Suddenly my mind went back to the high dark cliffs of Westminster Abbey, the blank doors and windows of endless streets, the devouring river, the cold gloom before dawn, and then with a shudder forgot them and saw the flowers and heard the birds with such a joy as when the ships from Tarshish, after three blank years, again unloaded apes and peacocks and ivory, and men upon the quay looked on; or as, when a man has mined in the dead desert for many days, he suddenly enters an old tomb, and making a light, sees before him vases of alabaster, furniture adorned with gold and blue enamel and the figures of gods, a chariot of gold, and a silence perfected through many ages in the company of death and of the desire of immortality. (*HE*, 18)

The pyramidal shape of 'the long swede pile', a construction that itself figures the unconscious, may have reactivated Thomas's Egyptian imagery.

8-9. *Christian men...God and monkey*: post-Darwinian irony.

11. *Amen-hotep*: the name of several eighteenth-dynasty pharaohs. The tomb of Amenhotep II, in the Valley of the Tombs of Kings, was excavated in 1898. Before the discovery of Tutankhamun's tomb in 1922, this was the only known tomb where a mummified pharaoh still lay in his own sarcophagus. The tomb had been much robbed, and the single object in *Swedes* that corresponds to its contents is 'blue pottery' or 'faience' (which appears in a *BL* draft). The passage in *The Heart of England*, and hence the poem, may involve 'snatches of memory of more than one discovery in the Valley of the Kings during the early years of the twentieth century'; the tomb of Tuthmosis IV contained fragments of animals, an alabaster face, and the dashboard of a war chariot. (See T.H.G. James, 'A Poetic Puzzle', *Hommages à Jean Leclant*, vol. 4 [Cairo: Institut français d'archéologie orientale, 1994], 147-51.) David and Caroline Gill cite an excavation reported in 1906: 'a boy was sent in [and finds included a] chariot, the...wheel rims of which shone through the darkness golden and scarlet' (*Notes and Queries* 53 [September 2003], 325).

11-12. *But dreamless...sweet as Spring.* This antithesis, the climax of dialectically poised sentences that resist sonnet-form, underlines the poem's status as an *ars poetica*. In contrasting the dead pharaoh's panoply with seasonal processes, and linking the latter with 'dream', Thomas prefers a biocentric, inner-directed aesthetic to an 1890s aesthetic of stylised display (see Introduction, 16). He attacks Walter Pater's prose for its 'exquisite unnaturalness', for making language seem to be as hard and inhuman a material as marble', for 'embalm[ing] choice things, seen at choice moments, in choice words' (*WP*, 220, 101, 108). Similarly, he compares the anthology *Des Imagistes* to 'a tall marble monument', in which the better poems 'are the green ivy beginning to climb the tall marble monument, and may well outlast it' (*New Weekly*, 9 May 1914).

Ms: *BL*. **Published text**: *P*. **Note on title**: Title is given in *BL*.

The Unknown Bird (55)

17 January 1915

'The strange bird lá-la-lá' (*FNB80*, early January 1915). In *The Happy-Go-Lucky Morgans* Mr Torrance remembers:

> Only one bird sang in [the cypress tree], and that was a small, sad bird which I do not know the name of. It sang there every month of the year, it might be early or it might be late, on the topmost point of the plume. It never sang for long, but frequently, and always suddenly. It was black against the sky, and I saw it nowhere else. The song was monotonous and dispirited, so that I fancied it wanted us to go because it did not like the cheerful garden, and my father's loud laugh, and my mother's tripping step: I fancied it was up there watching the clouds and very distant things in hope of a change; but nothing came, and it sang again, and waited, ever in vain. I laughed at it, and was not at all sorry to see it there, for it had stood on that perch in all the happy days before, and so long as it remained the days would be happy. My father did not like the bird, but he was often looking at it, and noted its absence as I did. The day after my sister died he threw a stone at it – the one time I saw him angry – and killed it. But a week later came another, and when he heard it he burst into tears, and after that he never spoke of it but just looked up to see if it was there when he went in or out of the porch. (*HGLM*, 146-7)

16-17. *I told / The naturalists.* '[T]he way in which scientific people & their followers are satisfied with *data* in appalling English disgusts me, & is moreover wrong' (*LGB*, 140); 'natural history, which is so often in danger of falling into the hands of mere takers of notes' (*RJ*, 118). The unclassifiable bird marks the point at which "Nature" takes on aesthetic meaning. Thomas salutes W.II. Hudson as 'the substantial miracle of a naturalist and an imaginative artist in one and in harmony' (*IPS*, 245). Many birds are named in his poetry (see note, 240), but this bird-Muse, like his equally elusive female Unknown, has no name.
21. *that La-la-la! was bodiless sweet.* Like Wordsworth's and Shelley's lark-Muses, the bird's call focuses strains between body and spirit, heaviness and lightness, perhaps prose and poetry. An aural counterpart to the 'desire of the eye' in *The Lofty Sky*, it pulls the poem towards Romantic transcendence: 'As if a cock crowed past the edge of the world', 'beyond my shore'. This otherworldly summons also parallels the unique 'light' in *An Old Song II*. Both images represent poetic vocation as a form of mysterious election: 'I alone could hear him'.
22-5. *Sad more than joyful...taste it.* These lines skirt self-parody with their convoluted insistence on the psychological, sensory and aesthetic *mot juste*.

Ms: *BC, BL.* **Published text:** *LP.* **Differences from** *CP1978*: 18 me, [*LP*] *me* [*RB* 2, 4 (June 1918)] **Note on title:** Title is given in *BL*.

The Mill-Pond (56)

18 January 1915

'The stream going helpless and fast between high banks is gloomy until it is turned to bright, airy foam and hanging crystal by the mill; over the restless

pool below hangs a hawthorn all white and fragrant and murmurous with bloom
…Over the green grass walks the farmer's daughter in a white dress…She is a
Lady May, careless, proud, at ease' (*HE*, 181-4); [of a 'ruined flock-mill' near
a weir] 'we could see its white wall of foam half a mile higher up the river,
which was concealed by alders beyond' (*HE*, 219).

15. *A girl came out*. After the girl's appearance, the poem's ominously intense
(perhaps erotically charged) sounds and images might seem to collapse into
sentimental anti-climax rather than consummate themselves in a bursting
'storm'. In *A Dream* and *The Mill-Water*, written at the time of Thomas's
enlistment, similar effects will find their full occasion. Yet if *The Mill-Pond*
somehow fails to be either a war poem or a love poem, 'teased the foam' and
'crouched / To shelter' may know this. The reader is left to speculate why the
speaker should 'now' remember that, all his senses absorbed in the moment,
he had to be warned to take dangers seriously.

Ms: *BC, BL*. **Published text:** *P*. **Note on title:** Title [unhyphenated] is
given in *BL*.

Man and Dog (56)
20 January 1915

Heightened reportage is a mode of Thomas's early poetry that fades away later
on. In May 1915 he wrote: 'I had got past poetical prose and my new feeling is
that here [in poetry] I can use my experience and what I am and what I know
with less hindrance than in prose, less gross notebook stuff and mere description
and explanation' (*SL*, 111). His friends had often told him, and he had told
himself, to stop keeping notebooks. The 'Other Man' in *In Pursuit of Spring* is
a notebook-victim (see note, 158). *Man and Dog* epitomises the initial alchemy
whereby Thomas turns 'notebook stuff' into poetry. *FNB79* contains this entry
for 21 November 1914:

> Going up Stoner in cold strong N.E. wind but a fine and cloudy sky at
> 3, overtook short stiff oldish man taking short quick strides − carrying
> flag basket and brolly and old coat on back and with a green ash stick in
> hand. Says it's a fine day and as I passed (agreeing) he decides to ask
> me for − I don't know, I stopped his request with questions, found him
> a 6d. He had a little bitch brown with spots of grey reminding me of a
> Welsh sheep dog − not much use, but company. He says the mother was
> almost pure (blue) Welsh. Hunts in Hangers, nearly got one this morn-
> ing 'he would and he wouldn't, 'twas like that.' 'They say those Welsh
> bitches will breed with foxes. He knew one the other side of Guildford
> and she had her litter of seven in a rabbit-hole. He had one. It [?]liked
> to bite anything it killed so hard it was useless: red mouth like a fox.' He
> has come from Childgrove where he's done two halfdays dock picking
> this week: is going to Alton and hopes for a lift from one of Crowley's
> men to Longmoor to look for a job. But perhaps he won't reach Alton −
> rheumatism in one leg − rubs oil they sell at harness makers and 'supples'
> it a bit − round face with white bristles all over and eyes with red rims.
> Has worked a lot at Southampton docks, navvying, but likes farm work

best, has promises of flint picking when sheep are out of field, <u>but</u> can't hang about – comes from Christchurch in the New Forest – did a year's soldiering in '74 in Berkshires. – has 3 sons at Front, one just come from Bombay had really finished his 8 years with the colours, one son a marine. If he can't reach Alton, will get a shakedown from a farmer.

Talked about the soldiers just coming to billet in Petersfield – he thought 2 or 3 thousand – 20, or so, in kilts – might be a Border Regiment.

A rustic, burring, rather monotonous speech, head a little hung down, but hardly a stoop, as he keeps on at his stiff quick short steps among crisp dry scurrying leaves up to Ludcombe Corner where I turned off.

He was thinking about soldiers in France – terrible affair – in cold weather, supposing they would be 'marching after the enemy' and surely not lying in trenches in this winter weather.

Farther behind the poem are passages in Thomas's prose, also based on note-taking, such as his depiction of an itinerant 'Umbrella Man': 'He was of middle height and build, the crookedest of men, yet upright, like a branch of oak which comes straight with all its twistings…He was a labourer's son, and he had already had a long life of hoeing and reaping and fagging when he enlisted at Chatham … He had lost his youth in battle, for a bullet went through his knee… He showed his gnarled knee to explain his crookedness…Labourer, soldier, labourer, tinker, umbrella man, he had always wandered, and knew the South Country between Fordingbridge and Dover, as a man knows his garden' (*SC*, 188-92). Archetypal aspects of the 'Umbrella Man' contribute to *Lob* (see note, 213). But in *Man and Dog*, as in *Up in the Wind*, the primary focus is social history compressed into an individual life-story. The man's career as casual labourer spans rural and industrial work amid the advance of modernity and the advent of war. This time frame, however, also sits within a longer eco-historical narrative implied by his relation to the land.

Man and Dog, which adapts oral history to couplets and *vice versa*, is a poetic apotheosis of the social portraiture for which Thomas admired *The Bettesworth Book* (1901) by 'George Bourne' (George Sturt):

At first the book may seem tame, a piece of reporting which leaves the reader not unaware of the notebooks consulted by the author. But in the end comes a picture out of the whole, painfully, dubiously emerging, truthful undoubtedly…which raises George Bourne to a high place among observers…Bettesworth had fought in the Crimea, and during sixty years had been active unceasingly over a broad space of English country – Surrey, Sussex, and Hampshire – always out of doors. His memory was good, his eye for men and trades a vivid one, and his gift of speech unusual… so that a picture of rural England during the latter half of the nineteenth century, by one born in the earlier half and really belonging to it, is the result. The portrait of an unlettered pagan English peasant is fascinating. (*IPS*, 85-6)

7. *flag-basket*: a basket made of reeds.
8-9. The equidistant *Alton* and *Chilgrove* (a village on the road from Chichester

to Petersfield) are in east Hampshire and west Sussex. 'Stoner' [Hill] in Thomas's notebook identifies the poem's setting as Steep. The man is walking cross-country by an old route.

10-24. *'Twere best...to another world I'd fall'*. Thomas's acute ear, transmuted into his hidden editorial presence, enables a seamless flow between direct speech, reported speech inflected by the man's 'mind...running', and the narrator's voice. For ''twere' etc., see note (153).

10. *'a money-box'*: savings. *BC*, less idiomatically, has 'the capital'.

12. *flint-picking*: removing stones to enable cultivation.

19. *couch*: couch-grass, a weed with creeping root-stalks.

28. *He kept sheep in Wales*. 'He' is the bitch's 'foxy Welsh grandfather'. Her pedigree adds to the ecological, historical and geographical ramifications of the poem.

38. *shakedown*: a makeshift bed, usually of straw.

39-40. *Many a man sleeps worse... 'In the trenches'*. Apparently casual allusions to the war (together with the man's 'year of soldiering') assimilate it to a continuum of labour and pain.

46. *the leaf-coloured robin*. On 23 November Thomas had noted: 'Robin is colour of twilight at 4.30 as soon as he leaves the ground and is seen in grey air among bare boughs over dead leaves and is invisible – you only know something moves, till he alights and is leaf-coloured' (*FNB79*).

46-8. *They passed...the twilight of the wood*. This valedictory finale resembles the 'disappearances' of 'Lob' and of 'Jack Noman' in *May 23*, although its point seems more purely historical. A nomadic way of life, which the poem values for its closeness to the countryside if not for its hardships, is 'passing'. Yet, as at the end of *As the team's head-brass*, elegiac cadences open up further vistas of obsolescence. The symbolic 'twilight of the wood' extends to current environmental fears.

   Ms: *BC, BL*. **Published text:** *LP*. **Note on title:** *CP1978* brackets the title; *CP2004* drops it. See Note on Text.

Beauty (58)

21 January 1915

This brief psychodrama exemplifies how a poem's speaker can switch between the roles of patient and analyst (see Introduction, 14). It also explicitly juxtaposes neurosis and art: the word 'beauty' survives from Thomas's youthful aestheticism to connect art with Nature and both with therapy. The neurotic symptoms set out in lines 1-10 correspond to Helen Thomas's accounts of her husband's black moods, and to his accounts of himself: 'there were terrible days when I did not know where he was; or, if he was at home, days of silence and brooding despair...often when he came in I was terrified by the haggard greyness of his face, and the weary droop of his body, as he flung himself into his study chair, not speaking or looking at me. Once, in one of these fits, after being needlessly angry with one of the children who cried and ran away from him, he rummaged in a drawer...where I knew there was...a revolver' (*HT*, 113; see note on *Rain*, 268). In October 1907 Thomas recorded: 'I sat thinking about ways of killing myself... Then I went out and thought what effects my suicide would have. I don't think I mind them. My acquaintances – I no longer have friends – would talk in a day or two (when they met) and try to explain and of course see suggestions in the past: W.H. Davies would suffer a little; Helen and the children – less in reality than they do now, from my accursed tempers and moodiness...I have no vitality, no originality, no love' (*SL*, 44). On 30 March 1908 he told Gordon Bottomley: 'An east wind or a wind from underground has swept over everything. Friends, Nature, books are like London pavements when an east wind has made them dry and harsh & pitiless. There is no joy in them. They are more dead than if they were in a Museum correctly labelled. And this is true not only this morning, but every morning, every afternoon & every night. I am now uniformly low spirited, listless, almost unable to work, & physically incapable. I have no idea what it means, but I crawl along on the very edge of life, wondering why I don't get over the edge' (*LGB*, 160). At that time, Thomas's condition was aggravated by the ban on his relationship with a young girl, Hope Webb (see notes, 238, 279). On 9 April he reported: 'I am now physically stronger, but as soon as my thoughts stray back to myself the same East wind blows. On the other hand the hour of sunset on Tuesday when I was walking back from Selborne through a steep valley with oaks...and no one about and the wind quite gone – that kept me quite unconscious and entranced' (*LWD*).

Beauty reads like a modern digest of Coleridge's 'Dejection: An Ode': 'I know so well the "grief without a pang" described with some flattery in Coleridge's "Dejection", so often had griefs not without a pang appeared to me almost delights by comparison, so often had I looked at things...as the poet was doing when he said "I see them all so excellently fair, / I see, not feel, how beautiful they are"' ('Ecstasy', unpublished essay, *BC*).

7-8. *like a river / At fall of evening*. Cf. a letter from Shelley to Mary Godwin quoted by Thomas: 'my mind, without yours, is as dead and cold as the dark midnight river when the moon is down' (*FIP*, 41). *Beauty* may be, in part, a hidden love poem or poem of frustrated desire.

10. *Cross breezes cut the surface to a file*. The criss-cross patterns on a file's blade add a metallic image of torment to the imagery of water and wind.

13. *misting, dim-lit, quiet vale*. Thomas quotes from Keats's notes on *Paradise Lost*: 'There is a cool pleasure in the very sound of vale. The English word is of the happiest chance. Milton has put vales in heaven and hell with the very utter affection and yearning of a great poet' (*K*, 15).

14-15. *Not like a pewit...but like a dove*. In *Oxford*, Thomas compares the beautiful voice of a solo chorister to 'a dove floating to the windows and away, away' (*O*, 9). The birds may represent alternative ways of dealing with neurosis: a regressive resort to nostalgia ('wailing' for 'something...lost'); or progress, however 'fractional', towards the grounded selfhood phrased as 'home and love'.

17-18. *There I find my rest...Beauty is there*. Framed by the affirmative 'there', this resolving couplet completes Thomas's adaptation of sonnet-structure to therapeutic purposes. The relation between lines 1-7 (four sentences) and 7-16 (a single sentence) parallels that between octet and sestet. In fact, the initial mood does not lift until l.11, when the sentence 'turns', as sonnets do, in a different direction. Its very unfolding, through a series of metaphors, enacts a curative process that identifies 'what yet lives in me' with creativity. 'Rest', inaccessible in *Over the Hills*, is 'found'. Thomas notes: 'Jefferies...says of beauty which only the imagination can hold that it is "an expression of hope...while the heart is absorbed in its contemplation, unconscious but powerful hope is filling the breast"' (*RJ*, 280). In its reflexive aspect, 'beauty' also covers Thomas's poetry so far.

Ms: *BL*. **Published text:** *SP, AANP, LP*. **Differences from** *CP1978*: 2 child alive *child, alive* 17 and through *as through* 18 me. *me:* **Note:** *CP1978* follows a typescript [*JT*] rather than *SP, AANP, LP*.

The Gypsy (58)

22 January 1915

FNB67 contains notes on East Grinstead Fair, 11 December 1913 (Thomas was staying with Vivian Locke Ellis at Selsfield House, East Grinstead):

> Gypsies coming in with sham flowers and 'My lucky gentleman' 'You've got a lucky face'. But she had a much luckier face in reality. Lots of caravans drawn up between Selsfield and Grinstead – begging money or half pipe of tobacco one caravan on Selsfield Common several down by Tickeridge, others by Hill Farm more at fork to Saint Hill. All beg. One boy and girl I ran away from. One boy playing rapid rascally Bacchanal tune on mouth organ while he drums on a tambourine and stamps feet and workmen grin. A few cart-horses at auction. Cheapjack, little black haired pale man of 30 who asks a man rough simple labourer if he's married and says 'You have my sympathy' and shakes hands and says 'Dyou love your wife' Lots of laughing, knives clocks jewellery etc.
> 17 December. 2 more gypsies with that rascally Bacchic music at Selsfield House door. One has mouth organ, the other drums on tambourine not lacking cymbals – they play 'Over the hills and far away' and 'If I were Mr. Balfour'.
> 4.15 p.m. How different 2 days ago when I looked from a highish road (? or from railway near Warnham) over a houseless lowish but hollow wooded country, nothing but gradations of inhuman (beginning to get misty at nightfall) dark, as of an underworld and my soul fled over it experiencing the afterdeath – friendless, vacant, hopeless.

In *The South Country* (265-71) Thomas had already tried to capture fair day: 'The main part of the fair consists of a double row, a grove, of tents and booths, roundabouts, caravans, traps and tethered ponies...there is a sound of machine-made music, of firing at targets, of shouts and neighs and brays and the hoot of engines...a gypsy woman on a stool, her head on one side, [is] combing her black hair and talking to the children while a puppy catches at the end of her tresses when they come swishing down...stalls full of toys, cheap jewellery and sweets like bedded-out plants, and stout women pattering alongside – bold women, with sleek black or yellow hair and the bearing and countenance of women who have to make their way in the world' (*SC*, 266-7). Thomas linked the threat to gypsy culture with that to the true 'countryman':

'Before it is too late, I hope that the Zoological Society will receive a few pairs at their Gardens. With them, or in neighbouring paddocks (or whatever, for the sake of human dignity, they are called), should be some Gypsies' (*TC*, 22). '[A]gainst the hedge a gypsy family pretend to shelter from the windy rain; the man stands moody, holding the pony, the women crouch with chins upon knees, the children laugh and will not be still. They belong to the little roads that are dying out: they hate the sword-like shelterless road, the booming cars that go straight to the city in the vale below' (*SC*, 215). George Borrow's interest in gypsies was central to Thomas's interest in Borrow: '[The Gypsies] connect Borrow with what is strange, with what is simple, and with what is free...Their mystery is the mystery of nature and life. They keep their language and their tents against the mass of civilisation and length of time. They are foreigners but as native as the birds' (*GB*, 237). In October 1914 some gypsies in Wales sparked off the urge to write poetry: 'I was meditating a poem about the Gypsies by the roadside, their gramophone and cosy lighted tent so near wind and stars, the children searching for coal in the refuse of the old mine, and me faintly envying them. I thought how feeble and aesthetic my admiration of the mountains was, when I knew nothing of life on them' (letter to Helen, 9 October 1914, *NLW*).

3-8. *'My gentleman...can you spare?'* Commenting on the possibility of hearing Thomas's hexameters as having either four or six stresses or both, Peter Howarth says of the speaker's conversation with the gypsy: 'It is quite impossible...to pronounce [l.7] as a six-stress line and not hear him pompous and afraid...The sense demands that the awkward second stress falls heavily on "you" (making the line sound like sarcasm directed at her lack of money) and lengthens the word "sovereign", as if relishing the sound of the large coin...If we are to believe in the speaker's good self and allow him four stresses, then [the gypsy] responds in a genuine question [l.8] with a rising tone at the end of the line... But if he is pompous, then her question becomes tired, petulant: her interest is elsewhere' (*British Poetry in the Age of Modernism* [Cambridge: Cambridge University Press, 2005], 97). The stumble in this transaction resembles a similar effect in *May 23* (lines 28-35). It is as if, given the gap between price and value thus exposed, dealings with nomadic people can never be commensurable on both sides.

17. *While his mouth-organ changed to a rascally Bacchanal dance.* For Thomas and folk music see general note to *An Old Song I* (166). Here the poem, too, changes its tune or pitch. It builds up to a climax of liberating abandon unique in Thomas's poetry. The 'rascally Bacchanal dance' counterpoints the 'slow' melody mimicked by the last quatrain of *The Penny Whistle*. *The Gypsy* is third in a series of poems that display Thomas's versatility with rhyming couplets, and the sensitive ear that shapes his rhythms. As the sentence-sounds of *Man and Dog* are inflected by its subject's speech, and those of *Beauty* by his own speech, so the hexameter couplets of *The Gypsy* take their cue from folk verses ('Over the hills and far away', 'Simple Simon') as well as from gypsy idioms. On another structural level, Thomas again nods to the sonnet. He bisects the twenty-eight lines between sister and brother, speaker and musician, and exploits the octet/sestet "turn" differently in each half. By thus hybridising

literary and folk forms, Thomas creates a 'music' which echoes his wish that 'English poetry [had] been founded…upon the native ballad instead of upon conceited ceremonious and exotic work' (*FIP*, 14).

19-22. *Outlasted all the fair, farmer and auctioneer…Romany.* Other notes on the fair include: 'A balloon-seller'; 'a bulging eyed, bulging cheeked cleanshaven auctioneer'; 'Drovers hang about with crooked sticks…cattle in High Street at foot of steps, some kneeling down opposite principal butcher's a cheapjack speaking on table on other pavement' (*FNB67*). As these lines give primacy – in memory and as Muse – to the visionary musician, they transmute notebook detail into symbol.

25-8. *The gradations of the dark…a crescent moon.* In line with the 'crescent' moon, this crescendo completes the transformation of Christmas into a pagan festival where Bacchus / Dionysus rules. The baby, the sardonic oxymoron 'Christmas corpses', and now a classical 'underworld' set up 'the Gypsy boy' to redeem 'the dark' by non-Christian and artistic means. That his 'eyes' surpass those of 'the kneeling ox' implies that the poem's disbelief exceeds that of Thomas Hardy's poem 'The Oxen', which can still imagine being invited on Christmas Eve to '"see the oxen kneel / / "In the lonely barton by yonder coomb / Our childhood used to know"'.

Ms: *BC, BL.* **Published text:** *LP.* **Differences from** *CP1978*: 21 corpses *Corpses* [misprint in *LP* and *CP1920*] **Note on title:** *CP1978* brackets the title; *CP2004* drops it. See Note on Text.

Ambition (59)

23 January 1915

Another day, a wide and windy day, is the jackdaw's, and he goes straight and swift and high like a joyous rider crying aloud on an endless savannah …Towards the end of March there are six nights of frost giving birth to still mornings of weak sunlight, of an opaque yet not definitely misty air. The sky is of a milky, uncertain pale blue without one cloud. Eastward the hooded sun is warming the slope fields and melting the sparkling frost. In many trees the woodpeckers laugh so often that their cry is a song…

It is not spring yet. Spring is being dreamed, and the dream is more wonderful and more blessed than ever was spring. What the hour of waking will bring forth is not known. Catch at the dreams as they hover in the warm thick air. Up against the grey tiers of beech stems and the mist of the buds and fallen leaves rise two columns of blue smoke from two white cottages among trees; they rise perfectly straight and then expand into a balanced cloud, and thus make and unmake continually two trees of smoke. No sound comes from the cottages. The dreams are over them… With inward voices of persuasion those dreams hover and say that all is to be made new, that all is yet before us, and the lots are not yet drawn out of the urn. (*SC*, 20-2)

Passages in *The Heart of England*, linked more closely with *Health* and *The Glory* (see notes 227 and 234), also anticipate *Ambition*. All three poems dramatise the gap between aspiration or desire and its realisation; between the speaker's capacity and high possibilities symbolised by early morning or early Spring or both. Not confined to Thomas's personal problems, these poems explore existential and cognitive questions that stem from Romantic ideology. In some respects, they parallel Yeats's dialogues between Self and Anti-Self. Like Yeats, and in a similar context of war, Thomas engages with the man of action, the Promethean hero: another 'Other' (see note on Thomas and Nietzsche, 227).

4-7. *Jackdaws began to shout and float and soar...sky.* Jackdaws also feature in 'January Sunshine' (which ends with the imperative 'Be beautiful and enjoy and live!'): 'In the immense crystal spaces of fine windy air...the jackdaws play. They soar, they float, they dance, and they dive and carve sudden magnificent precipices in the air, crying all the time with sharp, joyous cries that are in harmony with the great heights and the dashing wind' (*HE*, 156). In *Ambition* jackdaws stake out a zone of similar extremity. They initiate the poem's stark contrasts between 'black' and 'white', heights and depths. 'Warrior' (compare *Health*, l.30) and 'Challenges and menaces' add to their distance from Thomas's modes of self-doubt, banished to the 'ridiculed' owl. They may also allude to the war.

14-16. *A train...close-knit.* 'There was spring in the smoke lying in a hundred white vertebrae motionless behind the rapid locomotive in the vale' (*RU*, 5). 'The half-moon at the zenith of a serene, frosty night led in a morning of mist that filled up all the hollows of the valley as with snow: each current of smoke from locomotive or cottage lay in solid and enduring vertebrae above the mist' (*IPS*, 27-8).

17-22. *Time / Was powerless...Omnipotent I was. BL*'s 'I was omnipotent' is less telling than the inversion. Kirkham writes: 'This is, surely, a Lucifer's dream of usurpation, the pride that comes before the fall, *the* Fall...This Lucifer, besides, is a Romantic poet, blurring distinctions between perception and conception, imagining that his work reproduces the act of Creation. It is not the only passage in Thomas's poetry to present the Wordsworthian unitary view – mind and object dissolved into each other – as a delusion, and a seductive one for the solitary who seeks compensation for his impotence in the vicarious power exercised through the mastery of words.' For Kirkham, the pun on 'rime' may be Thomas's critique of his '*romantic* self...half believing that...no contrary reality obstructed free communication between dream and verse' (*MK*, 41-2). The 'white' aspect of the poem's colour dynamics brings 'clouds and rime', *via* chimney and train smoke, into 'pure' proximity. This portrait of the hubristic artist may be in dialogue with *The Gypsy*.

23. *the end fell like a bell.* Internal rhyme heralds the anticlimactic couplet in which 'Elysium', together with the interlacing rhyme scheme, finally collapses. Here a Romantic poem, Keats's 'Ode to a Nightingale', subverts Romantic ideology: 'Forlorn! The very word is like a bell / To toll me back from thee to my sole self!' The effect also hints at sexual detumescence.

26. *'twas:* see note (153).

Ms: *BC, BL.* **Published text:** *LP.* **Differences from** *CP1978*: 25 tell. [*LP*] *tell:* [*BC, BL*] **Note on title:** *CP1978* brackets the title; *CP2004* removes the brackets. See Note on Text.

House and Man (60)

3, 4 February 1915

> The name of Norgett on a stone called up Oldhurst into my mind, a thatched house built of flints in the middle of oak woods not far off – ancient woods where the leaves of many Autumns whirled and rustled even in June. It was three miles from the hard road, and it used to seem that I had travelled three centuries when at last I emerged from the oaks and came in sight of that little humped gray house and within sound of the pines that shadowed it. It had a face like an owl; it was looking at me. Norgett must have heard me coming from somewhere among the trees, for, as I stepped into the clearing at one side, he was at the other. I thought of Herne the Hunter on catching sight of him. He was a long, lean, gray man with a beard like dead gorse, buried gray eyes, and a step that listened. He hardly talked at all, and only after questions that he could answer quite simply. Speech was an interruption of his thoughts, and never sprang from them; as soon as he had ceased talking they were resumed with much low murmuring and whistling – like that of the pine trees – to himself, which seemed the sound of their probings in the vast of himself and Nature. His was a positive, an active silence. (*IPS*, 100-1)

The less 'positive' wood-dweller in the poem resembles the protagonist of Frost's 'An Old Man's Winter Night', written after *House and Man*, and perhaps in response to it. Frost presents a similar triangle of man, house, and encroaching natural forces: 'All out-of-doors looked darkly in at him / Through the thin frost, almost in separate stars, / That gathers on the pane in empty rooms'. Both poems reverse the human gaze at Nature. In *House and Man* 'forest silence and forest murmur' take on life in proportion as the man loses substance and speech, or becomes a thing ('half like a beggar's rag'). This wraith is antithetical to Thomas's Promethean self-projection in *Ambition*. The faintly Gothic symbolism hovers between ecological, psychological and cognitive suggestiveness.

1-3. *as dim...While I remember him*. When a poem by Thomas represents itself as memory-in-process, it moves either towards epiphany or towards its converse. Poetry's own integrative capacity is also on the line. 'Dimness' connects the speaker's difficulty in stabilising memory ('a reflection in a rippling brook') with the man's difficulty in maintaining selfhood, and the mind's difficulty in negotiating the natural world. All phenomena seem pulled towards 'the house darkness'. The poem's rhythm, notable for syntax that overrides or breaks the couplet, takes on an entropic momentum.

12-13. *half / Ghost-like*: see note on Thomas's 'ghosts' (202).

20. *A magpie like a weathercock in doubt*. On 1 February Thomas had noted: 'magpie in oak tip like weathercock' (*FNB80*). The poem ends with the image that ostensibly, and perhaps actually, sparked it off; but the arbitrariness of memory, like the image itself, is not reassuring. Cf. William Morris's 'The Message of the March Wind': 'And the vane on the spire-top is swinging in doubt'.

Ms: *BL*. **Published text:** *LP*. **Differences from** *CP1978*: 4 It was *'Twas*

8 'Lonely!' *'Lonely,'* 13 half like a beggar's *half a beggar's* **Note:** *CP1978* follows the version printed in James Guthrie's magazine [*RB* 1, 4 (nd)] rather than *BL/LP*, but the omission of 'like' seems an obvious misprint.

Parting (60)
11 February 1915

The parting was from Thomas's fifteen-year old son Merfyn, who left Steep on that day, *en route* for America, and with whom his relations were often tense. Two days later Thomas wrote to Bottomley: 'Merfyn is sailing to America today with the Frosts. I don't pretend to expect this or that of it but I believe the time had come to let him see what people were who couldn't make him do things as I can or a schoolmaster can but who nevertheless will expect him to give as well as take' (*LGB*, 243-4). Guy Cuthbertson points out that *Parting* is written in the quatrain (ABBA) of Tennyson's *In Memoriam*, and that it echoes another poem linked with Tennyson's grief for Arthur Hallam, 'The Passing of Arthur'. Here King Arthur leaves for 'the island valley of Avilion; / Where falls not hail, or rain, or any snow, / Nor ever wind blows loudly' (*Notes and Queries* 51, 2 [June 2004]).

7. *The perished self:* see note on Thomas's 'ghosts' (202).

10-12. *Remembered joy...sadden the sad.* Cf. lines 17-20 of *Home* (64), to which *Parting* seems closely related.

12-22. *So memory...spiritualised it lay.* Here 'ill' is sealed off from 'woe', and hence from hope of therapeutic transformation. Cf. Philip Larkin, 'Lines on a Young Lady's Photograph Album': 'in the end, surely, we cry / Not only at exclusion, but because / It leaves us free to cry'.

23-4. *the perpetual yesterday / That naught can stir or stain like this.* R. George Thomas notes that '"like this" refers to the poem' as well as to the speaker's state (*CP1978*, 389). The phrase aligns poetry with the 'suffering', rather than 'perished', self: with the 'today' of pain (and life) rather than a 'yesterday' that can only offer vain remorse and false transcendence ('bliss'). Just as the 'stirred' emotion cannot be contained, sentences spill over the quatrains in an edgily unexpected way.

Ms: *BL*. **Published text:** *LP* **Differences from** *CP1978*: 24 stain [*LP*] stain, [*BL*] **Note:** *CP1944* has 'strain': perhaps a misprint, although it is possible that Thomas considered this verb as an alternative. But it does not appear in *BL* or *LP*, the only extant sources. **Note on title:** Title is given in *BL*.

First known when lost (61)
11 February 1915

In *BL* the title appears as: First <u>known</u> when lost. Written in the same quatrain, though with different tones and rhythms, this poem can be read as a redemptive coda to *Parting*. Abrupt time-shifts invade the sealed-off past of *Parting*, and make 'the narrow copse' paradoxically present in absence. These shifts possibly led the *LP* editors to "tidy up" the sequence of tenses (see textual note).

4. *bill*: bill-hook.

12. *as if flowers they had been.* The *LP* editors (see textual note) could have understood this as a pluperfect (hence, 'made'), not as primarily a subjunctive form equivalent to 'as if they were flowers'. The usage may not only be for reasons of rhyme: the latent pluperfect makes 'faggot ends / Of hazel' continuous with, as well as analogous to, the copse's flowers.

14. *And now I see as I look.* Thomas sets high standards for 'seeing' (see note on a cognate poem, *Birds' Nests*, 163). Perhaps the retrospective insight here has further remedial implications (cf. 'amends', 1.11) for the absence that *Parting* mourns. In juxtaposing something paradoxically 'hidden…near' with 'small winding brook' and a 'rising' rhythm, the last quatrain figures access to sources in the psyche.

Ms: *BL.* **Published text:** *LP.* **Differences from** *CP1978*: 5 overgrown *o'ergrown* 16 tributary, *tributary* **Note:** *LP* has 'was' for 'is' [*BL*] in 1.8; 'made' for 'make' [*BL*] in 1.11. *CP1944* has 'is' and 'made'; *CP1978* 'is' and 'make'. It seems likely that the present tense always follows 'now'. Some intermediate typescript probably accounts for other differences between *BL* and *LP*. *CP1978* follows *BL* throughout.

May 23 (62)
15 February 1915

1-10. There never was a finer day…luck to endure. 'The Artist' (*LAT*, 130-9) anticipates the weather of *May 23* and *Haymaking*:

> This, said Adams to himself, staring strangely at the dry brushes and blank paper before him, this was the fairest day of the whole year, the youngest child of a long family of days, each fairer than its elder. First, there were two days following suddenly, hot and cloudless, upon weeks of storm, of sullenness, and of restless wind and rain vexing the new leaves and scattering the blossoms; and at the end of the second a thunderstorm out of the east ascended lightly and travelled rapidly away without silencing the birds…Adams found himself waiting day after day for the end and crown of this energy and change.
>
> There came a lustrous morning early assailed from all quarters of the sky in turn, as if the heavens were besieging the earth, by thunder and after long, brooding intervals, thunder again and again, now with cannonading and now one boom or blast followed by no sound except its echo and the challenge of the pheasants. The lark in the sky, the blackbird in the isolated meadow elms, the nightingale in the hazel and bluebell thickets, sang on; and before the last of the assault Adams set out, inwardly confident in the day's future. (130-2)

12-27. *Old Jack Noman…cress in his basket.* According to Helen Thomas, Jack Noman's original was 'a tramp who used to call asking for left-off clothes and selling watercress. He used to disappear for long periods, and then appear again as jaunty as ever. We thought his disappearances were spent in prison, for we knew he stole. But we liked him, and if Edward had a particularly warm but outworn garment – especially one he really had liked – he saved it until Jack came again' (Thomas, *Selected Poems* [London: Hutchinson, 1962], 112n.). At the beginning of *The Heart of England* (1906) a child in a London street views a 'Watercress Man' as the harbinger of romance and the countryside. Thomas's prose contains several other portraits of a watercress-seller/tramp under such names as Jackalone, Jack Runaway and Jack Horseman: 'close by stood the tall old watercress-man Jack Horseman, patiently waiting for the right moment to touch his cap. His Indian complexion had come back to the old soldier, he was slightly tipsy, and he had a bunch of cowslips in his hat' (*HGLM*, 176). 'What dreams are there for that aged child [Jackalone] who goes tottering and reeling up the lane at mid-day? He carries a basket of watercress on his back. He has sold two-pennyworth, and he is tipsy, grinning through the bruises of a tipsy fall, and shifting his cold pipe from one side of his mouth to the other. Though hardly sixty he is very old, worn and thin and wrinkled, and bent sideways and forward at the waist and the shoulders. Yet he is very young. He is just what he was forty years ago when the thatcher found him lying on his back in the sun instead of combing out the straw and sprinkling it with water for his use. He laid no plans as a youth; he had only a few transparent tricks and easy lies. Never has he thought of the day after tomorrow' (*SC*, 25).

'Jack' arrives in the poem like the spirit of May, like Autolycus in *The Winter's Tale*, combining in his appearance the freshness and heat of the season. He is related to 'Lob' by his name, earthiness and proverbial wisdom, by his roguery and generosity. But he personifies primal vitality rather than cultural evolution. The couplets of *Lob* have a different tune. Different again are those that characterise and historicise the 'old man' in *Man and Dog*.

25-34. *Fairer flowers...I say.* In saying 'Wait till next time' (for the speaker to give him 'something'), Jack retreats from the ordinary exchange and barter that he tentatively proposes in l.32, and thus fully matches his deed to the abundant day. John Lucas comments: 'The lovely anapaestic ripple of [lines 25-32] provides a kind of licensed gaiety of conversation, one that plays up the largesse of giving as opposed to selling, and which is reinforced by "Take them *and* these flowers, too, free". To honour that line's rhythmic movement you have to stress the surely unimportant word "and". In doing so, you realise how important it is: Jack Noman takes and gives flowers free because they come from "no man's gardens"' (Lucas, *Starting to Explain* [Nottingham: Trent Books, 2003], 116).

36. *roll-walk-run.* The elements of this compound function as verbs rather than nouns. The headlong rhythm epitomises how the poem's mainly four-stress line, with its mixed anapaests and iambics, fits its 'jaunty' subject.

37-8. *Oakshott rill...Wheatham hill.* Oakshott Stream and the hanger Wheatham Hill are north of Steep. Watercress flourishes in chalk streams, and English watercress production still centres on Hampshire: 'now there are only patches of the cress gone to weed in the Ashford and Oakshott Streams. Cowslips too have become rarer on the hangers' (*WW*, 28).

39-44. *'Twas the first day...like hops.* These packed lines consummate the rich textures and unusually intense happiness of the poem, which survive the shadow, mysterious rather than mournful, thrown into the sunlight by its final couplet. All phenomena acquire an equal sensuous value, relished by the assonance 'midges-bit-dust-sad-hid-ruts-seeds'. It is rarely that Spring, or any other season, can 'do nothing to make [Thomas] sad'.

45-6. *BL* ends less mysteriously: 'A fine day was May the 20th, / The day of old Jack Noman's death.' Criticism from W.H. Hudson seems to have precipitated the change: 'I must think about the sensation at the end of "May 20". I think perhaps it must come out' (letter to Hudson, *SL*, 108).

Ms: *BL*. **Published text:** *P.* **Differences from** *CP1978*: In punctuating lines 43-4, *CP1978* follows *P* [*copse. / hops,*] not *CP1920* [*copse, / hops,*]. The latter seems preferable, since the former [also in *PTP*] may be an inconsistent punctuation resulting from the change to the last couplet: see note above [*BL* has *copse. / hops.*]. **Note on title:** *May 23* is the title in *P*, *CP1920*, *CP1928* and *CP1978*; *May the Twenty-third* in *CP1944*.

The Barn (63)

22 February 1915

The Barn may involve a suppressed dialogue. It seems to merge the voice of an old (l.3) countryman or farm-labourer with that of an implied poet-listener. The first voice underlies the speaker's attitude to 'they'; his knowledge of the farm and its history; aspects of his idiom and mode of address: ''Twould not [*BL* ''Twouldn't'] pay to pull down' (see note on *The Signpost*, 153). Expressions like 'no other antiquity' and the account of the starlings are uttered in something closer to Thomas's 'own' voice. In *The Icknield Way* he writes about 'Lone Barn', near Wayland's Smithy on the Ridgeway, and tells the story of a deranged philosopher and his family who squatted there in miserable conditions. This 'black barn' contributes to both *The Barn* and *The Barn and the Down*: '[it] lies unexpectedly in a small hollow at one of the highest points of the downs, three miles from the nearest hamlet. It had long been deserted. The farmhouse was ruinous...An old plum tree, planted when barn and house were built, and now dead and barkless, stood against one end...The last of its doors lay just outside in the dead embers of the tramps' fire. Thus open on both sides to the snow-light and the air the barn looked the work rather of nature rather than of man. The old thatch was grooved, riddled, and gapped, and resembled a grassy bank that has been under a flood the winter through; covered now in snow, it had the outlines in miniature of the hill on which it was built' (*IW*, 237-40). In 'Earth Children', an old couple inhabit 'part of a farmhouse, the rest having fallen to ruin, and from human hands to the starlings, the sparrows, and the rats' (*HE*, 141).

18. *Making a spiky beard*: a characteristically brilliant piece of bird-observation. On 4 February Thomas had noted: 'starlings perch singly in hedge and talk and chatter and whistle with heads up, making a sort of spiky beard under beaks, bubbling throat' (*FNB80*).

23. *It's the turn of lesser things, I suppose.* The speaker traces, and seems to approve, a form of biodegradation whereby creatures take over, and Nature reclaims, an artefact.

Ms: *BL*. **Published text:** *LP*. **Note on title:** Title is given in *BL*.

Home (64)

23 February 1915

Thomas's first "home" poem is a metaphysical parable. He would write two other poems with this title: *Home*, which explores earthly dwelling, and *'Home'*, which explores 'fellowship' and nationality. But the quest for home always governs poetic travels that already span the dubiously 'homely' White Horse pub; 'powers / Coming like exiles home again' in *The Other*; the 'empty home' of *The Mountain Chapel*; the dove's ideal 'home and love' in *Beauty*. The dialectics of home in Thomas's poetry cross over between psychology and culture. 'Aurelius, the Superfluous Man' (Thomas took the concept from Turgenev's *Diary of a Superfluous Man*, 1850) is a relevant self-portrait: 'The superfluous are those who cannot find society with which they are in some sort of harmony. The magic circle drawn round us all at birth surrounds these in such a way that it will never overlap, far less become concentric with, the circles of any other in the whirling multitudes' (*HGLM*, 49-50). For Smith, Thomas's 'Superfluous Man' is 'the dispossessed rightful inheritor, equivocally retained by a civilisation guiltily unable to abolish him totally' (*SS*, 46). But, like Turgenev's diarist, Thomas tends to represent his psychic separateness as preceding and underlying other forms of alienation: 'with me, social intercourse is only an intense form of solitude' (*LCB*, 53). More positively, as in the case of Aurelius, he associates the 'superfluous' with visionary powers.

In 'A Note on Nostalgia' (*Scrutiny* 1 [1932], 8-19) D.W. Harding, cites *Home* when he charges Thomas with failure to 'probe his unhappiness' and with implying 'that its causes were remoter, less tangible and more inevitable, than in fact they were': 'The poem almost certainly springs from nostalgic feelings, but…Thomas gives them a much larger significance, larger than they deserve.' Cooke counters this critique by arguing that Thomas's poetry incorporates adequate 'resistance' to the regressive impulses it manifests (*WC*, 225-31). In *Home*, as in *Beauty* and *Parting*, the speaker ultimately refuses a regressive journey, perceiving its illusive nature. Whereas in *Parting* the 'strange land' of 'the Past' is disembodied, 'That land, / My home' remains un-embodied. Despite 'go back', it belongs to the future or the mind. *Home* may be less an expression of nostalgia – 'the ache for home' – than a poem *about* nostalgia and its limits.

1. *Not the end: but there's nothing more.* This elliptical opening marks an existential limbo between here and the hereafter, where life has no more 'meanings' to disclose.

2-4. *rude…solitude.* Thomas also rhymes these words in *The Other* and *Melancholy*.

6. *all that they mean I know.* Cf. the second quatrain of Hardy's 'To Life': 'I know what thou would'st tell / Of Death, Time, Destiny – / I have known it long, and know, too, well / What it all means for me.'

11-13. *No traveller tells of it…And could I discover it.* Direct allusion to Hamlet's 'To be or not to be' soliloquy ('The undiscovered country, from whose bourn / No traveller returns') exposes its presence in the poem. From the first line, 'the ache for home' has shown its other face as the death wish. 'I suppose every man thinks that Hamlet was written for him, but I *know* he was written for me' (*EF*, 12).

13-16. *And could I…things that were.* Cf. *The Signpost*, lines 20-30, and *Liberty*, lines 24-7; also *Hamlet*: 'For in that sleep of death what dreams may come'. Thomas's personae veer between desire for a condition free from suffering and re-attachment to the complex living moment.

17-20. *Remembering ills…what was well*. Cf. *Parting*, lines 10-12. Links between *Parting* and *Home* include Thomas's use of the quatrain. The move from an ABBA rhyme scheme to ABCB, with its greater potential to suggest progress, reflects the move from a speaker contemplating 'perpetual yesterday' to a speaker who builds on the earlier poem's recoil from sterile retrospect ('irremediable' picks up 'Not as what had been remedied' in *Parting*). Yet, unlike *Parting*, *Home* consists of end-stopped stanzas, and the speaker's ultimate decision 'to be', although more positive than his initial claim that life can yield no further 'meanings', projects stoicism rather than agency: 'I must wait'. Cf. *Hamlet*: 'And makes us rather bear those ills we have / Than fly to others that we know not of '.

Ms: *BL*. **Published text**: *LP*. **Note on title**: Title is given in *BL*.

The Owl (64)
24 February 1915

The carefully balanced triads of the first six lines, together with the equally careful discrimination between degrees of discomfort, prepare for the moral distinctions that the poem will establish. Later, 'telling me plain' defines the aesthetic of what proves to be a "war poem". His sense of 'what I escaped / And others could not' was a factor in Thomas's enlistment. Here the Hamlet of *Home* meets Fortinbras.

8-9. *cry/ / Shaken out*. The cross-stanza enjambment gives 'Shaken' a pivotal resonance.

10. *No merry note*: a reference to Winter's song 'When icicles hang by the wall' (*Love's Labours Lost* V, ii) which also features in *Lob* (lines 96-8): 'Tu-whit, Tu-who, a merry note'. The owl's cry, as inner 'voice', is no longer being 'ridiculed' (see *Ambition*, l.9).

13. *salted*. Scannell observes: 'It is the repeated word, *salted*, which is at once ambiguous yet absolutely right for [Thomas's] purposes. The owl grieves, lonely in the cold night, and the poet pities those who don't share the warmth and comfort that he is privileged to enjoy; but he is too honest to deny that, while his sympathy for the "soldiers and poor" is authentic, his awareness of their privation adds to his own pleasure and contentment while at the same time it awakens the sense of guilt…the word *salted* certainly means *flavoured* or *spiced*, but at the same time less comfortable connotations are invoked: the harshness of salt, the salt in the wound, the taste of bitterness, and of tears' (*VS*, 19-20).

Ms: *BL*. **Published text**: *P*. **Note on title**: Title is given in *BL*.

The Child on the Cliffs (65)
11 March 1915

Thomas spent childhood summer holidays in western Wales. In 'Edward Thomas and Wales' Sally Roberts Jones notes that 'the child in "The Child on the Cliffs" seems to be sitting on a Gower cliff, looking out over the drowned Coed Arian [Silver Wood] to the Devon coast' (*JB*, 81).

Westward, for men of this island, lies the sea; westward are the great hills. In a mere map the west of Britain is fascinating. The great features of that map, which make it something more than a picture to be imperfectly copied by laborious childhood pens, are the great promontories of Caernarvon, of Pembroke, of Gower and of Cornwall, jutting out into the western sea, like the features of a grim large face, such a face as is carved on a ship's prow. These protruding features, even on a small-scale map, thrill the mind with a sense of purpose and spirit. They yearn, they peer ever out to the sea, as if using eyes and nostrils to savour the utmost scent of it, as if themselves calling back to the call of the waves. (*SC*, 9)

Although 'sea-blue-eyed' like 'Lob', Thomas usually presents his 'land face'. His most extended prose meditation on the sea depicts it as 'unearthly' and unhistorical: 'a monster that has lain unmoved by time', 'that cold fatal element', 'a type of the waste where everything is unknown or uncertain except death' (*SC*, 162). Hence, perhaps, the darker orientation of this poem as compared with *The Child in the Orchard*, whose similar form suggests that Thomas's seachild and land-child are complementary. In *The Child on the Cliffs* the boy's perceptions seem to license indulgence of the death wish resisted in *Home*. The morbidly erotic scenario, which resembles certain Victorian images of childhood, includes a beckoning 'Belle Dame sans Merci' (in *BL* the phrase is 'white beseeching arm'). Thomas told Eleanor Farjeon: 'I like the Child on the Cliff. It is a memory between one of my young brothers and myself which he reminded me of lately. He was most of the child and I have been truthful. I think I can expect some allowances for the "strangeness" of the day' (*EF*, 127-8).

3. *Things are strange today on the cliff.* Thomas's deployment of 'strange', often in tension with 'familiar', resembles Freud's coupling of '*unheimlich*' (uncanny, disturbing) and '*heimlich*' (see note on *The Other*, 162). Freud also argues that the words are two sides of the same coin: 'on the one hand [*heimlich*] means what is familiar and agreeable, and on the other, what is concealed and kept out of sight' (Sigmund Freud, *Art and Literature*, Penguin Freud Library 14 [1985], 345). Here sunshine is paradoxically uncanny, prompting the surreal metamorphoses of the grasshopper; while, in the last stanza, 'lying under that foam' assumes the domestic aura of a child in bed. The poem may also be "Freudian" in the sense of Oedipal.

9. *Like a green knight*: a simile that adds to the Arthurian ethos.

13-16. *Fishes and gulls ring no bells...up in heaven.* This alludes to legendary drowned lands and cities off Britain's south-western coast, like Coed Arian, or Lyonesse between Land's End and the Scilly Isles, whose church bells can supposedly be heard: 'Outside, by the window, is the village idiot, with a smile like the sound of bells ascending from a city buried in the sea' (*BW*, 98).

Ms: *BL.* **Published text:** *LP.* **Differences from *CP1978*:** title: Cliffs [*LP*] *Cliff* 15 – hark! – [*BL*, *CP1920*] – *hark.* – [*LP*] **Note on title:** The title in *CP1978* is based on *EF*, quoted above. But Thomas's references to poems in letters cannot be seen as definitive [see Note on Text], and the singular, despite l.3, could imply a child climbing a cliff. The *LP* title, taken together with the *EF* reference, suggests that the *LP* editors were following a typescript [probably typed by Farjeon]. In l.15 *LP* seems to be in error.

The Bridge (66)

12 March 1915

'Next day I crossed the river. At first, the water seemed as calm and still as ice. The boats at anchor, and doubled by shadow, were as if by miracle suspended in the water. No ripple was to be seen, though now and then one emitted a sudden transitory flame, reflected from the sun, which dreamed half-way up the sky in a cocoon of cloud. No motion of the tide was visible, though the shadows of the bridge that cleared the river in three long leaps, trembled and were ever about to pass away. The end of the last leap was unseen, for the further shore was lost in mist, and a solitary gull spoke for the mist.' Thomas proceeds to meditate on a 'drowned dog' whose stillness 'gave me a strange suggestion of power and restraint', and which evokes 'the host of all the dead or motionless or dreaming things' (*BW*, 110-12).

Combining progress with suspension, the rhyme scheme of *The Bridge* is integral to its symbolism. The internal rhymes in the first and third lines of each stanza maintain a forward impetus, checked by the same-rhyming of the last two lines. Other forms of refrain and the long last line enhance the sense of hiatus, as if the poem refuses to move on to any further point but itself remains a 'bridge'. *The Bridge* holds in suspended animation key motifs of Thomas's poetry so far: strangeness; memory; travel; rest; the domains of Past and Future; opposed emotions, experiences and states ('smile or moan', 'kind'/ 'unkind', 'lights / And shades'); alternative 'lives'; dark depths. R. George Thomas speculates that the '"strange bridge"...may well refer to his first half-unconscious decision to enlist' (*CP1978*, 391).

10. *dark-lit*. This oxymoron, as applied to the 'stream' of consciousness, or perhaps to a zone where the conscious mind and the unconscious touch, is among the poem's 'bridges'.

11-15. *No traveller...or have been*. The benign sense of 'rest' or remission here is qualified by the idea that 'this moment brief between / Two lives' is suppressing ('hide') rather than dismissing an impossible third life, the synthesis of all Thomas's dialectics: 'what has never been'.

Ms: *BL*. **Published text:** *P*.

Good-night (66)

16 March 1915

Thomas grew up in London, but the whole direction of his life and art led away from it. *Oxford*, *The Heart of England* and *In Pursuit of Spring* all begin with a happy departure from city streets: 'Passing rapidly through London with its roar of causes that have been won, and the suburbs where they have no causes...' (*O*, 1). Conversely, his prose contains portraits of unhappily displaced people driven to London by the collapse of the English rural economy: 'He was a country-bred man with a distinct London accent. Once upon a time, it seems, he had charmed a snake, caught a tench of five pounds and lost a bigger one, and, like Jefferies, heard the song of the redwing in England; now he kept somebody's accounts and wore the everlasting mourning of clerks' (*TC*, 1). Yet Thomas spent much time in London, lodging with his parents, soliciting work from publishers and editors, researching books, seeing literary friends. In *Good-night*, in *The Childhood of Edward Thomas* and other autobiographical prose, he salutes his urban – and perhaps creative – origins: 'the Common...was large enough to provide us with many surprises and discoveries for years'; 'The streets were a playground almost equal to the Common' (*CET*, 39, 41). In moving from 'down' to 'suburb' to 'gardens of the town' (old 'inner suburbs'), *Good-night* reverses the course, and complicates the emotion, of a passage near the start of *In Pursuit of Spring*: 'Several times two or three children passed beneath the window and chattered in loud, shrill voices, but they were unseen. Far from disturbing the tranquillity, the sounds were steeped in it; the silence and stillness of the twilight saturated and embalmed them. But pleasant as in themselves they were entirely, they were far more so by reason of what they suggested. These voices and this tranquillity spoke of Spring. They told me what an evening it was at home. I knew how the first blackbird was whistling in the broad oak, and, farther away – some very far away – many thrushes were singing in the chill' (*IPS*, 19-20).

Thomas liked the concept behind Richard Jefferies's *After London* (1885), which begins with 'the relapse of England into barbarism, and the loss of everything characteristic of nineteenth-century civilisation' (*RJ*, 233). His reaction, like the book itself, belongs to the period when London's exponential growth was swallowing up formerly rural or semi-rural environments, creating new suburbs and marooning older ones: 'many suburbans have seen the paradise of their boyhood defaced' (*HS*, 103). Thomas was so deeply conditioned by all this as to make his poetry, in its ecological and metaphysical recoil, paradoxically "about" London: 'London is one of the immense things of the world, like the Alps, the Sahara, the Western Sea; and it has a complexity, a wavering changefulness along with its mere size, which no poets or artists have defined as they have in a sense defined those other things' (*RJ*, 106). He became negatively compelled by the puzzle of people 'living in no ancient way' (*HE*, 7), by the fact that 'we cannot make harmony out of cities' (*TC*, 11). He does not so much evade the modern city as insist that it sets poetry a cognitive problem:

[T]hese streets are the strangest thing in the world. They have never been discovered. They cannot be classified. There is no tradition about them. Poets have not shown how we are to regard them. They are to us as mountains were in the Middle Ages, sublime, difficult, immense; and yet so new that we have inherited no certain attitude towards them, of liking or dislike. They suggest so much that they mean nothing at all... They propose themselves as a problem to the mind, only a little less so at night when their surfaces hand the mind on to the analogies of sea waves or large woods...Once [in a new suburb] I came upon a line of willows above dead reeds that used to stand out by a pond as the first notice to one walking out of London that he was in the country at last; they were unchanged; they welcomed and encouraged once more. The lighted windows in the mist had each a greeting; they were as the windows we strain our eyes for as we descend to them from the hills of Wales or Kent; like those, they had the art of seeming a magical encampment among the trees, brave, cheerful lights which men and women kept going amidst the dense and powerful darkness. The thin, incompleted walls learned a venerable utterance. (*HE*, 4-6)

4. *the noise of man, beast, and machine prevails*. Stillness, for Thomas, is both a key quality of the countryside and a pre-condition of the aesthetic: 'To one bred in a town this kind of silence and solitariness perhaps always remains impressive. We see no man, no smoke, and hear no voice of man or beast or machinery, and straightway the mind recalls very early mornings when London has lain silent but for the cooing of pigeons' (*IW*, 145). While Thomas also imbues natural sounds with ominous force (see note on *The Penny Whistle*, 174), he invariably hears 'the roar of towns' (*Roads*) as unstructurable pandemonium: 'In the streets...the roar continued of the inhuman masses of humanity...Between the millions and the one, no agreement was visible' (*IPS*, 11). 'Somewhere far off I could hear an angry murmur broken by frantic metallic clashings. No one sound out of the devilish babble could I disentangle, still less, explain. A myriad noises were violently mixed in one muddy, struggling mass of rumbling and jangling...Above all, the babble was angry and it was inhuman...As I realised that it was the mutter of London, I sighed, being a child, with relief, but could not help listening still for every moment of that roar as of interlaced immortal dragons fighting eternally in a pit' (*HGLM*, 226-7).

6. *echo...echoing*. This word also appears twice in l.10. Thomas chose for *This England* William Blake's 'The Echoing Green', which evokes the playground of childhood, and ends: 'Many sisters and brothers, / Like birds in their nest, / Are ready for rest, / And sport no more seen / On the darkening green'.

9. *the ghost*: Thomas as a child. Smith comments: 'The ghost is one of the commonest tropes in Thomas's poetry. His English landscapes are in fact peopled primarily by ghosts, usually associated with memory and the return of the past' (*SS*, 66). In their psychological aspect, Thomas's ghosts are projections of the self: the 'ghosts' of tears in *Tears*; 'the 'half / Ghost-like' figure in *House and Man*; the 'ghost new-arrived' in *The Gypsy*; the 'perished self' of *Parting* who 'is in shadow-land a shade'. Cf. the 'ghostly double' that voices the prose origin of *Rain* (*IW*, 280). Thomas takes Hardy's 'hauntings' into new psychic as well as historical zones. When a proposal for a travel book fell through, he expressed his relief thus: 'I dread the new faces and new ways. I was born to be a ghost' (*JM*, 180).

11-16. *homeless...homely...a traveller's good-night*. See general note to *Home* (197). *Good-night* revisits the mood, language and imagery of *The Bridge* in more affirmative terms. Although the speaker remains in transit, this quasi-religious benediction, stronger than 'blest' in *The Bridge*, like his earlier sense of 'kingship' amid disparate phenomena, reconciles home and journey, friend and stranger, city and country, 'familiar' (*heimlich*) and 'strange' (*unheimlich*). These reconciliations also ratify Thomas's success in writing a "city" poem. In *Good-night* a reflexive sound track takes the speaker-as-poet to where urban 'noise' finally drowns birdsong, but the children's 'call' becomes a surrogate aural Muse.

Ms: *BL*. **Published text**: *LP*. **Differences from *CP1978***: 16 good-night *good night* **Note**: Inconsistencies in the spelling of 'good-night' have been regularised in this edition. **Note on title**: Title is given in *BL*.

But these things also (67)

18 March 1915

This poem's obliquely combative first line challenges conventions of the 'Spring' poem: the *BL* title is: *But these things also*. Judy Kendall sees the poem as also contesting Edward Garnett's criticism that some of Thomas's poems are 'petty in incident' (*JK*, 31). It may thus encode a long-held aesthetic belief: 'Anything, however small, may make a poem; nothing, however great, is certain to' (*MM*, 28).

5-8. *The shell of a little snail...purest white*. As in lines 4-16 of *November*, Thomas notices what other poets disregard. The 'minutiae' in this quatrain ('little', 'chip', 'mite', 'small') are kept distinct, and distinctive, by the itemising syntax, by monosyllabic diction, and by consonantal clashes ('chip of flint').

16. *And Spring's here, Winter's not gone*. The interpenetration of English seasons is a recurrent focus and symbol in Thomas's writings: 'Spring and summer and autumn had come – flowing into one another with that secrecy which, as in the periods of our life, spares us the pain of the irretraceable step' (*HE*, 157). But while some poems (*October*, *The Lane*) harmonise different seasons, *But these things also* is left unresolved by the adversative asyndeton that ends its single sentence, and which echoes the earlier spaces between words. The speaker's reading of misleading or ambiguous ('dung...purest') seasonal signs has an implied psychological counterpart. 'Keep their spirits up in the mist' prepares for *The New House*.

Ms: *BL*. **Published text**: *LP*.

The New House (68)

19 March 1915

The new house was at Wick Green (see general note to *Wind and Mist*, 209). This lyric doubly anticipates Thomas's more extended treatment of the same material in *Wind and Mist*, since it puts prophetically what the later poem examines retrospectively. The speaker/wind 'remembers the future'.

4. *moan*: a verb/noun that also signifies lament in *The Penny Whistle* (see note, 174) and *The Bridge*. Suppressed in the latter poem, it now resumes its sway. In August 1916 Frost told Thomas: 'You are so good at black talk that I believe your record will stand unbroken for years to come. It's as if somebody should do the hundred yards in five seconds flat' (*RFET*, 150).

13-16. *All was foretold me...should be*. This quatrain clinches the symbolism of a life or psyche trapped within a predestined narrative that can never become 'new'. Here the poem adds syntactical refrain to its ominous repetitions and sound-effects. Modal verbs (could, would, should) sweep the speaker from present incapacity to future doom. 'Should be' is both future perfect ('would have been') and a distant subjunctive that voices necessity.

Ms: *BL*. **Published text**: *AANP*, *LP*. **Note on title**: Title is given in *BL*.

The Barn and the Down (68)

22, 23 March 1915

See general note to *The Barn* (196). 'At end of Charles Street is a big slate-barn – you see the length of it and its ridge is in evening like Down against sky and sometimes I think How straight and firm that ridge, Down – sometimes I mistake a Down (which is also visible from thereabouts) for the barn – sometimes barn is exalted, sometimes Down humbled' (*FNB80*).

9-12. *Then the great down...black of night.* An alliterative crescendo dramatises the changing perspective and rising sense of menace: 'great'/'Grew', 'barn'/'black. The next quatrain's diminuendo begins with a flat repetition of 'barn'.

24. *So the barn was avenged.* The speaker's pride in 'new cautiousness' has gone before a fall. Thomas thought that the poem 'ought to have been 2 plain verses <u>implying</u> all I've had to explain' (letter to John Freeman, *ETFN* 38 [January 1998], 12). Yet this parable of perspective or proportion seems subtle enough. It applies both to making mountains out of molehills and to the reverse. Insofar as the down 'stored full to the ridge' figures the unconscious, its raids cannot be predicted. Smith comments: 'as the interchangeability of metaphor suggests, this is not a simple progress from error to enlightenment, but a recurrent confusion, intrinsic to the act of perception. "Critical eyes" develop their own species of error: scepticism can itself be an optical illusion' (*SS*, 102).

Ms: *M₁, BL.* **Published text:** *LP.* **Note:** R. George Thomas surmises that the 'first draft of this poem in the *M₁* notebook could be as early as 15 December 1914' [*CP1978*, 130]. For drafts, see *CP1978*, Appendix A. **Note on title:** Title is given in *BL*.

Sowing (69)
23 March 1915

In this 'perfect' lyric about perfection, physical and psychic ease seem one: an effect that recalls the integrated self in the eighth stanza of *The Other*. The 'hour' is 'tasted' and also a body that 'stretches'. Are the 'safely sown' seeds, on one level, Thomas 'early' poems? *Sowing* itself completes a sequence of four poems linked more than superficially by their form: quatrains whose line-length varies between two and four beats. Each poem has a distinctive rhythm. *Sowing*, in which sentence and stanza are co-extensive, counterpoints *But these things also* (a less positive Spring poem) in structure and cadence as well as mood. Its 'long stretched' assonances are still more contrary to the 'moan' of *The New House*.

10-11. *Nothing undone / Remained*: not identical with 'Nothing remained undone'.

13-16. *And now, hark...Saying good-night.* Smith comments: 'the synaesthesia is rounded off at the end in the appeal to "hark" (a much more kinetic act than merely hearing) which turns the rain even in its windless lightness into something which touches, as tear and kiss, in a language more intimate than that of speech. The "good-night" here is a kind of tucking-up after the physical satisfactions of labour' (*SS*, 144). Thomas was surely right to cut a fifth stanza: 'A kiss for all the seeds' / Dry multitude, / A tear at ending this / March interlude' (*BL*).

Ms: *BL.* **Published text:** *P.*

March the Third (70)

23 March 1915

Thomas was born on 3 March 1878. This poem has parallels with Robert Frost's 'The Valley's Singing Day' which ends with the poet-speaker saying, perhaps to an early-rising wife: 'I should be willing to say and help you say / That once you had opened the valley's singing day'. Both poems link a woman and birdsong with their own utterance. In *March the Third* 'she' announces and interprets 'this singing day'. As a birthday poem written shortly before Easter, *March the Third* subverts Christian celebration by making 'wild' and 'holy' interchangeable (cf. 'godsend'). A draft of lines 15-16 likens the birds' songs to 'canticles'. Thomas was dissatisfied with the poem: 'Perhaps I shall be able to mend March the 3rd. I know it must either be mended or ended' (*EF*, 132). His vein of quatrain poems may have worked itself out. The rhyme scheme seems over-emphatic.

Thomas writes of the chiffchaff: 'Nothing so convinces me, year after year, that Spring has come and cannot be repulsed, though checked it may be, as this least of songs. In the blasting or dripping weather which may ensue, the chiffchaff is probably unheard; but he is not silenced. I heard him on March 19 when I was fifteen, and I believe not a year has passed without my hearing him within a day or two of that date. I always expect him and always hear him' (*IPS*, 91). 'At the lower margin of the wood the overhanging branches form blue caves, and out of these emerge the songs of many hidden birds...All are blent into one seething stream of song. It is one song, not many. It is one spirit that sings' (*SC*, 21-2).

Ms: *BL.* **Published text:** *LP.* **Differences from *CP1978*:** title: March the Third *March the 3rd* 3-4 half-past [*BL*] *half past* [Farjeon typescript, *LP*] 6-8 When the birds do. I think they blend / Now better than they will when passed / Is this unnamed, unmarked godsend. *With the birds' songs. I think they blend / Better than in the same fair days / That shall pronounce the Winter's end.* 9 Or do all *Do men* 13 And when *When* 20 Because *Since now* **Note:** *CP1978* follows an Eleanor Farjeon typescript with ms. alterations [though with the title *March the Third*] rather than *BL/LP*. This edition prefers *BL/LP*, partly on aesthetic grounds; partly because, as in other cases, the possibility that Thomas re-thought his 'mending' of the poem [see general note above] cannot be discounted.

Two Pewits (70)

24 March 1915, revised 4 May 1915

According to Thomas, *Two Pewits* 'had to be as clear as glass' (*EF*, 134). His drafts (see *CP1978*, Appendix A) show how hard he worked at the poem – perhaps retuning his ear after *March the Third*. Clarity or apparent simplicity conceals complex art. With its single rhyme-sound and multiple refrains, *Two Pewits* displays a technical virtuosity to match that of the birds. 'Why? oh why', a yearning early love poem to Helen, mainly uses the same rhyme sound. It begins: 'O! dewy leaf that noddest high / 'Twixt the sod and Summer sky' (*NLW*, MS 22914C). Thomas's fascination with the aerial ballet of pewits (peewits/ lapwings) emerged as early as *The Woodland Life*: 'It is a beautiful sight to watch their facile turns of flight as each strives to surmount his rival. Now a couple seem as one bird, and again they part to soar and twist in opposite directions. As they race, the sun gleams on their crests and greenish bars, and the peewit swings in the air with his prowess of flight. In a straight steady motion, rare indeed with a peewit, their wings are soundless, but in the whirling dashes from side to side in combat or amorous display a strange wind-like rush is made as if their joints were stiff. Under a strong sun, when it is dazzling to look up, this rushing sound betrays the bird as it passes overhead' (*TWL*, 16).

The bird-artists, in their present-tense continuum, symbolise the liberation of creativity as realised through form. Fusing sound and movement, they differentiate Thomas-as-poet from his perplexed self: 'the ghost who wonders why', as he did in that youthful poem (see note on Thomas's 'ghosts', 202). For John F. Danby, *Two Pewits* is 'an exemplary instance of Thomas's polarised world...The birds sporting and crying midway between the moonlit sky and darkened earth intensify the light and darkness they reflect. In them, as if by their closer juxtaposition, the opposites are raised to a higher tension – a vivid, troubled, chequered activity against the discrete rest that sky or earth separately represent' ('Edward Thomas', *Critical Quarterly* 1 [1959], 309).

4. *dark surge*: 'black surf' in *M₁* and *BL* drafts. Cf. 'thine aery surge', Shelley, 'Ode to the West Wind'.

11. *ghost*: 'walker', then 'traveller' in the *M₁* drafts.

Ms: *M₁*, *BL*. **Published text:** *P*.

Will you come? (71)
25 March 1915

Most immediately, *Will you come?* is a love-song. Barker places it among those poems by Thomas that 'adapt the short song line and exploit its simplicity of cadence to good effect' (*JB*, 140). Yet, to quote John Pikoulis, the poem may equally be 'a direct and passionate appeal to the Muse' ('Edward Thomas as War Poet', *JB*, 123), and thus concern poetry's 'late' or reluctant advent as much as belated or frustrated love (see note on Thomas's love poems, 279). As a poem about poetry, or the inability to write it, *Will you come?* upsets the dynamic balance of *Two Pewits*. The poems are linked by the verb 'ride' and by chiaroscuro imagery; but the former, aligned with creative control, has ceased to govern the latter. The vocative case splits the double act of *Two Pewits*, and opposites no longer attract. The repeated 'come', the fruitless shifts of tense and time-setting, and the increasingly conditional mood dramatise an impasse. The reflexive dialectics between *Two Pewits* and *Will you come?* imply that form, like other kinds of integration, must be constantly renegotiated.

Ms: *M₁*, *BL*. **Published text:** *P*. **Differences from** *CP1978*: 25 come, [*BL*] *come* [*P*, *PTP*] The omission of the comma seems to be an error.

The Path (72)
26 March 1915

From Wick Green, Merfyn and Bronwen Thomas 'went daily to the junior school [of Bedales], walking and running down the steep Old Stoner Hill' by the path represented in the poem (*MT*, 13). In *The South Country* Thomas proposes 'a history of England written from the point of view of one parish, or town, or great house'. This would include 'the histories of roads':

> Every traveller in Hampshire remembers the road that sways with airy motion and bird-like curves down from the high land of clay and flint through the chalk to the sand and the river. It doubles round the head of a coombe, and the whole descent is through beech woods uninterrupted and all but impenetrable to the eye above or below except where once or twice it looks through an arrow [?a narrow] slit to the blue vale and the castled promontory of Chanctonbury twenty miles south-east. As the road is a mere ledge on the side of a very steep hill the woods below it hurry down to a precipitous pit full of the glimmering, trembling and murmuring of innumerable leaves and no sight or sound of men. It is said to have been made more than half a century ago to take the place of the rash straight coach road which now enters it near its base. (*SC*, 148-9)

1-3. *Running along a bank...there is a path*. As Thomas returns to blank verse and to the trope of the journey, he mimetically heightens the interplay between syntax and metre. The poem is itself a tricky 'path'. It begins by laying down fractal structures that will replicate themselves along the way, especially inversions of expected order: the first draft in *M₁* begins more conventionally: 'I know a path running along a bank, / A parapet that divides the level road / From the precipitous wood below'. Other structures initiated here are run-on lines; subordinate clauses placed in the foreground; an abrupt full stop. On one level, *The Path* presents a textual problem. The speaker, trying to make sense of it, stands in for both poet and reader.

3-15. *It serves / Children...year after year*. Motion says: 'Thomas clearly admires [the children's] youthful impatience with the second-hand, but he is careful to point out its vulnerability... [The] use of terms appropriate to military action ['parapet", 'invaded']... intensifies the menace of the surrounding wood. But having stressed this danger, Thomas goes on to insist that the children are more than a match for its encroachments... and are so closely identified with their path that they "wear it" as if they not only pressed it down but actually assumed it, like clothing' (*AM*, 160). For Smith: 'The aureate language with which the poet describes the path ("like silver", "gold, olive, and emerald", "silvered") suggests that he has travelled it and shares the children's values. They "wear" the path, but they have not "polished" it into insignificance; rather they have "silvered" it...endowing it with more not less value. Nevertheless, there is a hint of dispossession here too, for "the eye / Has but the road, the wood that overhangs / And underyawns it, and the path..."' (*SS*, 119-20).

17. *the eye*. In this visually oriented poem, the 'eye' that writes or reads must also negotiate an inner path between 'level road' and 'precipitous wood'. But it is hard to tell genuine vision (perhaps linked with the children's perspective) from mere appearance: the path only 'looks / As if it led on to some legendary / Or fancied place'. The reflexively 'sudden' ending leaves us with the riddle of 'where' the poem has actually 'led'.

Ms: *M₁*, *BL*. **Published text:** *P*.

The Wasp Trap (72)

27 March 1915

On 25 March Thomas had noted: 'Beautiful moonlight and in hedge glistens bottle put there long ago for wasps – old tins – old crockery opposite cottages – far [~~lakes~~] ponds etc.' (*FNB80*). A wasp trap is a sticky bottle or jam-jar that contains water to drown the wasps.

13-16. *For wasps meant....So glistening*. The 'loveliness' conferred by moonlight or imagination or the poem itself, like 'some legendary / Or fancied place' in *The Path*, may deceive (or we may want it to do so): the jar/star has been a death trap. 'Glistening' is not a wholly comfortable word, and 'From the dead apple-bough' anticipates a dark refrain in *The Gallows*.

Ms: *M₁*, *BL*. **Published text:** *LP*. **Note on title:** *CP1978* brackets the title; *CP2004* drops it. See Note on Text.

A Tale (73)

28 March 1915

The note that formed the basis of *The Wasp Trap* continues: 'Outside the [~~old~~] ruined cottage is periwinkle and when that is not flowering there is some blue and white china [?]peering/peeping among the leaves' (*FNB80*). In *BL* the poem as printed in this edition is cancelled, and the following version, dated 31 March, written below:

> Here once flint walls,
> Pump, orchard and wood pile stood.
> Blue periwinkle crawls
> From the lost garden down into the wood.
>
> The flowerless hours
> Of Winter cannot prevail
> To blight [?]those/these other flowers,
> Blue china fragments scattered, that tell the tale.

CP1978 prints both versions. That the cancelled version appears in *LP* suggests that Thomas had third thoughts. This edition prefers the cancelled version, which seems to have come quickly as a first draft in *M₁* before he began tinkering with the poem. Such a preference is supported by *LP* and by the only surviving typescript (*MET*). It also has an aesthetic basis. In the first two lines of the revised version, more is less: detail dissipates what 'ruined cottage' concentrates. Similarly, 'Blue periwinkle' is tautological (and pre-empts the adjective's later surprise), 'lost garden' superfluous. Conversely, omission of 'With flowers in its hair' removes a metaphor that, along with 'crawl', evokes the place's ghosts. In the revised second quatrain 'Of Winter' limits the scope of 'flowerless hours', while 'scattered' and the awkward 'cannot prevail / To blight' are also over-explanatory.

A Tale complements the aesthetic paradox of *The Wasp Trap* by posing questions about memory, art and Nature. The poem as commemorative 'tale' belongs to a series of traces left by the cottage and its inhabitants: 'the things are forgotten, and it is an aspect of them, a recreation of them, a finer development of them, which endures in the written words' (*RJ*, 298). Even so, the poem's 'endurance' is implicated in its dialectics. Thomas sets 'everlasting flowers' (not a wholly positive oxymoron) and, by analogy, poetic 'fragments' against the rooting periwinkle. The plant may be heading in the right or inevitable direction: 'into the wood'.

7. *everlasting*: a word that occurs only here and in *The Other* (see note, 161).

Ms: *M₁*, *BL*. **Published text**: *LP*. **Differences from** *CP1978*: see general note above.

Wind and Mist (73)

1 April 1915

In December 1909 the Thomases moved into a house (see *The New House*, 68, and notes) designed and built for them by Geoffrey Lupton, a young exponent of 'arts and crafts' principles. The house, in which they lived until August 1913, was at Wick (also Week or Wyke) Green on the Froxfield ridge above Steep. In the 1920s it acquired the name 'Red House'. The poem's autobiographical elements include the birth of Myfanwy Thomas (August 1910) and Thomas's breakdown in September 1911. He often complained about the house's position on top of the hangers: 'I am back again with the intolerable swishing of the trees in rain & wind which I have had ever since I came here last Christmas' (*LGB*, 206). Helen Thomas writes: 'somehow we could not love the house. The heavy oak was raw and new, and seemed to resent its servitude in beam and door, and with loud cracks would try to wrench itself free. There was nothing in that exposed position to protect us from the wind, which roared and shrieked in the wide chimneys, nor have I ever heard such furious rain as dashed vindictively against our windows...Often a thick mist enveloped us, and the house seemed to be standing on the edge of the world, with an infinity of white rolling vapour below us. There was no kindness or warmth or welcome about that house' (*HT*, 129). Helen's account may be coloured by Edward's writings, but Wick Green evidently became inseparable from the subjectivities of their time there. It shaped Thomas's depiction of Niflheim, cloud-world of the Nordic gods, in *Norse Tales*, and the myth may add resonance to the poem: 'The rain up here is incredible. It is like living before the creation, like the Niflheim that men ultimately emerged from: – when will they come?' (*LGB*, 226-7). In *Norse Tales* King Gangler 'remembers' an experience that helps him to understand Niflheim:

> He had just stepped out of his house after a night of rain and wind...
> Below him was the steep hill on the top of which stood his house, but
> the hill was blotted out by mist. Through the mist he could see moun-
> tains which he had never seen before, but either they, or he and his
> house, were moving...Then as he stood still thinking, he saw that the
> mountains were clouds. His house and the little piece of ground where
> he was standing seemed to be all that was left of the earth. The night's
> storm had washed away all the rest, and there he was shipwrecked in a
> sea of clouds and mist, rocking and swirling round about. This sea must
> have been like Niflheim. (*NT*, 12)

Like *Up in the Wind*, *Wind and Mist* has a generic affinity with Robert Frost's blank-verse dialogues. The parallels include people talking at cross-purposes; mingled 'inner' and 'outer weather' (to quote Frost's poem 'Tree at My Window'); the framework of a place or situation being explained to an outsider; deceptively simple speech. But *Wind and Mist* is more symbolic, less documentary, than Frost's eclogues, and closer to the poet's lyric voice(s). Thomas adapts Frostian structures, including the monosyllabic line, to create a psychodrama that, like some of his lyrics, might be set alongside Sylvia Plath's anatomies of mental breakdown. 'View' (lines 1 and 4) is a key word. The house, as analogue for the self, is looked both *from* and *at*; and the resultant 'views' or 'worlds' can differ as much as 'heaven' and 'chaos surging back'. The first speaker, partly Thomas's less disturbed or pre-breakdown 'Other', reads the landscape as an English microcosm (lines 6-8). The 'wind and mist' that dominate the main speaker's retrospect and introspection symbolise a double assault on the 'firm ground' of the self. Thomas represents cognitive collapse as confusion of the 'eye' followed by confusion of the ear (perhaps hearing voices). 'Mist' or 'cloud' denotes dissociation from 'reality'; 'wind', possession by another reality.

16-17. *Sometimes a man feels proud...one mighty thought'*. This echoes the Faustian fantasy of *Ambition* (see note, 191). In lines 60-1 such subjectivism assumes a delusive, paranoid shape: 'There were whole days and nights when the wind and I / Between us shared the world, and the wind ruled'.

25. *a castle in Spain*. Thomas may have recollected a drawing by his friend James Guthrie: 'Look again at his "Castle in Spain"; how it is perched up above that might of forest like a child that has climbed whence it cannot descend' (Thomas's preface to James Guthrie, *A Second Book of Drawings* [Edinburgh & London: T.N. Foulis, 1908]).

26-8. *I have thought...lived there then'*. In November 1906 Thomas wrote of Berryfield Cottage: 'We are now become people of whom passers by stop to think: How fortunate are they within those walls. I know it. I have thought the same as I came to the house & forgot it was my own' (*LGB*, 126).

46. *The clay first broke my heart, and then my back*. 'The garden improves but the clay breaks first the back & then the heart' (*LGB*, 211).

48-51. *a child / Was born...groans'*. The birth was difficult, and baby Myfanwy later contracted a mysterious illness. She recovered, but the period of anxiety 'more than ever increased our growing dislike of [the house]' (*HT*, 130). This passage conveys a peculiarly depressive state ('grey mind').

54. *cloud castle*. Thomas was a compulsive cloud-watcher: 'Round upon round [the hill] rose up, nodding but secure, until its summit overhung the rocky base and on this ledge was the likeness of a wall and turret in ruins. Such a castle it might have been as a child draws with its eyes out of nothing, when it reads for the first time of the Castle Perilous or Joyous Gard, set far above the farms and churches and factories of this world... And this mount, this mountain forest and overhanging brow, this incredibly romantic ruin upon the shelf of it, were built out of cloud in the violet western sky' (*CC*, 3-4).

54-68. *I had forgot the wind...wind and mist*. As with 'mist', 'earth' and 'cloud' in lines 35-43, the repeated words – often placed at the end of end-stopped lines as if blocking progress – dramatise obsession. The speaker's narrative tics signal that his neurosis continues: 'Pray do not let me get on to the wind'.

59. *quite unreal.* Despite his ironically phrased paranoia, the speaker, unlike his interlocutor (whose sanity approaches banality) or 'the house-agent's young man', may have learned something about 'reality'.

63. *My past and the past of the world were in the wind.* The other speaker projects the passing of time and the processing of memory on to a contrastingly harmonious vista (lines 9-12).

72-3. *would...could...should.* The modal verbs here echo the last quatrain of *The New House*, but with a more positive twist as befits the speaker's desire to 'try the house once more'.

Ms: *BL*. **Published text**: *AANP, LP*. **Differences from** *CP1978*: 16 proud of *proud at* [misprint in *AANP*, probably owing to 'at' in line above, corrected in *CP1928*] 43 *'You had a garden* dropped down a space in *CP1978* as in *BL* **Note**: in l.64 *LP* and *CP1944* print 'may' rather than 'will' [*BL, AANP*].

A Gentleman (75)

2 April 1915

Another poem of contrapuntal voices, *A Gentleman* takes a socio-linguistic approach to different 'views': to perception and 'judgment'. Although the latter seemingly goes against the judgmental 'stranger', we are invited to read between 'the Gypsy dame's' lines. In *The Happy-Go-Lucky Morgans* Mr Torrance recalls a similarly ambiguous character-witness: 'The Gypsy [here an inn-keeper's wife] was a most Christian body. She used to treat with unmistakeable kindness, whenever he called at the inn, a gentleman who was notoriously an atheist and teetotaler. When asked upbraidingly why, she said: "He seems a nice gentleman, and as he is going to a place where there won't be many comforts, I think we ought to do our best to make this world as happy as possible for him' (*HGLM*, 132). Smith observes that, for all Thomas's 'anxiety about being an "isolate self-considering brain", few collections of verse can have so many narratives of conversation and encounter, more vocatives, reported speech, or direct celebrations of the unique quiddity and otherness of other creatures and people' (*SS*, 159). Thomas was often an eavesdropper at 'inns': a passage in *The South Country* records an interchange between 'three labourers and the landlord... heated in conversation about some one not present' (*SC*, 246-9). In *A Gentleman*, as in *Man and Dog*, pentameter couplets provide a grid that casts the sentence-sounds of casual conversation into revealing postures. Formally, the poem functions as a bridge between *Wind and Mist* and *Lob*.

Ms: *M₁, BL*. **Published text**: *P*.

Lob (76)

3, 4 April 1915

Lob was 'very close to [Edward's] heart', and well received by his literary circle: Thomas told Eleanor Farjeon: 'Bottomley...agrees with everyone about "Lob"' (*EF*, 173, 147). Frost declared: 'The goodness is in Lob. You are a poet or you are nothing...I like the first half of Lob best: it offers something more like action with the different people coming in and giving the tones of speech.

But the long paragraph is a feat. I never saw anything like you for English' (*RFET*, 43). Edward Garnett found *Lob* 'a little breathless or rough' on the first reading, but Thomas confidently defended his methods: 'I am doubtful about the chiselling you advise. It would be the easiest thing in the world to clean it all up & trim it & have every line straightforward in sound & sense, but it would not really improve it. I think you read too much with the eye perhaps. If you *say* a couplet like "If they had reaped their dandelions and sold / Them fairly, they could have afforded gold" I believe it is no longer awkward. Then "because" at the end of a line looks awkward if one is accustomed to an exaggerated stress on the rhyme word which I don't think necessary' (*LEG*, 29).

Lob is as central to Thomas's "English" explorations as *The Other* to his poems of the inner road. Perhaps because it takes political nationalism to raise folklore's status, relatively few poems in the tradition of post-Romantic European cultural nationalism draw on English folkloric materials. But Thomas had long noted Yeats's exploitation of Irish lore and legend (see Introduction, 20); and William Morris, with his medieval and Nordic mythic scenarios, was a common literary ancestor. Another influence on Thomas was Charles M. Doughty (1843-1926), best known as the author of *Arabia Deserta*. He emulated neither Doughty's archaic vocabulary nor his jingoistic patriotism. Yet his massive epic poem *The Dawn in Britain* (1906-7), set in Celtic-Roman Britain, touched some (perhaps Anglo-Welsh) chord: '[Doughty's] picture of early Britain, vast, wild, sunlit, coloured, full of the songs of birds, with here and there a town and here and there the burial mounds of princes and unknown men – that picture would alone have made the poem deserve an undying name. It is a little matter, but I had no worthy sense of the rich great age of this home of my race until I found it here.' Thomas dreamed that the poem might give children 'such an harmonious view of early history and folklore and ancient monuments and the physical beauty of Britain as we can only grope after' (review of *The Dawn in Britain* V and VI, *Daily Chronicle*, 7 February 1907). Forced to admit, 'positively Doughty is an antiquarian', he went on praising him: 'Doughty is great. I see his men & women whenever I see noble beeches, as in Savernake Forest, or tumuli or old encampments, or the line of the Downs like the backs of a train of elephants, or a few firs on a hilltop' (*LGB*, 118-19, 135).

Although Leeds and Yorkshire are mentioned, the poem's "England" is Thomas's 'South Country': 'In a sense this country is all "carved out of the carver's brain" and has not a name. This is not the South Country which measures about two hundred miles from east to west and fifty from north to south. In some ways it is incomparably larger than any country that was ever mapped, since upon nothing less than the infinite can the spirit disport itself. In other ways it is far smaller – as when a mountain with tracts of sky and cloud and the full moon glass themselves in a pond, a little pond' (*SC*, 11). Yet Thomas's Welsh and western horizons make Wiltshire (which also features in *The Other*), rather than the Home Counties, his spiritual epicentre. He told W.H. Hudson: 'Wiltshire is almost my native county as my grandparents moved there [to Swindon] before my father left home and I spent all my holidays there for nearly twenty years' (*ETFN* 52 [August 2004], 8). He returned to Wiltshire while writing a book on his first literary love, Richard Jefferies: 'the genius, the human expression, of this country, emerging from it, not to be detached from it any more than the curves of some statues from their maternal stone' (*RJ*, 1). For Thomas, 'Jefferies came to express part of this silence of uncounted generations' (*RJ*, 20). His topography of the Jefferies country stresses its history (Celtic, Roman, Saxon) and pre-history: 'tumuli and earthworks that make the earth look old, like the top bar of a stile, carved by saunterers, bored by wasps, grooved and scratched and polished again' (*RJ*, 5).

Among Thomas's many visits to Wiltshire was a cycling tour in May 1911 with his son Merfyn. His notebook for the tour (*FNB53*), on which he drew for *The Icknield Way*, is headed: 'Marlboro', Pewsey, Amesbury, Salisbury, Tisbury'. One evening he visited Stonehenge (which he had adored as a child): 'sky very light and clear…I walk fast with a strange excitement under this sky and at length see 13 or 14 dark pillars [?] with great crosspieces and touching them on right a huge mound – Stonehenge'. Thomas's most recent field trip to Wiltshire had been in October 1914. He stayed in Avebury ('a village of obscure paths and roads that dwindle into paths'), and watched troops mobilising on Salisbury Plain: 'At Ludgershall I began to see soldiers and nothing else…soldiers in motors, on horses, driving artillery waggons, walking, everywhere, quiet whether busy or not…Suddenly at the end of the street is the Down or rather the camp – hundreds of bell-tents in rows, and marquees, and lines of mostly pack horses tethered' (letter to Helen, 5 October 1914, *NLW*).

Scattered through Thomas's prose are many prototypes of 'Lob' as an old countryman (see notes on *Man and Dog*, 185). He turns up first as 'A Wiltshire Molecatcher': 'It may be that he carries secrets which shall die with him; so, at least, his morose reserve suggests…Seated in the mound, between high double hedges, at noon over his "dinner", luxuriously pillowed among lush grass and golden pilewort, with his back leaning against an elm, he will converse intelligently on subjects that might have been deemed beyond his care, with a sharpness of sense and economy of words that bespeak a healthy mind cleansed by the pure hillside air' (*TWL*, 49-50). He becomes a wandering 'Umbrella Man': 'Every village, almost every farmhouse, especially if there were hops on the land, he knew, and could see with his blue eyes as he remembered them and spoke their names. I never met a man who knew England as he did' (*SC*, 192). Thomas can be sentimental about elderly 'Earth Children' (a chapter-title in *The Heart of England*) of both sexes. But he had been educated in rural culture by David Uzzell, his friend since childhood, who laid the deep foundations for 'Lob': 'I called [him] Dad, in the Wiltshire style, almost from the first day. I remember him first as a stiff straight man, broad-shouldered and bushy bearded, holding his rod out and watching his float very intently…He knew the names of most birds and could imitate their cries: his imitations of the jackdaw calling his name, and of the young rook crying and swallowing a worm at the same time, were wonderful. The flowers, too, he knew, both the common pretty flowers and those whose virtues he had read about in Culpeper's *Herbal*. With dried and powdered dock root and with extracts of leaves, flowers or bark, he composed dark medicinal-looking draughts' (*CET*, 129-31).

Thomas's fascination with the 'knowledge' possessed by old country people goes beyond the sociological approach of 'George Bourne' (George Sturt) in

The Bettesworth Book (see note, 185), and even Hudson's more holistic vision in his Wiltshire-based *A Shepherd's Life* (1910). It was a literary impulse like that which sent Yeats 'down into Connaught to sit by turf fires' and so gain access to 'the unwritten tradition which binds the unlettered...to the beginning of time and to the foundation of the world' (Yeats, *Essays and Introductions* [London: Macmillan, 1961], 4-6). The step from 'Lob' as rural archetype to 'Lob' as poetic tradition is clear in this passage where an exile from the country-side recalls 'an old, old man': 'You may be sure there were hundreds like him in Shakespeare's time and in Wordsworth's, and if there aren't a good sprinkling of them, generation after generation, I do not know what we shall come to, but I have my fears. I warrant, every man who was ever any good had a little apple-faced man or woman like this somewhere not very far back in his pedigree. Where else will he get his endurance, his knowledge of the earth, his feeling for life and for what that old man called God? When a poet writes, I believe he is often only putting into words what another such old man puzzled out among the sheep in a long lifetime' (*TC*, 9).

Thomas wrote *Lob* when completing *This England: An Anthology from her Writers* (see note, 165), conceived as a riposte to propagandist anthologies like *Songs and Sonnets for England in Wartime* (1914). He began a review of 'Anthologies and Reprints': 'The worst of the poetry being written today is that it is too deliberately, and not inevitably, English. It is for an audience: there is more in it of the shouting of rhetorician, reciter, or politician than of the talk of friends and lovers'. His article 'War Poetry', printed in the same issue of *Poetry and Drama* (2, 8 [December 1914]), similarly insists: 'I need hardly say that by becoming ripe for poetry the poet's thoughts may recede far from their original resemblance to all the world's, and may seem to have little to do with daily events.' *This England* has seven sections: This England, Merry England, Her Sweet Three Corners, London, Abroad and Home Again, Great Ones, The Vital Commoners. Thomas's brief 'Note' cuts to the chase: 'This is an anthology from the work of English writers rather strictly so called. Building round a few most English poems like "When icicles hang by the wall", – excluding professedly patriotic writing because it is generally bad and because indirect praise is sweeter and more profound, – never aiming at what a committee from Great Britain and Ireland might call complete, – I wished to make a book as full of English character and country as an egg is of meat. If I have reminded others, as I did myself continually, of some of the echoes called up by the name of England, I am satisfied.'

This England includes extracts from (among others) Anon., Chaucer, Shakespeare, Browne, Walton, Cobbett, Blake, Wordsworth, Keats, Clare, Hazlitt, Borrow, Dickens, Morris, Jefferies, Hardy, Doughty and Hudson. Thomas saw poetry as quintessential, and picked the kinds of prose that fed his poetry. In his essay 'England' he says of Walton's *Compleat Angler*: 'Since the war began I have not met so English a book, a book that filled me so with a sense of England, as this, though I have handled scores of deliberately patriotic works... In Walton's book I touched the antiquity and sweetness of England – English fields, English people, English poetry, all together' (*LS*, 109). That might be a template for *The Manor Farm* and *Haymaking*, the poems he sneaked into

This England under his pseudonym 'Edward Eastaway'. In *Lob* Thomas does the opposite: he sneaks *This England* into a poem, anthologises the anthology. At once *ars poetica* and cultural manifesto, this quirky quest-poem reaches more deeply into "England" than do 'deliberately patriotic works'. What Thomas says of Keats applies to himself: 'English literature, English poetry, the Muse of his native land, that "first-born on the mountains", as he calls her, was a main part of what England meant for Keats' (*K*, 16-17). *Lob* brings to the surface the historical sense of English poetry that permeates his poems. Yet this involves a test as well as a quest. Poetry, like other traditions, faces into 'No Man's Land' (see Introduction, 18).

Intermediary between 'Lob' as rural archetype and 'Lob' as poetic tradition is 'Lob' as folklore. Besides anthologising traditional songs (see note, 166), Thomas had compiled *Celtic Stories* (1911) and *Norse Tales* (1912). Closer to *Lob* is a more original work, *Four-and-Twenty Blackbirds*: 'I wish I had gone on where the Proverbs left off. Probably I never shall, unless "Lob" is the beginning' (*EF*, 172). In *Four-and-Twenty Blackbirds*, ostensibly a children's book, Thomas invents absurd origins for proverbs such as 'It's all my eye and Betty Martin'. He called this enterprise 'rather English, I fancy' (quoted, [ed.] Edward Garnett, *Selected Poems of Edward Thomas* [Gregynog Press, 1927], xii). But the tales eclectically relish English, Scottish, and Welsh place names and personal names. Proverbs transmit collective wisdom as idiom, as proto-poems. When Frost says 'I never saw anything like you for English', he recognises that *Lob* is a self-delighting linguistic *tour de force* marked by Thomas's attraction to demotic speech as the root of poetry. 'Lob', intriguingly, 'has thirteen hundred names for a fool'. The narrator, the 'squire's son', and 'Lob' as proverb-coiner all use proverbial expressions in the subversive spirit of 'Lydia Fairweather', a gypsy who speaks solely in proverbs. She replies to a vicar's complaint that this 'puts an end to conversation': 'You do no harm, though: you leap like a cock at a blackberry. Your wit's as long in coming as Cotswold barley, and without it you might as well live on Tewkesbury mustard. Were you born at Wotton under Weaver where God came never?' (*FTB*, 109-10).

'Lob' is a folk-name, more common in northern England, linked with Hob (hobgoblin) and Robin Goodfellow/Puck. The Fairy in *A Midsummer's Night's Dream* addresses Puck as 'thou lob of spirits', and asks this 'shrewd and knavish sprite': 'are you not he / That frights the maidens of the villagery; / Skim milk, and sometimes labour in the quern, / And bootless makes the breathless house-wife churn...?' In Rudyard Kipling's *Puck of Pook's Hill* (1906), Puck, 'the oldest old thing in England', represents continuity, the rural basis of English life, and the national *genius loci*. The attribution of 'Lob' to a spirit implies that he is not a small fairy, but of human size. Sometimes he is said to be the giant son of a witch and the Devil. Helpful as well as mischievous, he receives milk and a place by the fire for his services. In Milton's 'L'Allegro' the 'lubber fiend' or 'drudging goblin' lies down after threshing corn all night: 'And, stretched out all the chimney's length, / Basks at the fire his hairy strength' (see 'Lob-lie-by-the-fire', l.56). The etymology of 'Lob'/'lubber' seems to imply heaviness or dullness, but Thomas takes the name's associations and translations beyond any previous usage.

Alun Howkins relates Thomas's construction of 'Lob' to the historical moment when "village England" became an object of nostalgia; when 'Hodge', the stereotypical lumpen-labourer, was replaced by an archetypal repository of vanishing lore (see 'From Hodge to Lob: Reconstructing the English farm labourer, 1870-1914', in eds, Malcolm Chase and Ian Dyck, *Living and Learning* [Menston: Scolar Press, 1996], 218-35). Raymond Williams argues that Thomas romanticises the rural worker to create a dubious mystique of Englishness: 'All countrymen, of all conditions and periods, are merged into a singular legendary figure. The varied idioms of specific country communities – the flowers, for example, have many local names – are reduced not only to one "country" idiom but to a legendary, timeless inventor, who is more readily seen than any actual people' (*The City and the Country* [London: Chatto & Windus, 1973], 257). For David Gervais, however: 'What redeems [*Lob*] and distinguishes it from other exponents of "Englishness", is that it is honest enough not to pretend to some privileged vision of England...The poem is too subtle and too light to give us the option of falling back on words like "nation" and "race" to explain everything. We end simply in Wiltshire, with particular places and things, reminded of the battles still to come in Flanders' (*Literary Englands* [Cambridge: Cambridge University Press, 1993], 63). Yet Gervais, like Williams, sees Thomas as failing to 'give the social and political England of his time an adequate place in his verse' (63-4). According to Smith, the poem knows this, since it effectively 'admits' that 'Lob' is obsolescent or 'ghostly': 'the defiance [of "He never will admit he is dead"] is really the posthumous bravado of a ghost refusing his own mortality...the intangibility and evasiveness of Lob becomes the figure of a larger loss. This spirit of England is already no more than an image within the brain, an illusory site for all that the wandering subject feels dispossessed of' (*SS*, 82).

Thomas belonged to a Zeitgeist that collected folksongs and folklore (the Folklore Society was founded in the year of his birth), interviewed old country people, and artificially returned to Nature. But he was critically alert both to the economics of the countryside and to the contradictions inherent in 'that cultivation of the instinctive and primitive which is the fine flower of a self-conscious civilisation, turning in disgust upon itself' (*TC*, 39). There is self-satire in his portrayal of the narrator who twice goes 'In search of something chance would never bring'. At one level, second time round, the narrator has become an anthropologist on a field trip, frustrated and teased by his informants, pre-empted by the old man's opinion of archaeologists: 'They...couldn't find it, by digging, anywhere' (lines 11-12). 'It' remains elusive, and (cf. *The Other*) the quest may constitute the discovery. Just as 'the naturalists' miss something in *The Unknown Bird*, so the narrator – on another level, a poet – may get further than academic findings. Or, given the nature of his attention to the 'squire's son' (part-based on Richard Jefferies), the poet may be a more sensitive anthropologist. Further, as Gervais notes, 'particularity' deflects rhetoric.

In attaching *Lob* to Wiltshire, more specifically to the Vale of Pewsey, Thomas elaborates his wartime notion 'that all ideas of England are developed, spun out, from [a local] centre into something large or infinite, solid or aëry' (*LS*, 111; see notes on *The Manor Farm*, and *Adlestrop*, 165, 177). As 'an idea of

England', and idea of poetry, *Lob* sets death against metamorphosis. This tension, which can be read as a critique rather than denial of modernity, does not evade history in the shape of war. 'Lob' is elusive, and the poem allusive, partly because the Great War, conjoined with modernity, raises difficult questions about cultural memory and about memory as poetry.

4. *sweet as any nut*: perhaps an echo of W.H. Davies, 'The Child and the Mariner': 'An old seafaring man was he; a rough / Old man, but kind; and hairy, like the nut / Full of sweet milk'.

9. *opened up the barrows*. This may allude to a group of barrows and tumuli a mile north of Alton Priors (see note on lines 14-17), which includes the long barrow Adam's Grave, formerly 'Woden's barrow', excavated in 1860. But 'opening up the barrows' also condenses the history of archaeological digs in Wiltshire, and its implications.

10. *while I was scaring sparrows*. Birds used to be 'scared' away from seeds with wooden clappers, songs and shouts – proverbially, a child's first employment. William Cobbett recalls in his autobiography, in a passage that Thomas chose for *This England*: 'My first occupation was, driving the small birds from the turnip seed, and the rooks from the pease' (*TE*, 163).

12. *couldn't find it, by digging*: 'of these many folds in our nature the face of the earth reminds us, and perhaps, even where there are no more marks visible upon the land than there were in Eden, we are aware of the passing of time in ways too difficult and strange for the explanation of historian and zoologist and philosopher' (*SC*, 152).

14-17. *three Manningfords…Alton Barnes and Alton Priors*. FNB53 contains jottings on the Manningfords. 'Those villages' are in the Vale of Pewsey. The Vale extends from Devizes in the west to Savernake Forest in the east. 'This is the ford of Manna's people, from a Saxon original Manningaford. Abbots is from the Abbey of St Peter at Winchester, Bohun is from Henry de Boun who owned the manor in 1212, Bruce is from Briouze in Normandy.' 'First recorded as Aweltun in 825, [Alton] means the settlement at the source of a river [Saxon awiell, tun]…Alton Barnes takes its name from the Berners family, who were Norman landowners…Alton Priors reminds us that the land here was once owned by the priory of St Swithun, Winchester' (Martyn Whittock, *Wiltshire Place-names: their origins and meanings* [Newbury: Countryside Books, 1997], 95, 11). See also John Chandler, *The Vale of Pewsey* (Bradford on Avon: Ex Libris Press, 1991, 2000). Thomas exploits the mingled repetition and difference in the names to dramatise the trickery of language and 'memory': the narrator remembers being unable to remember. The villages 'Lurking to one side' belong to a mysterious confusion of actual and imagined landscapes.

18-30. *All had their churches…gold*. Thomas describes a Wiltshire village as 'an archipelago of thatched cottages, sprinkled here and there, and facing all ways, alongside an almost equal number of roads, lanes, tracks, footpaths, and little streams, so numerous and interlaced that they seemed rather to cut it off from the world than to connect it' (*HGLM*, 264). The poem's sequestered villagers seem caught in limbo: able neither to engage with what 'the road' and 'aeroplanes' represent, nor to maintain their own mode of 'dwelling'. Shooting the weathercock, a traditionally foolish act like the feats of the men of Gotham (see note below), becomes a parable of cultural self-harm. Like the failure to 'reap dandelions' and 'sell them fairly', it suggests that 'the people' – not only Wiltshire villagers – do not truly value their assets. Thomas's joke may make a precise economic and political point about 'the death of rural England'. English agriculture had entered a long depression in the 1870s (see Introduction, 23), partly because the government allowed the market to be flooded with cheap American wheat. The narrator's (unexplained) return after 'Many years' may both reflect Thomas's visit to Wiltshire in October 1914, and imply that, with war compounding socio-economic problems, the quest for 'Lob' has acquired new urgency.

36. *old Bottlesford*. Bottlesford is the name of another village in the area.

38-40. *White Horse…Walker's Hill*. What Thomas calls 'that very tame White Horse above Alton Priors' (*IPS*, 15) is near Adam's Grave, and 'lies in a shallow dip between Walker's Hill and Milk Hill…in the midst of a group of barrows and tumuli' (Kate Bergamar, *Discovering Hill Figures* [Princes Risborough: Shire Publications, 1997], 60).

40-2. *A girl proposed…Marked on the maps'*. The 'girl' and Thomas are both up to 'roguery'. In this special form of 'mapping', Adam's Grave on Walker's Hill evokes 'Adam Walker' – primordial man – to symbolise how humanity 'marks' the earth and *vice versa*. 'You will find "Welsh Ways" all over England. Walkers or Workaway Hill, where the Ridgeway descends southward from Wansdyke to the Pewsey Valley, is said to be a corruption of Weala-wege, and to have been called Walcway (or Welshway) by a shepherd not long ago' (*IW*, 22).

44-6. *Who loved wild bird…loved the earth*. His 'loves' identify the 'squire's son' with Richard Jefferies. Fishing was the only blood sport ever practised by Thomas, who ironically notices 'the sportsman's tenuous emotion of loving the hare that he has killed' (*RJ*, 38), but he accepted the contradiction built into any countryman's love of the earth: 'Where men and children are at close grips with nature, and have to wrest a living from the soil or the sea, there is apt to hide, like an imprisoned toad, at the very roots of their philosophy, if it does not flap like a crow in the topmost branches, a feeling that all the life that is not with them – as horse and sheep and cow are – is against them…[Jefferies] arose out of the earth, and he had its cruelty' (*RJ*, 34). See note on Thomas and hunting (178).

51. *His home was where he was free*. See general note to *Home* (197). This semi-paradox alludes to "liberty" as a peculiarly English value ('the free-born Englishman'), pushed to the margins by nineteenth-century capitalism. The 'wild', wandering aspect of 'Lob' associates that shift with Enclosure.

53. *Does he keep clear old paths…?* 'Untrodden but indelible old roads, worn by hoofs and the naked feet and the trailing staves of long dead generations'; 'East, south, and west flint-diggers' cartways, old roads, and hares' paths lead over the downs' (*RJ*, 4, 12).

56-7. *Lob-lie-by-the-fire / Came in my books*. In Beaumont and Fletcher's *The Knight of the Burning Pestle* (III, 423-6) the Citizen's wife informs her husband: 'there's a pretty tale of a Witch, that had the divels marke about her, God blesse us, that had a Giant to her sonne, that was cal'd *Lob-lie-by-the-fire*'. But this figure seems more likely to be first met in a children's book like Juliana Horatia Ewing's *Jackanapes, etc.* (1892), which includes the tale of 'Lob-lie-by-the-fire or the Luck of Lingborough' with the gloss that he is 'a rough kind of Brownie or House Elf'. Walter de la Mare wrote two poems called 'Lob-Lie-by-the-Fire'.

58-78. He has been in England...he might say. The verbal bravura of this passage makes its point. As Adam-like namer of flowers, birds and places, and translator of birdsong, 'Lob' becomes more openly a portrait of the artist. He rhymes 'cherry' with 'merry', finds metaphors for natural phenomena, and releases the latent qualities of 'English'. As naturalised man, 'Lob' bestows in turn names that humanise Nature ('Bridget-in-her-bravery') or link the animate and inanimate ('the Hog's Back'). All this implies that 'word' and 'thing' cohabit on earth (see note on *Old Man*, 151).

61. And in a tender mood he, as I guess. Replying to criticism from John Freeman, Thomas wrote: 'The...line is, I fear, echoed from a line in Adonais "He, as I guess, / Had looked on Nature's naked loveliness". But isn't it all right or mayn't Lob have been tender or have had a mood?' (*ETFN 38* [January 1998], 12). Like Shelley, he is also echoing Chaucer's recurrent tag and line-ending, e.g., 'But Venus is it soothly, as I gesse' (*Knight's Tale*, 1102). The phrase highlights Chaucerian qualities in Thomas's own couplets and his casting of *Lob* into this foundational English metre. 'At hawthorn-time in Wiltshire travelling' updates the start of *The Canterbury Tales* (a poem from which *This England* takes seven passages), with Chaucer himself now an object of pilgrimage. After 1.98, *BL* brackets the following lines, probably cut as over-explicit: 'Chaucer and Wordsworth and all true poets were / His friends, and Cobbett, Bunyan and Latimer'. (*This England* contains down-to-earth extracts from sermons by the martyred reformer Hugh Latimer.) In *M₁* Walton appears in the list of literary worthies, and 'Bunyan' replaces [Gilbert] 'White'. Cobbett eventually found his way into *Haymaking*.

59. 'By the way, we call wild cherry trees in these parts "Merry Trees"' (letter to W.H. Hudson, 2 May 1907, *ETFN 52* [August 2004], 7).

65-6. old herbal Gerard...Traveller's-joy. This England contains an extract from the *Herball* (1597) of John Gerard (1545-1612): 'The Traveller's Joy is found in the borders of fields among thorns and briers, almost in every hedge, as you go from Gravesend to Canterbury in Kent; in many places of Essex, and in most of these southerly parts about London, but not in the north of England that I can hear of...It is called commonly *Viorna quasi vias ornans*, of decking and adorning ways and hedges, where people travel, and thereupon I have named it The Traveller's Joy' (*TE*, 97).

67-70. Our blackbirds...rejoiced. Here birdsong, a proverb, and a poem by Hardy freely associate in the style of *Four-and-Twenty Blackbirds*. A male version of the proverb is more usual: 'Like lucky John (Jan) Toy – lost a shilling and found a tuppenny loaf'. Hardy's 'The Spring Call', included in *This England*, celebrates regional versions of the blackbird's call. It begins: 'Down Wessex way, when spring's a-shine, / The blackbird's "pret-ty de-urr!" / In Wessex accents marked as mine / Is heard afar and near.'

73. the Hog's Back. By repeating the name, the speaker endorses its fitness. 'I came in sight of the Hog's Back, by which I must go to Farnham. That even, straight ridge pointing westward, and commanding the country far away on either side, must have had a road along it since man went upright, and must

219

continue to have one so long as it is a pleasure to move and to use the eyes together' (*IPS*, 72).

74. *Mother Dunch's Buttocks*: the Sinodun Hills (a Celtic name), also known as the Wittenham Clumps, Berkshire Bubs or Bumps. 'Mother Dunch's Buttocks' comes from the Dunch family who once owned the land. Thomas refers to 'the clear heavings of the Sinodun Hills' (*IW*, 159). When sending *Lob* to *Blackwood's Magazine* Thomas substituted 'Happersnapper Hanger' for 'Mother Dunch's Buttocks', lest 'the disgusting line' should cause problems (*EF*, 145). The poem was still rejected.

76. *Totteridge and Totterdown and Juggler's Lane*. Totteridge is in Hertfordshire, Totterdown in Jefferies country 'where the Ermine Street...crosses the Ridgeway' (*RJ*, 3). Thomas himself partially "explains" Juggler's Lane: 'If [old winding roads] go out of use in a new or changed civilisation, they may still be frequented by men of the most primitive habit. All over England may be found old roads, called Gypsy Lane, Tinker's Lane, or Smuggler's Lane; east of Calne, in Wiltshire, is a Juggler's Lane; and as if the ugliness of the "uggle" sound pleased the good virtuous country folk, they have got a Huggler's Hole a little west of Semley and south of Sedgehill in the same county' (*IW*, 3).

77-8. *Why Tumbling Bay...he might say*. 'We have need of men like that to explain "Eggpie" Lane near the village of Sevenoaks Weald, or Tumbling Bay in a neighbouring parish far inland' (Thomas's preface to Isaac Taylor, *Words and Places* [London: J.M. Dent, 1911], ix). Here Thomas is criticising amateur etymologists, country people who have lost touch with their traditions. He says: 'Better pure imagination than rash science in handling place names.' At the point where even philologists must bow to the 'incalculable', 'Lob' or poetry does better: 'Studies like Canon Taylor's can only feed the roots of the imagination; they can colour or shape the flowers only by means beyond anticipation or estimate...Association is as strange as life: it absolutely distinguishes "guitar" from "catarrh", and helps to make the gulf between Amberley and Anerley' (ix-x). The name 'Tumbling Bay', that of a house in Seal parish near Tonbridge, remains 'incalculable'. See note on *If I should ever by chance* (285).

79-88. *'But little he says...forgot and done.* The contrast between 'Lob' and 'the sage' is not a piece of anti-intellectual primitivism but a comment on cultural and creative processes. It echoes two of Thomas's dicta on poetry, quoted above: 'When a poet writes, I believe he is often only putting into words what another such old man puzzled out among the sheep in a long lifetime'; 'I need hardly say that by becoming ripe for poetry the poet's thoughts may recede far from their original resemblance to all the world's'. Reviewing John Davidson's *The Triumph of Mammon*, Thomas says: 'We ought to guess the philosophy from the poetry no more than we guess the athlete's meals from the length of his leap' *(Daily Chronicle*, 30 April 1907); and, in another review of new verse: 'Poetry is a natural growth, having more than a superficial relation to roses and trees and hills. However airy and graceful it may be in foliage and flower, it has roots deep in a substantial past. It springs apparently from an occupation of the land, from long, busy, and quiet tracts of time, wherein a man or a nation may find its own soul. To have a future, it must have had a past' *(Daily Chronicle*, 8 February 1904).

85-6. Proverbial: 'Quietness is best, as the fox said when he bit the cock's head off'.

90-1. Proverbial: 'to skin a flint (stone) for a penny, and break a knife of twelve-pence' (hence 'skinflint'). In the poem's economics 'someone else's wife' contrasts with 'Jan Toy': another opposition between price and value.

96-8. *This is tall Tom...when icicles hung by the wall.* The preface to *This England* (see above) indicates that 'When icicles hang by the wall' from *Loves Labour's Lost*, which Thomas also quotes in *The Owl*, was central to the anthology's conception. Why he thought this wintry song 'most English' may be judged from its use here to clinch the transactions between environment, demotic culture and high literature that characterise *Lob*. It matters that 'Tom' and Shakespeare should 'talk'. Thomas had wanted to write 'a book on Shakespeare [giving] a background of the literature, social life and natural life, folk lore, and legend, and mythical natural history, and show how Shakespeare's pictures of nature and country life sprang from it' (*SL*, 89).

99. *Herne the Hunter.* The Shakespearean motif continues. Thomas first wrote about Herne in his short guide book, *Windsor Castle*: 'It is supposed to have been in [Elizabeth I's] childhood, in her father's reign, that the events which led to the story of Herne the hunter took place:

> There is an old tale goes, that Herne the hunter,
> Sometime a keeper here in Windsor forest,
> Doth all the winter-time, at still midnight,
> Walk round about an oak, with great ragg'd horns;
> And there he blasts the tree, and takes the cattle,
> And makes milch-kine yield blood, and shakes a chain
> In a most hideous and dreadful manner.

So speaks Mistress Page in opening her plans for the discomfiture of Falstaff. It is said that a yeoman hanged himself on a tree for fear of the king after hunting in the Forest without leave. The tree was cursed, and a ghostly stag haunted the place and butted at the tree and breathed smoke and fire as it tore the roots. There was also a story that Herne was a keeper and went mad after being gored by a stag. He tied a pair of antlers upon his head, ran naked through the Forest, and hanged himself on the tree near Shakespeare's Oak in the Home Park, which was called Herne's Oak for centuries' (*Windsor Castle* [London: Blackie, 1910], 51-2). Mistress Page's speech (*Merry Wives of Windsor* IV, iv) is in *This England*.

104-12. *When there were kings in Kent... So they were married.* Although 'our Jack' is not named until l.123, Thomas is already drawing on the English cycle of "Jack tales": 'Jack is not the dull moral prince of the fairy tale, but rather the folk hero, sharp, gaining his ends unscrupulously or even immorally, often through luck rather than virtue, often too lazy to work at ordinary pursuits. He is a trickster, or he is the clever younger son, or he is the unpromising hero, but always he is destined to turn events to his own account rather than having them shaped in his favour ' ([ed.] Maria Leach, *Standard Dictionary of Folklore, Mythology, and Legend* [New York: Funk & Wagnalls, 1949-50], 535). In 'The Princess of Canterbury' Jack, a foolish shepherd, wins the princess by passing various tests, one of which is to stay awake all night by her bedside. He entertains her by pretending to catch from his pocket fish that he has already placed there. In 'Lazy Jack' Jack takes a series of jobs to support his widowed mother but always loses or spoils, through his folly, the payments-in-kind he receives. Having dragged a piece of mutton home on a string, he promises to carry the next day's wages on his shoulders. The wages prove to be a donkey, and the sight of Jack with the donkey makes the deaf and dumb daughter of a rich man laugh for the first time in her life. Her father has promised that the man who achieves this feat shall marry her. (See, ed., Joseph Jacobs, *English Fairy Tales*, 1890-4 [repr. Bodley Head, 1968], 283-5, 95-6.)

113-22. *And while he was a little cobbler's boy...scraped his boots*. This "stupid ogre" tale, from Charlotte S. Burne's *Shropshire Folk-lore* (1883), appears in *This England*. Burne's version ends: 'But where [the giant] put down his load there stands the Wrekin to this day, and even the earth he scraped off his boots was such a pile that it made the little Ercall by the Wrekin side' (*TE*, 68-9). In Burne, the cobbler is a man. The change to a 'boy' accentuates the David and Goliath element, reinforced later by 'as Jack the giant-killer / He made a name'. As well as the archetypal invader, this giant may be a specific image of 'the German threat' (*WC*, 219-20).

123. *Gotham's sages*. The proverbial expression 'as wise as a man of Gotham' derives from tales based on the fabled idiocy of a village in Nottinghamshire. The men's exploits include hedging the cuckoo and drowning an eel (see Jacobs, *English Fairy Tales*, 279-82). In a nursery rhyme they go 'to sea in a bowl, / And if the bowl had been stronger / My song had been longer'; in a song by Thomas Love Peacock, which Thomas chose for his *Pocket Book of Poems and Songs for the Open Air*, they embark 'To rake the moon from out the sea'.

128-9. *ground up...The Yorkshireman*. Most English tales of giants and ogres include the war-cry: 'Fee, fi, fo, fum! / I smell the blood of an Englishman! / Be he alive or be he dead, / I'll grind his bones to make me bread!' The 'grinding' image (repeated l.142), like the story of Hob and the hog, uses a folk-motif to represent violence as intrinsic to English history – now symbolised in its internal aspect. Jacobs (whom Thomas possibly read) associates the cry with the two-headed giant Thunderdell, who 'comes from the northern dales to be revenged' on Jack the Giant-Killer (*English Fairy Tales*, 68). Thomas may allude to regional clashes in England, to the 'mills' of the industrial revolution, and (Cooke suggests) to war-profiteers (*WC*, 219). 'Yorkshireman' indicates that Thomas's historical geography resembles Kipling's: 'Kipling's history is rural and it is southern, as indeed is the project of many if not most of those who sought to change Hodge' (Howkins, 'From Hodge to Lob', 230).

133-41. *The man you saw...Lives yet*. As indicated above, some critics question the grounds for this climactic affirmation. Williams rebukes 'the casual figure of a dream of England, in which rural labour and rural revolt, foreign wars and internal dynastic wars, history, legend and literature are indiscriminately enfolded into a single emotional gesture. Lob or Lud, immemorial peasant or yeoman or labourer: the figure was now fixed and its name was Old England' (*The Country and the City*, 258). Yet lines 139-40 – written later than *BL* and *M₁* mss, and thus an interesting afterthought – seem calculated to cover a range of internal and external conflict. And 'Lob' does not remain embodied as 'peasant or yeoman' ('a mere clown, or squire, or lord', 1.132). In a fast-forward summation of the poem, he flickers between Nature, culture, politics, language, and literature. Linked by 'or' rather than 'and', this crescendo of 'naming' seeks, at least, to figure metamorphosis rather than 'fixity'.

133. *Jack Cade:* leader of Kent peasants and smallholders in rebellion (1450) against the economic policies of Henry VI; also a character in Shakespeare's *2 Henry VI*. In naming Cade and then Sedgemoor (1.140), Thomas again glances at current rural conditions. Smith comments: 'At Sedgemoor, in 1685, the West Country peasants who had flocked to support the pretender Monmouth's revolt against James II were wiped out in large numbers. Their insurrection had been brought about by an economic and social collapse beyond their capacity to understand, but linked, by [G.M.] Trevelyan [in *England under the Stuarts*, 1904] with a Waterloo which, in assuring British global hegemony, spelt the end for English agriculture' (*SS*, 83).

136. *Jack-in-the-hedge, or Robin-run-by-the-wall*: local names of several wild plants. Having accidentally omitted this line when he sent *Lob* to Eleanor Farjeon, Thomas remarked that it 'connects the Jacks and the Bobs too' (*EF*, 131).

137. *Robin Hood, Ragged Robin*. The outlaw, who reinforces the poem's anti-authoritarian tendency, does not intrude into this (seemingly) botanical catalogue. Robin Hood has lent his name to several plants, including the Ragged Robin – which implies poverty, as the plant-names in 1.136 imply a marginal, hidden, fugitive existence.

138. *One of the lords of No Man's Land*. Perhaps only in this poem could the name given to the ground between the British and German trenches realise its full significance as the translation of a rural term into a term of war. Thomas mentions 'a waste place of no man's land' (*SC*, 12) and 'No Man's Land' in 'the middle part of the South Downs' (*LPE*, 160).

141-5. *He never will admit…On to the road*. The poem has been turning back on its tracks since 'The man you saw', and will come full circle when the 'squire's son' morphs into the original 'ancient'. Here Thomas reintroduces the problematic 'weathercock' and the tension between 'lane' and 'road'. While these images confirm 'never', and affirm the perennial need for 'Lob' since 'millers' will always 'grind men's bones for bread', they also project a utopia.

144. *Lob* ends here in *M₁*. In *BL* Thomas cancels a full stop and continues.

Ms: *M₁*, *BL*. **Published text:** *P*. **Differences from *CP1978*:** 15 was, *was* 32 looked *I looked* 42 roguery, *roguery* 103 wrong, *wrong* 119 Of shoes for mending. The giant let fall from his spade *Of shoes. The giant sighed, and dropped from his spade* 128 He too *He, too,* 140 Sedgemoor too, – *Sedgmoor, too,* – **Note:** *CP1978* follows a typescript [*JT*] rather than *P*. In 1.148 *P* omits the comma after 'blood' present in *PTP*.

Digging (79)

4 April 1915

'Rich perfume of sage, dead grass and leaves, a mustard field and crumbling wild carrot seeds' (entry for 2 October, 'Open-Air Diary', in [ed.] Thomas, *British Country Life in Autumn and Winter* [London: Hodder and Stoughton,

1909], xi). His essay 'Flowers of Frost' ends: 'Frost seems also to play a part in sharpening the characteristic odours of winter, such as the smell of cherry-wood or the currant bushes freshly cut by the pruner, of tar when they are dipping hop-poles, the soil newly turned and the roots exposed by the gardeners... Above all, the fragrance of the weed-fire is never so sweet as when its bluish and white smoke heaves and trails heavily and takes wing at dawn over the frost and its crimson reflections of the flames and among the yellow tassels of the dark hedge' (*Country Life*, 13 February 1909). Like *Sowing*, a complementary "gardening poem", *Digging* is voiced by 'an inhabitant of the earth' (see note, 161). Once again, reciprocity with 'the dark earth' integrates mind and body, here in a lingering present-tense epiphany: 'I think / Only with scents' heals the Cartesian split. Yet 'wounds' and 'The dead, the waste, the dangerous' suggest that all reciprocities have been hard-won. 'Goutweed' is a pest; and it takes a figurative 'bonfire' to turn neurosis into poetry ('sweetness'). Interestingly, Thomas wrote this autumnal poem in Spring. In *Digging* he again remakes the quatrain for special purposes. He trellises an assonantal catalogue across three stanzas, and counterpoints shorter and longer lines to dramatise the diffusion of smells and thoughts. See Thomas's other poem with this title (99).

1-2. *I think / Only with scents*. 'He seemed to me to be able to use all his senses at once more acutely than most people use a single one... I remember that, for the whole of the last evening he spent with me, he at intervals pulled some mysterious object out of his pocket to smell. What it was I never saw, but it seemed to give him nearly as much satisfaction as his pipe' (J.W. Haines, 'Edward Thomas, As I knew him', *In Memoriam: Edward Thomas* [London: The Morland Press, 1919], 14-15).

3. *wild carrot's seed*: 'one of those clusters of wild carrot seeds, like tiny birds' nests, which are scented like a ripe pear sweeter and juicier than ever grew on pear-tree' (*HGLM*, 133).

5-8. *Odours that rise...celery*. Besides conveying sharp 'odours' in sharp sounds, onomatopoeia tracks the kinetic interchange between human energy and the natural world: 'wounds' / 'goutweed', 'spade' / 'raspberry'.

10-12. *a bonfire burns...all to sweetness turns*: 'the scent of the dying year is pungent as smoke and sweet as flowers' (*SC*, 44). 'All' could be both object and subject of 'turns'.

13-16. *It is enough...Autumn mirth:* 'empurpled evenings before frost when the robin sings passionate and shrill and from the garden earth float the smells of a hundred roots with messages of the dark world' (*SC*, 274). Other phrases from this passage will be recycled in *October*. As in *Sowing* ('the far / Owl's chuckling first soft cry'), birdsong is an aesthetic marker.

Ms: *M₁*, *BL*. **Published text:** *LP*. **Differences from** *CP1978*: 6 root [*LP*] roots [*M₁*, *BL*] **Note:** in l.6 two singular nouns make the relation between 'root' and 'tree' more conceptually and rhythmically coherent. **Note on title:** *CP1978* brackets the title; *CP2004* removes the brackets. See Note on Text.

Lovers (80)

5 April 1915

Lovers, including the irony of 'He has not got a gun...', and *In Memoriam (Easter,*

1915) prepare for the 'lovers' who 'disappear into the wood' in *As the team's head-brass*.

9. *'What a thing it is, this picking may'*. 'What a thing it is' was a favourite expression of Thomas's Wiltshire friend David Uzzell (see general note to *Lob*, 213). Uzzell's 'extraordinary freedom' educated the adolescent Thomas in sexual matters: 'he was the first man old enough to be my grandfather with whom I was on thoroughly good easy terms. He did not hide anything or invent a moral code for my benefit...he shook his head solemnly as he saw the once decent middle-aged gaffer from the works going up the canal-side with an obvious loose woman and later on emerging from the ash copse... At first I supposed him to be a wicked old man until I came to believe that all men were radically like him but most of them inferior in honesty. He was not in the least unseemly or obtrusive, but grave and roused very rarely to his Shakespearian laughter and the words, "Well, well, what a thing it is!"' (*CET*, 131-2). When Edward and Helen were secretly 'lovers', Uzzell let them stay in his Wiltshire cottage. Uzzell's voice seems to have licensed Thomas's most openly and happily sexual poem. His characteristic phrase marks genial assent, whether from the tolerant 'George' or some more mysterious source, to the erotic drives associated with 'picking may'.

Ms: *M1*, *BL*. **Published text:** *AANP, LP*.

In Memoriam (Easter, 1915) (80)

6 April 1915

Like *A Private*, this is no orthodox war memorial. An unexpected presence points to an absence. Insofar as the 'flowers left thick at nightfall' represent casualties, Wilfred Owen's rebuke in 'Insensibility' ('they are troops who fade, not flowers / For poets' tearful fooling') does not apply. If Thomas's woodland flowers are partly a wreath and partly a metaphor, they primarily mark a socio-ecological rupture: the loss of pre-war customs and futures. The dead may be 'far from home', but 'home' is also far from itself. The syntax of the last two lines prevents easy rhythmical or emotional resolution. R. George Thomas notes that *BL*'s 'long gap between *them* and *and* [suggests] a significant pause before the final phrase is read' (*CP1978*, 172). See note on Thomas's short poems (284).

Ms: *BL*. **Published text:** *P*. **Differences from** *CP1978*: title: Easter, *Easter*

Head and Bottle (81)

14 April 1915

This unsettling parable, which depends on a surreally disembodied 'head', features another of Thomas's doubled pairs. The drinker and 'I' stake out an implied choice – which is ultimately no choice – between voluntary oblivion and inevitable death. The drinker's suspended animation, in what could be either farmyard or graveyard, shuts down the faculties that define life. Yet his state appears more seductive than natural decline, tracked by the asset-stripping assonances 'lose...lose...alyssum...bees' hum...beeless flowers': 'it had early been observed, as by the Chinese Chuang Tzu, that a drunken man who falls out of a cart does not die: "His spirit is in a condition of security. He is not conscious of riding in the cart; neither is he conscious of falling out of it. Ideas of life, death, fear, etc., cannot penetrate his breast; and so he does not suffer from contact with objective existence"' ('Ecstasy', unpublished essay, *BC*). Thomas counterpoints entropy and suspension by adapting the limping couplet, also used in *After Rain*.

1. *alyssum*. 'Sweet Alyssum' is a four-petalled white garden flower, also a garden escape, which grows in clusters and has a honey-like scent that attracts bees. '"Snow on the mountains", *Alyssum Saxatile*, a fleecy show in cottage-gardens' (*TWL*, 229).

Ms: *BL*. **Published text:** *P*.

Home (81)
17 April 1915

See *Home* (64), and notes. Thomas's most affirmative 'home' poem ('"Twas home') is set in Steep. On 12 April he had written: 'Evening of misty stillness after drizzly day – last thrushes on oaks – then man goes by a dark white cottage front to thatched wood lodge and presently began sawing and birds are all still' (*FNB80*). Considered as epiphany, *Home* reverses the centrifugal structures of *Adlestrop*: birdsong dies into 'silence'; each self-contained stanza, with its apt mix of no rhyme and full rhyme, spirals inwards towards the two-stress final line and a 'point of home' (see note, 177). At one level, like *Adlestrop*, the poem enacts the discovery of its own aesthetic bearings: 'all / That silence said'. 'Eve' (l.8) suggests a beginning as much as the end of day.

4-6. *one nationality...One memory.* These lines are succinctly radical. At a time when oneness in, and the oneness of, 'nationality' and 'memory' was propagandised, Thomas gives the words local and ecological 'meaning'.

10-11. *familiar...and strange too.* Cf. *Good-night*, lines 5-8 (where 'welcome' also occurs); *Words*, lines 23-7; and see note (245).

20-4. *A labourer...silence said.* Smith stresses the communal dimension of 'home' in this poem, which ends with 'the sound of human labour': 'If silence speaks, it is no longer a threat to the isolated self, but is rendered harmless, even comforting, by a community of labour within which solidarity can be rediscovered' (*SS*, 89-90). The speaker's solidarity with birds also makes him 'an inhabitant of the earth' (see note, 161). The poem absorbs birdsong and sawing into its own sound-system. Jonathan Bate notes that the sawing implies localised 'dwelling': '"The sound of sawing" is not that of a sawmill, of mass consumption and destruction..."Sawing" is also a word for thrush song; and a thrush, like a labourer, takes wood to make its dwelling' (Bate, *The Song of the Earth* [London: Picador, 2000], 275-6).

Ms: *M₁*, *BL*. **Published text:** *LP*. **Differences from** *CP1978*: 13 oaktop *oak top* 21 weariness, *weariness* **Note:** *CP1978* follows a typescript [*MET*] rather than *LP*. **Note on title:** Title is given in *BL*.

Health (82)
18 April 1915

'The best and worst of sickness is to think how glorious health is or [?]might / must be. – glorious ambitious feeling on April 18 when Butser [Hill] was but a great jump away over hollow land early in morning and sky all blue but one white cloud' (*FNB80*). The proximity here of 'glorious / health / ambitious' links *Ambition*, *Health* and *The Glory*: all early morning poems that measure the distance between desire and fulfilment, aspiration and achievement. This provides a basis for dialectics between different selves, and between versions of the mind's relation to the world. On 28 April Thomas told Eleanor Farjeon: 'I was rather ill for 4 days with a chill…a chill and a boil together' (*EF*, 31). His tendency to small ailments, fatigue and boils supports the surmise that he had 'an incipient diabetic condition' (*RGT*, 243). But, partly owing to his psychological problems, Thomas conceived 'health' as more than physical well-being: 'I have long thought that I should recognise happiness could I ever achieve it. It would be health, or at least unthwarted intensity of sensual and mental life, in the midst of beautiful or astonishing things which should give that life full play and banish expectation and recollection' (*HE*, 91). A later passage prefigures *The Glory* as well as *Health*:

The sun has been up for an hour without impediment, but the meadows are rough silver under a mist after last night's frost. The greens in cottage gardens are of a bright, cold hue between blue and grey, which is fitter for the armour of heaven, or the landscape of some strong mystic, than for one who loathes to leave his bed. The blackbirds are scattering the frost, and they live in glittering little hazes while they flutter in the grass.

But the sky is of an eager, luminous pale blue that speaks of health and impetuousness and success. Across it, low down, lie pure white clouds, preserving, though motionless, many torn and tumultuous forms; they have sharp edges against the blue and invade it with daggers of the same white; they are as vivid in their place in that eager sky as yews on a pale, bright lawn, or as lightning in blue night. If pure and hale intelligence could be visibly expressed, it would be like that. The eyes of the wayfarer at once either dilate in an effort for a moment at least to be equal in beauty with the white and blue, clear sky, or they grow dim with dejection at the impossibility. The brain also dilates and takes deep breaths of life, and casts out stale thought and coddled emotion. It scorns afterthought as the winds are flouting the penitent half moon. ('The Pride of the Morning', *HE*, 135)

Thomas copied into a 'Golden Book' of literary touchstones, which he began compiling in 1901, Sir William Temple's reflections on 'Health and long life'. Temple links 'health, peace, and fair weather': 'health in the body is like peace in the state, and serenity in the air: the Sun, in our climate, at least, has something so reviving, that a fair day is a kind of sensual pleasure, and of all others the most innocent' (Bodleian Library, MS. Don. e. 10). Thomas's large concept of 'health' also owes much to Richard Jefferies, who is 'on the side of health, of beauty, of strength, of truth', and who presents Nature as 'a great flood of physical and spiritual sanity' (*RJ*, 297). Thomas read Nietzsche when working on his Jefferies biography: 'Isn't Nietzsche magnificent? & so necessary these days? Yet he damns me to deeper perdition than I had yet bestowed myself'; 'Nietzsche will have to come in later. *The Genealogy of Morals* is a very great book. But I kick at his too completely aristocratic view' (*LGB*, 152, 154). Discussing Jefferies's *The Story of My Heart*, Thomas says: 'This dream of a master-mind and his regret over the death of Julius Caesar and Augustus recall [Nietzsche's] words: "This man of the future who will redeem us from the old ideal...as also from what had to grow out of this ideal;...this bell of noonday and the great decision which restores freedom to the will, which restores to the earth its goal and to man his hope...he must come some day"' (*RJ*, 189). In proclaiming creativity, the life-force, the will-to-power, and a future *Übermensch*, Nietzsche was reacting against personal and cultural 'sickness'. Thomas prefers Jefferies to Nietzsche because he 'would not have made the mistake of so admiring the unfettered great man's prowess as not to see the beauty of the conquered and all the other forms of life which the powerful would destroy if they might' (*RJ*, 189). *Health* can be read as a dialogue between Nietzschean principles and resistance to them. It sits between *Ambition* (where a fantasy of 'omnipotence' is undercut) and *The Glory* (where it never gets off the ground).

The surprisingly Nietzschean element in *Health* is matched by the poem's formal surprise. For once, perhaps to make visionary 'leaps', Thomas employs free verse – a variety somewhere between Whitman and Pound. The sections (three to thirteen lines) and lines (four to sixteen syllables), into which he divides the poem, have different rhythms as well as lengths. Yet sound and sense unite to hold line and poem together, as in the repetition of key words, often at the end of end-stopped lines.

13. *what blue and what white is.* 'The sky seems to belong to this land, the sky of purest blue and clouds that are moulded like the Downs themselves but of snow and sun' (*SC*, 35).

17-18. *Wiltshire...Wales*: significant horizons of 'desire'.

29-34. *With health...sunlight upon dew.* In *The Icknield Way* one of Thomas's personae thrills to the sound of a woman singing: 'Oh, for a horse to ride furiously, for a ship to sail, for the wings of an eagle, for the lance of a warrior or a standard streaming to conquest, for a man's strength to dare and endure, for a woman's beauty to surrender...for a poet's pen!' (*IW*, 142). Later, Thomas imagines swifts 'racing and screaming when the Danes harried this way a thousand years ago, and thus went they over the head of Dante in the streets of Florence. In the warriors and in the poet there was a life clearly and mightily akin to that in the bird's throat and wing, but here all was grey, all was dead' (*IW*, 168). 'Warrior' links *Health* with *Ambition* (l.6).

31-2. *Caesar, Shakespeare, Alcibiades, / Mazeppa, Leonardo, Michelangelo.* Nietzsche names Julius Caesar, Shakespeare, Leonardo da Vinci and Michelangelo among models for his *Übermensch*. In Yeats's Nietzschean poem 'Long-legged Fly' (1937-8), Caesar, Michelangelo and Helen of Troy exemplify the utmost power of 'mind'.

32. *Mazeppa*: Ivan Stepanovich Mazep(p)a (1644?-1709), Hetman of the Cossacks in Ukraine under Russian imperial rule, which he eventually challenged. Byron's poem *Mazeppa* draws on the legend that Mazeppa, when he 'had no other gem nor wealth / Save nature's gift of youth and health', seduced a count's wife, and the count had him tied to a wild horse. 'Byron's poetry without his

life is not finished; but with it, it is like a statue by Michael Angelo or Rodin that is actually seen to grow out of the material. He was a man before he was a poet... There are finer poems than his "Mazeppa", but the poet is the equal of that wild lover and of the great King who slept while the tale was told' (*SC*, 111-12). If Byron is both poet and man of action, 'Mazeppa' is both fact and Romantic icon: he also inspired Pushkin's epic poem *Poltava*, Tchaikovsky's opera based on the poem, a painting by Géricault, a Liszt *étude*. Thomas, like Nietzsche and Yeats, is interested in the energies common to the creative artist, art itself, powerful men, and beautiful women.

35-46. I could not be...four yards. Unlike achieved 'health and...power' (1.29), whether worldly or artistic, discontent keeps possibilities open. In suggesting that Nietzschean 'mightiness' has its blind spots, Thomas may imply the value of his own literary vantage-point.

39. As the hand makes sparks from the fur of a cat. On 4 April Thomas had noted: 'One of the prettiest Spring things is the wagtail running up and down the warm tiles twittering as if the sun made the song as one's hand on a cat's back makes sparks' (*FNB80*). 'I passed some examination in chemistry but, as with other things, cared nothing for it, except for doing as well as most at it. For a while I played with magnets and amber, and rubbed the cat's fur in the dark' (*CET*, 83).

Ms: *M₁*, *BL*. **Published text**: *LP*. **Differences from** *CP1978*: 22 still be *be still* [?misprint] **Note on title**: *CP1978* brackets the title; *CP2004* removes the brackets. See Note on Text.

The Huxter (83)

20 April 1915

Here a countryman, a bottle, and a cart combine more healthily than in *Head and Bottle*. They also put paid to dreams of the *Übermensch*. A prose proto-type for the 'huxter' (huckster, seller of cheap goods) is a 'carter': 'Though a slight man he had broad shoulders and arms that hung down well away from his body, and this, with his bowed stiff legs, gave him a look of immense strength and stability: to this day it is hard to imagine that such a man could die...he did nothing but work, except that once a week he went into the town with his wife, drank a pint of ale with her, and helped her to carry back the week's provisions' (*HGLM*, 142-3). The poem relishes a less respectable figure, itinerant and carnivalesque. Like Jack Noman in *May 23* and the lovers in *Lovers*, the huxter personifies May-time. Thomas aptly reverts, as in his next poem, to a folksong model.

2. a plentiful lack. Hamlet teases Polonius by pretending to rebuke a satirist who says that old men 'have a plentiful lack of wit' (*Hamlet* II, ii).

9. And they laugh as down the lane they bump. Praising the vivid country characters in Jefferies's *Amateur Poacher*, Thomas writes: 'The great heavy-laden wagon of life goes rocking down the lanes, and the artist gathers up some of the wisps from the elm trees when it has passed' (*RJ*, 123).

Ms: *M₁*, *BL*. **Published text**: *P*.

She dotes (84)

21 April 1915

Thomas plays on the double meaning of 'dotes'. He may still have *Hamlet* in mind. Discussing 'those mad maids and their songs that are so characteristic of English poetry', he says: 'Such are Ophelia, Wordsworth's Ruth, and Herrick's Mad Maid...These maids...are always love-lorn and always flower-lovers wandering in the free air' (*FIP*, 87-8). *She dotes* echoes the 'old tunes' sung by Ophelia after Polonius's death: 'They bore him barefaced on the bier.../ And on his grave rained many a tear'; 'And will he not come again? / No, no, he is dead, / Go to thy death-bed, / He never will come again'. Thomas makes birds (and *their* songs), rather than flowers, the focus of obsessive grief and its search for meaning.

8-10. *childishness...carelessness...loverless*. This consonantal rhyme/refrain mimetically suggests the woman's obsession and frustration ('woodpecker' is the only other tri-syllabic word in the poem).

Ms: *M₁*, *BL*. **Published text:** *LP*. **Note on title:** *CP1978* brackets the title; *CP2004* drops it. See Note on Text.

Song (84)

22 April 1915

CP1978 prints a first stanza not cancelled in *M₁* or *BL*:

She is beautiful
With happiness invincible:
If cruel she be
It is the [*M₁* She has a] hawk's proud innocent cruelty.

It seems likely that Thomas dropped the stanza, which does not appear in *AANP*. Its tone, rhythm, vocabulary, and lack of refrain detach it from what follows. In the remaining quatrains, song conventions (of the court rather than the folk) depersonalise emotion as Thomas again links love, death and birdsong. He wrote the poem while 'under a thick cloud of [his life of] Marlborough'. Sending it to Eleanor Farjeon, Thomas calls it 'a sort of a song' and asks: 'Does it make you larf?' (*EF*, 132). The question may imply that Farjeon, herself in love with Thomas, will realise that the poem alludes to some secret passion. See note on Thomas's love poems (279).

6. *the cuckoo spoils his tune*: proverbial, and perhaps reflexive. In June, as Thomas would have known, the male cuckoo ceases to sing his mating song, and the female's different call is heard.

8. *And yet she says she loves me till she dies*. The song behind *Song* is an Elizabethan favourite of Thomas's: 'There is a Lady sweet and kind, / Was never face so pleased my mind, / I did but see her passing by / And yet I love her till I die' (Anon.).

Ms: *M₁*, *BL*. **Published text:** *AANP*, *LP*. **Differences from *CP1978*:** see general note above.

A Cat (85)

24 April 1915

Bird-murder is calculated to attract Thomas's deepest 'loathing', yet he accords the cat ambiguous respect and even some compassion (lines 2-4). A line in *M₁* tells us that the speaker 'From a stranger's dog once saved this pest'. The human who drowns her kittens belongs less excusably to the same murderous scheme of things. 'God gave her rest', one of the barbed references to 'God' in Thomas's poetry (see note, 274), questions Christian constructs more than it deplores animal Nature. Cf. the hawk's 'cruelty' in the cancelled stanza (above) of *Song*. 10. *One speckle on a thrush's breast*: 'the hedges are full of strong young thrushes which there is no one to frighten – is there any prettier dress than the speckled feathers of their breasts and the cape of brown over their shoulders and backs, as they stir the dew in May?' (*SC*, 103). Later in the same passage Thomas condemns 'the spirit of one who, having been disturbed while shaving by a favourite cat in the midst of her lovers and behaving after the manner of her kind, gives orders during the long mid-day meal that she shall be drowned forthwith, or – no – tomorrow, which is Monday' (*SC*, 105).

Ms: *M₁*, *BL*. **Published text:** *LP*. **Note on title:** *CP1978* brackets the title; *CP2004* removes the brackets. See Note on Text.

Melancholy (85)

25 April 1915

Since 'melancholy' is one of Thomas's names for his neurosis, he usually updates its meaning (see notes on *The Other*, 161; *October*, 259). Yet the hexameter couplets of this near-sonnet linger over Romantic melancholy – which includes lingering and malingering – especially as patented by Keats:

> Love for vanished, inaccessible, inhuman things, almost for death itself – regret – and the consolations offered by the intensity which makes pleasure and pain so much alike – are the principal moods of these poems... The 'Ode on Melancholy' is one of the central poems of this period, admitting, as it does so fully, and celebrating, the relation between melancholy and certain still pleasures. Nowhere is the connoisseurship of the quiet, withdrawn spectator so extremely and remorselessly put. The 'rich anger' of the mistress is to be a precious, delicious object; her 'peerless eyes' are to be devoured as roses. Richer juice could not be extracted from poison-flowers. (*K*, 51-4)

In Keats's 'Ode on Melancholy', 'the melancholy fit shall fall / Sudden from heaven like a weeping cloud'. Thomas also takes 'rave' and 'soft' from the 'Ode' ('Or if thy mistress some rich anger shows, / Imprison her soft hand, and let her rave'); 'fever' and 'despair' from 'Ode to a Nightingale'; 'wild' and 'strange' from 'La Belle Dame sans Merci'. Wordsworth contributes 'a distant cuckoo' to the poem; Coleridge, the 'dulcimer' of 'Kubla Khan'. Thus the speaker's neo-Romanticism is highly self-conscious, as is his yielding to "reverie" (in the quotation above, Thomas reads Keats in *fin-de-siècle* terms). His condition recalls the decadent mood of Thomas's early prose, perhaps his intermittent opium-habit. In 1902 Thomas was 'so much in sympathy' with De Quincey's *Confessions of an English Opium-Eater* and the Celtic Twilight Yeats that they seemed 'to belong to my own experience' (*LGB*, 40).

In the last five lines of *Melancholy*, spatial and temporal shuttles between 'distant', 'near', and 'remote' enact a disturbing recession from 'history'. The syntax opens out to confirm a paradoxically 'withdrawn' state: solitude as solipsism. This does not help the symptoms implied by 'raved', 'fever', 'fear', 'despair', 'wild' and 'foes'. For Kirkham, *Melancholy* is 'one of [Thomas's] very few unsatisfactory poems', because it 'induces and condones more than it presents and analyses the "strange sweetness" of abandoning oneself to despair' (*MK*, 36). Thomas certainly figures more as patient than analyst. But, as Kirkham recognises, there is still a gap between the poem's attitude and the speaker's surrender to narcotic 'poison-flowers'. His deliberate embrace of melancholy is itself placed as symptomatic.

3-4. *solitude...rude*: words also rhymed in *The Other* and *Home* (64).

6-7. *What I desired I knew not...I knew*. This pivotal sentence almost parodies (again consciously, perhaps) Thomas's capacity to block all hopeful exits. It revisits the problem of 'desire' as posed in *The Other* (lines 33-7), and echoes that poem's syntactical twists.

8. *wild air*: a phrase that also occurs in *The Source* and *The Sheiling*.

Ms: *M₁*, *BL*. **Published text:** *P*.

Tonight (86)
30 April 1915

'Now it is when Kate comes to me –' (among notes that point towards *April*, *FNB80*). In *M₁* and *BL* this song-like lovers' duet begins: 'Margaret, you know at night'. Thomas may simply have made a mistake when transcribing the poem, a mistake that reflects some earlier stage in its composition: in *M₁* l.7 originally read: 'Come soon, my heart, tonight'. Yet *Tonight* appears to dramatise forbidden love, whether heterosexual or homosexual. The contrapuntal stanzas contrast an open, "natural" relationship ('the true sun above a summer valley') with one hidden from the world ('electric light'). The larks and 'ask no light' resolve the opposition.

Ms: *M₁*, *BL*. **Published text:** *LP*. **Differences from** *CP1978*: 7 Kate: *Kate;*

April (86)
2 May 1915

For Thomas's youthful love poem set in 'over-sweet' April, see note on *No one so much as you* (278). 'Emily' is a mystery, though see note on his love poetry (279). The notebook jotting quoted above with reference to *Tonight* ('Now it is when Kate comes to me') occurs amid notes for *April*, beginning: 'As we met, the nightingale sang / As we loved – / As we parted – the same' (*FNB80*). Read as a sequence, *Song*, *Melancholy*, *Tonight* and *April*, all of which include bird-call mood-music, may encode some erotic narrative. Thomas wrote to Frost on 3 May: 'Two pairs of nightingales have come to us. One sings in our back hedge nearly all day & night…I hope the gods don't think I'm the sort of poet who will be content with a nightingale, though. You don't think they could have made that mistake do you? What does it mean?…Am I really ripe for being all round content, or what?…Are the children at school now? Or are you still "neglecting" them? God bless them all. By the way, there was a beautiful return of sun yesterday after a misty moisty morning, & everything smelt wet & warm & cuckoos called, & I found myself with nothing to say but "God bless it". I laughed a little as I came over the field, thinking about the "it" in "God bless it"' (*RFET*, 51-2). Cooke thinks that Thomas might have 'suppressed' *April* (*WC*, 248). Scannell finds the poem 'almost maudlin in its sentimentality', although partially redeemed by 'an essential innocence of feeling' (*VS*, 29).

1. *The sweetest thing.* The problem with *April*, and perhaps with a soft spot in Thomas's poetry, hinges on the adjective in the first line of each stanza. 'Sweet' is one of the recurrent words (like 'joy', 'pain', 'strange', 'tears', 'mirth') that reflect his effort to evoke basic feelings in basic English. Its appearances so far include: 'Yet I would rather give up others more sweet, / With no meaning, than this bitter one' (*Old Man*); 'The sailors' song of merry loving / With dusk and sea-gull's mewing / Mixed sweet' (*An Old Song II*); 'an April morning, stirring and sweet / And warm' (*Tears*); 'This is a dream of Winter, sweet as Spring' (*Swedes*); 'that La-la-la! was bodiless sweet' (*The Unknown Bird*); 'just / As sweet and dry was the ground / As tobacco-dust' (*Sowing*); 'sweet as any nut' (*Lob*); most recently and self-consciously, 'sweeten the strange sweetness' (*Melancholy*). Ahead lie: 'Strange and sweet / Equally', 'Make me content / With some sweet-ness / From Wales' (*Words*); 'the sweet last-left damsons' (*There's nothing like the sun*); 'The past is the only dead thing that smells sweet' (*Early one morning*); 'a song / As sweet as a blackbird's, and as long' (*If I were to own*); 'All plea-sure and all trouble, / Although most sweet or bitter' (*Lights Out*); and, above all, the celebrated climax of *Tall Nettles*: 'I like the dust on the nettles, never lost / Except to prove the sweetness of a shower'.

'Sweet' transfers between physical sensations, emotional states and aesthetic responses. The word works best when contrary qualities or images ('bitter', 'Winter', 'dry…dust', 'strange', 'dead') avert over-sweetness. The letter quoted above shows Thomas to be wary of 'all round content': a condition implicitly bad for poetry, like the nightingales that do get into the poem along with fur-ther sweetish words ('smile', 'God bless', 'rapture', 'lovelier').

9-10. *When earth's breath…richest oven's.* 'A richness, now first felt, in the atmosphere, as if the sun drew fragrances from the earth' ('Diary', 21 March 1896, *TWL*, 231).

10. *loudly rings 'cuckoo'*: an echo of Thomas's favourite medieval lyric, with which he ended *The Pocket Book of Poems and Songs for the Open Air*: 'Sumer is icumen in, / Lhude sing cuccu!'

Ms: *M₁*, BL. **Published text:** *LP*. **Differences from** *CP1978*: 11 'tsoo, troo, troo, troo': *'tsoo, troo, tsoo, troo';* [*LP* has 'tsoo, tsoo, tsoo, tsoo':] **Note:** R. George Thomas speculates that the *LP* editors 'misread' l.11 in *BL* [*CP1978*, 196]. That seems probable – 'sharply' does not fit a continuous 'tsoo' – but the third word in *M₁* and *BL* may also be 'troo'. This sound is the source of the link between the nightingale's song and the legend of Tereus and Philomela.

233

John Clare's transcription of the song includes: 'tee rew tee rew tee rew' [ed. Alice Oswald, *The Thunder Mutters: 101 Poems for the Planet* (London: Faber & Faber, 2005), 36]. **Note on title**: Title is given in *BL*.

The Glory (87)

? early May 1915

The Glory, undated, precedes *July* in *M₁*, and a page is cut from *BL* between the revised version of *Two Pewits* (4 May) and *July* (7 May). On 2 May Thomas noted: 'Soft raindrops pit the clean pale dust' (*FNB80*, cf. l.15). Other notes that prefigure *Tonight*, *April*, *The Glory*, *July* and *Two Houses* occur together in *FNB80* between 18 April and 23 May (see *CP1978*, 396). *The Glory* has thematic links with *Ambition* and *Health*. The following passage continues Thomas's meditation on 'happiness', quoted with reference to *Health* (227):

> I never achieved [happiness], and am fated to be almost happy in many different circumstances, and on account of my forethought to be con- temptuous or even disgusted at what the beneficent designs of chance have brought... [for example] polluting, by the notice of some trivial accident, the remembrance of past things, both bitter and sweet, in the company of an old friend...Also, the flaw in my happiness which wastes it to a pleasure is in the manner of my looking back at it when it is past. It is as if I had made a great joyous leap over a hedge, and then had looked back and seen that the hedge was but four feet high and not dangerous. Is it perhaps true that those are never happy who know what happiness is? (*HE*, 91-2)

With its quasi-religious keyword, *The Glory* (like *Health*) may refer to the mystical ideals of Richard Jefferies: ideals that inspired Thomas but which he usually represents as beyond his scope. Thomas says of Jefferies's *The Story of My Heart* (1883): 'He thinks of nature as supplying men with strength and desire and means for soul life. He has rediscovered the sources of joy in nature, and foresees that what has fed his lonely ecstasy in the downs will distribute the same force and balm among the cities of men below. They are, indeed, perennial sources, but his passionate love of the beautiful and joyous fills him with longing for the day when they shall be universal too' (*RJ*, 187). In Chapter 5 of *The Story of My Heart* Jefferies writes: 'I drank the beauty of the morning; I was exalted. When it ceased I did wish for some increase or enlargement of my existence to correspond with the largeness of feeling I had momentarily enjoyed.' Jefferies's 'ecstasy' is in the Romantic tradition. *The Glory* revisits Romanticism's original 'invitation' to internalise the 'sublimity' of Nature: the set of ideas that lies behind the emotions aroused by similar morning landscapes in *Ambition* and *Health*. On one level, the poem dramatises a clash between Romantic idealism and literary modernity.

The speaker ponders Romantic precepts for life ('be') and art ('do') figured by 'the lovely of motion, shape, and hue': a phrase that spans Nature and artistic creation. Aesthetics – 'beauty' – may take precedence over 'happiness', although each word occurs four times. Thus *The Glory* begins with Thomas also revisiting earlier poems: *Melancholy* and *April* (cuckoo), *Beauty* (dove), *Adlestrop* ('White clouds ranged even and fair as new-mown hay'), and *Tears* ('heat...stir'). He pulls these images towards an arena seemingly prepared for a grand Romantic encounter between subjectivity and the phenomenal world: 'the sublime vacancy / Of sky and meadow and forest and my own heart'. But 'vacancy' already sabotages the 'sublime'. It anticipates the different aesthetic model (not wholly negative) implied by the speaker's unresolved self-interrogation: his five questions might be scenarios for other poems. All these dialectics are mediated by sonnet structure. *The Glory* is a double sonnet with unpredictable rhymes and 'turns'. 'Start' ends the first sonnet.

15. *And tread the pale dust pitted with small dark drops.* At the opposite pole from 'sublime vacancy', this monosyllabic, onomatopoeic line aptly 'embodies' the speaker's recasting of his relation to 'beauty' as a step-by-step empirical quest.

19-20. *Or must I be content with discontent / As larks and swallows are perhaps with wings?* Kirkham calls this 'a comparison that effectively "clips the wings" of human aspiration, since the ability to fly, especially the climbing and darting flight of these birds, is a natural image for freedom from limits' (*MK*, 101). However, the simile could work the other way: by raising the status of 'discontent'.

21-2. *And shall I ask...once more / What beauty is.* Cf. *Beauty*, and: 'I am not sure that I consider anything in nature (on a grand scale) beautiful. Beauty is it seems to me inferior to the sublime which is irregular, worn, or finer in intention than execution. "Lycidas" is beautiful. "Ode to West Wind" not. I find most people call "beautiful" what I call "pleasant"...but what is beauty. I don't find answer in Burke, or Ruskin' (*Diary*, 27 April 1901, *NLW*).

26. *fast pent*: spiritually imprisoned. The phrase echoes Keats's sonnet beginning 'To one who has been long in city pent', which also includes the lines: 'Who is more happy, when, with heart's content, / Fatigued he sinks into some pleasant lair / Of wavy grass...'

28. *I cannot bite the day to the core.* This seeming inconclusiveness, like the sense that 'beauty' and 'happiness' are no longer absolute, marks a shift in aesthetic horizons. 'It is interesting to note that although [Thomas] cannot "bite the day to the core", the language and the image that he uses to tell us this have a strength and a sharpness which show at least that he knows fully what "biting" means and involves' (*HC*, 201).

Ms: *M₁*. **Published text**: *P*.

July (88)

7 May 1915

Thomas associated rivers and lakes with reverie and psychic harmony: 'The hazy sky, striving to be blue, was reflected as purple in the waters. There, too, sunken and motionless, lay amber willow leaves...Between the sailing leaves, against the false sky, hung the willow shadows' (*RAP*, 25); 'The morning was already hot...At the river I took a dinghy and sculled for nearly two hours... Hardly a thought or memory shaped itself. Nevertheless, I was conscious of that blest lucidity, that physical well-being of the brain, "like the head of a mountain in blue air and sunshine", which is so rarely achieved except in youth' ('On the Evenlode', *HS*, 166); 'There is nothing like the solitude of a solitary lake in early morning, when one is in deep still water' (*RFET*, 145).

Like *Two Pewits*, *July* calls attention to the balancing-act of form. It is as if the mirrored stanzas, the 'doubled' images and words (including the word 'image') and the self-enclosed rhyme-scheme (ABABBA) extravert the artistic processes behind the poem. They establish a fine equilibrium between subjectivity and Nature, between control ('stirs...break') and unconscious absorption ('drowse'). Cf. Yeats's 'A Long-legged Fly': 'Like a long-legged fly upon the stream / His mind moves upon silence'. *July* dissolves tensions active in *The Glory*, from which it repeats 'clouds', 'stirs', 'heat', 'sky' and 'content'. 'Naught moves' is a positive variation on 'naught to travel to' at the end of *The Glory*.
12. *still*: at once adjective and adverb.

Ms: *M1*, *BL*. **Published text:** *LP*. **Note on title:** Title is given in *BL*.

The Chalk-Pit (88)

8 May 1915

For Thomas's fascination with pits and hollows, see general note to *The Combe* (170). 'The chalk of Froxfield and Steep was extensively used in the past to lighten the clay soils, and there are at least four or five large chalk pits... The one in "The Chalk-Pit"... is most likely that at the foot of Wheatham Hill. Along its rim an ancient road climbs, probably pre-Roman, making for Old Litten Lane and Week Green' (*WW*, 28). Thomas begins his essay 'Chalk Pits': 'It is sometimes consoling to remember how much of the pleasantness of English country is due to men, by chance or design...among the works of men that rapidly become works of Nature, and can be admired without misanthropy, are the chalk and marl pits' (*LS*, 27-8). Among 'lesser' pits, he distinguishes two types: the pit scooped from a hillside and the 'hollow pit' that can become a dell:

> One or two of the best of them are half-way between the hollow pit and the hill-side scoop. One in particular, a vast one, lies under a steep road which bends round it, and has to protect its passengers by posts and rails above the perpendicular. At the upper side it is precipitous, but it has a level floor, and the old entrance below is by a very gradual descent. It is very old, and some of the trees, which are now only butts, must have been two centuries old when they were felled. It is big enough for the Romany Rye to have fought there with the Flaming Tinman. But in [George] Borrow's days it had more trees in it. Now it has about a score of tall ash trees only, ivy covered, and almost branchless, rising up out of it above the level of the road. Except at midsummer, only the tops of the ash trees catch the sunlight. The rest is dark and wild, and somehow cruel. The woodmen looked tiny and dark, as if working for a punishment, when they were felling some of the trees below. That hundred yards or so of road running round the edge of the ancient pit is as fascinating as any other of similar length in England. From the rails above

you could well watch the Romany Rye and the Flaming Tinman and fair-haired Isopel. But except the woodmen and the horses drawing out the timber, no one visits it. It is too gloomy. This is no vineyard, unless for growing the ruby grape of Proserpine, the nightshade. Though roofed with the sky, it has the effect of a cave, an entrance to the under-world. (*LS*, 32-3)

As a poetic dialogue, *The Chalk-Pit* has structural links with *Up in the Wind* and *Wind and Mist*; but the poem is also an "eclogue" in the further sense that it debates aesthetic questions. The speakers stake out alternative ways of reading (and writing) the human imprint on landscape. The first speaker (A) fits the scene into ready-made slots: 'amphitheatre', 'tragical', 'tale', 'play'. The second speaker (B) 'should prefer the truth / Or nothing'. While it is tempting to see A as Thomas the fanciful prose-writer (cf. the passage quoted above), B as Thomas the empirical, plain-speaking poet, their dialectics may be more complex. In *The Isle of Wight*, in a passage that also underlies *Up in the Wind*, Thomas already broaches issues raised by the poem. He distributes different attitudes among 'two or three' friends contemplating 'a solitary yew...ruinous in outline, tortured and bleak [that] added a wild and tragic note to the gentle slopes and masses':

'It is unfair of that old tree to air its misery in such a place,' said one, 'but it is not the first time that any of us, I dare say, has seen a tree or a rock play such tricks. Sometimes one finds a landscape that is changed in this way so as to become for ever after the legitimate setting for some poem or romance. Ruskin, you may remember, regarded it as something curious and precious...that his wandering over England took him to places where "his romance was always ratified to him by the seal of locality – and every charm of locality spiritualised by the glow and the passion of romance". We have to be fortunate to have any such experience; for we must come early to the scene, and the hour and every circumstance must conspire if we are not to fail utterly to connect the visible scene with its imagined inhabitants. Most of us have more often constructed our own setting for tales without any effort and usually by accident...' 'Some books leave the mind with a picture so clear and singular that we are sure to recognise it if ever we meet it on our travels...' 'Yes; and there are other places which immediately strike us as fit scenes for some tragic or comic episode out of the common. I know a little white inn standing far back from the road, behind a double row of noble elms...[for the continuation of this passage see notes on *Up in the Wind*, 145]. 'I don't know why you should want to fit a story to a scene like that. I am quite willing to wait until the tragedy or comedy arrives, provided that my enquiries as to what may have happened already have been fruitless. Very likely you might learn some history for which your inn, and the trees, are the perfect arena. Try! You people have such loose fancies, and you make the world a jumble of books, and men, and Nature, like a pantomime. Still, I will grant you one scene that did move me exceedingly in something like the way you speak of...' (*IOW*, 27-30)

In the poem, B speaks for 'waiting until the tragedy or comedy arrives'. He starts from observation, a name, the available data: 'But see: they have fallen'; 'It is called the Dell. / They have not dug chalk here for a century'; 'I will ask'. Thomas's third persona, the 'man of forty' recalled by B, obliquely backs up this perceptual caution: 'The wren's hole was an eye that looked at him / For recognition'. Here, too, B evokes not fictive 'ghosts' but actual people who disturb A's 'fancies'. The last word, the genuine 'mystery', is his. Yet A and B may merge in lines 30-4, which reflect memory's difficulty in separating experience from representation, and both from subjectivity. Perhaps A voices the extent to which Thomas's poetry remains 'haunted' by Romantic possibilities. He works up the curiosity on which B's mystery depends.

10. *the smack that is like an echo*. 'Men felling trees and the sound of axe is like an echo because it comes after the stroke' (1 January 1915, *FNB80*). 'Echo' echoes 'smack', which echoes 'axe'.

43-50. *A man of forty…A girl of twenty…glinting eyes.* R. George Thomas writes: 'These lines are based on memories of [Thomas's] open-air courtship of Helen Noble' (*CP1978*, 397). But this squares neither with the age-gap nor with A's disapproval of 'free thought, free love'. The lines more probably encode Thomas's bitterness about his aborted relationship with Hope Webb (see note on *The Unknown*, 279; *HT*, 120-1; *RGT*, 144-7). In January 1908, while working on *Richard Jefferies* at Minsmere in Suffolk, he 'got very fond of a girl of 17 with two long plaits of dark brown hair & the richest grey eyes, very wild & shy'; 'I dimly foresee a guttering candle…Yet you are partly right when you propose the consolation of an unassailable vision of her'; 'the night before I left Minsmere I was pedantically asked not to go on writing to the girl who was away at school…So there is a more unhappy raw truncation' (*LGB*, 156-61). In fact Hope was eighteen (*ETFN* 26 [February, 1992], 12). It seems that this history, these 'ghosts', invaded the scenario as originally conceived, to become the 'tragical' experience that really haunts the chalk-pit as poem (see textual note).

44. *orts and crosses*: noughts (oughts) and crosses. '40 years had crisscrossed his cheeks with pain and pleasure' (*FNB80*, after 18 April).

56-8. *imperfect friends, we men / And trees…mystery'*. Instead of co-opting trees for an anthropomorphic drama, B invokes the partly problematic eco-history which connects 'men / And trees'. Yet 'mystery' invests this nexus with quasi-religious feeling: 'I cannot walk under trees without a vague powerful feeling of reverence. Calmly persuasive, they ask me to bow my head to the unknown god. In the evening, especially, when the main vocation of sight is to suggest what eyes cannot see, the spacious and fragrant shadow of oak or pine is a temple which seems to contain the very power for whose worship it is spread' (*HS*, 183). 'What they worshipped at Avebury temple, no one knows, but the human mind is still fertile in fantasy and ferocity – if it no longer draws blood – when it worships within walls. To me the sycamores that gloom at the entrance to the temple are more divine' (*RJ*, 8). Thomas mourned trees destroyed to make way for new suburbs: 'The elms had come unconsciously to be part of the real religion of men in that neighbourhood' (*SC*, 64). Another passage from *The South Country* prefigures the tree symbolism in his poetry:

I like trees for the cool evening voices of their many leaves, for their cloudy forms linked to earth by stately stems – for the pale lifting of the sycamore leaves in breezes and also their drooping, hushed and massed repose, for the myriad division of the light ash leaves – for their straight pillars and for the twisted branch work, for their still shade and their rippling or calm shimmering or dimly growing light, for the quicksilver drip of dawn, for their solemnity and their dancing, for all their sounds and motions – their slow-heaved sighs, their nocturnal murmurs, their fitful fingerings at thunder time, their swishing and tossing and hissing in violent rain, the roar of their congregations before the south-west wind when it seems that they must lift up the land and fly away with it, for their rustlings of welcome in harvest heat – for their kindliness and their serene remoteness and inhumanity, and especially the massiest of the trees that have also the glory of motion, the sycamores, which are the chief tree of Cornwall, as the beeches and yews are of the Downs, the oaks of the Weald, the elms of the Wiltshire vales. (*SC*, 168-9)

Ms: *M₁*, *BL*. **Published text:** *LP*. **Differences from *CP1978*:** title: The Chalk-Pit *The Chalk Pit* 2, 37 chalk-pit *chalk pit* 4,7 briar *brier* 17/18, 28/9, 52/3 *stanza breaks in CP1978* **Note:** Lines 47-51 and 53-8 are present only in *LP*. *BL* and *M₁* end: "'You may know the breed [*M₁* sort]." / "Some literary fellow, I suppose. / I shall not mix my fancies up with him.'" The first two stanza breaks introduced in *CP1978* are detectable in *BL*, but *LP* [for which, given the added lines at the end, there must have been a further source] has no such breaks. **Note on title:** Title as given in *BL* is unhyphenated, but see note above *re LP*.

Fifty Faggots (90)

13 May 1915

Writing to Frost on 15 May, Thomas copied out *Fifty Faggots* and told him: 'One of my reliefs in this week's work was to write these lines founded on carrying up 50 bunts (short faggots of thin & thick brushwood mixed) & putting them against our hedge'. He asks of the lines: 'Are they <u>north</u> of Boston only?' (*RFET*, 53-4). In alluding, however humorously, to Frost's collection *North of Boston*, the question betrays 'anxiety of influence'. Yet it may also have a precise point. *Fifty Faggots* can be read as responding to Frost's poem 'The Wood-Pile', with which it shares the verb 'warm' as well as a focal symbol for eco-historical relations between 'men / And trees' (see above). The poems conceive history from different angles, perhaps English and American. In 'The Wood-Pile' a 'small bird' leads the way to a 'cord of maple', 'older sure than this year's cutting, / Or even last year's or the year's before'. The speaker wonders why it should have been abandoned – possibly by 'Someone who lived in turning to fresh tasks' – 'To warm the frozen swamp as best it could / With the slow smokeless burning of decay'. This retrospective riddle envisages greater human 'control' ('fresh tasks') over Nature and events than does *Fifty Faggots*. And whereas Frost's actors (speaker, bird, wood-pile builder) seem distinct from one another, Thomas – still hesitating between going to America and going to war – projects

239

a collectively uncertain future. Linguistic variants track the mutations of a mini-ature eco–system ('underwood', 'faggots', 'thicket', prospective nesting-place or fire-lighters). On 15 August 1916, with the war not yet 'ended', he admitted to Frost: 'My faggot pile is pretty nearly used up, but it wasn't fair. We have been saving coal by wood fires out of doors, or it would have lasted the war out I believe' (*RFET*, 145). The poem's uncertainties are mediated by deviations from sonnet-form: assonance rather than rhyme, an unresolving seven-line sestet.

1. *faggots*: 'bunts' in letter to Frost.

3. *Jenny Pinks's Copse*: 'Pinks Copse is a Steep place name, at the top of Ridge Hanger' (*WW*, 13). '[F]ortunately science cannot destroy the imagination which kindles...at the infinite variety of significance in names like...Palfrey Green, Happersnapper Hanger, Jenny Pink's Copse' (Thomas's Introduction to Isaac Taylor, *Words and Places* [London: J.M. Dent, 1911], x).

14-15: in *BL* and letter to Frost: 'Have ended that I know not more about / And care not less for than robin or wren'.

Ms: *BL*. **Published text:** *P*.

Sedge-Warblers (90)
23 May 1915

The text printed in this edition (and in *SP*, *AANP*, *LP*) is cancelled in *BL*, and a revised version dated 24 May (here, *SW2*) apparently preferred. *CP1978* / *CP2004* prints both versions. Significant differences are noted below. That *SP* and *AANP* print the cancelled version gives it a priority that also seems war-ranted on aesthetic grounds. *SW2* omits l.14. In reducing *Sedge-Warblers* to 28 lines, Thomas may have wanted to stress its structure as a double sonnet (like *The Glory*, with which it has other links), while also destabilising the first sonnet's clinching couplet ('water'/'daughter'). But the original version does equally interesting things with sonnet-form: l.15 floats freely between the rhyme schemes of two sonnets. Hence, perhaps, Thomas's vague answer to a query from Eleanor Farjeon: 'I expect that line ending in pair [*sic*] was intended to rhyme with two lines higher up [i.e. "desire"]' (*EF*, 146).

FNB80 contains the following entry for 23 May 1915: 'beyond Warnford [in Hampshire]. Water crowfoot and marigolds iris <u>leaf</u> and clear swift combing water but no nymph only the sedgewarblers in willows more continuous than lark and clearer than sweetest voice singing sweetest <u>words</u> I know, though often grating or shrill and always jerky and spasmlike with rare sweet gentle iterations and 3 or 4 together or in turns'. This is followed by notes for a poem: 'Long ago it would have borne a nymph / – cloudless clear sail / Now it [?]drifts the chestnut petals from the distant park / She could / Love all day long and never hate or tire / the best of May / Buttercups brighter than brass / – soft'.

Sedge-Warblers is one of the poems quoted by James Fisher to support his view that 'the major English bird poet of our century was Edward Thomas' (*The Shell Bird Book* [London: Ebury Press and Michael Joseph, 1966], 208). Birdsong can have a wholly transcendental value in Thomas's poetry, as when the haunting 'notes' of *The Unknown Bird* and the 'pure thrush word' in *The Word* symbolise the Muse or perhaps symbolism itself. But, as in *Fifty Faggots*, birds are also closely observed co-inhabitants of the earth. Between their Wordsworthian poles of 'heaven' and 'home', birds often stand in for the poet or – as in *Two Pewits* – provide aesthetic models. This is not just anthropomorphism. Thomas assumes (rightly) that birdsong, the most complex utterance by any other species, and the lyric poem have a common evolutionary origin. Here the sedge-warblers' song re-attaches the speaker-as-poet to the earth, and mediates the aesthetic self-correction whereby he exchanges 'desire' for 'wisdom': a nostalgic 'dream' of 'beauty' for 'clearer' vision with utterance 'to match'. Another portrait of the divided artist, *Sedge-Warblers* adjusts the mainly visual focus of *The Chalk-Pit* by moving from voyeuristic fantasy to sensory and imaginative balance. The speaker 'looks into' while 'hearkening': a verb repeated from *The Glory*. The sedge-warblers' stripped-down song resolves some of the problems associated with 'beauty' in that poem, where one curative possibility is: 'Hearkening to short-lived happy-seeming things'. 'Hearken' means more than 'listen'.

3. *any brook so radiant*: 'river of such radiance' (*SW2*).

8. *Child to the sun, a nymph whose soul unstained*: 'Child of the sun, whose happy soul unstained' (*SW2*). 'Nymph' fits the classical-pagan (and erotic) character of the 'dream', and see next note.

8-10. *nymph...immortal kin*. This is the idiom of Thomas's floweriest prose: 'Nymph-like the brook brightens and curves its crystal flesh and waves its emerald hair under the bridges at field corners, where the brambles dip their blossoms, and the nightingale sings and the sedgewarbler has its nest. For it the lonely willows in the flat fields shed their yellow leaves most pensively, like maidens casting their bridal garments off' (*HE*, 98-9).

10. *A lover*: 'Lover' (*SW2*).

12. *poison*. Cooke links 'poison' with Thomas's remark, 'Victor Hugo has called reverie a poison of the brain' (*HS*, 6), although that passage continues with a defence of reverie. Later he would describe Keats's 'Ode on Melancholy' as juice 'extracted from poison-flowers' (see note on *Melancholy*, 231).

13. *So that I only looked into the water*. In ceasing to impose 'Another beauty' on the scene, the speaker renews a traditional trope: '"Fool", said my Muse to me, "look in thy heart and write"' (Sir Philip Sidney, *Astrophil and Stella*, I).

14. Omitted in *SW2*.

15-17. *combed...water-crowfoot*. '[T]he kingfishers were in pairs on the brooks, whose gentle water was waving and combing the hair of the river moss' (*BW*, 122). 'The water of the pond was entirely hidden by the flowers of the water crowfoot like a light fall of snow' (*IOW*, 26).

17. curdled to: 'curdled in' (*SW2*, 1.16).

19-20. *And sedge-warblers, clinging so light / To willow twigs, sang longer than the lark*: 'The sedgewarblers that hung so light / On willow twigs, sang longer than any lark' (*SW2*, lines 18-19). 'Clinging' makes the birds' persistence more precarious and hence more meaningful. It also prepares musically for 'sang longer'.

21. *Quick, shrill, or grating*. As the notes for this poem indicate, Thomas often tries to reproduce birdsong (cf. *The Unknown Bird*, *The Owl*, *April*): '[The turtle dove's] voice is a soft purring, sounding as if half buried and very warm and luxurious, far softer & less articulated than the woodpigeon's "take two cows Taffy". The stockdove is a third species, about the same size as the woodpigeon but not ringed round the neck & with a coo that is more of a grunt as a rule

than the woodpigeon's, a soft grunt, but it has other very pretty notes which I can't describe' (*LGB*, 193).
25. then: 'now' (*SW2*, l.24).
25-6. *sweetness…sweetest…sweet*: see note on *April* (233). Here Thomas may criticise his inclination towards 'sweetness'. Compare Frost's 'Oven Bird' (this poem also appears in *AANP*), which 'knows in singing not to sing'.
28. *Wisely reiterating endlessly*. 'As to the 3-word line I thought it was right somehow, but there was nothing intentional about it' (*EF*, 146).
   Ms: *M1*, BL. **Published text:** *SP*, *AANP*, *LP*. **Note:** See general note above. Title is unhyphenated in *AANP*, but a hyphen appears in the text.

I built myself a house of glass (91)
25 June 1915

Speaking as both patient and analyst, Thomas compresses his psychological history into a disturbing parable. On the same date he wrote to Edward Garnett, ascribing his difficult behaviour to 'self consciousness and fear': 'What you call superiority is only a self defence unconsciously adopted by the most faint-hearted humility – I believe. It goes on thickening into a callosity which only accident – being left to my own devices perhaps – can ever break through. I long for the accident but cannot myself arrange to produce it! However, perhaps landing in New York quite alone, and under some stress, may do the trick' (*ETFN* 52 [August 2004], 16). Poem and letter indicate that, despite poetry, neurosis continued, as did Thomas's hope of salvation from outside (see Introduction, 17). Earlier, he had told Eleanor Farjeon: 'the central evil is self-consciousness carried as far beyond selfishness as selfishness is beyond self denial …and all I have got to fight it with is the knowledge that in truth I am not the isolated selfconsidering brain which I have come to seem – the *knowledge* that I am something more, but not the belief that I can reopen the connection between the brain and the rest' (*EF*, 13).
1. *a house of glass*. 'I discovered the joy of throwing stones over into the unknown depths of a great garden and hearing the glass-house break' (*CET*, 43). 'People who live in glass houses shouldn't throw stones' is one of the proverbs featured in *Four-and-Twenty Blackbirds*, where it becomes a parable of paranoia. Archie Flinders, a tell-tale who spies on other children, throws stones at passing boys until they retaliate by breaking the glass-house in his garden. One boy quotes the proverb, and later Archie 'dreamed that he was living in an enormous palace with rooms and halls too many for him to count. They were full of beautiful things and all were his. Nevertheless Archie was not happy; for the walls, the floors, and the roof of his palace were made of glass. Nobody else was in the palace; yet he kept looking round, out of the glass walls, up out of the glass roof, and down through the glass floor; he was afraid to do anything lest he should be peeped at, and somebody should tell tales about him.' Unable to find 'a corner where there was no glass', Archie eventually rushes out of the palace: 'Without a pause he picked up a stone and hurled it at the walls. A crash, a hundred clashes, and a long clattering dissolved the palace to a heap like a pyramid' (*FTB*, 67-9).
6. *No neighbour casts a stone*. This line cryptically fuses two of Christ's injunctions:

'Thou shalt love thy neighbour as thyself'; 'He who is without sin among you, let him cast the first stone'.

Ms: *B.* **Published text:** *LP.* **Note:** The absence of a stanza-break in *LP* seems to be a misprint. **Note on title:** *CP1978* brackets the title; *CP2004* drops it. See Note on Text.

Words (91)
26-8 June 1915

In *B*, *Words* is headed: 'Hucclecote – on the road from Gloster to Coventry'. Like *I built myself a house of glass*, it was written when Thomas was on a brief cycling-tour and visiting his solicitor-friend J.W. (Jack) Haines in Hucclecote, Gloucestershire. Hence the poem's western tilt, further influenced by a trip to May Hill (from which Wales can be seen) on the Gloucestershire-Herefordshire border. In 1914 Thomas had walked there with Frost. Like *Lob*, *Words* mingles cultural defence, *ars poetica*, and more mysterious vistas. As cultural defence, it marks a fresh turn to history, as if certain kinds of introspection have indeed been 'broken' by *I built myself a house of glass*. The first person plural is to the fore. As *ars poetica*, too, *Words* moves away from subjectivity. Thomas affirms the primacy of language, traces its evolutionary and historical accretions, and proposes an aesthetic of listening for what it encodes. Placed at the end of *P*, *Words* complements *Lob* by turning tradition outside in, by locating it in the linguistic and lyrical grain:

> [John Clare] reminds us that words are alive, and not only alive but still half-wild and imperfectly domesticated. They are quiet and gentle in their ways, but are like cats – to whom night overthrows our civilisation and servitude – who seem to love us but will starve in the house which we have left, and thought to have emptied of all worth. Words never consent to correspond exactly to any object unless, like scientific terms, they are first killed. Hence the curious life of words in the hands of those that love all life so well that they do not kill even the slender words but let them play on; and such are poets. The magic of words is due to their living freely among things, and no man knows how they came together in just that order when a beautiful thing is made like 'Full fathom five'. And so it is that children often make phrases that are poetry, though they still more often produce it in their acts and half-suggested thoughts; and that grown men with dictionaries are as murderous of words as entomologists of butterflies. (*FIP*, 85-6)

> Life itself is fleeting, but words remain and are put to our account. Every action, it is true, is as old as man and never perishes without an heir. But so are words as old as man, and they are conservative and stern in their treatment of transitory life. Every action seems new and unique to the doer, but how rarely does it seem so when it is recorded in words, how rarely perhaps it is possible for it to seem so. A new form of literature cannot be invented to match the most grand or most lovely life. And fortunately; for if it could, one more proof of the ancient lineage of our life would have been lost. (*GB*, 40)

243

Cooke relates *Words* to Thomas's critical 'themes' (*WC*, 137-45). The poem condenses insights from the complementary studies of Maurice Maeterlinck, Algernon Charles Swinburne and Walter Pater that helped Thomas to recognise and exorcise the 'murderous' propensities of his own style. '["Serres Chaudes"] is hardly more than a catalogue of symbols that have no more literary value than words in a dictionary. It ignores the fact that no word, outside works of information, has any value beyond its surface value except what it receives from its neighbours and its position among them' (*MM*, 27). 'Hardly before [Swinburne's *Atalanta in Calydon*]...had words been so self-contained, so much an end in themselves, so little fettered to what they could suggest but not express ...The words in [*Atalanta*] have no rich inheritance from old usage of speech or poetry, even when they are poetic or archaic or Biblical' (*ACS*, 20-2). '[Pater's] words have only an isolated value; they are labels; they are shorthand; they are anything but living and social words...Pater was, in fact, forced against his judgment to use words as bricks, as tin soldiers, instead of flesh and blood and genius. Inability to survey the whole history of every word must force the perfectly self-conscious writer into this position. Only when a word has become necessary to him can a man use it safely; if he try to impress words by force on a sudden occasion, they will either perish of his violence or betray him. No man can decree the value of one word, unless it is his own invention; the value which it will have in his hands has been decreed by his own past, by the past of his race' (*WP*, 213-15).

5-9. *As the winds use...crack...drain...whistle through*: a downbeat version of the Romantic metaphor for inspiration, as in Shelley's 'Ode to the West Wind': 'Make me thy lyre, even as the forest is'. See general note to *Aspens* (251). Thomas also re-orients this trope by invoking 'English words' as poetry's moving spirit. The rhyme 'drain' / 'pain' echoes Hardy's 'In the Cemetery': 'as well cry over a new-laid drain / As anything else, to ease your pain!'

13-14. *light as dreams, / Tough as oak*. 'Lighter than gossamer, words can entangle and hold fast all that is loveliest, and strongest, and fleetest, and most enduring, in heaven and earth... They outlive the life of which they seem the lightest emanation – the proud, the vigorous, the melodious words...the things are forgotten, and it is an aspect of them, a recreation of them, a finer development of them, which endures in the written words' (*RJ*, 298).

14-16. *Tough as oak, / Precious as gold, / As poppies and corn*. Cuthbertson connects these similes with Thomas Fuller's *History of the Worthies of England* (1662) and Thomas Traherne's *Centuries of Meditations,* written at the same period but not printed until 1903. *This England* 'contains a passage on "The Oak of Gloucestershire" from Fuller's *Worthies* [in which] Fuller records that "The best [oak] in England is in Dean Forest in this country, and most serviceable for shipping, so tough that, when it is dry, it is said to be as hard as iron"' (*GC*, 133). *This England* also includes Gilbert White's reflection on the Selborne oak, destroyed in 1703, and Cowper's 'Yardley Oak'. Thomas often quotes this passage from Traherne: 'The corn was orient and immortal wheat, which never should be reaped, nor was ever sown. I thought it had stood from everlasting to everlasting. The dust and stones of the street were as precious as gold' (*SC*, 132).

17. *Or an old cloak*: a line absent from two typescripts in which these lines follow l.31: 'To the touch / As a man's old cloak'. Perhaps Thomas felt that 'To the touch' made it too obvious that his similes associate words with all the senses.

20. *the burnet rose*. J.W. Haines (a botanist) explains that on their ride to May Hill he had misled Thomas as to the name of a 'thick wild rose in the hedge, not the ordinary pink "dog-rose"' (quoted *GC*, 135). The Burnet Rose is creamy white, and grows by the sea. The actual rose may have been Sweet Briar (Eglantine), a deeper pink than the Dog Rose and more strongly scented. Its 'sweetness' derives primarily from the leaves.

23-31. *Strange...familiar...lost homes*: see note on Thomas and the *Unheimliche* or uncanny (199). In *Words* the paradox that 'strange' and 'familiar' can change places is tracked to the very sources of language. 'Lost homes' compresses some ideas about words (their 'half-wild' night-life and 'ancient lineage') explored by Thomas in passages quoted above.

33. *oldest yew*. During his Cotswolds trip Thomas visited Painswick: 'the place with 100 yews in the churchyard where no one can count beyond 99' (26 June, *LWD*). Wordsworth's 'Yew-trees' appears in *This England*: 'There is a Yew-tree, pride of Lorton Vale...This solitary Tree! A living thing / Produced too slowly ever to decay'.

35. *Worn new*. This succinct oxymoron suggests what happens to language in history and poetry, and also how "tradition" works. Judy Kendall points out the link with Thomas's 'pseudo-translation "Eluncd"' in *Beautiful Wales*: 'She is dead, Eluned, / Who sang the new songs / And the old; and made the new / Seem old, and the old / As if they were just born and she had christened them' (*BW*, 82; *JK*, 67).

40-1. *the earth which you prove / That we love*. Cf. 'The magic of words is due to their living freely among things', quoted above from *Feminine Influence on the Poets*. As in *Old Man*, echoed in 'the names, and the things' (l.50), Thomas conceives the non-identity of word and thing in associative (and ecological) rather than post-structuralist terms.

43-5. *some sweetness / From Wales...nightingale*s. 'After all, Wales is good for me. In spite of my accidentally Cockney nativity, the air here seems to hold in it some virtue essential to my well-being, and I always feel, in the profoundest sense, at home' (*SL*, 16). See Sally Roberts Jones, 'Edward Thomas and Wales' (*JB*, 77-83). Here Thomas's Anglo-Welshness slips over a supposed border with such ease that he virtually elides the English and Welsh languages. He uses the fact that nightingales' habitat stops short of Wales to attribute a special music to Welsh speech and names. In *Beautiful Wales* Thomas quotes George Borrow's reference to the Welsh poet Huw Morus (1662-1709) known as Eos Ceiriog: the Nightingale of Ceiriog (*BW*, 5-6).

56. *ecstasy*. 'Where a man's life culminates in some hidden or famous deed of love, heroism, poetry, where he is exalted out of himself, out of the street, out of mortality, there is ecstasy' ('Ecstasy', unpublished essay, *BC*).

57-8. *Fixed and free / In a rhyme*. Another succinct oxymoron defines poetic form, perhaps with an implied critique of 'free' verse. The poem's own form makes the point: one- or two-beat lines that give each word enormous space; rhymes that may be adjacent or twenty-four lines apart ('dreams' / 'streams'). Cf.

245

Keith Douglas's 'Words' (1943): 'I keep words only a breath of time / turning in the lightest of cages'.

Ms: *B*. **Published text:** *P*. **Differences from** *CP1978*: 36 again: [*P*] *again;* [*B*] **Note:** From *CP1920* to *CP1949* there is no stanza-break after l.51: an error due to the fact that it ends a page in *P*.

The Word (93)

5 July 1915

Thomas's letters during the first half of 1915 show him trying to make up his mind, with increasing urgency, about a future in which he seemed ever more likely to join Frost in America (see general note to *I built myself a house of glass*, 242). On 26 June he told Walter de la Mare: 'I am planning to go to America in a month or 2 to see if there is anything to be had there' (*LWD*). Perhaps the Cotswolds trip that produced *Words* drew him back to England. On 11 July he wrote to Frost: 'Last week I had screwed myself up to the point of believing I should come out to America & lecture if anyone wanted me to. But I have altered my mind. I am going to enlist on Wednesday if the doctor will pass me' (*RFET*, 78). On 14 July Thomas was passed fit for military service, and by 19 July he had joined the Artists' Rifles: 'a territorial corps which trains men to be officers' (*LGB*, 252). From late June (*Words*) to 23 July (*Cock-Crow*) his poetry seems to deliberate, at a deep level that implicates its own aesthetic, the meaning of such a decision. He would revisit these deliberations in *This is no case of petty right or wrong* and other poems.

In *FNB80* origins of *The Word* and *Haymaking* are intermingled: 'Things forgotten – / I have forgotten the names of the stars, the big above the little / and to one side – and dates of wars etc. / But I remember / Those little copses of blackcaps nettles bramble where / a man might hide forever dead or alive' (after 2 June). *The Word* responds dialectically to *Words*: the biblical, transcendental ring of its singular title being set against language (and poetry) as a historical and cultural phenomenon. Midway through the poem (l.11), the speaker moves from forgotten human names to 'remembered' birdsong, from the 'abyss' of history to the perennial present tense of poetry. A 'pure thrush word' recalls the bird-Muse of *The Unknown Bird*, and might seem to represent poetry as music, as 'pure' sound. Yet the second half of *The Word* has also opened up an evolutionary vista in which 'singing' and 'saying' converge. All these dialectics bear on the question of "war poetry".

5. *Abyss*: a word that will recur in *A Dream* (l.10).

6-9. *I have forgot, too...Some things I have forgot that I forget*. Here, in contrast with *Old Man* (another dialectical point of reference), 'forgetting' acquires a positive value because it sorts out mnemonic, and poetic, priorities. To retain 'lesser things' cuts 'mighty men' and 'old wars' down to size, as does the reversal of expected order in 'lost or won'. This may imply that lyric – 'pure thrush word' – rather than epic, or any other heroic brand of "war poetry", remembers what really matters and is itself remembered. In thus playing with proportion and scale, Thomas applies his critical dictum, 'Anything, however small, may make a poem; nothing, however great, is certain to' (*MM*, 28), to the context of war.

16. *only the name*. Cf. *Adlestrop* (l.8) and *'Home'* (l.28).

17-19. *thinking of the elder scent...the wild rose scent...like memory*. 'The air smells like the musky wild white rose; coming from the west it blows gently, laden with all the brown and golden savours of Wales and Devon and Wiltshire and Surrey which I know, and the scent lifts the upper lip so that you snuff deeply as a dog snuffs' (*HE*, 95); 'the pink roses which have the pure, slender perfume connected by the middle-aged with youth' (*IW*, 107). To 'think of' a scent, and make 'memory' a simile, is to give the senses a cognitive centrality that again unsettles hierarchies. The poem's reflexive ending suggests that the inspiration and impact of poetry ('a pure thrush word' surprises the reader too) dissolve barriers between mind and body, thought and memory.

Ms: *B*. **Published text:** *AANP*, *LP*. **Note:** *CP1928* and *CP1944* print 'will' [*B*] for 'can' in l.5.

Under the Woods (94)

5 July 1915

'Lazy keeper in cot under woods – smokes and has one green shrivelled stoat, he killed ages ago when trees were young – never shoots now' (after 2 June, *FNB80*). In *The Happy-Go-Lucky Morgans* Mr Torrance recalls: 'Now, home and the garden were so well known, so safe, and so filled with us, that they seemed parts of us, and I only crept a little deeper into the core when I went to bed at night, like a worm in a big sweet apple. But the woods on the hills were utterly different, and within them you could forget that there was anything in the world but trees and yourself, an insignificant self, so wide and solitary were they. The trees were mostly beeches and yews, massed closely together. Nothing could grow under them...Nobody took heed of the woods except the hunters... The last keeper had long ago left his thatched cottage under the hill, where the sun shone so hot at midday on the reed-thatched shed and the green mummy of a stoat hanging on the wall' (*HGLM*, 149-51). In *Under the Woods*, as in *House and Man*, trees shadow a precarious human presence. Despite 'children', 'old' does not seem to 'wear new' (*Words*) for people as for thrushes. In some respects, *Under the Woods* reverses the trajectory of *The Word*.

3. *sung*. It is odd that Thomas, who often half-rhymes, should use 'sung' not 'sang', but 'sung' appears in all three extant texts.

18-22. *Out of most memories...no scent at all*. The stoat is a stark little omen that contrasts with the final images/self-images of *The Word*, where memory and strong scents interpenetrate.

Ms: *B*. **Published text:** *LP*. **Differences from** *CP1978*: title Under the Woods *Under the Wood* **Note on title:** *CP1978* follows a typescript [*JT*], in which 'Wood' is singular, rather than *LP* [no title in *B*]. But see Thomas's plural in source-passages and in the poem itself.

Haymaking (94)

6-8 July 1915

Copious notes for *Haymaking* include the following: 'Park mead of thin grass... grove of low squat elms and long grass and men under – a solitary yew – also on the slopes of chalkpit wych hazel and flowering elder – a stack in midfield

– tosser idle – men lean on rakes – oldfashioned as Crome and Constable. How old it is! I seem to see it now as someone long years hence will see it in a picture' (after 2 June, *FNB80*). *Haymaking* was first published in *This England* together with *The Manor Farm*, written six months before (see notes, 165, 214). More self-conscious than its precursor, this summer farm-landscape encapsulates not only pastoral England but also English pastoral. As *Lob* tracks English tradition, and *Words* celebrates its linguistic mode and poetic medium, so *Haymaking* distils Thomas's reading of country books. The prose passages and notes behind the poem also implicate landscape painting. Here lyric memory rescues more from the 'abyss' (*The Word*) than in *Under the Woods*. Thomas had often tried to capture the 'spirit' of rural scenes shaped by 'centuries of peace and hard work and planning for the undreaded future...The spirit of the place, all this council of time and Nature and men, enriches the air with a bloom deeper than summer's blue of distance' (*SC*, 13). A related passage prefigures *The Cuckoo* and *Cock-Crow* as well as *Haymaking*:

> [T]he sun is once more in the sky, the mist has gone... The swallows flying are joyous and vivid in colour and form as if I had the eyes of some light-hearted painter of the world's dawn. Where the gleam was, that haunt of the sun's, that half hour's inn to which he turns from the long white road of the sky to rest, is seen to be the white farm house that stands in the midst of woods and ricks.
>
> Yet, though so clear, the house, half a mile off, seems to have been restored by this fair and early light and the cooing of doves to the seeming happy age in which it was built. The long, tearing crow of the cock, the clink of dairy pans, the palpitating, groaning shout of the shepherd, *Ho! ho! ho! ho! ho!* now and then, even the whirr of the mowing machines, sound as if the distance that sweetens them were the distance of time and not only of space. (*HE*, 71-2)

1-2. *After night's thunder...cold*: cf. the weather-setting of *May 23*. Both poems have sources in Thomas short story 'The Artist' (see note, 194): 'clouds, the most delicate of toppling marble mountains...Round about the sun itself hung a mass of...blue-grey, edged with fiery gold' (*LAT*, 133-4).
5. A draft of this line, 'And joyous bathed in Homer's sea' (*FNB80*), suggests that Thomas has long European vistas in mind.
8. *the holly's Autumn falls in June*: 'The little June Autumn of the hollies' (*FNB80*). Here Thomas blends seasons more subtly than in *The Manor Farm* (lines 18-20). Cf. 'kernel sweet of cold' (l.2).
13-15. *And in the little thickets...garden warbler.* These lines are anticipated in jottings for *The Word* (see note, 246): 'Those little copses of blackcaps nettles bramble where / a man might hide forever dead or alive' (*FNB80*). The blackcap is closely related to the garden warbler.
16-18. *shrill shrieked...The swift...arrow.* The aural and visual 'sharpness' of this impression prepares for the writers and painters in l.35, and for the final 'Uttered' and 'picture'. In 'The Artist' the eyes of Adams the painter delight 'in the flight of the swift which was as if the arrow and bow had flown away together' (*LAT*, 133).

35. *Older than Clare and Cobbett, Morland and Crome.* 'Older than Clare and Wordsworth Morland and Crome' (*FNB80*). Thomas writes of John Clare (1793-1864): 'To enumerate the flowers was a pleasure to him, and he did so in a manner that preserves them still dewy, or with summer dust...No man ever came so near to putting the life of the farm, as it is lived, not as it is seen over a five-barred gate, into poetry' (*LPE*, 234-5). 'William Cobbett is one of those names which have come to symbolise the bearer's character to perfection. It is now impossible to say how much of the character of the name was given to it by this one man in his seventy-two years of life (1763-1835). It was an altogether English name to begin with, thoroughly native and rustic; and English it remains, pure English, old English, merry English... William Cobbett is the only Cobbett in the *Dictionary of National Biography*, but through him speak a thousand Cobbetts, too horny-handed to hold a pen, hairy, weather-stained, deep-chested yeomen and peasants, yet not one of them, I dare say, a better man than this Farnham farmer's boy, whose weapons included the sword, the spade, the voice, and the pen' (*RR*, vii). Thomas praises Cobbett's style in terms central to his own and Frost's ideas about speech and poetry (see note, 298). *This England* contains four extracts from Cobbett's writings, and twice juxtaposes Clare and Cobbett.

Thomas quotes from George Borrow's *Wild Wales*: 'Such was the scene [a water-mill and pigs] which I saw from the bridge, a scene of quiet rural life well suited to the brushes of two or three of the old Dutch painters, or to those of men scarcely inferior to them in their own style – Gainsborough, Moreland [*sic*], and Crome' (*GB*, 283). George Morland (1763-1804), a painter of landscape and animals, gets a sympathetic mention in *The Isle of Wight*: 'This most English – old English – of painters knew every corner of the island, especially those parts which are still least accessible, as he knew every fisherman and publican...There is no cruciform or other stone to his memory: nothing left but his paintings, his pleasant name, and the stories of his merriment and after wretchedness' (*IOW*, 43). Thomas applies the simile 'as English as Morland' to 'a perfect type of the dark ancient house in a forest' (*HGLM*, 72). John Crome (1768-1821), often called 'Old Crome', to distinguish him from his son, founded the 'Norwich school' of painting.

37. *A white house crouched at the foot of a great tree.* This powerful symbol, which interweaves the human or animal body with house and tree, condenses aeons of agriculture, culture, and pastoral representation. 'White' links the house with 'empty road' and 'mill-foot water'.

41-2. *out of the reach of change – / Immortal.* The poem's permanence seems indexed to the obsolescence of what it depicts. The 'undreaded future' (see quotation above) no longer applies. As in his preliminary sketch – 'I seem to see it now as someone long years hence will see it in a picture' – Thomas pans away from the framed scene, which freezes into an icon as landscape becomes "landscape". This ambiguous, elegiac and self-elegiac ending is conditioned by 'the death of rural England' (see Introduction, 23) as well as by war.

42. *grange*: originally a granary, then a country house with farm buildings attached.

Ms: *B*. **Published text**: *TE*, *P*. **Differences from** *CP1978*: 24 team, *team;*

35 Cobbett *Cowper* **Note:** *CP1978* follows *TE* rather than *P.* In *PTP*, however, Thomas has changed 'Cowper' to 'Cobbett'. In *CP1928* and *CP1944* 'stiff up' [l.9] is changed to 'up stiff' [*B*].

A Dream (96)

7, 8 July 1915

On 9 July Thomas talked to 'a sergeant of the Artists' Rifles at their H.Q.' (*SL*, 115). On 22 July he wrote to Frost: 'A month or two [ago] I dreamt we were walking near Ledington but we lost one another in a strange place & I woke saying to myself: "somehow someday I shall be here again" which I made the last line of some verses' (*RFET*, 83). In May he had listed among possible topics for poems: 'Somehow someday I shall be here again (waking from dream of deep pool. Full of water revolving and plunging – dream of Frost too and a walk to this.) I woke with this line of farewell to the place' (*FNB80*). 'Thomas recorded many dreams in his various notebooks, all carefully worked over… often with clear indications of their source in waking experience' (R. George Thomas, *CP1978*, 400). Thomas draws on dreams for the elements of fantasy and fable in his prose. *A Dream* may allude to another poet's dream vision: its underground stream, a symbol at once psychological and historical, recalls the 'deep romantic chasm', 'mighty fountain', and sacred river's 'mazy motion' in Coleridge's 'Kubla Khan'.

A Dream is Thomas's first sonnet (see note on his sonnets, 294), although he has written double sonnets, such as *The Glory*, and been ever alert to sonnet-form as a deep structure of lyric. Given Rupert Brooke's *1914* sequence, and Thomas's rivalry with Brooke (see Introduction, 17), it is interesting that his first sonnet should be a "war sonnet". But Thomas reinvents the genre. The syntax of the opening lines dramatises departure from 'known fields': from the past; from all that *Haymaking* represents; perhaps from Brooke's 'corner of a foreign field / That is for ever England'. Then ominous 'waters' ruffle the rhythm until 'Heaving and coiling' erupts into the sestet. At the sonnet's centre, between daylight and underworld, stands the poet-speaker 'thinking'. The transition from 'thinking' to 'bemused' suggests that, at an unconscious level where a decision or poem may be forming, he is drawn to 'the abyss'. Hence 'I forgot my friend'.

3-8. *dark waters…white.* In 'Penderyn' Thomas writes of the Welsh river Neath as seen in October 1914: 'the river, fresh from a waterfall, poured out into the light under ash trees…in one place [it] ran black underground, and in another danced down a quarter of a mile of cascades white as milk' (*COE*, 24).

9. *So.* Placed at the sonnet's turn, this word serves a double grammatical function. It both intensifies 'bemused' and makes that state a consequence of what has occurred.

14. Two drafts of this line are: 'Saying "Someday, somehow, I shall be here again["]' and 'Saying "I shall be here, someday, somehow, again["]' (*FNB80*).

Ms: *B.* **Published text:** *LP.* **Differences from** *CP1978*: 7 birth; [*B, LP*] *birth:* [*JT*]

The Brook (96)

10 July 1915

Notes in *FNB80* indicate that *The Brook* comes from the same matrix as *The Word*, *Haymaking* and *A Dream*. This sequence of July 1915 poems is also formally interconnected. All are written in rhyming couplets; and *Haymaking* (42 lines) and *The Brook* (28 lines) are further linked with *A Dream* by elements of sonnet-structure. As in earlier poems, like *Man and Dog*, *Beauty* and *Lob*, Thomas counterpoints couplet and syntax. *The Brook* begins with slow-paced sentences that establish a Zen-like meditation. The placing of 'Unseen', 'mugwort dull' and 'A butterfly alighted' adds to an impression that all the speaker's senses are engaged yet somehow detached. Thomas's landscapes and rhythms vary according to the perspectives on history that enter his thinking about the war: the problematics of memory in *The Word*, human settlement stacked up as 'a great tree' in *Haymaking*, the apocalyptic symbolism of *A Dream* in which sonnet-structure 'turns' on a decisive moment. *The Brook* holds several time-frames in questioning ('as if') balance: a timeless present, which ambiguously involves 'loss'; history as 'the gleam,/ The motion, and the voices, of the stream' – 'motion' and 'stream' being repeated from *A Dream*; eco-history (the butterfly); prehistory (the horseman). The relation between the contemporary 'cart-horse' and 'the horse with silver shoes' is among the poem's riddles.

1, 25. *child*: '"Nobody's been here before" says Baba [Myfanwy Thomas] paddling in sandy brook – so she thinks' (*FNB80*). Baba's remark connects with the concept of time represented by 'the brook' in Richard Jefferies's writings. Thomas quotes the brook in Jefferies's *Wood Magic* as saying: 'that which has gone by, whether it happened a second since, or a thousand years since, is just the same; there is no real division betwixt you and the past...the world is not old; it is as young as ever it was' (*RJ*, 147-8).

15. *I was divided*: a reflexive start for the second sonnet.

17. *frizzled*. In suggesting how the 'waters' look, sound and move, this adjective epitomises the poem's synaesthetic clarity.

22. *barrow*. A draft in *FNB80* refers to 'the Bramdean tumulus': a long barrow. This places the setting of *The Brook* as Bramdean Common, near Steep. Myfanwy Thomas recalls the poem's occasion (*MT*, 45-6).

   Ms: *B*. **Published text**: *AANP, LP*.

Aspens (97)

11 July 1915

For Thomas and trees, see note (238). The aspen, *populus tremula*, belongs to the willow family. Strongly flattened leaf stems cause its leaves to twist and shake in the slightest breeze. Hence the folk name 'old wives' tongues'. The tree was thought to have been punished with eternal quaking for not bowing its head at the Crucifixion, or, alternatively, for supplying the wood for the Cross. Another tradition stresses the aspen's protective qualities, owing to ancient use of its wood for shields. Thus (as here) aspens were often planted near settlements. Strong root systems ensure that aspen colonies survive 'all sorts of weather, men, and times'. *Aspens* is Thomas's most complete revision of the Romantic analogy between inspiration and a wind-tossed tree. Rather than representing the poet as acted upon by a cosmic power, he reflexively connects the aesthetics of poetry with its prophetic openness to history: 'Increasing complexity of thought and emotion will find no such outlet as the myriad-minded lyric, with its intricacies of form as numerous and as exquisite as those of a birch-tree in the wind' (*Daily Chronicle*, 27 August 1901). Later Thomas wrote of Christina Rossetti: 'For hers was an instrument having the power to make out of little words and common things, including a discontent with this earth and life which is not too deep for tears or words and "goes not to Lethe", a music more enduring, perhaps not less monotonous or more really sorrowful, than that of a larch tree sighing in the wind' (*LS*, 70). Urging Bottomley to take the poem for *AANP*, Thomas said: '"Aspens", I have thought, was decidedly one of the better pieces' (*LGB*, 265).

2. *the inn, the smithy, and the shop*: not just literal buildings but also the loci of human community: social life, manufacture, commerce. 'Blacksmith's cavern' (l.5) has a prehistoric ring. Although this scene may be based on the cross-roads near Thomas's house (Yew Tree Cottage) in Steep (*WW*, 33), see next note.

7. *The clink...random singing*. In Thomas's prose-sketch 'The Doves' (the name of an inn) he figures as a traveller among 'deep red buildings in parallel rows and symmetrical blocks, a solitude inhabited by unknown multitudes', where 'music streamed out of the Inn at the cross-roads'. He enters this inn, 'of a red, unmellowed, unmellowable brick', and sits apart in a small room: 'The clink of the bar, the heavy groaning walk of the landlord, the bright sun...the lively joyless music of the young soldiers, gave me a strange ecstasy without pleasure...[The music] made mockery of home, parents, wives, ambitions, joys, sorrows, debts' (*RB* 1, 3 [nd, ?1913/1914], 40-1).

12-16. *ghosts...ghostly room*. See note on Thomas's 'ghosts' (202). The quotation in the previous note indicates that symbolic 'talk of rain' covers more than "village England" threatened by modernity and war. As the cross-roads becomes 'a ghostly room', it portends a larger human absence which implicates modernity itself. Our tenure as 'inhabitants of the earth' may be in question. In part, an ecological elegist, the Cassandra-like speaker is haunted by the future.

22-4. *We cannot other... like a different tree*. 'About "Aspens" you missed just the turn that I thought essential. I was the aspen. "We" meant the trees and I with my dejected shyness' (*EF*, 152-3). Despite this, and despite its ghostliness, *Aspens* is Thomas's most assertive self-portrait as an artist. Those who 'like a different tree' are put on aesthetic and historical notice. The sibilant music that spreads out from the word 'aspens', and reaches its climax in 'ceaselessly, unreasonably', prevails over 'every other sound' in the poem.

Ms: *B*. **Published text**: *SP*, *AANP*, *LP*.

The Mill-Water (98)

12 July 1915

Among the poem's sources may be 'the tempestuous sixteen-foot fall of Steep Mill, which ceased its trade at the beginning of [the twentieth] century...[T]he Old English...called the Ashford Stream the Ludburn or Loud-bourne' (*WW*, 38-9). 'Mill full sound – heard by those alone – who are thinking and stop suddenly – and by those who watch long – so that they seem to feel with all who ever listened to it when mill was there' (after 2 June, *FNB80*). Earlier, Thomas had written:

> One by-road went to a lifeless mill, a tall house with upper windows of ample prospect. Above the wheel the waters no longer slid fast with awful repose, but cried and leapt through the broken flood-gates into a pool in the shadow of steep banks and underwood. The house was peopled only by the beautiful machinery of polished wood, now still and morose. The wheel too was still. Callosities of dry moss on the spokes, little by little, took the place of the weed which the river had combed into such excellence. And I could not but wonder that these things had, according to Hecuba's wish, voices 'in hands and feet and hair', the eloquence of death. The place would have been sad, had it not been for the meadow cranesbill at the door, a mournful flower, but here, as part of the ceremonial of decay by which this desolation was made perfect, it left one thought, 'How beautiful is death'. Each evening, just when the first nightjar was skimming the wood, the sedge-warblers began to sing all together round the pool. The song might have been the abstract voice of some old pain, feebly persistent. It went far into the night with a power of ghostly alarms, and attuned to such thoughts as come when night in certain places is malign, reverses the sweet work of the day, and gives the likeness of a dragon to the pleasant corner of a wood. The birds were full of prelusive dark sayings about the approaching night. (*HS*, 177-9)

Links between *The Mill-Water* and *Aspens*, as 'prelusive dark sayings about the approaching night', include the repeated 'moonlight', 'gloom', 'drowned' and 'sound' – the latter two, a repeated rhyme. Sound plays an equally important part in *The Mill-Water*, where the longest line often mimics the water's power, and the rhyme scheme (ABBA) sets up an ominous sequence of echo-systems. If *The Mill-Water* elegises 'a work-place and a home', dissolution also turns inwards. As with 'Solitude' and 'company' in the syntactically tangled fifth quatrain, cognitive and communal states are intertwined. Although a 'thought' (the poem itself) may emerge from the water's 'sound', Thomas's water-symbolism, muted in *The Brook* and *Aspens*, resumes the apocalyptic 'surge' of *A Dream*.

7-8. *mocks...busy roar*: cf. 'Hushing the roar of towns' (*Roads*, l.63). Thomas's visions of human obsolescence are all the more unsettling because he half-welcomes the end of 'busy roar': 'Man seems to me a very little part of Nature and the part I enjoy least' (*SL*, 51); 'I like to see grass and flowers come down softly to take possession of any London soil...the flowers and grass are related to me as the bricks, mortar, and iron are not, and I have a kind of far-off share in their victories' (*TC*, 12); 'It is a curious pleasure to see [raw settlements] besieged by docks and nettles, and, as sometimes happens, quietly overcome by docks and nettles' (*IW*, 125). Thomas's language of war and conquest sides with natural forces. In the poem, Nature 'reigns' and 'mocks', its 'idleness' suggesting more than the end of old-style rural technology.

Ms: *B*. **Published text:** *LP*.

For These (99)

13, 14 July 1915

Thomas completed *For These* on the day he 'passed the doctor' as fit for enlistment (*LGB*, 252). He refers to the poem as a 'prayer' (*EF*, 152). If so, like most of Thomas's poetic dealings with God or 'fate', it has an ironical tilt. *For These* belongs to the lyric genre that expresses desire for an idyllic rural retreat, but to its self-subverting wing (exemplified by Horace's second epode). Thomas includes more straightforward instances in the 'Village and Inn' section of his *Pocket Book of Poems and Songs for the Open Air*: poems such as John Clare's 'Proposals for Building a Cottage' (rechristened 'Clare's Desire'), to which *For These* may allude:

> Beside a runnel build my shed,
> With stubbles cover'd o'er;
> Let broad oaks o'er its chimney spread,
> And grass-plats grace the door...
>
> A little garden, not too fine,
> Inclose with painted pales;
> And woodbines, round the cot to twine,
> Pin to the walls with nails...
>
> And as the sweeping swallows stop
> Their flights along the green,
> Leave holes within the chimney-top
> To paste their nest between...

For These concludes a trio of quatrain-poems. It resembles *Aspens* in line-length, *The Mill-Water* in rhyme scheme. Here the ABBA scheme helps Thomas to dwell on an ideal "home". The delayed main verb and final stanza do not wholly negate the cumulative force of a catalogue that restores the balanced earthly (and poetic) habitat threatened in *Aspens* and lost in *The Mill-Water*: 'Where what the curlew needs not, the farmer tills'. This Arcadian microcosm may also be a prospectus for 'content': home in its psychological aspect.

   Ms: *B*. **Published text:** *AANP, LP*. **Differences from *CP1978*:** title For These [*AANP, LP*] *For these* [*Prayer*] **Note on title:** The title in *CP1978* incorporates Thomas's allusion to the poem in the letter quoted above.

Digging (99)

21 July 1915

'Finding an old pipe and one of mine in garden. Someone / will assuredly find mine when I am not – / He created the elephant' (*FNB80*, before 25 March 1915). This poem begins where the happier poem of the same name leaves off, reversing the rhyme 'earth'/'mirth'. The switch from present-tense epiphany to archaeological and eco-historical vista (see note on l.9) reflects the fact that the digger has become a 'soldier'. This may have activated Thomas's notebook jottings, and recalled *Tears*: another poem with soldiers. 'Tears or mirth' defines the human condition through the ages. But Thomas neither segregates these emotions, nor invokes a timelessness that excludes critique. 'Mirth' and 'laughed' convey anti-war irony as much as joy. He uses the clay pipes to question how dead soldiers are 'represented', and to offer a sardonic self-memorial. 'Living air' – the earthly biosphere – challenges the oppressions signified by 'Almighty God' (see note on *February Afternoon*, 274).

2. *clay pipes*. Thomas was a connoisseur of clay pipes (see *IPS*, 120-6).

4. *Blenheim* [1704], *Ramillies* [1706], and *Malplaquet* [1709]: victories of the Duke of Marlborough in the War of Spanish Succession. This line is the only obvious mark left on Thomas's poetry by his last and most uncongenial book-commission: *The Life of the Duke of Marlborough*. Yet the biography mediates his response to the current war, as when he calls the panegyrics after Ramillies 'verses of praise and flattery that never died because they never lived' (*LDM*, 173). Coombes sees 'his view of the Duke's times and campaigns' as 'coolly and consistently disenchanted' (*HC*, 42). Cooke highlights passages that criticise the military and political establishment, and identify with the common soldier (*WC*, 85-7).

9. *mastodon*. 'How little do we know of the business of the earth, not to speak of the universe; of time, not to speak of eternity. It was not by taking thought that man survived the mastodon. The acts and thoughts that will serve the race, that will profit this commonwealth of things that live in the sun, the air, the earth, the sea, now and through all time, are not known and never will be known. The rumour of much toil and scheming and triumph may never reach the stars' (*SC*, 26).

10. *in this same light of day*: once, 'at what earth had to bear' (*EF*, 153).

Ms: *B*. **Published text:** *LP*.

Two Houses (100)

22 July 1915

The 'house' is central to Thomas's metaphysics of inhabiting the earth and the body. Here it takes on a consciously emblematic shape. In *The South Country* he describes a thatched cottage, and continues: 'The one other house is not so high; nor has it eyes; nor do an old man and a girl and two children go in and out of it; it is, in fact, not a house of the living, but of the dead, a round tumulus at the edge of the hill' (*SC*, 197). At one level, *Two Houses*, like *Digging*, is a poem of departure for war. The trope of "leaving England" becomes a dreamlike diptych. Thomas's symbolic abodes split down the middle, into 'sunny' and 'dark', as if *The Manor Farm* and *The Combe* were clamped together. In fact, not every aspect of the poem is symmetrical: in each stanza the rhymes are differently distributed, and line-lengths vary. Smith argues that Thomas deconstructs the larger opposition he sets up, because this parable echoes his critique of a great house: 'Only a thousand years of settled continuous government, of far-reaching laws, of armies and police, of roadmaking, of bloody tyranny and tyranny that poisons quietly without blows, could have wrought earth and sky into such a harmony. It is a thing as remote from me here on the dusty road as is the green evening sky and all its tranquillity of rose and white' (*SC*, 116). Smith comments: 'The poem…rips the ideological "surfaces" of "harmony" away from this vision of England, to reveal that it is in reality a haunted landscape, full of ghosts and dark echoes of historic brutality and oppression' (*SS*, 66).

5/24. *So pleasant to look at... Dark echoes reply*. Since *Haymaking*, where the 'swift' holds visual and aural effects in balance, and where painting and writing cooperate to create pastoral, sight has become the main sensory medium for landscapes of peace (cf. 'visible' in *For These*, l.3); sound, the medium of history on the move.

7. *warm tiles*. Cf. *The Manor Farm* (l.12): 'tiles duskily glowing'.

14. *like a wasp at the muslined peach*: ripening peaches are protected by light material such as muslin. This simile focuses the scene's insulation, whether in the speaker's mind or in ideological terms, from a road that may 'lead to France' (*Roads*). 'Wasp' implies anger as well as desire; 'dusty thought' (l.11) is equivocal too.

21. *black dog*. 'Dog that [?]barks / barked so hoarse and old by Luff's house (near old farmyard and trees) and also by river – ?Rother [a Hampshire river] under echoing banks' (nd, *FNB80*). 'And presently it was dark, but for a lamp at an open door, and silent, but for a chained dog barking, and a pine tree moaning over the house...I could just hear the river Frome roaring steadily over a weir far off' (*IPS*, 178-9). In the poem, this complex of images evokes Cerberus and the river Styx.

26-7. *the dead...half hidden lie*. Thomas writes of the Cornish moors: 'On every hand lie cromlech, camp, circle, hut and tumulus of the unwritten years...It is a silent Bedlam of history, a senseless cemetery or museum...There are enough of the dead; they outnumber the living; and there those trite truths burst with life and drum upon the tympanum with ambiguous fatal voices' (*SC*, 159-60).

Ms: *B*. Published text: *LP*. Differences from *CP1978*: 7 under the warm *under warm* 14 the muslined *a muslined* **Note:** *CP1978* follows *B* and a typescript [*JT*], rather than *LP*, which must reflect another typescript, and seems conceptually and rhythmically preferable. 'The warm tiles' keeps a particular farmhouse in view; 'the muslined' generalises the simile.

Cock-Crow (101)

23 July 1915

Cock-Crow harks back to a prose passage also linked with *Haymaking* (see note, 248): 'the long, tearing crow of the cock, the chink of dairy pans' (*HE*, 72). After the splits of *Two Houses*, sound and sight come together again, but not straightforwardly. F.R. Leavis writes:

> To present a 'wood of thoughts' as being 'cut down' by an 'axe of light' looks like a bold indulgence in the pleasures of stylisation. Yet we have to recognise that 'wood' with its suggestions of tangled and obscure penetralia, stirring with clandestine life, is not an infelicitous metaphor for the mental life of sleep. And when...we come to 'silver blow' we have to recognise a metaphorical subtlety...'Cleaving' identifies the effect of the sound with that of the axe, the gleam of which gives an edge to the 'silver' of the blown trumpet. The silver-sounding trumpet is a familiar convention, and the element of wilful fantasy in this translation of the cock-crow becomes overt in the heraldically stylised twin trumpeters...We are prepared so for the ironical shift of the last line where daylight reality asserts itself. (Leavis, 'Imagery and Movement', *Scrutiny* 13, 2 [September 1945], 133-4)

Cock-Crow is one of Thomas's best-known short poems (see note, 284). Donald Davie praises it by invoking Imagism, a compliment that Thomas might not have relished (see Introduction, 20): 'This has all the "hardness" and "dryness" that T.E. Hulme had asked for...It is a great pity, and cause for wonder, that neither Pound nor anyone else apparently should have recognised that, if Imagism means anything, it surely means a small impersonal masterpiece like this' (*Times Literary Supplement*, 23 November 1979).

Thomas's parable could apply to many transactions between the unconscious and the conscious mind. Yet, at one level, *Cock-Crow* reviews the process that has led to his enlistment. Cf. the link between cock-crow and summons to war in Hardy's '"Men Who March Away"' ('Men who march away / Ere the barn-cocks say / Night is growing grey'), an 'impersonal song' that Thomas admired (see note on *The Trumpet*, 312). On 21 July he explained to Bottomley: 'It was not at all a desperate nor yet a purposed resolution but the natural culmination of a long series of moods & thoughts' (*LGB*, 253). The poem condenses 'moods & thoughts' into images that move from perplexity to decision (given a mock-heroic glamour) to the point where action must begin. The sequence of end rhymes and internal rhymes ('night' / 'light' / 'night' / 'bright') intensifies a rhythmic momentum to which the last line may be climax, anti-climax, or reality-check. This is the first poem of Thomas's to feature a martial call. Along with another eight-line parable, *I built myself a house of glass*, it demarcates his month of decision. He did not write another poem for nearly three months.

Ms: *B*. Published text: *SP, P*.

October (101)
15, 16 October 1915

As with the summer landscape of *Haymaking*, Thomas had often tried to capture Autumn. An early essay speaks in *fin-de-siècle* style of being 'troubled tenderly by autumnal maladies of soul' (*RAP*, 28). 'The leaves are falling from the poplars steadily one by one...It is this dead stillness and gloom that makes the fall of the leaves so arresting; no flutter of wind drifts them through the air...as they glide through the stirless space from branch to earth Even as we gaze on this wondrous scene of colour, the mist disperses and the sunbeams pour down, further to enliven what was already gay...the earth is strewn with gorgeous hues lit up anew. As the light varies, the shadows shift, and now the orange, now the gold, is all aflame' ('In Autumn Woods', *TWL*, 85-7). 'This is the beginning of the pageant of autumn, of that gradual pompous dying which has no parallel in human life, yet draws us to it with sure bonds. It is a dying of the flesh, and we see it pass through a kind of beauty which we can only call spiritual...[and which] awakens the never more than lightly sleeping human desire of permanence...The motion of the autumn is a fall, a surrender, requiring no effort, and therefore the mind cannot long be blind to the cycle of things as in the spring it can when the effort and delight of ascension veils the goal and the decline beyond...Pauses there are, of course, or what seem pauses in the declining of this pomp...mornings full of the sweetness of mushrooms and blackberries from the short turf among the blue scabious bloom' (*SC*, 272-4).

Cooke uses *October* to illustrate the 'number of influences which may impinge on Thomas's consciousness in the course of a single poem' (*WC*, 192-4). Here the major influence is Keats: not only 'To Autumn' and 'Hyperion' ('No stir of air was there / ...where the dead leaf fell, there did it rest') but everything that comes together in the odes where 'the poet made for himself a form in which the essence of all his thought, feeling, and observation, could be stored without overflowing or disorder' (*K*, 57); 'To Autumn' is 'a landscape that is the very picture of his mind' (*FIP*, 38). *October, There's nothing like the sun, The Thrush* and *Liberty* represent Thomas's most sustained effort to translate Keats's 'essence' into his own 'mind'. Autumn 1915 may have been his optimum moment for Keats, who presides over a return to poetry amid circumstances liable to sharpen a sense of mortality. *October* was the first poem that Thomas wrote in army camp (High Beech, Essex). It germinated in a letter to Frost (3, 5 September):

> But now I can't think of writing. The country is a little strange to me. It seems as if in my world there was no Autumn though they are just picking hops in Kent. On Hampstead Heath the other day I watched the bees at the bramble flowers & green blackberries & they looked so unfamiliar & with a kind of ugliness, partly but not wholly due to the fact that the earth around about was dirty London earth... As it happened I had 2 hours sleeplessness the night I was on guard after writing this & made it tolerable by making blank verses suggested by what I had just written to you. I had to. But I couldn't finish them & now they are practically gone. (*RFET*, 95-6)

This explains why Thomas told Eleanor Farjeon that 'the original version [of *October*] was in blank verse, but quite different' (*EF*, 169). *October*, like *There's nothing like the sun* and *Liberty*, is not stanzaic. But moving away from blank verse may have brought Thomas texturally closer to Keats's odes. With their intricate patterns of rhyme, assonance, and syntactical unit, and their nods to sonnet-structure, these three poems rework aspects of Keatsian 'form' along with Keatsian 'essence'.

1. *one great bough of gold*: 'elms (many with several isolated boughs all yellow while the rest was green)' (letter to Helen, 5 October 1914, *NLW*).

4. *Harebell and scabious and tormentil.* 'Hasn't Bronwen taught you tormentil, the tiny yellow flower in short hill grass, a flat buttercup or avens with rather separate petals? Tormentilla it is. The accent is on the 2nd syllable' (*EF*, 169). Among the flowers listed for 3 October 1895 in Thomas's 'Diary in English Fields and Woods' are 'Harebells...sheep's scabious...tormentil' (*TWL*, 199). His poetic catalogues of flowers or birds, in which simplicity belies intensity, are the apotheosis of field notes. Thomas says of Keats's art: 'It ["Ode to a Nightingale"] and the "Ode on a Grecian Urn" are of a texture so consummate and consistent that the simple line, "The grass, the thicket, and the fruit-tree wild", in one of them, and an equally simple line in the other, "With forest branches, and the trodden weed", both gain from their environment an astonishing beauty, profound and touching' (*K*, 56).

8. *The gossamers wander at their own will.* '[T]he promise [of a timeless moment]

is deceptive, for the equilibrium is easily disturbed...The hesitant rhythm of a line like "The gossamers wander at their own will" (I think it is a line of Wordsworth's that leads one to expect "*sweet* will") co-operates to produce an effect of fragility' (see John Burrow, 'Keats and Edward Thomas', *Essays in Criticism* 7 [1957], 404-15).

10-11. *fresh again.../As Spring*: 'the gold of the leaves had an April freshness' (*RAP*, 31).

11-12. *cool...warm*. This adjectival paradox is repeated from l.7 of *Two Houses* in a way that re-opens channels between the senses as well as the seasons.

12. *and now I might*. Here *October* 'turns' like a sonnet from evocation to introspection, though rhythm (in a sense the poem's subject) connects the two. Thomas proceeds to remix concepts from earlier poems such as *The Other* (title and lines 82-3), *Beauty*, *The Glory* and *Melancholy*.

17. *gorse that has no time not to be gay*: cf. *If I should ever by chance*, l.9, and see note (286).

18-20. *happiness...melancholy*: see note on *The Other* (161), and general note to *Melancholy* (231). 'Tomorrow I shall remember I was happy today' (before 7 September 1915, *FNB80*); 'a mood long blackened and obscured by the name of melancholy' (after 7 September, *FNB80*). '[M]elancholy is the mood most easily given an appearance of profundity, and, therefore, most easily impressive' (*IPS*, 150). 'I fell in with a philosopher who seemed to be equally moved [by an evening scene] yet could not decide whether his condition was to be described as happiness or melancholy...He was a lean, indefinite man; half his life lay behind him like a corpse, so he said, and half was before him like a ghost' (*IW*, 137). '[M]elancholy (in spite of the ode) is too disparaging a name for this mood ...we have been deceived in suspecting evil of ["Ode to a Nightingale"] because it is beautiful and attributes divinity to what we think a weakness' (*K*, 55). In testing the unstable frontier between 'happiness' and 'melancholy', Thomas adapts Romantic language to mutations within the psyche, and to traffic between the unconscious and the self that 'thinks' and 'names'.

Ms: *B*. Published text: *P*. Differences from *CP1978*: 2 one by one, – *one by one*. – 10 rich scene *late year* 11 Spring *Spring*, 18 happiness, – *happiness,* Note: *CP1978* follows *B* rather than *P*, whose text is vindicated by *PTP*. From *CP1920* to *CP1949* there is no stanza-break after l.9: an error due to the fact that it ends a page in *P*. Note on title: Title is given in *B*.

There's nothing like the sun (102)

18, 19 November 1915

This is the first poem that Thomas wrote at Hare Hall Camp, Gidea Park, Romford, Essex, where he was a map-reading instructor. He would be based there until August 1916. The poem reflects 'Beautiful cold sunny days, and the earth thick with clean snow' (*EF*, 171). 'Sweet as last damsons on spangled tree when November starling imitates the swallow in sunny interval between rain and all is still and dripping' (1 November 1915, *FNB80*); 'There's nothing like the sun in January – / While a man lives there's nothing like the sun' (?16 November, *FNB80*).

1. *There's nothing like the sun as the year dies*. Playing on the phrase 'nothing

259

like', Thomas splices the first line of Shakespeare's *Sonnet CXXX* ('My mistress' eyes are nothing like the sun') with his response to the last stanza of Keats's 'To Autumn': 'something light, thin, cold and vanishing' (*K*, 53). Keats rhymes 'dies' / 'skies'; Thomas, 'dies' / 'flies'.

2. *this...so*. '"This world being made so" is 5 heavy syllables unaccented' (*EF*, 175). Accents are important throughout the poem. The next line's monosyllabic (and monotonous) iambics place all earthly phenomena, from 'men' to 'flies', on the same level. More varied rhythms, as in the evocation of damsons, relish the diversity of months and days. 'Last-left damsons from the bough' echoes 'last oozings hours by hours': the phrase quoted by Thomas from 'To Autumn' to illustrate Keats's effects of 'mellowness and slowness' (*K*, 53). Cuthbertson argues that *There's nothing like the sun* is consciously belated in both literary history and the annual cycle: 'Thomas is taking some of the fruit from Keats's fruit-filled autumn scene; and it appears to be significant that Thomas's autumn comes after Keats's...The swallows have already gone' (*GC*, 243).

10-11. *whistling what / Once swallows sang*: a variation on Keats's 'The redbreast whistles' and 'gathering swallows twitter' in 'To Autumn'.

20. *There's nothing like the sun till we are dead*. As the poem turns back on itself, the blunt rhyme word, together with other contrasts between 'as the year dies' and 'till we are dead', makes no bones about the earthly condition. A draft has 'till a man's dead' (*EF*, 172).

Ms: *B*. **Published text:** *P*. **Note:** *B*, *CP1928* and *CP1944* begin l.15 'August' rather than 'And August' [*P*]. Thomas tinkered with the poem, and Eleanor Farjeon typed several versions [see *CP1978*, 248].

The Thrush (102)

November 1915

Thomas wrote this poem 'the day I was in as hut-orderly while the rest went to South Weald'. The thrush may be a Londoner: 'How I noticed the one thrush near the tip of poplar 250 yards away beyond Nightingale Lane in opening of Rusham Road – he was singing, the only one' (1 February 1915, *FNB80*). The thrush is the bird that Thomas most often aligns with, or carefully differentiates from, the poet (cf. *The Word* and *The Green Roads*). Similarly, he differentiates his own thrush-poem from Hardy's 'The Darkling Thrush', which proposes that the thrush's winter song carries 'Some blessed Hope, whereof he knew / And I was unaware'. For Thomas, 'awareness' and its responsibilities are human. *The Thrush* may also criticise Keats's 'translation of a thrush's song that told him he was "right to have no idea but of the morning"'. Keats makes the thrush say: 'O fret not after knowledge! I have none'. Thomas comments: 'The great odes, the poem to Autumn, and "The Eve of St Agnes" could never have been translated out of a thrush's song' (*K*, 51).

The Thrush is a choric interlude in this Keatsian sequence. It dwells on the burden of consciousness that detaches humanity (and poetry) from 'alternation of violet and rose' (*October*). The parallels with 'Ode to a Nightingale' are obvious. But where Keats stresses human suffering, Thomas stresses cognition, memory and language. He begins with a question about 'reading', and speculative syntax complicates lines that might have been songlike. Rhythmic counterpoint, including different kinds of refrain, backs up the distinction between poetry and birdsong.

5. *I hear the thrush*. Originally this quatrain addressed the thrush: 'I hear you alone and see / You alone' etc (*FNB80*). Besides injecting some appropriate distance, the change to the third person may have complicated the 'you' of the first quatrain, making it partly inner-directed or equivalent to 'one'.

17. *I know the months all*. Thomas has just proved this in *There's nothing like the sun*. Months feature in the title of eight poems; others incorporate their date-lines: 'It was late June' (*Adlestrop*); 'At hawthorn-time' (*Lob*); 'This early May morn' (*The Cherry Trees*); 'the harvest blue' (*How at once*). Thomas's sense of the seasons and sense of history seem to be converging. 'November' in *The Thrush* is more time-bound than in *November*, written a year earlier.

Ms: *B*. **Published text:** *LP*. **Differences from** *CP1978*: 22 in April [*CP1920-CP1949*] *into April* [*B, LP*]: the latter seems awkward in grammar and rhythm **Note on title:** In *B* the title is 'A Thrush'.

Liberty (103)
26 November 1915

Liberty concludes Thomas's autumnal meditation on 'things that have an end', his psychological and metaphysical journey from the 'green elm with the one great bough of gold' to 'the tall elm's shadow'. This soliloquy brings meditation itself centre-stage, and 'Ode to a Nightingale' sets the scene: 'haply the Queen-Moon is on her throne / ...But here there is no light, / Save what from heaven is with the breezes blown / Through verdurous glooms and winding mossy ways'. Thomas may also echo Anne Finch's 'A Nocturnal Reverie' (see note on *The Other*, 160), which ends: 'When a sedate Content the Spirit feels, / And no fierce Light disturbs, whilst it reveals... In such a *Night* let Me abroad remain, / Till Morning breaks, and All's confus'd again; / Our Cares, our Toils, our Clamours are renew'd, / Our Pleasures, seldom reach'd, again pursu'd.' He had written similarly himself: 'The past day is long past, the day of fighting, digging, buying, selling, writing; and if there are still men on the earth they are all equal in the trances of passion or sleep; the day to come is not to be thought of. The moon reigns; you rule. The centuries are gathered up in your hand' (*HE*, 167).

5. *unforgotten and lost*. This phrase governs the items in the next line and a half. Cf. *The Word*, lines 1-9, where Thomas explores the priorities and politics of memory. Thus *Liberty* revisits something 'thought' at the time of his enlistment. John F. Danby calls 'unforgotten' 'a typical surprise. It does not mean "still remembered". It means in fact the very opposite: these things have never been even admitted into memory...The present moment is thus apprehended as a datum from a memoriless and unremembered world, the world of the other admitted into the pure now' (Danby, 'Edward Thomas', *Critical Quarterly* 1 [1959], 310).

9-18. *liberty...free or not*. Here 'liberty' is checked by 'dream', and 'free' appears highly contingent: 'the second half of the poem meditates on the delusoriness of freedom from involvement in delusions' (Danby). The speaker confronts a paradox: actions that tie one down (joining an army, perhaps) may be liberating whereas too much choice can paralyse the will. A year earlier, like Hamlet envying Fortinbras, Thomas had contrasted the attitudes of 'the men who are fighting or going to fight' with those of 'morbid people in whom the balance or fusion of mind and body is impossible, and who admire frantically what is impossible to themselves' (*LA*, 13).

15. *mind. If every hour.* A quasi-division as between two sonnets occurs here, just as something akin to a sonnet's 'turn' occurs in the middle of lines 9 and 21.

24-7. *And yet I still...dark within the door.* Catalogue – lists of flora and fauna, naming the months – is a deep structure in these poems. *Liberty* ends with a comprehensive catalogue that rearranges key terms of Thomas's poetry, and redefines an 'inhabitant of the earth' (see note, 161). The affirmative (on balance) tone chimes with his summation of Keats: 'though a lover of the moon, a most sublunary poet, earthly, substantial and precise, a man, but for his intensity, singularly like his fellow-men' (*K*, 39).

24. *half in love with pain*: cf. 'half in love with easeful Death', 'Ode to a Nightingale'.

25. *With what is imperfect, with both tears and mirth.* '[Jefferies] has learned... that things may be imperfect and yet better than the perfection of cloistered nullity' (*RJ*, 227). 'Tears and mirth' alludes to Thomas's two *Digging* poems. 'Mirth' and 'earth' are rhymed in both, and in *The Other* and *The Source*. Thomas uses (almost) every possible rhyme for 'earth'.

Ms: *B*. **Published text**: *P.* **Note**: In l.8 *CP1944* has 'a grave' [*B*].

This is no case of petty right or wrong (104)
26 December 1915

This poem returns to the roots of Thomas's thinking about the war. On 3 September 1914 he wrote: 'I don't quite know what will happen. The obvious thing is to join the Territorials but I can't leave other people to keep my family ...I am slowly growing into a conscious Englishman' (*LJB*, 74). On 19 September he mentioned to Frost that he was adding to an article ['This England'] based on the experience that also generated *The sun used to shine* (see note, 296): 'the new moon of August 26 & you & me strolling about in the sun while our brave soldiers &c. I doubt if I shall get nearer soldiering than I did then, chiefly for fear of leaving many tangles behind' (*RFET*, 26). On 11 October he reflected: 'I suppose writers generally have been people who tasted far more things than they ever swallowed and digested. But Shelley bothered for a time about politics...Tennyson started at any rate to join a body of volunteers to fight (I think) in Spain. And I – dig in the garden. I suppose it is something. I only feel how far too little it is to give my imagination of the lives of men reality' (letter to Helen, *NLW*). At the end of October Thomas told Frost: 'I have just made myself almost ill with thinking hard for an hour, – going up to my study & sitting there, – that I ought to enlist next week in town...I go on writing, unlike all the patriots, or rather as the patriots feel they oughtn't to' (*RFET*, 30). On 20 November he told W.H. Hudson: 'As you will have supposed, I have not enlisted, tho I should have done if I had been in company that had encouraged me. At least I think so. Not that I pretend to be warlike or to think except with blank misgiving of any sort of life different from my past: only I can't justify not making an effort, except by saying that if I did go it would be hard to put and leave things straight at home' (*ETFN* 52 [August 2004], 10).

For Thomas's enlistment, see Introduction (17) and general note to *The Word* (246). If *Liberty* suggests that his poetry is still reviewing that decision, *This is no case* reads like a polemical reprise of the decision-making process. Despite 'Dinned / With war and argument', the first line speaks as from the midst of an argument: an argument pursued on two fronts, against both patriots and pacifists. Thomas may also be subtextually quarrelling with himself, and thus over-egging his love for England. But one reason why he 'hated' jingoism was because it had stolen patriotism. He and the poet Ralph Hodgson agreed not to meet again until after the war because 'I am not patriotic enough for his exuberant taste' (*LGB*, 243). In December 1914 he told Harold Monro: 'Hodgson flung off today labelling me pro-German. I almost enlisted afterwards in repentance' (*ETFN* 42 [January 2000], 9). As for his father's politics: 'People get fined occasionally for speaking well of the Germans at private parties – under the Defence of the Realm Act. I don't wonder. My father is so rampant in his cheery patriotism that I become pro German every evening' (9 August 1915, *RFET*, 89); 'In town I saw my father too...he treats me so that I have a feeling of shame that I am alive. I couldn't sleep after it... We argued about the war & he showed that his real feeling when he is not trying to be nice & comfortable is one of contempt' (2 January 1916, *RFET*, 115).

'Argument' brings to the poetic surface (and thus simplifies) the complex of psychological, ethical, cultural and literary factors that shaped Thomas's commitment to the war. This is the only poem of his that proclaims its status as a war poem, but he had been pondering an aesthetic of "war poetry" since Autumn 1914. Reviewing his own literary situation, while wondering 'whether I can in reason and decency enlist', he told Walter de la Mare: 'The question is what to do with spare time. It is not easy – if possible – to go on writing as if the County Council ran the world: otherwise it would be a good time for doing what one really wants to do, provided one can really discover now what that is' (*LWD*, September 1914). Between October and December, while preparing his review article 'War Poetry', he noted: 'Poetry: The war national but as yet dark and chaotic in brain – e.g. no good poems early in Napoleonic wars. Some writers can't go on with old work but no reason why they should at once be able to admit war into subject matter. Poetry excepting cheapest kind shows this dark chaotic character. People expressing all sorts of <u>views</u> and trumping up old canting catchwords, but not yet the compact essential real truth to this occasion alone. Statesman may say "No price too high when honour and freedom are at stake" etc. But it can't be translated into poetry' (*FNB79*).

This England marks a further stage in Thomas's thinking – or feeling: the proper ratio between thought and feeling is itself at issue. Like *Lob*, *This is no case* condenses passages from the anthology but with a bias towards explicitly "national" content. A crucial model for the poem was Coleridge's 'Fears in Solitude: written in April 1798, during the alarm of an invasion'. In *This England* Thomas juxtaposes 'Fears in Solitude' with his own *Manor Farm* and *Haymaking*; and in 'War Poetry' he says: 'no newspaper or magazine, then or now, would print such a poem, since a large part of it is humble' (*Poetry and Drama* 2, 8 [December 1914], 341). After recording his anxieties about invasion and 'all the crash of onset', Coleridge appeals:

O native Britain! O my Mother Isle!
How shouldst thou prove aught else but dear and holy
To me, who from thy lakes and mountain-hills,
Thy clouds, thy quiet dales, thy rocks and seas,
Have drunk in all my intellectual life,
All sweet sensations, all ennobling thoughts,
All adoration of the God in nature...?
There lives nor form nor feeling in my soul
Unborrowed from my country!

This is no case also takes concepts from Thomas's prose reflections on 'England': from the pre-war *Happy-Go-Lucky Morgans*; from essays commissioned by the *English Review* in August 1914 ('Tipperary', 'England', 'It's a Long, Long, Way'); and from 'This England'. The *English Review* commission entailed research. From 29 August to 10 September 1914 Thomas 'travelled through England, from Swindon to Newcastle-on-Tyne, listening to people, in railway carriages, trams, taverns, and public places, talking about the war and the effects of it' ('Tipperary', *LS*, 113). This exceptional field trip may have contributed to his becoming a poet. It is interesting that Thomas should now return to that moment, to his first thoughts about the war, and (in the final lines) to the rhyming couplets he had favoured in July 1915, his month of decision (see note, 251). A letter to Eleanor Farjeon reveals that he wrote the couplets several weeks after the earlier lines (*EF*, 180). Uniquely in his work, the couplets of *This is no case* serve discursive purposes – a package Thomas disliked in eighteenth-century poetry. He thus courts his own censure of those who write 'under the direct pressure of public patriotic motives' ('War Poetry', 341). But if he slips into rhetoric (as in the final gloss on 'hate'), or strays into Rupert Brooke territory, at least he tries to make the patriotic poem inner-directed rather than aggressive. Thomas published *This is no case* in *SP*, which may explain its absence from *P*; although *Cock-Crow* appears in both, and Farjeon seems to think the omission significant.

This is no case may show signs of strain partly because it adapts to England/ Britain at war a patriotic idea predicated on Wales. Before the war Thomas had noted: 'what with Great Britain, the British Empire, Britons, Britishers, and the English-speaking world, the choice offered to whomsoever would be patriotic is embarrassing' (*SC*, 71). Some years earlier, he had 'walked to Wimbledon' with his friend Arthur York Hardy, who was about to join the South African police, 'talking of patriotism of which I never felt a spark unless it be [?]perhaps to love a few acres in Wales. A Frenchman is to me the same as an Eng[lishman]' (*Diary*, 29 September 1901, *NLW*). Similarly, he writes: 'I do not easily believe in patriotism, in times of peace or war, except as a party cry, or the result of intoxication or an article in a newspaper, unless I am in Wales' (*BW*, 174); and he says of 'Land of My Fathers': 'It was exulting without self-glorification or any other form of brutality. It might well be the national anthem of any nation that knows, and would not rashly destroy, the bonds distinguishing it from the rest of the world without isolating it' (*HGLM*, 224-5). Thomas's reading of "England" through Wales or Ireland may work best where it bases itself on 'a few acres'. The following extracts suggest the poetic possibilities (*Adlestrop*, *Lob*) and limits (*This is no case*) of "nationality":

Someone with a precocious sneer, asked if England was now anything more than a geographical expression, and Mr Stodham preached a sermon straight away: 'A great poet [Wordsworth] said once upon a time that this earth is "where we have our happiness or not at all". For most of those who speak his language he might have said that this England is where we have our happiness or not at all. He meant to say that we are limited creatures, not angels, and that our immediate surroundings are enough to exercise all our faculties of mind and body: there is no need to flatter ourselves with the belief that we could do better in a bigger or another world. Only the bad workman complains of his tools... [after a quotation from Wordsworth's 'To a Skylark', "Type of the wise who soar but never roam, / True to the kindred points of heaven and home"] Well, England is home and heaven too. England made you, and of you is England made. Deny England – wise men have done so – and you may find yourself some day denying your father and mother – and this also wise men have done. Having denied England and your father and mother, you may have to deny your own self, and treat it as nothing, a mere conventional boundary, an artifice, by which you are separated from the universe and its creator... He is a bold man who hopes to do without earth, England, family, and self.' (*HGLM*, 220-2)

I should like to know what the old soldier meant by 'England', if it was anything more than some sort of a giant with Gloucestershire for its eyes, its beating heart, for everything that raised it above a personification. His was a very little England. The core and vital principle was less still, a few thousand acres of corn, meadow, orchard, and copse, a few farms and cottages; and he laughed heartily over a farmer's artfulness who had hid away some horses wanted by the War Office. If England was against Germany, the parish was against Germany, England, and all the world. ('It's a Long, Long, Way', *LS*, 136)

In times of peace and tranquillity the vocabulary of patriotism is not much used...If England lies like a vast estate calm around you, and you a minor, you may find faults without end. If England seems threatened you feel that in losing her you would lose yourself...

I believe the man who thought it a 'quaint' idea to love England would feel very much as I do about these passages and about Walton altogether. I believe that England means something like this to most of us; that all ideas of England are developed, spun out, from such a centre into something large or infinite, solid or aëry, according to each man's nature and capacity; that England is a system of vast circumferences circling round the minute neighbouring points of home. ('England', *LS*, 91, 111)

At one stroke, I thought, like many other people, what things that same new moon sees eastward about the Meuse in France... I was deluged, in a second stroke, by another thought, or something that overpowered thought. All I can tell is, it seemed to me that either I had never loved England, or I had loved it foolishly, aesthetically, like a slave, not having realised that it was not mine unless I were willing and prepared to die rather than leave it as Belgian women and old men and children had left their country. Something I had omitted. Something, I felt, had to be done before I could look again composedly at English landscape... ('This England', *LS*, 221 [see general note to *The sun used to shine*, 296])

2-3. *That politicians or philosophers / Can judge.* In l.17 the capacity of future 'historians' to make judgments about the war is also doubted. Cf. the limitations of 'naturalists' in *The Unknown Bird.* 'Philosophers' may allude to Bertrand Russell's pacifist campaigning.

4. *to please newspapers.* The speaker is both 'reading', and refusing to write for, the jingoistic press. 'In print men become capable of anything. The bards and the journalists say extraordinary things...They feel they are addressing the world; they are intoxicated with the social sense' ('England', *LS*, 92). 'It is the hour of the writer who picks up popular views or phrases, or coins them, and has the power to turn them into downright stanzas. Most newspapers have one or more of these gentlemen' ('War Poetry', 344).

12. *Two witches' cauldrons roar.* In 'Fears in Solitude' Coleridge hopes that 'the vaunts / And menace of the vengeful enemy' may 'Pass like the gust, that roared and died away / In the distant tree'. As with 'gong' (l.7) and 'Dinned' (l.9), Thomas continues to associate war, and its rhetoric, with noise. Cf. the opening of Yeats's 'A Prayer for My Daughter' (1919): 'Once more the storm is howling'.

15-26. *like her mother... She...her foe.* 'The old phrases come back alive in wartime. I have heard a farmer's wife refer to England as She' ('England', *LS*, 92). Thomas himself calls England 'her' in the same essay (see quotation above). Despite damning 'Britannia' as 'a frigid personification' (see Introduction, 21), he may have felt that such gendering fleshed out 'ideas of England'. *This England* is subtitled: 'An Anthology from her Writers'.

19. *serene...ken*: a slightly odd echo of Keats's 'On First Looking into Chapman's Homer'.

20-6. *But with the best...foe.* The epigraph to the 'This England' section (the first section) of *This England* is Prince Arthur's patriotic outburst in the *Faerie Queene* (II. x. 69) after reading 'Briton moniments':

Dear Country, O how dearly dear
Ought thy remembrance and perpetual band
Be to thy foster Child, that from thy hand
Did common breath and nouriture receive?
How brutish is it not to understand,
How much to her we owe, that all us gave,
That gave unto us all, what ever good we have.

21. *I am one in crying, God save England.* 'One' is at odds with Thomas's criticism of the 'writer of hymns or patriotic verses...who feels himself always or at the time at one with [a] class, perhaps the whole nation, or...who can simulate or exaggerate this sympathy' ('War Poetry', 343).

22. *what never slaves and cattle blessed.* A draft of lines 21-2 is: 'Cry God save England else we lose our souls / And shall [be] live clothed and fed like animals' (26 November 1915, *FNB80*). Cf. 'like a slave' in the passage quoted above from 'This England', and 'brutish' in the quotation from *The Faerie Queene. This England* contains several celebrations of English 'liberty' by Milton and others, including Lord Mansfield's claim: 'The air of England has long been too pure for a slave, and every man is free who breathes it'.

23. *The ages made her that made us from the dust*: 'But do know that bone of her bone I am' (*FNB80* draft). Eleanor Farjeon writes: 'when we were walking in the country...I asked him the question his friends had asked him when he joined up, but I put it differently. "Do you know what you are fighting for?" He stopped, and picked up a pinch of earth. "Literally, for this." He crumbled it between finger and thumb, and let it fall' (*EF*, 154).

Ms: B. Published text: *SP, LP.* **Note on title:** *CP1978* brackets the title; *CP2004* drops it. See Note on Text.

Rain (105)

7 January 1916

For Thomas and rain, see general note to *After Rain* (154). A passage in *The Icknield Way* is perhaps best known of 'the uncut stones which are scattered about his books' (*VS*, 12):

> I lay awake listening to the rain, and at first it was as pleasant to my ear and my mind as it had long been desired; but before I fell asleep it had become a majestic and finally a terrible thing, instead of a sweet sound and symbol. It was accusing and trying me and passing judgment. Long I lay still under the sentence, listening to the rain, and then at last listening to words which seemed to be spoken by a ghostly double beside me. He was muttering: The all-night rain puts out summer like a torch. In the heavy, black rain falling straight from invisible, dark sky to invisible, dark earth the heat of summer is annihilated, the splendour is dead, the summer is gone. The midnight rain buries it away where it has buried all sound but its own. I am alone in the dark still night, and my ear listens to the rain piping in the gutters and roaring softly in the trees of the world. Even so will the rain fall darkly upon the grass over the grave when my ears can hear it no more...I am not a part of nature. I am alone. There is nothing else in my world but my dead heart and brain within me and the rain without...There is nothing to be seen or heard, and there never was. Memory, the last chord of the lute, is broken ...Now there is neither life nor death, but only the rain...the rain falls for ever and I am melting into it. Black and monotonously sounding is the midnight and solitude of the rain. In a little while or in an age – for it is all one – I shall know the full truth of the words I used to love, I

267

knew not why, in my days of nature, in the days before the rain:
'Blessed are the dead that the rain rains on.' (*IW*, 280-3)

Cooke discusses the development from prose to poem (*WC*, 177-82). Thomas's incantatory prose already aspires to the condition of poetry: 'finally a terrible thing, instead of a sweet sound and symbol'. *Rain* does what this says. Its seamless symbolism blends sound, image, cadence and the voice of the 'ghostly double' into a prospect of 'annihilation' or nihilism now intensified by war. The repeated 'rain' (rhyme, refrain, rhetoric, onomatopoeia) fuses outward bombardment with inner dissolution. Here the apocalyptic waters of *A Dream* and *The Mill-Water* reach a new pitch. *Rain* relates dialectically to the poems that precede it: to *Liberty* as a darker soliloquy; to *This is no case of petty right or wrong* as a 'bleaker' war poem. Noting Frost's response to 'some verses I had sent – dismal ones, I gather', Thomas says: 'Perhaps one was called "Rain", a form of excrement you hoped it was when you said "work all that off in poetry & I shan't complain"' (*RFET*, 126).

2. *bleak hut*: an army-hut at Hare Hall Camp.

6. *this solitude*: perhaps global as well as personal.

14. *Myriads of broken reeds all still and stiff*: the war dead. B has 'A million' for 'Myriads of'.

16. *the love of death*: cf. 'half in love with pain' (*Liberty*). Thomas needed no cue from Keats to be more than 'half in love with easeful Death': 'Yet I brood too much for suicide; the thought to kill myself kills itself by its intensity. How many sedentary people do commit suicide?' (*Diary*, 2 May 1901, *NLW*). But in 1908 and 1913 he nearly did more than brood (see Introduction, 13). On the first occasion he noted in his diary: 'Up 7. Reading. After tried to shoot myself. Evening reading. Read Marlowe. To bed 11' (*Diary*, 29 November 1908, *NLW*; *ETFN* 27 [August 1992], 4). Three weeks earlier he had written: 'How nice it would be to be dead if only we could know we were dead. That is what I hate, the not being able to turn round in the grave & to say It is over. With me I suppose it is vanity: I don't want to do so difficult a thing as dying without any chance of applause after having done it' (*LGB*, 174-5). See general note to *Beauty* (186).

Thomas uses these experiences in his prose: 'As will happen with men who love life too passionately, [Morgan Rhys] was often in love with death. He found enjoyment in silence, in darkness, in refraining from deeds, and he longed even to embrace the absolute blank of death, if only he could be just conscious of it; and he envied the solitary tree on a bare plain high up among the hills, under a night sky in winter where the only touch of life and pleasure was the rain. And now, with his fantastic belief that the corpse is life's handiwork and its utmost end, he is humanised only by a dread of the blank to which he is going...He has made a heaven and he fears it' (*BW*, 94-5). 'The Attempt', a fictionalised account of Thomas's suicidal episode in 1908, features another Welsh *alter ego*: '[Morgan Treharon] was called to death, but hardly to an act which could procure it...Death was an idea tinged with poetry in his mind – a kingly thing which was once only at any man's call. After it came annihilation...There was also an element of vanity in his project; he was going to punish himself and in a manner so extreme that he was inclined to be exalted by the feeling that he was now about to convince the world he had suffered exceedingly' (*LAT*, 165-6; cf. *HT*, 113-14).

17-18. If love it be towards what is perfect...disappoint. This again counterpoints *Liberty* ('half in love.../ With what is imperfect'). The difference between the poems' endings turns on structure and tone. *Rain* ends, not with an inclusive, if ambivalent, catalogue, but with a series of qualifying clauses that echo the self-irony in Thomas's prose portraits – Morgan Treharon is said to practise 'luxurious self-contempt' (*LAT*, 163). The notion of death as 'perfect' makes its lover an aesthete.

Ms: *B*. **Published text:** *P*. **Note:** In l.17, *B* [followed by *CP1928* and *CP1944*] has 'for' not 'towards' [*P*]. While 'towards' might seem unidiomatic, it carries a resistant emphasis amidst the assonantal build-up: 'Myriads / reeds / wild rain / dissolved / what is perfect'. **Note on title:** Title is given in *B*.

The clouds that are so light (105)
15 January 1916

Thomas takes another image from *The Icknield Way* which (in *Roads* too) he seems to be recalling: 'The air was now still and the earth growing dark and already very quiet. But the sky was light and its clouds of utmost whiteness were very wildly and even fiercely shaped, so that it seemed the playground of powerful and wanton spirits knowing nothing of earth. And this dark earth appeared a small though also a kingly and brave place in comparison with the infinite heavens now so joyous and so bright and out of reach' (*IW*, 137). In the poem, the paradox of cloud-shadows and Thomas's most habitual polarities (dark/light, earth/sky) enrich the trope of beauty's dependence on the lover and on the poem itself ('this small dark spot' covers both). *The clouds that are so light* simultaneously invokes a Muse – perhaps a new one, given the present tense – that counters the depressive 'love' in *Rain*. It heralds the sequence of love (and hate) poems, mainly in quatrains, that Thomas would write between 8 February and 4 March. A letter to Helen Thomas shows that it also heralds her reception of them (see note, 277): 'Fancy your thinking I might have someone in view in those verses beginning "The clouds that are so light". Fancy your being pleased at the idea. Well, perhaps you wouldn't be, if there really were someone, in which case I would hardly write verses, I think' (?24 January, quoted *CP1978*, 408).

Ms: *B*. **Published text:** *P*. **Differences from *CP1978*:** title: The clouds that are so light [*P*] *Song* [title in *B*] [2] **Note:** In *CP1928* the poem begins: 'As the clouds' and l.5 begins: 'Even so' [*B*]. In *CP1944* the poem is re-titled from the change in its first line, and the *B* and *P* versions confused in the text: 'As the clouds...And even so'.

Roads (106)
22 January 1916

The epigraph to *The South Country* is a speech by Paul Ruttledge in Yeats's play *Where There is Nothing*: 'As I can't leap from cloud to cloud, I want to wander from road to road. That little path there by the clipped hedge goes up to the high road. I want to go up that path and to walk along the high road, and so on and on and on, and to know all kinds of people. Did you ever think that the roads are the only things that are endless; that one can walk on and on, and never be stopped by a gate or a wall? They are the serpent of eternity. I wonder they have never been worshipped. What are the stars beside them? They never meet one another. The roads are the only thing that are infinite. They are all endless.' 'The little roads, so old, wind among the fields timidly as if they marked the path of one creeping with difficulty through forest coeval with the world' (*HE*, 128). Thomas follows many roads in *The South Country*, *In Pursuit of Spring*, and the first chapter of *Richard Jefferies*, but his road-worship reaches its prose apotheosis in *The Icknield Way*:

> Today I know there is nothing beyond the farthest of far ridges except a signpost to unknown places. The end is in the means – in the sight of that beautiful long straight line of the Downs in which a curve is latent – in the houses we shall never enter, with their dark secret windows and quiet hearth smoke, or their ruins friendly only to elders and nettles – in the people passing whom we shall never know though we may love them…I could not find a beginning or end of the Icknield Way. It is thus a symbol of mortal things with their beginnings and ends always in immortal darkness. I wish the book had a little more of the mystery of the road about it. (*IW*, 'Dedication', vi-vii)

> Much has been written of travel, far less of the road. Writers have treated the road as a passive means to an end, and honoured it most when it has been an obstacle; they leave the impression that a road is a connection between two points which only exists when the traveller is upon it…Yet to a nomadic people the road was as important as anything upon it…We still say that a road "goes" to London, as we "go" ourselves. We could not attribute more life to them if we had moving roads with platforms on the sidewalks. We may go or stay, but the road will go up over the mountains to Llandovery, and then up again over to Tregaron. It is a silent companion always ready for us, whether it is night or day, wet or fine, whether we are calm or desperate, wet or sick. It is always going; it has never gone right away, and no man is too late…old roads will endure as long as the Roman streets, though great is the difference between the unraised trackway, as dim as a wind-path on the sea, and the straight embanked Roman highway…The making of such roads seems one of the most natural operations of man, one in which he least conflicts with nature and the animals…Why go straight? There is nothing at the end of any road better than may be found beside it, though there would be no travel did men believe it. (*IW*, 1-5)

Thomas's 'Dedication' (to Harry Hooton) is ironically aware that his walking has become a professional function. He says of youthful walks with Hooton: 'I am glad they are in ghostland and not fettered in useless print' (vi). Yet roads and walks condition his deepest imaginative structures. In *Roads* the trope of the journey, always latent in his poetry, re-emerges to be given an emblematic stamp.

270

During its half-anthropomorphic, half-animistic course, *Roads* 'lightly' touches many bases. For Thomas, the body links walking and writing: '[Cobbett's] sentences do not precisely suggest the swing of an arm or a leg, but they have something in common with it' (*RR*, xi). He also maps roads on to cognitive processes and *vice versa*: a point that the fourth quatrain makes explicit. As a self-image for Thomas's poetry, *Roads* attaches its windings and back-tracks to earth-history, to the road-network, to his criss-crossings of England and Wales. Sinuous syntax loops over the quatrains like paths over the downs. The ABBA rhyme-scheme, and the way in which end-stopped quatrains melt into run-on quatrains, further dramatise twists and turns, stops and starts.

25-8. *The next turn...Hell conceal*. Like the poem more generally, its most allegorical stanza has absorbed Bunyan: '*Pilgrim's Progress* is full of the sense of roads...When Christian comes to the Hill Difficulty you see the primitive man deciding to go straight uphill, turning not to the left by the way called Danger into a great wood, nor to the right to Destruction...How full of plain English country wayfaring is the passage where Hopeful and Christian take a road by a river-side, and then when it turns away from the water they see a stile leading into a path which keeps on, as a path would do, along the bank through By-path Meadow: only, as it happens, the river is in flood and they must turn back again towards the stile. This man knew roads' (*IW*, 6). Other literary referents for *Roads* are '*Cymbeline*...and some of the historical plays of Shakespeare', which 'give a grand impression of wide tracts of country traversed by roads of great purpose and destiny' (*IW*, 7). *Cymbeline*, perhaps owing to its Anglo-Welsh "Britishness", was a favourite play of Thomas's.

29-32. *Often footsore...As it winds on for ever*. The last line, rhythm and key rhyme of this quatrain recast the ending (and refrain) of Tennyson's 'The Brook': 'And out again I curve and flow / To join the brimming river, / For men may come and men may go, / But I go on for ever'. Like 'winding stream' (l.15), the echo renders roads fluid as water.

33. *Helen of the roads*: 'Helen is the lady in the Mabinogion, the Welsh lady who married Maxen the Emperor and gave her name to the great old mountain roads – Sarn Helen they are all marked on the maps. Do you remember the "Dream of Maxen"? She is known to mythologists as one of the travelling goddesses of the dusk' (*EF*, 182). Thomas recounts 'The Dream of Maxen' in *Celtic Stories* (121-5) and *The Icknield Way*. Maxen dreams of a beautiful girl in a castle, and finally tracks her down after years of searching: 'She became his bride, and he gave her three castles – one at Arvon in North Wales, one at Carleon, and one at Caermarthen in the South. Then, says the tale, "Helen bethought her to make high-roads from one castle to another throughout the Island of Britain. And the roads were made. And for this cause are they called the roads of Helen Luyddawc, that she was sprung from a native of this island, and the men of the Island of Britain would not have made these great roads for any save her"' (*IW*, 7-8).

35. *the Mabinogion tales*: Welsh tales 'written down at the end of the Middle Ages, and translated from Welsh into English by Lady [Charlotte] Guest in the nineteenth century [1849]. The original Welsh manuscript (called "The Red Book of Hergest"...) belongs to the fourteenth and fifteenth centuries,

but the stories had been told over and over again, and probably written down many times, before they were copied into "The Red Book"' (*CS*, 126).

50-6. *Troops that make loneliness...the dead / Returning lightly dance.* 'I wish you had liked "Roads" more. I thought the particular ghosts came in comfortably enough after the ghosts in general' (*LGB*, 260). This is one of Thomas's most eerily *unheimlich* effects (see note, 199). Subtly, 'ghost' does not appear in the poem, although its landscape has been haunted from the outset: 'invisible', 'Forgotten', 'fade', 'dream', 'dawn's twilight', 'the dead'. Again 'Troops' occurs in what might seem to be the wrong stanza. 'Lightly dance' is both a critique of the war and an unsettling (*danse macabre*) image for the war dead.

53. *Now all roads lead to France.* Frost told Edward Garnett after Thomas's death: 'His poetry is so very brave – so unconsciously brave. He didn't think of it for a moment as war poetry, though that is what it is. It ought to be called Roads to France' (*SLRF*, 217).

59. *They keep me company.* '"They" in [stanza] 15 refers to "the dead"' (*EF*, 184).

61-2. *the solitude / Of the loops over the downs.* 'Jefferies often thought of the sea upon these hills...There is something oceanic in their magnitude, their ease, their solitude – above all, in their liquid forms, that combine apparent mobility with placidity...They are never abrupt, but, flowing on and on, make a type of infinity' (*RJ*, 13).

63. *roar of towns*: see note on *Good-night* (202).

64. *brief multitude.* This oxymoron challenges conventional ideas of scale. Doubly paradoxical, in combining temporal and spatial concepts, it magnifies remembrance of the dead and cuts the city down to size. Thomas writes of London: 'A sense of multitude surged about and over me – of multitudes entirely unknown to me – collected by chance – mere numbers – human faces that were at that moment expressing innumerable strange meanings with which I had nothing to do' (*HE*, 6).

Ms: *B*. **Published text:** *AANP, LP*. **Note on title:** Title is given in *B*.

The Ash Grove (108)

4-9 February 1916

'I don't quite know why, but the ash is becoming my favourite tree' (letter to Helen, 5 October 1914, *NLW*). Drafts of this poem contain further stanzas. In one ms. (kept by Eleanor Farjeon) the first four stanzas, which precede drafts of the last three existing ones, are as follows:

In an ash grove among the mountains once, I was glad
Exceedingly, walking under the trees, notwithstanding I had
Naught that I knew to be glad of. Bare and decayed,
Their few leaves shaking in silence, the trees were not sad

Though half of them stood dead and the living made
Little more than the dead ones made of shade.
If it led to a house the house was long since gone,
But the ash grove welcomed me and my feet delayed

From where I saw the first of the stony roots clasp the stone
And I forgot myself and the past and future, on
To where the last of the shadows fell and the blaze
Of the sun returned, and outside I walked alone.

Before and after nothing was worth my gaze
Or my thought. For emptiness it was a day of days,
Except that moment under the ash trees tall
Which then to have understood would have been to erase.

This second 'journey' poem again plays with scale, space, and time. Whereas the short lines of *Roads* go an infinite distance, the long lines of *The Ash Grove* (up to sixteen syllables) stretch out 'Paces each sweeter than sweetest miles'. 'Interval' (1.5) applies to time, space, inner space and the poem itself. As in *The Bridge*, Thomas adapts rhythm and stanza to a state of hiatus or remission. Like the long lines, the same-rhymed stanzas (AABA, BBCB etc.) 'delay' over fleetingly fulfilled 'desire'. But the final unrhymed line ending, which points beyond the poem, is 'die'.

6. *sweeter...sweetest*: see note on *April* (233).

8-9. *wall // That I passed through at either end without noticing*. This reflexive stanza-break mirrors one of the rare moments of integration in Thomas's poetry when a bar or barrier unconsciously melts.

10-11. *can bring / The same tranquillity*. Thomas revises Wordsworth's definition of poetry as 'emotion recollected in tranquillity' (Preface to *Lyrical Ballads*, second ed. [1800]) by celebrating tranquillity recollected in tranquillity and by maximising 'recollection': the nexus of memory and epiphany; good memory driving out bad; the mnemonic role of poetry – his own 'song' of the ash grove.

11-12. *ghost...ghostly*: see note on Thomas's 'ghosts' (202). Like the ash grove's history, the speaker's 'ghostly gladness' is extraordinarily 'veiled', elusive and recessive. It depends on a secondary epiphany, on a notional singer and her 'lost' song, on love redeemed only in simile.

13. *The song of the Ash Grove*. 'Llwyn Onn' or 'The Ash Grove' is a traditional Welsh harp melody to which various Welsh and English words have been set. 'Restless wing' (1.7) and the poem's anapaestic rhythms suggest that Thomas has in mind the version by 'Talhaiarn' (John Jones, 1810-70), of which this is the first stanza:

Shine, blessed sun, on the home of my boyhood,
Bright be thy rays on the famous 'Ash Grove',
Dear to my heart is the home of my parents,
Home of my infancy, home of my love;
Far, far away I have sailed o'er the ocean,
Still guided by fate on the wings of unrest;
Oh! that I had the swift wings of the swallow,
To fly to my home, to return to my nest.

15. *something unwilling to die*: cf. 'what yet lives in me' (*Beauty*, 1.18). There are also parallels between 'Llwyn Onn' and the end of *Beauty*.

Ms: *B*. **Published text**: *LP*. **Note on title**: Title is given in *B*.

February Afternoon (109)

7, 8 February 1916

See note on Thomas's sonnets (294). Thomas's second sonnet, like his first (*A Dream*), is a war-sonnet. He told Eleanor Farjeon: 'you didn't realise it was a sonnet I suspect' (*EF*, 187). In the octet the Petrarchan structure, tightened by similar rhyme sounds, helps to suggest the suspension or obliteration of time: 'making as a day / A thousand years'. But history and politics are not absent. As in *Digging* (99), long eco-historical perspectives bring agriculture, culture and war into an unstable pastoral frame. Thomas uses millennia to focus a day in 1916; a day in 1916 to focus millennia. With its starlings' 'parliament', 'rooks' and 'gulls', *February Afternoon* is also a bird-fable of war. Some details recall his "explanation" of the proverb 'Birds of a feather flock together': 'In the clear hard weather men were ploughing in the Thames valley... The earth was turned up in rich, dark clods like the inside of a frosted cake, and on to the furrows descended hundreds of white gulls. When Bob [a little boy] shouted, the birds rose up and whirled in the air like snow. Wherever the fields had been striped black by the plough there was a dappling of white gulls on the black.' Later [Bob] 'saw the black clergy-birds flocking together here and there, just as the jackdaws did overhead' (*FTB*, 71-3).

1. *parleying starlings*: '4 February 1915. Sometimes dozens of starlings – separately in hedge and in oaks of meadow behind are talking at same time – the sweetest voiced democratic crowd imaginable. The sweetest democracy imaginable' (*FNB80*).

4-5. *first are last...last are first*. 'But many that are first shall be last; and the last shall be first' (Matthew XIX, 30).

8. *shaw*: a strip of wood or underwood forming the border of a field.

10-11. *the broad ploughland oak / Roars mill-like*. This emblem evokes several oppressive forces: 'the roar of towns' (*Roads*) and of industry; the 'dark Satanic mills' in Blake's 'Jerusalem'; 'the mills of God'.

13-14. *And God...stone-deaf and stone-blind*. The last two lines bring an anti-religious undercurrent to the surface. The only positive mentions of God in Thomas's poetry occur at moments of untypical sentiment: 'God bless you' (*April*) and 'God save England' (*This is no case of petty right or wrong*). Here Thomas queries the latter. He had deplored Hardy's 'most tyrannous obsession of the blindness of Fate, the carelessness of Nature, and the insignificance of Man' (*IPS*, 194), but war may have made Hardy's 'God' more credible: 'He sank to raptness as of yore, / And opening New Year's Day / Wove it by rote as theretofore, / And went on working evermore / In his unweeting way' ('New Year's Eve', 1906). Cf. Thomas's fable, 'The Chessplayer', in which an old man sits alone in a mountain cave above the earth, playing 'with chessmen of ivory and ebony', and thus 'making the days and nights and all the hours, and never looking out to behold his handiwork' (*COE*, 12). In depicting the war as conditioned by Judaeo-Christian patriarchy, Thomas parallels Wilfred Owen. While Nature's 'law' may itself be territorial, it has its checks and balances, and only human beings wrap violence in transcendental 'array'. Thomas's mother had been 'reading Revelations' to him while he was ill in London (*CP1978*, 409). *February Afternoon* may specifically dispute Revelation XX, which dwells on

Satan's 'thousand years' of imprisonment: prelude to 'a new heaven and a new earth'. Thomas's vision of blind recurrence holds out no such millenarian prospect. Before the war, he had written: 'What they worshipped at Avebury temple, no one knows, but the human mind is still fertile in fantasy and ferocity – if it no longer draws blood – when it worships within walls' (*RJ*, 8).

Thomas was a cradle agnostic, son of generally secular parents, a Darwinian. In Swindon his 'bigoted, worldly, crafty, narrow-minded, and ungenerous' grandmother 'first took me to church. Clad in those uncomfortable clothes, I walked beside her, who looked more uncomfortable in her layers of black. I felt that everyone enjoyed being stiff, solemn, black, except myself. On entering the church she bent down to pray, dragging me down with her to blur my sight for a similar period...It was an inexplicable conspiracy for an hour's self-torture. The service was a dreary discomfort in which the hymns were green isles' (*CET*, 47-8). Later, his parents attended a Unitarian chapel: 'Perhaps my weariness in chapel was mingled with something that specialists would label as religious. I only know that where people were sad and solemn I was overcome, half-suffocated by the sadness and solemnity. What was read and preached was to me airy nothing' (*CET*, 75). Before going up to Oxford, Thomas thought of joining the Church of England because he felt he needed 'religion...an informing spirit in all I do and am...I want, as Milton says in those pathetic closing lines of his Epic, "a place to rest"' (letter to Harry Hooton, *LTH*, 128). Nothing came of this plan, although he later regretted not attending the college chapel. In 1902, writing to Jesse Berridge (who became an Anglican clergyman in 1906), Thomas called himself 'a devout agnostic' (*LJB*, 34). In 1912 he warned Berridge: 'don't label me *anima naturaliter christiana* while I am alive. It seems so particularly a privilege of the unresisting dead to have someone come down upon them & pin that order onto their breasts. It won't matter then' (*LJB*, 67). On 23 March 1917 Thomas recorded in his 'War Diary': 'Rubin...believes in God and tackles me about atheism – thinks marvellous escapes are ordained. But I say so are the marvellous escapes of certain telegraph posts, houses, etc' (*CP1978*, 478).

Ms: *B*. **Published text**: *LP*. **Note**: in l.11 *B* has 'or bear'. **Note on title**: Title is given in *B*.

I may come near loving you (109)
8 February 1916

Addressed, but never posted, to Thomas's father Philip Henry Thomas (1854-1920), *I may come near loving you* remained unpublished until *CP1949*. It is interesting that this poem should follow the hostile portrayal of God the Father in *February Afternoon*. R. George Thomas comments: 'The relation between father and son was a difficult one but not as implacable as this poem suggests' (*CP1978*, 409). John Pikoulis, however, charges him with softening the poem's impact for the family's sake (*JP*, 53). Thomas's recent arguments with his father about the war – 'He treats me so that I have a feeling of shame that I am alive' (*RFET*, 115) – may have re-activated deeper-seated problems (see note on *This is no case of petty right or wrong*, 263). They had quarrelled bitterly over Thomas's comparative academic failure, his refusal to follow his father into the Civil Service, his early marriage, his decision to write: 'bad words with father who takes every chance of insulting me' (*Diary*, 28 February 1901, *NLW*). Thomas's older male friends, like the writer James Ashcroft Noble (Helen's father, who died in 1896) and 'Dad' Uzzell, can be seen as surrogate fathers. Yet his father did come round to the marriage, and Thomas often stayed in his parents' London home. Again, some childhood memories seem warm enough; although, in depicting his parents as opposites, Thomas implies their role in his psychological conflicts: 'He was eloquent, confident, black-haired, brown-eyed, all that my mother was not…I can hear but never see him telling me for the tenth or hundredth time the story of the Wiltshire moonrakers…and many another comic tale or rhyme'; 'My father and I made merry over the Devil and the folly of believing in him as we supposed many did. He used to try different chapels or different preachers, sometimes taking me with him, more especially when he had become an almost weekly attendant at a Unitarian Chapel' (*CET*, 17-18, 31). The poem's succinct plain-speaking may target paternal 'eloquence'.

Thomas's entire career might be read as a reaction against his father's values. 'Undo' (l.11) represents those values as destructive. Thomas senior, who liked 'directly elevating philanthropic and progressive literature' (*CET*, 104), was disappointed by his son's lack of worldly ambition. A Liberal Party activist and skilled public speaker, he knew Lloyd George, and stood (unsuccessfully) for parliament after retiring from the Civil Service. His interests were philosophical as well as political: 'he became prominent in Positivist circles' (see *RGT*, 4-5). His father's jingoism caused Thomas to dub him the 'Public Man' or PM. After Thomas's death, a reviewer criticised his 'dislike of committing himself', calling him 'a non-combatant of letters'. His father riposted in terms that might have annoyed Thomas: 'Just as little was he non-combatant in literature as in war' (*The Nation* 13 [20 October 1917]).

3. *nothing to do.* 'Do', as in l.11, obliquely contrasts the 'Public Man', the man of action, with the truth-telling poet who gets the last word.

10. *impotence.* Here Thomas may consciously invoke, rather than unconsciously substantiate, Freud's theory of the 'Oedipus Complex'.

Ms: *B*. **Published text:** *CP1949*. **Differences from** *CP1978*: title: I may come near loving you [*P.H.T.*] 7 you [*B*, *CP1949*] *you*, [typescript given to R. George Thomas by Helen Thomas] **Note on title:** This edition names the poem for its first line. In *CP2004* the poem has no title. See Note on Text.

Those things that poets said (110)
9 February 1916

What poets say 'Of love' is a central theme in *Feminine Influence on the Poets* (see general note to *The Unknown*, 279). Here, between poems of 'loving not', Thomas raises theoretical questions about 'love and poetry'. For the speaker, love poetry's truth-claims have been discredited. Yet he proceeds to 'prove' love's existence by a negative. Despite his ironical tone, the felt 'difference' between loving and not loving extends the definition of love (and love poetry) to 'something varying infinitely' (see note on l.7). Thomas uses the trope of a poem that denies its own genre.

4. *love and poetry equally.* 'How many times has Shelley – Shelley and the daffodils of Devon or the wild thyme of Wiltshire – been the half of a first

276

love? To how many does his poetry not seem, during a great lovely tract of life, to have been the half of spring and summer and autumn, of night and dawn and noon, and of youth enjoying these things? At the time when youth is most exultant, this poetry is thumbed night and day; a page is opened at random, as Virgil used to be, for a word big with fate' (*FIP*, 78).

7. *Or if mine were the true.* See letter to Helen Thomas, 24 February, quoted with reference to the next poem: 'You know how unlike I am to you, and you know that you love, so how can I? That is if you count love as any one feeling and not something varying infinitely with the variety of people' (*SL*, 119).

16. *loving not.* Again, see letter to Helen: 'you know that my usual belief is that I don't and can't love and haven't done for something near 20 years' (*SL*, 119).

Ms: *B*. **Published text:** *LP*. **Differences from** *CP1978*: title and l.1: Those *These* **Note:** In all editions from *LP* to *CP1978* the title is *These things that poets said*. But the first line of *B* [where the poem is untitled] begins with 'Those'. No other ms. or typescript survives, and the *LP* editors may have misread 'Those' [which seems more appropriate to the tense of the first quatrain] as 'These'. **Note on title:** *CP1978* brackets the title; *CP2004* drops it. See Note on Text.

No one so much as you (110)
11 February 1916

This poem was first published in *CP1928* under the above title. In *CP1978* R. George Thomas titles it '[M.E.T.]', citing 'Helen Thomas's statement to me that the poem was about the poet's mother [Mary Elizabeth Thomas]' (*CP1978*, 276). Presumably, Helen based this statement on Thomas's letter of 24 February:

> Fancy your thinking those verses [*I may come near loving you*] had anything to do with you. Fancy your thinking, too, that I should let you see them if they were. They are not to a woman at all. You know precisely all that I know of any woman I have cared a little for. They are as a matter of fact to father. So now, unless you choose to think I am deceiving you (which I don't think I ever did), you can be at ease again. Silly old thing to jump so to conclusions. You might as well have concluded the verses to Mother were for you. As to the other verses about love you know that my usual belief is that I don't and can't love and haven't done for something near 20 years. You know too that you don't think my nature really compatible with love, being so clear and critical. You know how unlike I am to you, and you know that you love, so how can I? That is if you count love as any one feeling and not something varying infinitely with the variety of people. (*SL*, 119)

Yet, as John Pikoulis notes, 'most readers have assumed' that the poem is 'about Helen herself' (*JP*, 53). Did Thomas 'deceive' Helen, or even himself, as to the source – or one source – of the emotional scenario that his letter paraphrases? Their marriage was put under huge stress not only by the economic need for Thomas to keep writing, but also by his need for child-free peace in which to do so and to develop his own talent. Hence his frequent working absences from home, during one of which he formed an unwise passion (see note on *The Chalk-Pit*, 238, and general note to *The Unknown* below). But strains may have predated the marriage (June 1899). A letter to Harry Hooton (8 May 1898, *LTH*, 126-8) included a poem that anticipates *No one so much as you* in more than form:

Weary of April's over-sweet –
Anemone and marigold –
I turned my feet
To her the meek and bold.

'Let me but speak to thee, or thou
To me unhastily, of naught:
Of love not now,'
I moaned with heart distraught (!)

Wistfully smiling, then, she stept
To lift me with love's best, though I
Unheeding wept
And cared not to reply.

Ah! when repose came – cruel bliss –
To her sweet toil she turned and wove,
And bitter 'tis
We cannot always love.

The bracketed exclamation mark is Thomas's own, and he offers an alternative version of the last two lines: 'And would not kiss: / Twas she owned pain I could not move'. In 1903 he recorded in his diary: 'No one knows how difficult I find it to live with Helen, though I admire her, like her, perhaps love her' (*SL*, 31). In 1904 he wrote to Helen: 'If I could only love *you* and show my love as much as you deserve how happy would you (and I) be! But with all my silly head and trembling body and rotten soul I do love you' (*SL*, 35). In 1905 he told Jesse Berridge: 'What I really ought to do is to live alone. But I can't find courage to do the many things necessary for taking that step. It is really the kind H[elen] & the dear children who make life almost *impossible*' (*LJB*, 47).

On 24 January 1916 Thomas had already tried to deflect Helen's anxieties about *The clouds that are so light* (see note, 269). Besides exclaiming 'Fancy your thinking I might have someone in view in those verses' ('Fancy' also seems uneasy in the letter of 24 February quoted above), he says: 'Oh, you needn't think of another lady. There would have to be 2 to make a love affair and I am only one. Nobody but you would ever be likely to respond as I wished. I don't like to think anybody but I could respond to you. If you turned to anybody else I should come to an end immediately' (*CP1978*, 409). Here, verbal anticipations of *No one so much as you* suggest, at least, that the perspectives dramatised in this series of love poems closely mesh with Helen's reactions to the poems, and with Thomas's reaction to her reactions. See, too, *And you, Helen*. As for his relations with his mother: he wrote to Frost in July 1915: 'There is no one to keep me here [in England] except my mother. She might come too' (*RFET*, 82). In October 1913, when Thomas decided against suicide:

'The final argument was my mother who has received nearly all the other blows possible' (*LWD*). Nonetheless, his letters to Helen until the end are signed off 'All and always yours'.

1-3. *you...you.* Thomas repeats this form of rhyme in the third and fifth quatrains. The vocative that separates 'I' from 'you' becomes a refrain at once tender and relentless.

33-6. *Till sometimes...here.* This partly unrhymed, partly off-rhymed quatrain lends emphasis to the full rhymes of the final quatrain, as if the speaker, at some subterranean level, is moving towards a decision.

36. *linger here.* Arthur Ransome remembers Thomas saying: 'I run away from home every day, but I always come back for tea' (*The Autobiography of Arthur Ransome* [London: Cape, 1976], 99).

Ms: *B*. **Published text**: *CP1928*. **Differences from** *CP1978*: title [see general note above]: No one so much as you [*M.E.T.*] 17 My eyes scarce *Scarce my eyes* 25 For I at most *I at the most* 28 Only a fretting *A helpless fretting* **Note**: *CP1978* follows a typescript [retained by Eleanor Farjeon] rather than *B* and *CP1928*, but the phrasing in *B* seems more likely to be the revised version. **Note on title**: In *CP2004* the poem has no title.

The Unknown (112)

14 February 1916

In a rather obvious dialectical move, Thomas reworks Richard Crashaw's love-and-Muse poem, 'Wishes to His Supposed Mistress':

> Whoe'er she be –
> That not impossible She
> That shall command my heart and me...

Thomas calls Crashaw's poem 'remarkable for its grave original beauty and its being apparently inspired by the thought of a woman who may some day appear before him, and also because the woman is to be not merely beautiful and virtuous, but intelligent' (*FIP*, 264). His own stanza (rhymed ABCBA) differs from Crashaw's, but echoes its slow tempo and self-enclosed rhyme-scheme. All this befits a dream vision as opposed to the valedictory momentum of *No one so much as you*.

The poems in which Thomas speaks as lover are poems of desire or lost love or both. His self-representations to Helen, including the idea that his nature is not 'compatible with love' (*SL*, 119), appear disingenuous. For instance, Hope Webb, the young girl he met in 1908, when working on *Richard Jefferies* at Minsmere, Suffolk, and with whom his relationship was abruptly terminated, seemingly haunts his love poetry (see note on *The Chalk-Pit*, 238). In this set of poems, *The Unknown* and *Celandine* bear or track her traces, proving Bottomley astute when he 'propos[ed] the consolation of an unassailable vision of her' (*LGB*, 160). Before being forbidden to write to Hope (who had gone to boarding school), Thomas told Walter de la Mare: 'She is 17 [actually 18], a particularly lovely age to me because when I was that age I knew only two of my coevals, one I married and the other is in South America, and in the presence of this new one I had the sharpest pains and pleasures of retrospection, longing and – I am now making absurd attempts to return to that period by means of letters' (*SL*, 50). This implies that an aspect of his sexuality remains arrested at, and hence fixated on, the adolescent moment – also, that premature domesticity caused the arrest. 'The Fountain' is one of several prose sketches that evoke Hope in a Suffolk moorland setting, and identify her beauty with Nature's (cf. 'A Return to Nature', *SC*, 81-3; 'The End of a Day', *LAT*, 52-7). The idealisation or sublimation in these writings survived Thomas's switch to poetry:

> As a boy it was of such a being that I used to think – though my imagination was not energetic enough to body it forth quite clearly – when I felt, in loneliest places among the woods or clouds, that my foot-falls had scared something shy, beautiful, and divine...she was akin to the spirit abroad on many days that had awed or harassed me with loveliness – to the spirit on the dewy clovers...to the spirit in mountain or forest waters, in many unstained rivers, in all places where Nature had stung me with a sense of her own pure force, pure and without pity...She was in sight for less than a minute as I went up from the sea over the moor, and when I turned in one of its hollows she had disappeared and I saw nothing but sea and sky, which were as one. (*RU*, 143-4)

See Martin Haggerty, 'Hope amidst Dejection' (*ETFN* 26 [February 1992], 5-15); Richard Lowndes, '"Louder the heart's dance"' (*ETFN* 27 [August 1992], 17-22).

Yet, as Thomas himself insists in *Feminine Influence on the Poets*, love poetry is not autobiography: 'Many love-poems were never shown to their begetters, many would not have moved them nor were in a sense meant for them at all. The love-poem...is written in solitude, is spent in silence and the night, like a sigh with an unknown object. It may open with desire of woman, but it ends with unexpected consolation or with another desire not of woman' (76). The 'maidens' that flit through his prose and poetry are shaped by literature as well as sex: by Romantic poetry; by Richard Jefferies's dewy rural heroines; by George Meredith's Nature-goddesses; by the ethereal icons of the *fin-de-siècle*; by traditions of the "Muse". Thomas's poetry of 'desire' has parallels with Yeats's poems to Maud Gonne. He writes in 'Isoud with the White Hands' (1902): 'something floated under the trees, turning an unknown face towards me; then passed away as softly as the day was fading. I just saw the pale glorious face' (*HS*, 184). In 'The End of a Day' he imagines Hope similarly: 'She might some day be a Helen, a Guinevere, a Persephone, an Electra, an Isoud' (*LAT*, 56).

In *Feminine Influence* Thomas stresses the dynamics between love poetry as a genre and the whole poetic 'impulse': 'individual women...give the impulse and the subject. When the subject changes the impulse will remain, and the influence, though not easily definable, is not the less great' (5). '[A]ll poetry is in a sense love-poetry' (86). 'The sight of a fine landscape, recovery from sickness, rain in spring, music of bird or instrument or human voice, may at any time evoke as the utterance of our hearts the words long ago addressed to a woman who never saw them, and is now dead. And as these things revive poems in the mind of a reader, so certainly they have given birth to some of those poems in the minds of poets; and the figure of a woman is introduced unwittingly, as a symbol of they know not what, perhaps only of desire' (77). '[Women's] influence in love has been exerted by the stimulation of desire – desire to possess not only them but other known and unknown things deemed necessary to that perfection of beauty and happiness which love proposes. It is a desire of impossible things which the poet alternately assuages and rouses again by poetry, in himself and in us' (91).

Ms: *B*. **Published text:** *AANP, LP*.

Celandine (113)
4 March 1916

Celandine recasts 'July' (*LAT*, 96–116): a tale of doomed lovers that may also draw on Thomas's feelings for Hope Webb in January-February 1908 (see notes above). In 'July', 'one of those crude mixtures of experience & invention which prove me no artist' (*LGB*, 206), the narrator watches his past self walking in a wood of 'mossy-footed beeches' with the dead 'Margaret': 'his eyes could not distinguish the ghost of the living from the ghost of the dead...As she used to do, years before, she flowed beside him swiftly, and with a motion as if she trod not upon the earth but upon the south wind that was always blowing in that land'. The tale depends on a contrast between 'the July land' and 'a low, grey winter sky and a flat white winter land'. The poem more subtly sets images of a 'bright' vigorous body against 'shadow', 'phantom' and 'winter hues'. Perhaps this is Hope as 'Persephone' (see general note to *The Unknown*, 280). Like *It rains*, which also shuttles between past and present, *Celandine* has parallels with Hardy's love poems to his dead wife.
6. *phantom*. 'As I have told you I don't like the country on the whole, only the two or three miles of moor, sandy cliff, flat marsh & sea visible from here, & even that is a remembered dream now that the child I told you of has become a phantom face & a kind but moderate letter writer...more than a whole hour do I lie in the morning twilight daily, struggling to sleep & put away worthless thoughts & images but vainly...Yet you are partly right when you propose the consolation of an unassailable vision of her. That, I dread to think, will be a possession after she is gone right away below the horizon' (*LGB*, 159-60).
9-10. *Her nature and name / Were like those flowers*. 'Hope' would fit the bill.
18. *locks sweeping the mossy sod*: accounts of Hope stress her long hair.
23. *like a never perfectly recalled air*: cf. *The Ash Grove*, lines 12-14. This fine simile again pulls elusive memory towards art figured by folksong. Thomas's suite of love poems ends with the speaker relinquishing fantasy.

Ms: *M₂, B*. **Published text:** *LP*. **Differences from** *CP1978*: 21 its juice *the juice* **Note:** in l.21 *B* and *M₂* have 'its'; printed versions from *LP* to *CP2004* 'the'. Although there must have been some intermediate version [since *B* and *M₂* have 'But 'twas' at the start of l.19], 'its' in the existing mss could be read as 'the'. 'Its' seems more attuned to the sound-system of the final lines. **Note on title:** Title is given in *B*.

'Home' (113)

7 and 10 March 1916

Thomas's most direct poetic reflection on his life as a soldier is set in the environs of Hare Hall Camp: 'Somebody said something about homesickness the other day. It is a disease one can suppress but not do without under these conditions' (letter postmarked 27 February 1916, *EF*, 188). Previously, in camp at High Beech, Thomas had 'found I could get on with people I had nothing in common with & almost get fond of them. As soon as we were in London the bond was dissolved & we had blank looks for one another' (*LGB*, 255-6). A letter to Frost (5 March) prefigures *'Home'*:

> I have been restless lately. Partly the annoyance of my promotion being delayed. Partly the rain & the long hours indoors…here I have to like people because they are more my sort than the others, although I realise at certain times they are not my sort at all & will vanish away after the war. What almost completes the illusion is that I can't help talking to them as if they were friends…Well, the long & short of it seems to be that I am what I was, in spite of my hopes of last July. The only thing is perhaps I didn't quite know what I was. This less active life you see gives me more time & inclination to ruminate. Also it is Sunday, always a dreary ruminating day if spent in camp. We got a walk, three of us, one a school-master, the other a game-breeder who knows about horses & dogs & ferrets. We heard the first blackbird, walked 9 or 10 miles straight across country (the advantage of our uniform – we go just where we like): ate & drank (stout) by a fire at a big quiet inn – not a man to drink left in the village: drew a panorama…which is an amusement I have quite taken to – they say I am a neo-realist at it. (*RFET*, 124)

Later, there was to be deeper contact with some new arrivals at Hare Hall, including Bottomley's friend, the painter Paul Nash: 'He is a change from the 2 schoolmasters I see most of. He is wonderful at finding birds' nests. There is another artist, too…a Welshman…I am really lucky to have such a crowd of people always round & these 2 or 3 nearer: you might guess from "Home" how much nearer' (*RFET*, 132). Nash (whose painting 'Spring in the Trenches' is on the cover of this edition) recalls Thomas thus: 'I believe I saw one of the happiest bits of his life while we were in the Artists – he was always humorous interesting and entirely lovable but others who knew him speak of him as the most depressed man they ever met' (*Poet & Painter: Letters between Gordon Bottomley and Paul Nash 1910-1946* [1955; repr. Bristol: Redcliffe, 1990], 89).

The letter to Frost quoted above may also disclose an aesthetic seed of *'Home'*: 'Your talking of epic & play rather stirred me. I shall be careful not to <u>indulge</u> in a spring run of lyrics. I had better try again to make other people speak' (*RFET*, 124). While Thomas went on writing lyrics, and *'Home'* is more mono-logue than dialogue, the poem prepares for *As the team's head-brass* in being acutely conscious of how 'people speak' in wartime. The inverted commas in title and text are ironical and interrogative as well as conversational. Thomas's third "home" poem confronts the strains between personal, regional and national affiliations. It does so in dialogue with *Home* (81), which explicitly affirms an

282

ecocentric localism, and other poems where "England" implicitly figures as a subjective 'system of vast circumferences circling round the minute neighbouring points of home' (*LS*, 111). But army life may have led Thomas to question even so fluid a 'system', let alone his patriotic high-water mark in *This is no case of petty right or wrong*. His pre-war short story 'Home' had already problematised home and nation. Here a soldier from London dreams, as he dies in the Boer war, not of Africa or London or imperial Britain but of a childhood trip to Wales: 'The country that he had been fighting for was not [the] solitude of the marsh, the mountains beyond, the farms nestling in the beards of the mountains, the brooks and the great water, the land of his father and of his father's fathers' (*LAT*, 37).

3-5. *the untrodden snow…wild and rustic and old*. 'It is fine and wintry here, very dirty though underfoot. The hills look impassable and make me think they must have looked like that 2000 years ago' (letter, 'probably March 11th', *EF*, 191). 'We were in a primitive world. In those short days the world seemed to have grown larger; distance was more terrible. A friend living thirty miles off seemed inaccessible in the snow. The earth had to be explored, discovered, and mapped again; it was as it had been centuries ago, and progress was not very real to our minds' (*HE*, 157). It is as if 'untrodden snow' recreates the original Eden, Arcadia, pastoral landscape or earthly home. 'Fair' makes no distinction between man and Nature. Later, history and geography will disturb the harmony.

12. *the cold roofs*: Hare Hall Camp, not just literally 'cold'.

14-15. *fellowship / Together long*. With dramatic fitness, enjambment breaches the sonnet-like structure of the first fourteen lines. Overall, the poem consists of two and a half ragged sonnets. After l.21 ('We were divided'), a sonnet in couplets traces the speaker's further self-extrication from any soldierly collective.

20-1. *Between three counties…We were divided*. 'Such an endless variety of men & accents & names…Business men, clerks, teachers, pianists, schoolboys, colonials …all mixed up & made indistinguishable at first by the uniform. Until you know a new man fairly well you think of him simply as a soldier. I daresay I have been mistaken for one myself' (*RFET*, 117-18). In the poem diversity 'divides', but "England" could connect Thomas with fellow-soldiers: 'I furbish up my knowledge of England by finding some place that each man knows & I know & getting him to talk. There isn't a man I don't share some part with' (*LGB*, 259).

22. *we knew we were not friends*. Cf. 'I can't help talking to them as if they were friends' in the letter to Frost quoted above.

28. *only the word*: a fraught echo of 'only the name' in *Adlestrop* and *The Word*.

30-5. *If I should ever… an evil dream*. Here 'we' becomes 'I'. Apart from contingent co-operation, 'fellowship' has broken down, while 'union' may also be queried in a broader political sense (Thomas favoured "Home Rule all round"). Thus, compared with 'I am one in crying, God save England' (*This is no case of petty right or wrong*), meanings have become incommensurable. 'Strangeness', which has already moved from landscape to relationships ('We…looked strangely each / At the other'), now mutates into self-estrangement as 'other' begets an old motif: 'else I should be / Another man'. *'Home'*, like Thomas's correspondence, disproves the myth that, in enlisting, 'he had changed his whole attitude to life, shaken hands with the past and shut his eyes to the future, so that he was troubled neither with regrets nor apprehensions' (*JM*, 228). The army could irritate him on a petty level: his promotion to full corporal (which came through at the end of March) had been 'delayed' because he had covered up a man's absence. More crucially, inner turmoil continued: 'I am what I was, in spite of my hopes of last July' (see letter to Frost). In November 1915, after a difficult visit home, he had already asked Frost: 'Does one really get rid of things at all by steadily inhibiting them for a long time on end? Is peace going to awaken me as it will so many from a drugged sleep? Am I indulging in the pleasure of being someone else?' (*RFET*, 107). The spectre of the Other ensures that Thomas's inner life, and the war's role in it, will continue to be volatile and dialectical. In August 1916 he wrote more positively to Frost: 'I don't believe I often had as good times as I have had, one way & another, these past 13 months' (*RFET*, 145). Yet there is always a distinction between what Thomas says to friends, or even to himself, and his poetic psychodrama as conditioned by war. 'Home', which broaches the unspoken and inadmissible, implies this too.

30-2. *If I should ever more admit...captivity.* In his second-last letter to Helen (6 April 1917) Thomas says: 'I, you see, must not feel anything. I am just as it were tunnelling underground and something sensible in my subconsciousness directs me not to think of the sun. At the end of the tunnel there is the sun. Honestly this is not the result of thinking; it is just an explanation of my state of mind which is really so entirely preoccupied with getting on through the tunnel that you might say I had forgotten there was a sun at either end, before or after this business...for a time I have had my ears stopped – mind you I have not done it myself – to all but distant echoes of home and friends and England' (*SL*, 163).

Ms: *M₂*, B. **Published text:** *P*. **Differences from** *CP1978*: 6 Fair, too, *Fair too* 8 for, except need, *for except need*. 12/13 no stanza break *stanza break* 16 words *word* 30 stanza break at 'If' *no stanza break* **Note:** *CP1978* follows *B* rather than *P*. **Note on title:** Title is given in *B*.

Thaw (114)
10 March 1916

Set in the same landscape, *Thaw* is an upbeat coda to '*Home'*. On 16 March Thomas told Frost: 'the weather is changing at last. The snow has melted. The sun is very warm. The rooks in the camp trees are nesting' (*RFET*, 126). Thomas wrote four poems that consist of one quatrain, the others being *In Memoriam (Easter, 1915)*, *The Cherry Trees* and *When he should laugh*. If his poems are 'like quintessences of the best parts of my prose books' (*JM*, 326), his short poems, especially his single-quatrain poems, are quintessences of a quintessence. Thomas did not share *fin-de-siècle* objections to the long poem. Nor did he approve the Imagist aesthetic whose soul was brevity (see Introduction, 20; note on *Cock-Crow*, 257). Yet, in an otherwise negative review of the anthology *Des Imagistes*, he writes: '[Ezra] Pound...has seldom done better than here under the restraint imposed by Chinese originals or models' (*New Weekly*, 9 May 1914). Whether or not Thomas internalised Imagism, he mastered the testing high-wire act of the short poem. In fact, his short poems differ from most Imagist poems in being miniatures rather than fragments. That is, all his structures (image, ordering of syntax relative to line, dialectics of tone or perspective) are stripped to their bones. *Thaw* is the most symbolically concentrated of Thomas's 'Spring' poems – as in the slow release of 'Winter pass'.

3. *delicate as flower of grass*: a simile that might apply to the poem itself. 'The beeches that were yesterday a brood of giantesses are now insubstantial and as delicate as flowers of grass' ('Flowers of Frost', *Country Life*, 13 February 1909). 'Delicate' echoes 'freckled' and 'speculating': all three adjectives span the human and natural worlds.

Ms: *M₂*, *B*. **Published text**: *P*.

If I should ever by chance (115)
29 March – 6 April 1916

Discussing the selection of his poems for *AANP*, Thomas says: 'The household poems ought perhaps to appear as a bunch' (*LGB*, 266). Although the poems in question (*If I should ever by chance*, *If I were to own*, *What shall I give?* and *And you, Helen*) did not make the cut, they eventually 'appeared as a bunch' in *P*. On the basis of the letter, R. George Thomas gives them the overall title 'Household Poems' in *CP1978*. But, aside from the *PTP* evidence (see textual notes), Thomas's phrase suggests a genre rather than a title. As contrasted with the wholly interior world of his recent love poems, this sequence explores affiliations that the Anglo-Saxon word 'household' might encode. These are 'will and testament' poems spoken in wartime by 'an inhabitant of the earth' (see note, 161). The apotheosis of Thomas's catalogues, the poems at once celebrate earthly things (flowers, birds, places, place names, 'copses, ponds, roads, and ruts') and add symbolic value. In substituting poetic complexity for legal intricacies, in playing with ideas of 'leasehold' and 'freehold' as well as 'household', Thomas explores the responsibilities that earthly dwelling incurs. One way in which he does this is by attaching conditions to the speaker's 'gifts', as tests accompany fairy gifts in folklore. Such traditional motifs (tradition being part of the legacy) consort with the poems' strongly rhymed couplets, anapaestic rhythms, nursery-rhyme echoes, refrains. Apart from 'Steep', the names – of house, farm, hall, park, village, parish, field, lane, and brook – are taken from the area around Hare Hall Camp (Romford, south-east Essex). See Basil Reitz's 'Notes on the Place Names' (*ETFN* 40 [January 1999], 3-4). The folk-idiom of the first three poems allows Thomas to raise serious issues lightly. Discussing price and value in his poetry, Smith writes: 'Ownership is both an absurdity and a disgrace for Thomas' (*SS*, 149). In *Rose Acre Papers* he whimsically asserts his imaginative right to a great estate: 'the gardens are really mine... I have sometimes wondered when the "owner" will acknowledge my right. Yet I am in no haste to enter into possession: that in itself would be barbarous... I prefer to be outside, innocently investing the place...never was such cheerful communism, such wholesome confusion of meum and tuum' (*RAP*, 9).

2-3. *Codham...Lapwater*. 'If only those poems which are place-names could be translated at last, the pretty, the odd, the romantic, the racy names of copse and field and lane and house. What a flavour there is about the Bassetts, the Boughtons, the Worthys, the Tarrants, Winterbournes, Deverills, Manningfords, the Suttons: what goodly names of the South Country – Woodmansterne,

285

Hollingbourne, Horsmonden, Wolstanbury, Brockenhurst, Caburn, Lydiard Tregoze, Lydiard Millicent, Clevancy, Amesbury, Amberley (I once tried to make a beautiful name and in the end it was Amberley, in which Time had forestalled me)...' (*SC*, 148). What Thomas calls 'the fascination of a roll-call of country names' (*IW*, 22) is itself an embryonic poetry in his prose, and place names are central to his thinking about 'word' and 'thing'. He writes of London street-names: 'They are the elements of a puzzle map of England, which gradually we fill in, now recognising from a bus-top the name of a Wiltshire village, and again among the Downs coming upon a place which had formerly been but a name near Clapham junction' (*IPS*, 39). Further, the fact that place names often defy 'translation' (in a different sense) gives them a quasi-autonomous status. In these poems, up to a point, they are legacies in themselves. Yet the names also bear out Thomas's "associative" concept of language: they evoke 'things', however arbitrarily ('Cockridden, and Childerditch'). As his orchestration of sound releases their poetry, he conjures up microcosmic landscapes.

4. *my elder daughter*. Rachel Mary Bronwen Thomas, usually called 'Bronwen', was born on 29 October 1902. She died in 1975.

8. *find them before I do*. 'Bronwen was Edward's most eager sharer of wild-flower lore; she knew as many as he did, had an eye almost as quick...In his happiest poem...Edward offers to bestow on his elder daughter half a dozen sweet-named places...provided she finds the first white violet of the year before he does. Every spring it was a race between them' (*EF*, 22).

9. *if she finds a blossom on furze*: a generously easy condition to fulfil since furze (gorse, whin) flowers all year round. Cf. 'gorse that has no time not to be gay' (*October*, l.17). These phrases 'have their origins in the country saying, "When gorse is out of flower then kissing's out of fashion"' (*MT*, 289).

Ms: *M₂, B*. **Published text:** *P*. **Differences from *CP1978*:** title: If I should ever by chance *Household Poems [1 Bronwen]* 11 absent in *CP1978*, as in *P* and *CP1920*; present in *B, CP1928* and *CP1944* **Note:** It is unusual for this edition to go against *P* and *PTP*, but it does so with regard to l.11. Elsewhere Thomas never leaves a couplet incomplete [here he would also fail to complete a kind of sonnet], and single lines can be omitted in transcription or typing. **Note on title:** In *PTP* the poem is given a first-line title.

If I were to own (115)

1-7 April 1916

See general note to *If I should ever by chance* (285).

4-14. *Wingle Tye...untranslatable*. This catalogue, the most amplified in the sequence, works centripetally. It moves from the outer reaches of an estate to a sheltered garden, from plurality to 'single trees', from Nature and culture to poetry (the thrush). 'Proverbs untranslatable' reflexively aligns the poem itself with birdsong, and figures meanings encrypted even more deeply than in place names. Poetry is also implicated in the murkier matter of the blackbird (see below).

3. *the Tyes*. In Essex 'tye' seems originally to have meant an outlying common, then an enclosed field.

5-7. *Skreens...Lillyputs*. The names ending in 's' either stem from a local manorial name or have been assimilated to this form.

15. *my son.* Philip Merfyn [Mervyn] Ashcroft Thomas, the Thomases' first child, was born on 15 January 1900. He died in 1965.

23-5. *unless I could pay, for rent...not I.* The 'rent' specified here revitalises the idiom 'for a song', making it the measure of true value. If the speaker should despoil this currency, he will lose his residual rights in the heritage. Bird-killing seems to symbolise some form of violation; song/poetry some form of redemption. Violence and the prospect of being 'left old and alone' probably reflect Thomas's difficult relations with Merfyn (see general note to *Parting*, 193). As with his attitude to his own father in *I may come near loving you*, there are Oedipal overtones. Yet this complex 'proverb' of inheritance, property and power may also allude to the war (as does the killing of creatures in *The Combe* and *The Gallows*), and echo the question posed by E.M. Forster's *Howards End* (1912): 'To whom does England belong?' In any case, Thomas's legacy in the male line, with its ultimate focus on 'the house', takes a different turn from the poems for his daughters.

30. *till the cart tracks had no ruts*: i.e., forever.

Ms: *M₂*, *B*. **Published text**: *P*. **Differences from** *CP1978*: title: If I were to own [*2 Merfyn*] **Note on title**: In *PTP* the poem is given a first-line title.

What shall I give? (116)
2-8 April 1916

See general note to *If I should ever by chance* (285). *What shall I give?* belongs to the poetic genre that expresses wishes for a girl's future – traditionally, dynastic wishes, as in Andrew Marvell's 'Upon Appleton House'. Some poems invert that emphasis. W.H. Davies's 'Sweet Stay-at-Home', which Thomas would have known, begins: 'Sweet Stay-at-Home, sweet Well-content, / Thou knowest of no strange continent'. But whether grand or modest, such wishes usually represent a socio-political vision that denies female agency. Thomas may avoid this trap by subverting both 'power' and 'contentment'. His 'queen / Who ...sat in Havering Bower' anticipates Yeats's 'A Prayer for My Daughter' (1919), where the ideal woman is no 'great queen' but 'Rooted in one dear perpetual place'. Philip Larkin's 'Born Yesterday (*for Sally Amis*)', which redefines 'ordinary', seems aware of Thomas's and Yeats's poems.

1. *my daughter the younger*: Helen Elizabeth Myfanwy Thomas, 'Baba', born on 16 August 1910. Myfanwy Thomas died in 2005.

3. *I shall not give her anything.* The poem proceeds to contradict this statement. Its trajectory from 'South Weald and Havering' to 'the Pleiades' at least giftwraps the values of 'Steep and her own world'.

4-9. *Havering...Havering Bower.* Reviewing Reginald A. Beckett's *Romantic Essex*, Thomas remarks: 'We are grateful...for the mere repetition of such names as Ashingden, Cressing, Havering-atte-Bower' (*Daily Chronicle*, 2 May 1901). The Crown held the Royal Manor or Liberty of Havering for six centuries. Two palaces were built there. 'Bower' indicates that Havering was particularly associated with queen consorts: Eleanor, wife of Henry III, who added it to the royal property in 1267; Isabelle of France, child-bride of the deposed Richard II; and Joan, widow of Henry IV, who was imprisoned on a charge of treason

and witchcraft and returned to Havering to die (1437) in the palace of Pyrgo.
11. *Samarcand*: more usually 'Samarkand'. James Elroy Flecker's *The Golden Journey to Samarkand* (1913) may have brought this exotic city to mind, although – or because – Thomas had reviewed Flecker's 'Parnassian' collection unfavourably (*Bookman*, October 1913). There is aesthetic point to his deconstruction of the opposition 'Samarkand'/'Steep' (as of 'Romantic Essex'). But if he demystifies the former as a spur to poetry, he does not sentimentalise the latter.

Ms: *M₂*, *B*. **Published text**: *P*. **Differences from** *CP1978*: title: What shall I give? [*3 Myfanwy*] **Note on title**: In *PTP* the poem is given a first-line title.

And you, Helen (117)

9 April 1916

See general note to *If I should ever by chance* (285). Along with Essex place names, the cultural aspect of Thomas's will-making has been receding. 'Self' at the end of *What shall I give?* brings its psychological aspect into the foreground. The poems can be read as family therapy for neurosis that derives from the speaker: as compensating for all he has failed to 'give'. Thomas's own self-reproaches and Helen Thomas's memoirs evidence his difficulties in belonging to any 'household'. In autumn 1912, after leaving home for a time to board with Vivian Locke Ellis, he told Bottomley: 'My habit of introspection & self contempt has at last broken my spirit. Intense irritability made life intolerable in a cottage where I could not suffer without making 4 others suffer with me' (*LGB*, 226). Above all, compensation was owed to Helen: 'Helen usually gets a share of my depression, & in fact has done so for so many years now that she is always too near the edge, has lost her buoyancy & is thin & often poor-spirited: but she still has a lot of courage & whenever I let her, gets hopeful again' (*LGB*, 162). *And you, Helen*, the only vocative poem in the sequence, reintroduces the 'I' and 'you' of *No one so much as you*. 'Yourself' and 'myself' are again in mutual question as Thomas elaborates his regret that 'I could not return / All that you gave'. He imagines giving Helen back her life.

7. *A clear eye as good as mine*. Helen Thomas was short-sighted. 'The amazing keenness of Edward's sight was brought home to me on these walks; he would remark on some bird in a distant tree when to me the tree was only a blur on the landscape. (Once when we were riding on an open bus-top in town, he pointed out to me the curious difference in the two eyes of a dog sitting in a window. I took his word for it)' (*EF*, 24). 'The clearness of the physical is allied to the penetration of the spiritual vision. For both are nourished to their perfect flowering by the habit of concentration. To see a thing as clearly as [Jefferies] saw the sun-painted yellow-hammer in Stewart's Mash is part of the office of the imagination' (*RJ*, 44).

Ms: *M₂*, *B*. **Published text**: *P*. **Differences from** *CP1978*: title: And you, Helen [*4 Helen*] **Note on title**: In *PTP* the poem is given a first-line title.

The Wind's Song (117)

22-30 April 1916

See note on Thomas's sonnets (294). His third sonnet returns to the Romantic equation between wind and poetic inspiration, last reworked in *Aspens*. Specifically, Thomas returns to Shelley's 'Ode to the West Wind' where the symbolic wind brings dead things to life: 'Drive my dead thoughts over the universe / Like withered leaves to quicken a new birth'. *The Wind's Song* seems to diagnose the speaker's initial 'dullness' or depression as compounded of creative sterility and sexual tristesse ('nunneries', 'a mere stump'). It is as if the Muse has withdrawn. 'Lone pine clump' echoes the ominous 'close pine clump' (cf. 'close copses' here) in *Roads*, and Thomas's self-image as a 'pine in solitude' in *No one so much as you*. The sonnet's strong contrasts are accentuated by its couplet-form, and by the sestet's marked 'turn' from 'sad' to 'glad'.

2. *anemones*. During his courtship of Helen, Thomas called her 'my anemone maiden' (*SL*, 8).

7. *branchless and flayed and prone*. This self-flagellating phrase recalls the psychological terrain of *The Hollow Wood*.

13-14. *My heart...was made free*. Cf. the ending of *Beauty*, with which the poem has other parallels.

Ms: *M₂*, B. **Published text**: *CP1928*. **Note**: *CP1928* has 'Dull thoughted' in l.1, but 'Dull-thoughted' [*B*, *M₂*] seems preferable. **Note on title**: this may have been given to the poem when it was first published in *CP1928*. *CP1978* brackets the title; *CP2004* drops it. See Note on Text.

Like the touch of rain (118)

23-30 April 1916

Like the touch of rain and *When we two walked* are linked by the motif of 'walking'; by emotional retrospect; by form (three quatrains rhymed ABAB); and by dialectics that oppose doomed passion to lesser 'happiness'. In part, the poems may reprise the narrative of Hope Webb (see notes 238, 279).

5. *love of the storm*: 'everything annihilated save the wind, the rain, the streaming road, and the vigorous limbs and glowing brain and what they created...We and the storm were one' (*IW*, 13). The weather-imagery and 'sings' echo the climax, perhaps also in a sexual sense, of *The Wind's Song*. Cf. *The Mill-Pond* too.

8. *'Go now'*: in *M₂* 'I'll go now'.

Ms: *M₂*, B. **Published text**: *P*. **Differences from** *CP1978*: title: Like the touch of rain [*P*] *'Go now'* **Note on title**: *CP1978* follows a reference to the poem in a letter to Eleanor Farjeon [*EF*, 194]. *PTP* provides no warrant for this.

When we two walked (118)

23 April - 1 May 1916

See general note to *Like the touch of rain* above. R. George Thomas refers this poem to 'a long walk taken by the poet and his wife before Easter 1914' (*CP1978*, 414). But, whether applicable to their marriage or not, its 'Lenten' setting seems primarily metaphorical. Thomas's most nuanced gloss on 'happiness' (as so often, a recollected rather than present condition) gives the quatrain here a very different sound from the tones of extremity in *Like the touch of rain*. 7-8. *Who acted...Juno and Jupiter*. An 'exile' returning to childhood scenes says: 'We forgot that ours had been the sin of Alcyone and Ceyx who, in their proud happiness, called one another Zeus! and Here!' (*HE*, 49-50). Zeus (Jupiter) punished the sinners by turning Alcyone into a kingfisher, Ceyx into a gannet. In *The Happy-Go-Lucky Morgans* a 'cottage woman' recalls the young Morgans, several of whom die: 'You never saw the like of them for happiness. When I used to stop at the gate and see them in the grass, perhaps soaking wet, tumbling about and laughing as if they weren't Christians at all, I said to myself: "Oh, dear, dear me, what trouble there must be in store for those beautiful children, that they should be so happy now. God preserve them, if it be his will." I whispered: "Hush, children, be a bit more secret-like about it." It don't do to boast about anything, let alone happiness' (*HGLM*, 270).

Ms: *M*₂, *B*. **Published text:** *P*. **Differences from** *CP1978*: 9 Gods *gods*

Tall Nettles (119)
24 April - 1 May 1916

See note on Thomas's short poems (284). *Tall Nettles* is a corner of his poetry that many readers 'like most'. 'The walnut tree among the ricks is dead...deep in the brittle herbage underneath it lean or lie broken wheels, a rude wooden roller, the lovely timber of an antique plough, a knotted and rusted chain harrow' (*HE*, 108); 'the barn and sheds, apparently tumbling but never tumbledown, were...surrounded by a disorderly region of nettles' (*HGLM*, 130). Like *But these things also* and *The Word*, *Tall Nettles* tests Thomas's critical dictum: 'Anything, however small, may make a poem; nothing, however great, is certain to' (*MM*, 28). Here one starting-point may have been the fourth line of *The Mill-Water*: 'On the prone roof and walls the nettle reigns'. But dereliction and Nature's victory now co-exist with a 'farmyard', and springy rhythms pull all the poem's elements together. The symbol lacks its earlier aura of apocalyptic foreboding mixed with desire for a post-human earth.
7. *dust*. 'Cobwebs and wholesome dust – we needed some of both in the corners of our minds' (*HS*, 112).
8. *sweetness*. Braced by 'dust', 'prove', and its climactic position, this problematic word powerfully justifies its use (see note, 233).

Ms: *M*₂, *B*. **Published text:** *P*.

The Watchers (119)
24 April - 1 May 1916

That *Tall Nettles* and *The Watchers* appear on the same page of *B* suggests their proximity in Thomas's head, and the extent to which they comprise an *ars poetica*. Like the similarly paired poems that precede them, both are written in an ABAB quatrain. The stanzas of *The Watchers*, with their different rhythms, are themselves dialectically opposed. MacDonald Emslie comments: 'The visitor at the inn watches from behind glass. The stuffed creatures on the walls of his room watch him from behind an inner layer of glass... This watching of the visitor who is watching the carter who is watching his horse provides three kinds of watching and three different worlds, each reflecting critically on its neighbour' ('Spectatorial Attitudes', *Review of English Literature* 5, 1 [1964], 67). *The Watchers* condenses Thomas's critique of Walter Pater and 'the contemplative aesthetic life, too refined for the contamination of experience' (*WP*, 147). Pater's 'spectatorial attitude' makes him 'forget that the thing seen is not a picture' (cf. 'no fire, but a view', l.7). Such 'sequestered egotism' ends in inhumanity: 'Thinking of the noble attitudes of men – heroes of novels – in their strife with circumstance, he asked whether men would fret against their chains if they could see at the end "these great experiences", these noble attitudes, these tragical situations...One more step, and he would bid the dying gladiator be comforted by the stanzas of Childe Harold' (*WP*, 172, 149, 174, 74). Lafcadio Hearn has the same faults:

> The book [*Chita*] is not without humanity, but the attitude towards human things, the most tragic and the most simple, is usually spectatorial. He describes, for example, the jetsam of a storm which destroyed an island and all its holiday population...The impression given by the passage is that Hearn had never got beyond the point of view that this scene was a good subject for description. He was writing as a detached aesthetic artist and this cold figure is as conspicuous as the storm and its havoc. In a different key is the description of yellow fever which ends the book. Hearn himself had nearly died of the disease in New Orleans: in *Chita* it kills a man but it gives some life to the style... (*LH*, 51-2)

In criticising Pater and Hearn, Thomas was exorcising an earlier literary self. His spectatorial *Horae Solitariae* (1902) includes an essay that represents rural people as 'the Caryatids of life' (*HS*, 115). The war added a further edge to his critique, as when he rebukes himself for loving England 'aesthetically' (*LS*, 221). The letter to Helen in which Thomas reflects on writers and the war, along with his own failure 'to give my imagination of the lives of men reality' (see note, 262), begins by describing his room in a Welsh inn: 'dignified by a black [?] cock in a glass case as well as a fantastic heavy armchair, presumably for a president to sit in, a fretwork ship in a glass case and a portrait of a pointer (I think)' (10 October 1914, *NLW*). Thus a subtext of *The Watchers* may be his desire for more active service. On reaching France, he told Helen that it was 'impossible' to write 'in this new disturbing world where I am so far only a spectator' (quoted *JM*, 253).

3-4. *The carter smokes... Watching the water press in swathes about his horse's chest.* 'It may be going to far to give [symbolic value] to the fire the visitor's world lacks (and the smoking carter possesses); but certainly the fourth line's qualities are to be contrasted with the dry catalogue-effect of line eight' (Emslie, 68). Pater's 'hard visual treatment of life and nature' (*WP*, 150) has points of contact with Imagist poetry, which Thomas and Frost criticise as being written by, and for, the eye (see Introduction, 20). Here, the onomatopoeic and kinetic fourth line exemplifies sensory life pressing into literature; rhythm created by the mutual pressure between speech and form; poetry written by, and for, the ear.

8. *And many cases of stuffed fish, vermin, and kingfishers*: 'grown men with dictionaries are as murderous of words as entomologists of butterflies' (*FIP*, 85-6). 'Pater was, in fact, forced against his judgment to use words as bricks, as

tin soldiers, instead of flesh and blood and genius...Pater's influence has tended to encourage meticulosity in detail and single words, rather than a regard for form in its largest sense' (*WP*, 215).

Ms: *M₂, B*. **Published text:** *TP, CP1928*. **Note on title:** *The Watchers* and *The Lane* may have been given their titles when they were published together in *TP. CP1978* brackets the title; *CP2004* drops it. See Note on Text.

I never saw that land before (120)

5 May 1916

Like *The Mountain Chapel* and *A Dream*, this poem may recall Thomas's visit to Wales in October 1914, and the essay 'Penderyn': 'Excepting when I crossed it the river Neath was generally hidden either by oak, ash or elder lining it... Then I came to a village...As the river was now little more than a brook, the hills of its valley sides were now mountains...The fields down by the river were very green, enclosed and protected by a few farmhouses and trees' (*COE*, 23-4). As in *Home* (81), which starts with a precisely contrary line ('Often I had gone this way before'), epiphany takes a traveller by surprise. As in *The Bridge* and *The Ash Grove*, the rhyme scheme (here ABABA) befits a moment prolonged between past and future, expectation and memory: in part, the creative moment. But, compared with these poems, *I never saw that land before* is the most harmonious in mood and form. The last stanza draws out the implication that the speaker has come upon a 'land' that symbolises poetry itself – strangely foreknown, instantly "home". On one level, Thomas's journey from poem to poem repeats his unknowing search for its starting-point. The phrase 'equal interval' could allude to verse, and the poem's syntax underlines its own poise: the chiasmus 'hinted all and nothing spoke'; the placing of 'Endeared' amid the prepositions it governs, of 'anything' amid the verbs that govern it. The initial three-stanza sentence allows the catalogue of the landscape to unfold without check – thus reversing the syntactical and emotional trajectory of *For These*. The relation between the first three stanzas and the last two (also one sentence) corresponds to the structural ratio of sonnet-form.

17-18. *some goal / I touched then*. Cf. *The Other* ('the unseen moving goal') and *Some eyes condemn* ('I had not found my goal'). Coombes finds 'something relatively immature in the way Thomas...refers to happiness and beauty as "goals" that can conceivably be reached and retained, as if he hoped a golden land existed at the end of a journey' (*HC*, 209). But the 'goal' seems provisional and strategic. It discloses itself only in its fleeting realisation: perhaps as a poem.

22. *A language not to be betrayed*. This reflexive phrase seals the reciprocity between mind and world that the poem manifests, and which the 'aesthetic spectator' of *The Watchers* can neither experience nor express. As in *Aspens*, recalled by 'whisper', such reciprocity ultimately depends on the ear rather than the eye: the inspirational 'breeze / That hinted all and nothing spoke'. Thomas sets the bar high for the 'language' that poetry constitutes. The repeated 'what', 'whisper' and 'hid', together with 'betrayed', challenge the reader.

Ms: *M₂, B*. **Published text:** *LP*. **Note on title:** *CP1978* brackets the title; *CP2004* drops it. See Note on Text.

The Cherry Trees (120)

7, 8 May 1916

See note on Thomas's short poems (284). Myfanwy Thomas traces this poem's source to a walk with her father when she said of scattered cherry petals: 'Someone's been married' (*MT*, 43). Written a year after *In Memoriam (Easter, 1915)*, *The Cherry Trees* echoes its form, imagery of paradoxical flowers, reminder of peacetime custom. Taken together, the poems move between courtship and funeral with no intermediate 'wedding'. Elegiac cadences accelerate as 'old road' folds the war dead into the death of rural England. A likely literary context for *The Cherry Trees* is '1887', the poem with which A.E. Housman begins *A Shropshire Lad* (1896). The first part of the poem celebrates Queen Victoria's Golden Jubilee by 'remembering friends of ours' who died for the empire: 'It dawns in Asia, tombstones show / And Shropshire names are read'. The better-known second part celebrates the cherry tree: 'Loveliest of trees, the cherry now / Is hung with bloom along the bough'. *The Cherry Trees* breaks down Housman's bipartite structure.

1. *The cherry trees*. B begins: 'The cherry tree leans over and is shedding'. In later opting for the plural, Thomas may have sought to differentiate his poem from Housman's.

4. *when*: 'though' in *B*.

Ms: *B*. Published text: *P*.

It rains (121)

11-13 May 1916

For Thomas and rain, see general note to *After Rain* (154). 'One shower I remember that wrought marvels in a London garden... At the bottom of the garden, beyond the lawn, was an enclosed space of warm rank grasses and rising over them a vapour of cow-parsley flowers. A white steam from the soil faintly misted the grass to the level of the tallest buttercups. Rain was falling, and the grasses and overhanging elm trees seemed to be suffering for their quietness and loneliness...For the time, that garden was the loneliest place on earth, and I loved and feared its loneliness' (*RAP*, 46-7). 'Far away a gate is loudly shut, and the rich blue evening comes on and severs me irrevocably from all but the light in the old wood and the ghostly white cow-parsley flowers suspended on unseen stalks. And there, among the trees and their shadows, not understood, speaking a forgotten tongue, old dreads and formless awes and fascinations discover themselves and address the comfortable soul, troubling it, recalling to it unremembered years not so long past but that in the end it settles down into a gloomy tranquillity and satisfied discontent, as when we see the place where we were unhappy as children once' (*HE*, 55). 'The white cow-parsley flowers hovered around me on invisible stalks' (*HE*, 217).

Evidently cow-parsley was an image that haunted Thomas – an image of haunting. 'Fallen petals' also seem to be pursuing him from *The Cherry Trees*. Eerily insubstantial, *It rains* is a landscape of memory as distinct from a remembered landscape. In 'searching the wilderness', crossing a psychic threshold, the speaker haunts his past rather than *vice versa*. Similarly, the poem re-enters its own pre-history: the mood of *fin-de-siècle* 'loneliness' in *Rose Acre Papers*, the troubling 'forgotten tongue' discovered in *The Heart of England*. Smith calls the first stanza of *It rains* 'a whole complex of negatives...What is there is defined in terms of what is not – "nothing stirs.../Anywhere", "untrodden", "there is none to break", just as, later, the poet is defined by the absence of the loved one or all those other absences implicit in the qualification "Unless alone". A large number of Thomas's poems open thus, with a negative construction in the first sentence which inserts absence right into the heart of an achieved and actual world' (*SS*, 99-100).

8-9. *To think of two walking, kissing there, / Drenched*. This effect strangely combines elements from *Like the touch of rain* and *When we two walked*. If *It rains* shakes up the kaleidoscope of the Hope Webb affair (see notes, 238, 279), or recalls other lost loves or Thomas's courtship of Helen, it may do so under the influence of Hardy's love poems to his dead wife. There are parallels (rain, lovers walking, ghostliness) with Hardy's 'At Castle Boterel':

> As I drive to the junction of lane and highway,
>   And the drizzle bedrenches the waggonette,
> I look behind at the fading byway,
>   And see on its slope, now glistening wet,
>   Distinctly yet
>
> Myself and a girlish form benighted...
>
> I look and see it there, shrinking, shrinking,
>   I look back at it amid the rain
> For the very last time; for my sand is sinking,
>   And I shall traverse old love's domain
>   Never again.

13. *the parsley flower*: a phrase appropriately 'suspended' at the end of one of the mid-stanza unrhymed lines. This five-line stanza contrasts with that of *I never saw that land before*.

14. *ghostly white*: see note on Thomas's 'ghosts' (202).

Ms: *M₂, B*. **Published text:** *P*.

Some eyes condemn (121)

13, 14 May 1916

'I am glad you liked the sonnet, I suppose it was one. My fear was that it ended with a click. "One" is, I suppose, a weakness' (*EF*, 198). 'I suppose it was one' seems disingenuous: more than Thomas's other sonnets, *Some eyes condemn* calls attention to itself as such. He wrote only six sonnets (seven, if *If I should ever by chance* is counted), but secretly flirts with the form by writing double or even treble sonnets (*The Glory, Haymaking*) and non-stanzaic poems of between ten and eighteen lines. In other ways, too, his poetry reproduces the sonnet's structural importance in the history of English lyric. But Thomas's wariness of the 'click' has roots in Romantic doctrine; in his view of the sonnet as an invader that displaced the folk tradition; in his boredom with Victorian auto-pilot sonneteering. When (November 1902) he wrote a tough critique of a sonnet sequence sent to him by Jesse Berridge, he partly blamed the form for encouraging Berridge's 'aerial tendency':

> Personally, I have a dread of the sonnet. It must contain 14 lines, & a man must be a tremendous poet or a cold mathematician if he can accommodate his thoughts to that condition. The result is – in my opinion – that many of the best sonnets are rhetoric only. I think most of Rossetti's are. Rossetti too is responsible for introducing the sesquipedalian-word sonnet...Sesquipedalian [polysyllabic] words are all very well...But once under the spell, sense & concreteness are apt to disappear...[Rossetti's] sonnets are often like big men in pompous clothing. They are impressive without saying anything...I don't mean that every sonnet should contain a fresh & striking idea that would look well in a leading article. I mean that if a sonnet fails to produce an impression of strength and unity, & if, on analysis, it still seems to lack unity & strength, then it is inconsiderable. (*LJB*, 36)

As a reviewer, Thomas had to endure interminable sonneteers: 'Many of [Lloyd Mifflin's] sonnets are so long that we can scarce believe our eyes which see only fourteen lines' (*Daily Chronicle*, 16 February 1904); 'It had become, thanks to Canon Rawnsley's industry, almost impossible to read a new sonnet without a slight measure of contempt' (*Morning Post*, 9 August 1909). Sending *Digging* (99) to Eleanor Farjeon, he remarked: 'I suppose it should have been a sonnet, but I can't Rawnsleyise yet' (*EF*, 154). In *Feminine Influence on the Poets* he hedges his bets: 'The sonnet had, in fact, become so powerful a thing of itself [in Elizabethan England] that the chances were against a man who set out to use it as a medium of "emotion remembered in tranquillity". He might as well hope to be the saviour of mankind in a well-ironed silk hat'; 'As the sonata can be true-hearted as the folk-song, so the elaborate sonnet or epithalamium can be no less so than "Whistle and I'll come to ye, my lad"' (*FIP*, 98, 104).

Two of Thomas's sonnets are written in couplets (*A Dream, The Wind's Song*); two are Petrarchan (*February Afternoon, Some eyes condemn* [with variation in the octet]); his last two are Shakespearean (*It was upon, That girl's clear eyes*): he took Shakespeare's sonnets with him to France. *Some eyes condemn* proclaims its form by ending with ending-tropes of the Elizabethan love sonnet: the lover-poet's consuming obsession; the beloved's eyes doing damage; her power over his mind and utterance. Cf. 'alas the race / Of all my thoughts has neither stop nor start, / But only Stella's eyes and Stella's heart' (Sidney, *Astrophil and Stella*, XXIII). The sonnet as a whole mimics an Elizabethan or Jacobean conceit. The slightly grotesque focus on the 'eye' is a synecdoche for diverse perspectives and philosophies. Notably, eyes never meet.

3-7. *some laugh...waking.* Cf. *When he should laugh.* In Thomas's poetry 'laughter' usually has a mirthless implication, as does 'mirth'.

10. *many I have loved watching.* As his prose indicates, voyeurism played a part in Thomas's somewhat vicarious love life: 'My thoughts were much on a girl whom I saw for half a minute at Horsmonden...pale and fragile, holding up a pink muslin skirt with one hand...But I cannot now be excited except sentimentally by young women. My affections are grown those of a troubadourish

eunuch, and I want merely freedom to admire and not to possess them' (*Diary*, 22 July 1901, *NLW*). Helen worried about 'dream girls' (*SL*, 124).

13. *thinking of your eyes, dear.* Thomas may again allude to Hope Webb (see notes 238, 279). His portraits of her dwell on her grey eyes.

Ms: *M₂, B*. Published text: *P*.

The sun used to shine (122)

22 May 1916

In August 1914 the Thomases holidayed at Oldfield House (now Old Fields), Le[a]dington, Dymock, on the Gloucestershire-Herefordshire border. Robert Frost and his family occupied a nearby house, Little Iddens. On 25 August Thomas wrote: 'Purple crocus with white stem and a sharp division between it and the pale but not unwholesome purple of the mostly folded bloom among short grass just up to flower's base'; on 26 August: 'a sky of dark rough horizontal masses in N.W. with a 1/3 moon bright and almost orange low down clear of cloud and I thought of men east-ward seeing it at the same moment. It seems foolish to have loved England up to now without knowing it could perhaps be ravaged and I could and perhaps would do nothing to prevent it' (*FNB77*). The next stage was an essay, 'This England' (*The Nation*, 7 November 1914), about 'the new moon of August 26 & you & me strolling about in the sun while our brave soldiers &c.' (*RFET*, 26):

> The sun shone, always warm, from skies sometimes cloudless, sometimes inscribed with a fine white scatter miles high... Three meadows away lived a friend, and once or twice or three times a day I used to cross the meadows, the gate, and the two stiles...
>
> How easy it was to spend a morning or afternoon...strolling with my friend, nearly regardless of footpaths, in a long loop, so as to end either at his house or my lodging. It was mostly orchard and grass, gently up and down...many [of the meadows] had several great old apple or pear trees. The pears were small brown perry pears, as thick as haws, the apples chiefly cider apples, innumerable, rosy and uneatable, though once or twice we did pick up a wasp's remnant, with slightly greasy skin of palest yellow, that tasted delicious. There was one brook to cross, shallow and leaden, with high hollow bare banks...
>
> If talk dwindled in the traversing of a big field, the pause at gate or stile braced it again. Often we prolonged the pause, whether we actually sat or not, and we talked – of flowers, childhood, Shakespeare, women, England, the war – or we looked at a far horizon, which some dip or gap occasionally disclosed...
>
> Then one evening the new moon made a difference...The sky was banded with rough masses in the north-west, but the moon, a stout orange crescent, hung free of cloud near the horizon. At one stroke, I thought, like many other people, what things that same moon sees eastward about the Meuse in France. Of those who could see it there, not blinded by smoke, pain, or excitement, how many saw it and heeded? I was deluged, in a second stroke, by another thought, or something that

overpowered thought. All I can tell is, it seemed to me that either I had never loved England, or I had loved it foolishly, aesthetically, like a slave, not having realised that it was not mine unless I were willing and prepared to die rather than leave it as Belgian women and old men and children had left their country. Something I had omitted. Something, I felt, had to be done before I could look again composedly at English landscape, at the elms and poplars about the houses, at the purple-headed wood-betony with two pairs of dark leaves on a stiff stem, who stood sentinel among the grasses or bracken by hedge-side or wood's-edge. What he stood sentinel for I did not know, any more than what I had got to do. (*LS*, 216-21)

A trope of Great War literature is the incongruity between 1914's golden summer, a symbolic last or lost summer, and the outbreak of war on 4 August. For Thomas, the birth of his poetry, latent in 'This England', obliquely celebrated by *The sun used to shine*, provides a further twist. The poem implies that his creative matrix – Frost, English landscape, 'poetry', war – cohered in August 1914. A year later, three weeks after enlisting, Thomas told Frost: 'I am a real soldier now, inoculated and all...Ledington & White leaved Oak seems purely paradisal, with Beauty of Bath apples Hesperidean lying with thunder dew on the warm ground. I am almost old enough not to make any moan of it' (*RFET*, 88-9). On 21 May 1916 the war and Frost again coincided. Having been upset by not hearing from Frost, Thomas received a letter, now lost, enclosing 'Not to Keep': a poem about a dead soldier. His reply (the same day) anticipates becoming more deeply involved in the war: 'Something may happen. A pension or grant is still just possible [in June the Royal Literary Fund gave him a £300 grant]...Also I may possibly get a job which will take me out into the firing line yet not into the worst risks & give me more money – as an officer' (*RFET*, 133). Written next day, from the future that its notebook origins conceive, *The sun used to shine* has an intricate time-frame. The speaker mediates between the embryonic poet who hears 'rumours of the war remote' and the soldier poet for whom the war, ever less remote, has come 'back to mind' in a different sense. *The sun used to shine* recreates/creates an epiphany, an Eden, where time is on hold but also running out: 'an apple wasps had undermined'. Images in the landscape remember the 'to be' as well as the 'late past'.

Thomas notes: 'men have written little poetry upon love for their friends' (*FIP*, 50). In fact, *This England* contains an extract from the supreme English example of this genre: Tennyson's *In Memoriam*. Frost and Ledington may have disposed Thomas to choose a section (LXXXIX) that evokes literary and political 'talk' during a summer picnic (it also refers to 'The gust that round the garden flew, / And tumbled half the mellowing pears'). *The sun used to shine* echoes Tennyson's four-beat line, elegiac cadences and final rhyme-words:

> ...we glanced from theme to theme,
> Discuss'd the books to love or hate,
> Or touch'd the changes of the state,
> Or threaded some Socratic dream...

We talk'd: the stream beneath us ran...

And last, returning from afar,
Before the crimson-circled star
Had fall'n into her father's grave,

And brushing ankle-deep in flowers,
We heard behind the woodbine veil
The milk that bubbled in the pail,
And buzzings of the honied hours.

The sun used to shine commemorates a literary or "Parnassian" friendship as intense as that of Tennyson and Arthur Hallam. For Michael Hofmann, the letters between Thomas and Frost exemplify the 'romance of friendship' (see 'Foreword', *RFET*, xxxi-xxxix). Thus Thomas says: 'The next best thing to having you here is having the space (not a void) that nobody else can fill' (*RFET*, 98). Frost could be difficult, but everything he writes to or about Thomas is wholly loving: 'Whats mine is yours. I say that from the heart, dear man...My whole nature simply leaps at times to cross the ocean to see you for one good talk' (*RFET*, 142); 'Edward Thomas was the only brother I ever had...I hadn't a plan for the future that didn't include him'; 'He more than anyone else was accessory to what I had done and was doing. We were together to the exclusion of every other person and interest all through 1914 – 1914 was our year. I never had, I never shall have another such year of friendship' (*SLRF*, 217, 220). He told Helen Thomas: 'He was the bravest and best and dearest man you and I have ever known. I knew from the moment when I first met him at his unhappiest that he would someday clear his mind and save his life. I have had four wonderful years with him. I know he has done this all for you: he's all yours. But you must let me cry my cry for him as if he were <u>almost</u> all mine too' (*RFET*, 189). Yet there was mutual jealousy between Frost and Helen. He says of her memoir *As It Was* (1926): 'I wonder if she wasnt in danger of making E.T. look ridiculous in the innocence she credited him with. Mightnt men laugh a manly laugh? E.T. was distinguished at his college in Oxford for the ribald folk songs he could entertain with – not to say smutty' (*SLRF*, 351). Frost wrote three elegies for Thomas: 'To E.T.', 'A Soldier', and 'Iris by Night' where 'we two' again walk together in western England: 'One misty evening, one another's guide, / We two were groping down a Malvern side'. The poem symbolises the poets' friendship as a rainbow ring: 'And we stood in it softly circled round / From all division time or foe can bring / In a relation of elected friends'.

Thomas's and Frost's poems for one another also ratify a shared aesthetic (see Introduction, 14). *The sun used to shine* is a virtuoso performance of what Frost calls 'sentence tones...thrown and drawn and displayed across spaces of the footed line' (*SLRF*, 191-2). Run-on lines and stanzas exemplify, as well as dramatise, the poets' reciprocity. Similarly, the rhyming of 'walked' and 'talked', and the kinetic rhythm that fuses these activities, embody "body language": 'The movement of [Cobbett's] prose is a bodily thing. His sentences do not precisely suggest the swing of an arm or a leg, but they have something in common with it. His style is perhaps the nearest to speech that has really survived' (*RR*, xi). David Constantine writes: 'Walking for a poet like Thomas or Wordsworth or Clare or Frost is a condition of being in, of progressing through the actual substance of poetry. And the feel of walking, its rhythms, the response of the feet to the changing demands and textures of the path, the continual stimulation of all the senses, the sustained interplaying of the mind and the imagination with the realities under foot and before the eyes – all this is so analogous to the composition of a certain kind of poetry as actually to become the condition and process of composition itself' (*ETFN* 40 [January 1999], 12).

1. *we two walked*: cf. the first line of *When we two walked* and 'two walking' (*It rains*, 1.8). Thomas associates love as well as talk with walking. 'A Walk', an early love poem to Helen, has the lovers walking 'hand in hand thro' the blossomed whin' and 'By the swift brook trickling bright'. The poem ends with them crossing the 'last meadow-stile' while 'the pale moon smiles down' (*NLW*, MS 22914C).

13. *a sentry of dark betonies*. 'The nicest flower all the way was the wood betony at the edges of the woods. It looks so wise – a purple flower like basil, but darker, with dark leaves, rather stiff' (letter to Helen, 16 August 1912, *SL*, 75). See 'This England', quoted above.

15-17. *crocuses...sunless Hades fields*: 'the tenderest green and palest purple of a thick cluster of autumn crocuses that have broken out of the dark earth and stand surprised, amidst their own weak light as of the underworld from which they have come' (*SC*, 271). The image is an autumnal version of the Persephone myth.

28. *like memory's sand*. As 'like' changes in usage (now prefacing a simile), the poem reflexively aligns poetry with memory. In effect, *The sun used to shine* 'remembers' August 1914 twice. Second time round, the faster rhythm and shorthand noun–clauses suggest poetry holding on as memory 'fades'.

31-2. *under the same moon / Go talking*. The poem's diurnal scheme, reinforced by 'yellow' apples, 'Pale purple' crocuses and 'dark' betonies, encompasses longer time-spans: life and death, including the self-elegiac tone; history ('the Crusades / Or Caesar's battles'); literary history ('sometimes mused'). Similarly, the landscape is a microcosm – at one level, of the poets' work. As in Frost's 'After Apple-Picking', the 'fallen apples' may have something to do with poems, while the crocuses hint at Thomas's oddly belated poetic 'birth'. The climactic intensity of 'the same moon' suggests that it partly figures the imagination, turning the poem into one of Thomas's valedictory testaments. His poetic birth and death merge as he hands on a rich legacy to 'other' poets.

Ms: *M₂*, *B*. **Published text:** *P*.

No one cares less than I (123)

25, 26 May 1916

In this dissident, dissonant poem, war and poetry clash. The long refrain lines, with their flat rhythm, suggest that the speaker's perplexities will never reach any resolution, formal or otherwise. The ironical rhyme 'God'/'clod' parodies more conclusive poems, including two of Rupert Brooke's *1914* sonnets: 'III. The Dead' ('Blow out, you bugles, over the rich Dead') and 'V. The Soldier'

('If I should die, think only this of me: / That there's some corner of a foreign field / That is for ever England'). For Thomas and Brooke, see Introduction (17). Pressed by Frost for his 'final opinion' of Brooke's poetry, Thomas replied: 'I think he succeeded in being youthful & yet intelligible & interesting...more than most poets since Shelley. But thought gave him (and me) indigestion. He couldn't mix his thought or the result of it with his feeling. He could only think about his feeling. Radically, I think he lacked power of expression. He was a rhetorician, dressing things up better than they needed' (*RFET*, 151, 153-4). Brooke's war-sonnets assume a providence (and an audience) that 'knows' and 'cares'. Through the conceit of fitting an unpatriotic poem to a bugle call Thomas posits that an indifferent universe writes its own scripts.

2. *Nobody knows but God*. Cf. the 'God' of *February Afternoon*, and see note (274).

Ms: *M₂*, B. **Published text:** *LP*. **Note:** *CP1978* omits the commas after 'God' (l.2) and 'clod' (l.4) present in *LP*. **Note on title:** *CP1978* brackets an editorially chosen title: *Bugle Call*. In *CP2004* the poem has no title. This edition retains the *LP* title. See Note on Text.

As the team's head-brass (123)

27 May 1916

On 28 May Thomas wrote to Helen: 'I set out [from Hare Hall camp] with a meal in my haversack for a long walk, but didn't go more than 6 miles all day. I sat down a good deal, both in the fields and at an inn, and passed or was passed by the same pair of lovers 3 or 4 times. It was very pleasant too, warm and cloudy. I wrote some lines too and rewrote them' *(NLW; ETFN* 27 [August 1992], 4). This celebrated poem marks a further stage in Thomas's second phase of decision-making about the war. On 9 June he wrote: 'I have been trying for an artillery commission but without military influence it looks as if I might have a long wait' (*EF*, 198). In July he was accepted for training, and turned down a permanent position at Hare Hall. By September he was an officer cadet at the Royal Artillery School in London. The Royal Artillery did not compel Thomas to seek service overseas nor, once in France, to leave HQ to rejoin his battery. But from mid-1916 he was evidently impatient for 'change'. On 15 August he told Frost: 'This waiting troubles me. I really want to be out' (*RFET*, 144). On 29 October he told de la Mare: 'I hope I shall be preserved from Coastal Defence. I want a far greater change than I have had so far' (*LWD*). In a letter to Frost (2 March 1917) Helen Thomas says: 'Edward wants the real thing and won't be happy till he gets it' (*ETFN* 46 [January 2002], 10). Thus 'Have you been out?' in l.18 of *As the team's head-brass*, a question that identifies the poem's speaker as a soldier, attaches his conversation with the ploughman to Thomas's inner dialectics. Perhaps, as the previous poem suggests, the Rupert Brooke model of the "soldier poet" still bothered him.

A summation of Thomas's "Home Front" poetry, *As the team's head-brass* symbolises war's intrusion into rural England, and into English (and European) pastoral. Before the war he had written: 'How nobly the ploughman and the plough and three horses, two chestnuts and a white leader, glide over the broad swelling field in the early morning! Under the dewy, dark-green woodside they wheel, pause, and go out into the strong light again, and they seem one and glorious, as if the all-breeding earth had just sent them up out of her womb – mighty, splendid, and something grim, with darkness and primitive forces clinging about them, and the night in the horses' manes' (*HE*, 21). Ploughing might seem to represent the opposite of war: agriculture, oneness with 'the all-breeding earth'. Yet this opposition proves as unstable in *As the team's head-brass* – Thomas's last "eclogue" – as in *February Afternoon*. Moving on from *Haymaking*, and placing speech rather than a silent image at the poem's centre, Thomas now fully historicises an iconic rural scene. In so doing, he challenges Hardy's 'In Time of "the Breaking of Nations"' (1915) as a vision of history:

I
Only a man harrowing clods
  In a slow silent walk
With an old horse that stumbles and nods
  Half asleep as they stalk.

II
Only thin smoke without flame
  From the heaps of couch-grass;
Yet this will go onward the same
  Though Dynasties pass.

III
Yonder a maid and her wight
  Come whispering by:
War's annals will cloud into night
  Ere their story die.

Whereas Hardy segregates archetypal narratives from 'War's annals', Thomas exposes them to historical contingency and situates his persona in its midst. He also lets rural labour speak for itself. The dialogue that interrupts the ploughman's circuits establishes a template for all the poem's structures: for the collapse of cyclical paradigms; for war-talk (including talk of dismemberment) breaking up blank verse; for the imagery and back-story linked with the 'fallen elm'; for gaps, discontinuities and absences.

1. *As the team's head-brass flashed out on the turn*: 'there was a pretty show of horse ornaments of brass among the saddlery. I almost counted these ornaments, crescents, stars, and bosses, as flowers of Spring, so clearly did I recall their May-day flashing in former years' (*IPS*, 230). In the placing of 'turn', as later in l.6, Thomas exploits a formal corollary to the symbolism whereby sword is taking over from ploughshare. 'Verse', as a line of poetry, derives from the ploughman's 'turn' (*versus*): an origin that enters the poem's structures. As war penetrates pastoral, line-turns become more jagged.

5. *Watched*: cf. *The Watchers*, and see note (290). This verb, repeated in l.35, may obliquely criticise the speaker for being a spectator of rural England, and of the war.

7-11. *Instead of treading me down... Scraping...screwed*. This oddly violent language implies that farming and war are not wholly discrete products of human culture.

20-1. *I could spare an arm…leg…lose my head.* On 21 November 1915 Thomas had written to his aunt: 'I really hope my turn will come and that I shall see what it really is and come out with my head and most of my limbs' (*LA*, 18). *This England* includes the speech in which Williams says to the disguised Henry V: 'But if the cause be not good, the king himself hath a heavy reckoning to make when all those legs and arms and heads, chopped off in a battle, shall join together at the latter day and cry all, We died at such a place…' (*Henry V*, IV, i).

25. *One of my mates is dead.* This absent 'mate' (cf. *A Private*) is an *alter ego* who haunts both the ploughman and the implied soldier poet.

26. *they killed him*: an interestingly impersonal or impartial, as well as colloquial, usage. Cf. 'they killed the badger' in *The Combe*.

31. *Another world'.* 'Ann says there is another world. "Not a better," she adds firmly. "It would be blasphemous to suppose that God ever made anything but the best of worlds. Not a better, but a different one, suitable for different people than we are now, you understand, not better, for that is impossible, say I" ' (*HGLM*, 299).

33. *The lovers came out of the wood again.* The lovers' simply stated return contrasts with Hardy's rhetorical claim, and does not re-inscribe a cyclical view of history.

34-6. *for the last time…stumbling team.* 'For the last time', which reverberates in several directions, is pivotal to the symbolism of the 'last' two lines. Thomas thought of calling the poem 'The Last Team' (*EF*, 144). Horses, like farm-labourers, were being recruited for war, while modernity threatened the plough along with other traditional staples of rural England: 'teams of plough horses …had been taken for service in France…in the wake of the newly invented tank, tractors and steam ploughs belched and rumbled across English fields' (Caroline Dakers, *The Countryside at War 1914-1918* [London: Constable, 1987], 19). That 'time' rhymes with 'team' hints that the former may be running out for the latter. 'For the last time' also shadows the speaker's possible future as one of those 'gone / From here'. Thomas ends where Hardy begins. He reworks 'clods' and 'stumble' in a way that leaves his own poem open to the hinted trenches and to history.

Ms: *M₂*, *B*. **Published text:** *P*. **Differences from** *CP1978*: 1 [and in title] head-brass [*P*] *head brass* [*B*] 23 Yes: a [*P*] *Yes, a* [*B*]

After you speak (124)

3 June 1916

See note on Thomas's love poems (279). The irregularly rhymed one- or two-beat lines of this and the next poem mark a rhythmic shift, a kind of metrical sorbet, after three poems weighted with war (although war infiltrates *Bright Clouds*). As in *Words*, the movement creates space for single words, mainly monosyllables. *After you speak* has structural parallels with *The clouds that are so light*. But here the Romantic 'lark', also a metaphor for the poem itself ('A mote / Of singing dust'), collapses the distance between desire and the transcendental beloved. The oxymorons 'black star' and 'singing dust' set up the identification of 'lust' with, or as, 'love'. In this most erotic of Thomas's love poems, 'eyes' uniquely 'meet'.

Ms: *M₂*, *B*. **Published text:** *P*.

Bright Clouds (125)

4, 5 June 1916

See general note to previous poem. The Zen-like focus on the pond, 'bright' images set against 'shade', a moment suspended between 'calls', and 'criss-cross bayonets' suggest that *Bright Clouds* alludes to Thomas waiting for action: 'Naught's to be done'. 'Frets' and 'scum' make 'may-blossom' a less positive image than usual, and hint at discontent beneath the poem's surfaces. Perhaps the pond also mirrors "waiting for the end" on a broader symbolic front. This suspense is not the idyllic suspension of *July* where 'still' has a different nuance.

7. *Like criss-cross bayonets*: a simile that first appeared in 'Birds in March' (1895), an article by Thomas in the Sunday School Association magazine *Young Days*: 'Wandering along, we come to a woodland mere, and amidst the reeds and rushes growing along the shore, or in the shallow water at the edge, we spy a moor-hen's nest approaching completion. It is made of the long bayonet-like reeds and other water plants' (reprinted, *ETFN* 53 [January 2005], 13). In *The Woodland Life* Thomas calls bluebell leaves 'dark green sword-like blades', and notes in a field 'Diary' entry for 21 April 1895: 'Reeds piercing the ripples of the brook, with twin blades, curved and meeting like callipers' (*TWL*, 36, 165).

Ms: *M₂, B.* **Published text:** *P.* **Differences from *CP1978*:** title: Bright Clouds [*P*] *The Pond* **Note on title:** the title in *CP1978* derives from a letter to Eleanor Farjeon: 'Did I send you the short lines on a pond?' [*EF*, 199]. *PTP* provides no warrant for this.

Early one morning (126)

8-11 June 1916

See note on Thomas and folksong (166). 'I am sending you a sober set of verses to the tune of Rio Grande, but I doubt if they can be sung' (*EF*, 199). Thomas had included 'Rio Grande', whose 'glorious tune' he then 'preferred to Westminster Abbey' (*LGB*, 94), in his *Pocket Book of Poems and Songs for the Open Air*:

> O where are you going to, my pretty maid?
> > O, away to Rio;
> O where are you going to, my pretty maid?
> > We're bound for Rio Grande.
> Away to Rio, away to Rio;
> So fare thee well, my bonny young girl,
> We're bound for Rio Grande...

'Early one morning' is the title and opening phrase of another song, also included in the *Pocket Book*: 'Early one morning, just as the sun was rising, / I heard a maid sing in the valley below: / "O don't deceive me! / O do not leave me! / How could you use a poor maiden so?"' The drafts of *Early one morning* [*M₂*] retain the songs' "deserted maiden" narrative, except that the speaker represents himself as leaving a woman because of her father's opposition: 'She was lovely and young and her father unkind. / She could wait but I was hasty inclined'. The drafts also contain detail such as 'The baker's cart passed with a smell of new bread' (see *CP1978*, 332, 452). Partly on Eleanor Farjeon's advice, Thomas purged narrative and descriptive elements. He also cut a refrain from between the lines of each couplet (*B* begins: 'Early one morning in May I set out. / Away for ever / And nobody I knew was about, / Away somewhere, away for ever'). The cuts have made the poem more cryptic, surreal and ominous as an adaptation of the 'going away' folksong.

3-4. *I'm bound away for ever, / Away somewhere, away for ever.* The refrain (with its internal refrains) attached to the first and last couplets concentrates the ambiguity of the speaker's project. In juxtaposing 'bound' and 'away' from the refrains of 'Rio Grande', Thomas creates a semi-oxymoron. He insinuates the contrary meaning of 'bound', as if 'liberty', with its uncertain horizons ('somewhere'), might actually be necessity or a dark destiny. 'Bound' resonates with 'burnt' and 'banged': all three sound disturbingly final.

6. *burnt my letters.* Thomas would do a lot of this from August onwards, as his family prepared to leave Steep and he cleared the decks for joining the Royal Artillery. The phrase has the ring of 'burning my boats'.

Ms: *M₂, B.* **Published text:** *P.* **Differences from *CP1978*:** title: Early one morning [*P*] [*Song 3*] **Note on title:** In *CP2004* the poem has no title.

It was upon (126)
21 June 1916

See note on Thomas's sonnets (294). 'A score years' connects the poem with his field 'Diary' entry for 30 June 1895 in *The Woodland Life*: 'Grass of the rising aftermath or "lattermath" beautifully green after a quickening rain, whilst the thistled pastures are grey' (*TWL*, 185). The 'lattermath' is the second or later mowing of grass for hay. In the poem, the resurrected image aptly figures delayed 'accomplishment'; while the oxymoron 'hoar Spring' encompasses all the paradoxes of Thomas's second chance, his becoming a poet or soldier poet. In August 1914 he had asked Eleanor Farjeon with regard to poetry: 'Did anyone ever begin at 36 in the shade?' (*EF*, 81). The sequencing of phrase and clause is integral to how *It was upon* shuttles between past, a past future, present and future. The upbeat momentum of the octet (the pulse of youth) climaxes in assonantal words strategically placed: 'Drenched...Flushed...outspread...possessed'. Here Thomas sexualises youthful ambition, and 'possessed' encloses 'the future'. The maturely speculative sestet dramatises 'recall...and question' by delaying those verbs until two or three lines after their object, as the open-ended last line distances the incalculable 'lattermath'. The future is becoming a more explicit theme in Thomas's poems.

Ms: *M₂, B.* **Published text:** *P.* **Differences from *CP1978*:** 6 rest, *rest*

Women he liked (127)
22 June 1916

In *The Happy-Go-Lucky Morgans* Mr Torrance says of an old-fashioned squire: 'he was pure rustic English, and his white hair and beard had an honourable look as if it had been granted to him for some rare service...I think he knew men as well as horses; at least he knew everyone in that country, had known them all when they and he were boys. He was a man as English, as true to the soil, as a Ribston pippin' (*HGLM*, 148-9). 'Shovel-bearded Bob' suggests that 'Lob' 'lives yet' in Thomas's poetry, but the poem is tinged by his darker concerns at this period. Smith writes:

> 'Women he liked' seems full of the presence of human beings. Its 'slow-climbing train' from which travellers hear the stormcock singing in the elms seems to dominate the landscape. The elms themselves testify to that presence, for long ago Farmer Hayward planted them out of love. But it is in this very act, in this love, that the displacement of the human begins. The man himself is an ambiguous patriarch, at once an earth spirit, liking women and loving horses, altering the landscape by his acts, and, at the same time, an unintentionally negative force... There is an omen here of an England changing for the worse, as a result of acts which are intended to be beneficial but actually destroy... It is only in retrospect that the shift from nightingales to stormcock becomes an omen of an England itself moving from calm to turbulence... In June 1916...the slough and gloom of a lane which was once named and claimed by no one, could not but call up the desolation of another No Man's Land, in Flanders. Bob's love and labours have not reclaimed the landscape; rather, they have turned 'a thing beloved' into something else, alien and negative. (*SS*, 76-8)

2. *Old Farmer Hayward of the Heath*. The poem may have begun as a dual gloss on Hayward's Heath in Sussex and some actual Bob's Lane. Considered as etymology, it acts on Thomas's belief: 'Better pure imagination than rash science in handling place names' (see note, 220).

7. *stormcock*: the missel-thrush whose song is said to presage bad weather.

16. *the name alone survives*. In Thomas's *M₂* draft 'Only the name survives' is changed to the final version. Perhaps he felt that 'Only the name' too closely echoed the last line of *Old Man*: also occupied with names and a dark vista. This poem's 'gloom' may be mitigated by the fact that 'the name', so unpredictably acquired, 'survives'. Thomas's key idea about language (previously quoted with reference to *Old Man* and *A Tale*) is that 'words outlive the life of which they seem the lightest emanation...the things are forgotten, and it is an aspect of them, a recreation of them, a finer development of them, which endures in the written words' (*RJ*, 298). The achieved naming of 'Bob's Lane' reflexively applies to the poem and its author. Insofar as *Women he liked* (following *It was upon*) ponders the paradoxes of creativity, Thomas has proved to be a 'stormcock', rather than 'nightingale', poet.

Ms: *M₂*, B. **Published text**: *P*. **Differences from** *CP1978*: title: Women he liked *Bob's Lane* **Note on title**: the title in *CP1978* derives from a letter to Eleanor Farjeon: 'Bob's Lane I liked' [*EF*, 201]. *PTP* provides no warrant for this – and the 'name' should come as a surprise.

There was a time (128)

23 June 1916

There was a time probes Thomas's metamorphosis from anguished introvert to soldier (its plot parallels the twist of fate in *Women he liked*). His letters, many of which are summed up by 'I sought yet hated pity' (l.11), frequently propose that only some external agent can change his life. Here he acknowledges war as a paradoxical saviour, a perversely accepted test. A month before enlisting he told Frost: 'Frankly I do not want to go, but hardly a day passes without my thinking I should...How much of it comes of unwillingness to confess I am unfit' (*RFET*, 66-7). More recently (21 May) Thomas had reported: 'actually I find less to grumble at out loud than 10 years ago: I suppose I am more bent on making the best of what I have got instead of airing the fact that I deserve so much more' (*RFET*, 131). Occupied with the nature of 'strength', 'weakness' and 'might', the poem also implicates broader questions, such as the relation between the artist and the man of action (for Thomas and Nietzsche, see note 227). Formally, *There was a time* is an extended Shakespearean sonnet with an extra quatrain before the 'turn'.

1. *There was a time when*: a conscious echo of the opening words of Wordsworth's 'Ode on Intimations of Immortality'. Time-lags are on Thomas's mind.

8-9. *Because it was less mighty than my mind / Had dreamed of*. This psychological reflex is common to the Romanticism of Thomas, Yeats and Philip Larkin. Cf. Yeats, 'The Man who Dreamed of Faeryland', and Larkin: 'I never like what I've got' (ed. Anthony Thwaite, *Selected Letters of Philip Larkin 1940-1985* [London: Faber & Faber, 1992], 165).

10, 15. *weakness*: cf. *The Other* (l.85).

16-17. *wage... gives up eyes and breath*. Cf. Rupert Brooke's sonnet, 'III. The Dead': 'These laid the world away... gave up the years to be /...Honour has come back, as a king, to earth, / And paid his subjects with a royal wage'. Despite Thomas's critique of Brooke's war sonnets in *No one cares less than I* (see note, 299), in this quasi-sonnet he takes their language a little more seriously while still contesting it. Here the speaker speaks only for himself; 'wage' is allowed to find its own value; 'gives up eyes and breath' is no euphemism; and 'what' makes the object of the whole exercise radically uncertain.

Ms: *M₂*, *B*. **Published text:** *LP*. **Differences from *CP1978*:** 18 would [*B, CP1928, CP1944*] *can* [*LP, CP1920*] **Note:** The nuances of 'would' seem more complex and powerful. In *M₂* 'can' is substituted for 'might'. **Note on title:** *CP1978* brackets the title; *CP2004* drops it. See Note on Text.

The Green Roads (128)

28 June 1916

'The forest is a fragment left 6 miles from here [Hare Hall Camp], the best of all this county. I go there every time I can. There is a cottage not far off where you might like to stay some day. The people have been there 53 years. You can't imagine a wilder quieter place' (*EF*, 202). *The Green Roads* continues the symbolic journey that Thomas's poetry has resumed in fresh guises. Like *The Other*, the poem is an emblematic landscape with fairy-tale features ('goose feathers', 'forest', 'castle keep'), archetypal inhabitants, and a mix of *heimlich* and *unheimlich* prospects (see note, 162). Its mythic aura owes something to Thomas's depiction of 'Iron Wood' in *Norse Tales*: 'The trees were oak-trees, twisted, bare and black, and he could not see far into the wood. All was black, except one tiny blot of orange on a low branch of one oak-tree. All was silent except one tiny song which came from that blot of orange. It was a robin singing, and [King

Gangler] stood watching it. Nothing was moving inside the wood...Years went by, and he forgot the forest. Now he remembered it, and shuddered at the thought of the old Giantess and her wolf children that would some day devour the sun and moon' (*NT*, 16). Formally, too, Thomas summons the folk-ghost, recently heard in the different couplets and refrains of *Early one morning*. Ear as well as eye draws the reader towards the 'forest' – the word itself being relentlessly repeated. The variable line length, un-rhyming couplets and the second line's wandering internal rhyme (a trap that trips up the ear) add to the unease.

3-4. *Like marks...To show his track.* 'I do not know how much I may have dwelt on the story in later years, but Grimm's *Hansel and Grethel*, the children going out into the wood to be lost, dropping a trail of stones behind them and finding their way back, but failing to do so when they used breadcrumbs which the birds ate, came to be to my mind one of the great stories of the world' (*CET*, 57).

6. *the nettle towers*: cf 'the nettle reigns' (*The Mill-Water*, 1.4).

12. *middle deep*. Each word could be either noun or adjective.

16. *Excepting perhaps me.* This suggests that poetry remains mnemonically vigilant when 'all things' are pulled towards an oblivion for which their own 'forgetting' may be partly responsible. As in *The Thrush*, memory distinguishes the poet (and his modes of refrain) from his 'repetitive' bird-counterpart. Thomas changed a repeated 'twiddle' to 'repeat' (*EF*, 206).

Ms: *M₂*, *B*. **Published text**: *P*.

The Gallows (129)

3, 4 July 1916

The Thomases were staying with Vivian Locke Ellis at Selsfield House, East Grinstead: 'At Ellises I could not help writing these 4 verses on the theme of some stories I used to tell Baba there' (*EF*, 202). The stories must have been rather macabre, as is an earlier 'dream' in which rural 'men and women' are seen 'in a kind of heaven where all day long for ever they did those things which had most pleased or most taken hold of them in life':

> The gamekeeper stood, with smoking gun barrels, and a cloud of jay's feathers still in the air, and among the May foliage about him. Pride, stupidity, servility clouded his face as in his days of nature, and above him in the oaks innumerable jays laughed because beauty, like folly, was immortal there.
>
> The squire, more faint, and whether to his joy or not I could not discern, was standing under a bough on which hung white owls, wood owls, falcons, crows, magpies, cats, hedgehogs, stoats, weasels, some bloody, some with gaping stomachs, some dismembered or crushed, some fleshless, some heaving like boiling fat, and on them and him the sun shone hot. (*HE*, 193-4)

Thomas disliked gamekeepers – rarely popular with Nature-lovers – and had come to associate them with war (see note on *An Old Song I*, 168). He remarks that Richard Jefferies's veneration for keepers might induce 'disgust with such a policeman god' (*RJ*, 117). Even if it was probably too soon for him to have grasped the enormity of the Somme (on 1 July, 20,000 British soldiers had been killed), *The Gallows* turns a familiar rural image into a powerful fable of mass slaughter. This misnamed 'keeper' or hanging judge has something in common with the 'God' of *February Afternoon*. But the 'things' on the tree also accuse humanity as a species. Thomas uses folksong structures to transmute anger into cosmic irony. Intricate refrains build up the horror and the indictment.

Ms: *M₂*, *B*. **Published text:** *P*.

The Dark Forest (130)

1, 5 and 10 July 1916

'The other 3 [verses] I believe are no good, the forest is perhaps a too obvious metaphor'; 'I suspect it is a bad Maeterlinckian thing' (*EF*, 202, 219). Thomas had attacked Maeterlinck's 'entirely conscious symbolism' (*MM*, 33). Coombes writes: 'Forest' is one of the most frequent symbols in the poetry, but when we attempt to fix its significance we find not only that it varies subtly according to the context, but also that our terms of explanation tend to sound heavy and clumsy in comparison with the poet's touch' (*HC*, 220). One context for *The Dark Forest* may be the increasing 'multitudes' of war dead. The *M₂* draft ends with an explicitly elegiac stanza:

> Not even beloved and lover or child and mother,
> One from within, one from
> Without the forest could recognise each other,
> Since they have changed their home.

9-10. *foxglove...marguerite*: cf. the symbolic flora of *The sun used to shine*. The 'purple' foxglove, like the crocuses in the earlier poem, may be linked in Thomas's mind with 'sunless Hades fields' and Persephone.

Ms: *M₂*, *B*. **Published text:** *LP*. **Note on title:** *CP1978* brackets the title; *CP2004* drops it. See Note on Text.

When he should laugh (130)

15 July 1916

See note on Thomas's short poems (284). In this aphoristic quatrain 'laughable' sums up the coldly ironical aspect of Thomas's vision. Cf. *Some eyes condemn*, lines 3-8. Perhaps the 'wiser' man protects the feelings of 'all such as are foolish and slow of thought and slower of speech, and laugh at what they love because others do and then weep in solitude' (*HE*, 151).

Ms: *B*. **Published text:** *P*.

How at once (131)

10 August 1916

This poem was written when Thomas was 'upset by vaccination' and bored in hospital (*LGB*, 270). 'I...shall be lucky to do more [verses] till the swifts are back again' (*EF*, 209). By 'next May' Thomas had been killed. He told Eleanor Farjeon: 'By the way, you misread that poem you didn't so much like – about the swifts – missing the point that year after year I see them, realising it is the last time, i.e. just before they go away for the winter (early in August). Perhaps it is too much natural history' (*EF*, 213). In fact, there is less and less 'natural history' in the poems of this period. Perhaps because they constitute "poetry of preparation" (in whatever form), their symbolic skeleton is more visible. *How at once* re-opens questions of 'seeing', 'knowing' and absence previously explored in *First known when lost*, but here they take on a self-elegiac cadence.

Ms: B. **Published text:** *P*. **Differences from** *CP1978*: title: How at once *The Swifts* **Note on title:** the title in *CP1978* derives from the letter to Eleanor Farjeon quoted above. *PTP* provides no warrant for this.

Gone, gone again (131)
3 September 1916

Gone, gone again starts by brooding on the last word of *How at once*. The bleakly repeated 'gone' and 'again' are echoed by 'oranges', 'young', 'began' and 'dung'. Thomas was now an officer cadet with the Royal Artillery in London, which may have prompted this gloomy retrospect. Lines 15-16 constitute a stark *summa* of the war (a month after its second anniversary); and images of fallen apples and broken glass, now given a darker tinge, recall *The sun used to shine* and *I built myself a house of glass*, poems linked with his decision to enlist. *Gone, gone again* also looks back to *The Mill-Water* and *The Thrush*: poems that similarly consist of eight quatrains and mainly two-beat lines. While the former is rhymed ABBA and the latter mostly ABCA, the rhyme scheme of *Gone, gone again* runs through six variations. This fits the unresolved way in which Thomas revisits material from the earlier poems. The urban 'old house', like 'the old mill' in *The Mill-Water*, focuses anxieties about the dissolution of home and the self: anxieties that seem to have become still less controllable. In *The Thrush* the poet-speaker's power to 'read' different months figures the complexity of human consciousness at work on the world. The entropic first quatrain of *Gone, gone again* flattens out difference: an effect replicated by 'Youth, love, age and pain'. 'Not memorable' switches off the faculty that distinguishes man and poet from thrush. There is also no hint, in this depressive scenario ('empty quays'), that poetry itself might be a therapeutic agent.

11. *Blenheim oranges:* a large yellow eating apple with orange flecks, given its martial name by the subject of Thomas's *Life of the Duke of Marlborough*.

12. *grubby*. Cooke points out that this word 'combines the sense of "dirty" and "eaten by grubs"' (*WC*, 141).

14. *the lost one*: possibly Hope Webb (see notes 238, 279), although the seasonal context does not fit her.

17-24. *Look at the old house...age and pain.* See general note to *Two Houses* (255). This London house, in the first of three London poems, identifies the speaker's state with the vanishing landscape of Thomas's childhood. He mourned 'the charm of the older suburban houses and gardens, yielding nothing to the tide that has surrounded them on every side, until one day their cedars fall and the air is full of mortar and plaster, flying from ceiling and wall, and settling on the grass and prostrate ivy' (*RJ*, 105-6). As Thomas comes closer to departure for France, his symbolic houses represent tenancy of the mind, body and earth as ever more precarious. He speaks as the ghost of haunted houses:

> Hanging from the wall in rags, too wet even to flap, are the remains of an auctioneer's announcement of a sale at the house behind. Mahogany – oak chests – certain ounces of silver – two thousand books – portraits and landscapes and pictures of horses and game – of all these and how much else has the red house been disembowelled. It is all shadowy within, behind the windows, like the eyes of a corpse, and without sound, or form, or light...
>
> A house is a perdurable garment, giving and taking of life. If it only fit, straightway it begins to chronicle our days. It beholds our sorrows and our joys; its untalebearing walls know all our thoughts, and if it be such a house as grows after the builders are gone, our thoughts presently owe much to it; we have but to glance at a certain shadow or a curve in the wall-paper pattern to recall them, softened as by an echo... It is aware of birth, marriage and death; and who dares say there is not kneaded into the stones a record more pleasing than brass? (*SC*, 235-6, 239)

Ms: *B*. **Published text:** *P*. **Differences from** *CP1978*: title: Gone, gone again *Blenheim Oranges* **Note on title:** the title in *CP1978* derives from a reference to 'those last verses – the Blenheim Oranges – of mine' in a letter to Eleanor Farjeon [*EF*, 213]. *PTP* provides no warrant for this.

That girl's clear eyes (132)
10 September 1916

See note on Thomas's sonnets (294). In its opening and closing lines, assonantal rhyme-sounds tighten the mesh of this Shakespearean sonnet. *CP1944* has 'Handel Street' in brackets after the title. Thomas was now attending the Royal Artillery School in Handel Street, Camden: 'I am not enjoying this half & half cadet stage a bit' (*LJB*, 80). The School was close to the Foundlings' Hospital for which Thomas Coram received a royal charter in 1739. The composer Handel gave his name to the street and money to the Hospital. The Hospital site is now a children's playground: Coram's Fields. The 'stony square sunlit' is Brunswick Square, built as recreation grounds for the Hospital. It still has a particularly splendid plane tree, which might have sheltered Thomas. The sonnet brings together disparate people: an anonymous 'girl', 'children' from the Hospital, and 'us': implicitly, Thomas and his fellow cadets. It may be the reader's job to join up the dots since the point is non-communication and disjunction – which extend to the speaker's psychology and to the 'sealed', coded quality of the poem itself. In *Roads* 'reveal' is linked with 'Heaven', 'conceal' with 'Hell'. For Thomas, the failure of 'eyes' to meet denotes rifts, secrets or denials, whether about sexual attraction or war. 'Like tombs' gives some of the show away. The men 'at [their] tasks' are 'sealed' off from their environment as well as from each other, although or because that environment seems complicit in their situation. Cf. Wilfred Owen, 'The Send-Off': 'So secretly, like wrongs hushed-up, they went'.

1-8. *concealed... In spite of many words*. Thomas wrote to Walter de la Mare from France (9 March 1917): 'One is absolutely friendless here. Everybody has something to conceal and he does so by pretending to be like everybody else. All the talk is shop or worse' (*SL*, 147).

10. *pleasure and pain*: cf. a refrain of *The Gallows*.

11. *tasted... sunlit*: cf. 'tasted sunlight', *The Other* (l.15).

13. *children, line after line*. Sunlight, music, and regimented children ambivalently recall one of the epiphanies ('Soldiers in line') by which the speaker in *Tears* is moved, perhaps towards war (see note, 178). London, scene of that epiphany, now hub of the war, has become 'stony' as well as 'sunlit'. And while (as in *Tears*) the most expressive language is that of the senses, this poem implies their power to deceive. Coombes notes: 'the blazing music, the marching children, are themselves hiding a reality; in their attractiveness they (almost) blot out the memory of the pity and profound devotion of the founder of the hospital' (*HC*, 224).

Ms: *B*. **Published text:** *LP*. **Note on title:** *CP1978* brackets the title; *CP2004* drops it. See Note on Text.

What will they do? (133)

15 September 1916

'Gone', implicit in *That girl's clear eyes*, resurfaces in this blend of valediction and malediction. A truncated sonnet, *What will they do?* reads between the lines of its precursor. Thomas set high standards for friendship: 'I sometimes thought...of how there is now no man living with whom I can be completely myself – Frost nearest of all, but I think not quite, because I am a little anxious to please him' (letter to Helen, 11 October 1914, *NLW*). He often suffered from the paranoid belief that he was less visible or necessary to other people than they to him. At a performance of Bottomley's *King Lear's Wife* he was perversely pleased when the changes effected in his appearance by the army confirmed this: 'Nobody recognises me now. Sturge Moore, E[dward] Marsh, & R.C. Trevelyan stood a yard off & I didn't trouble to awake them to stupid recognition' (*RFET*, 132). More darkly, the poem's solipsistic, self-answered question echoes Thomas's suicidal thoughts in 1907: 'I sat thinking about ways of killing myself... Then I went out and thought what effects my suicide would have... My acquaintances – I no longer have friends – would talk in a day or two (when they met) and try to explain and of course see suggestions in the past' (*SL*, 44). The indifferent 'they' in 'the loud street' may also represent more public forms of 'insensibility' – Wilfred Owen's word.

12. *Until that one turned back and lightly laughed*. Cf. Virginia Woolf: 'It's not catastrophes, murders, deaths, diseases that age and kill us; it's the way people look and laugh, and run up the steps of omnibuses' (*Jacob's Room* [London: Penguin Books, 1992], 69).

Ms: *B*. **Published text:** *LP*. **Note on title:** *CP1978* brackets the title; *CP2004* drops it. See Note on Text.

The Trumpet (133)

26-8? September 1916

On 20 September Thomas had moved to firing camp: the Royal Artillery Barracks at Trowbridge, Wiltshire: 'We are in tents and so we see the night sky. The trumpet blows for everything and I like that too, tho the trumpeter is not excellent' (*EF*, 214); 'I have written some verses suggested by the trumpet calls which go all day. They are not well done and the trumpet is cracked, but the Reveillé pleases me (more than it does most sleepers)' (*EF*, 219). Cooke observes that, because *The Trumpet* stands first in *P* and hence in most editions of *CP*: 'it is sometimes read as a poem of the "visions of glory" category. It is, however, wholly different from such poems and testifies more to the ambiguity of Thomas's commitment. It was as if he had to pervert his own nature to adapt himself to the war, and the impotent climax of the first stanza...amounts almost to an act of desecration against the lovers, who represent a norm of sanity in his other poems...A phrase like "the old wars" cuts right across any optimistic belief in a "war to end war"' (*WC*, 235). Here Cooke alludes to the fact that *The Trumpet* also stands first in the first section ('Visions of Glory') of I.M. Parsons's anthology of Great War poetry, *Men Who March Away* (London: Chatto, 1965). Parsons takes his title from Hardy's '"Men Who March Away"': Song of the Soldiers', praised by Thomas as 'an impersonal song which seems to me the best of the time, as it is the least particular and occasional' ('War Poetry', *Poetry and Drama* 2, 8 [December 1914], 345; see note on *Cock-Crow*, 257). *The Trumpet* seems aware both of Hardy and of A.E. Housman's 'Reveille', with which Thomas begins his (pre-war) *Pocket Book of Poems and Songs for the Open Air*:

Wake: the silver dusk returning
  Up the beach of darkness brims,
And the ship of sunrise burning
  Strands upon the eastern rims.

Wake: the vaulted shadow shatters,
  Trampled to the floor it spanned,
And the tent of night in tatters
  Straws the sky-pavilioned land.

Up, lad, up, 'tis late for lying:
  Hear the drums of morning play;
Hark, the empty highways crying
  'Who'll beyond the hills away?'...

Whereas Housman backs his rhetoric of early rising with a martial metaphor, Hardy brings war, and pro-war sentiment, into the foreground: 'What of the faith and fire within us / Men who march away / Ere the barn-cocks say / Night is growing grey, / Leaving all that here can win us'. Thomas reverts to Housman's metaphorical scheme and imperative mood: mimicry of the trumpet-call boosts 'Rise up'. But he switches the focus to dawn itself as a revelation of 'this earth newborn'. Here 'rising' means something more radical than getting up or getting on with it. Thomas absorbs Reveillé, as he does the bugle of *No one cares less than I*, into the dialectics of his own voice. It is indeed a subversive trumpet call that refers to 'the old wars' (cf. *The Word*, 1.7), and urges 'men' (perhaps those who 'march away') to forget 'everything' except earth's loveliness. Yet, for Thomas, a visionary moment can be as problematic as a 'vision of glory'. If *The Trumpet* revisits the dewy landscape of *The Glory*, as well as *Cock-Crow*, a poem bound up with his decision to enlist, it does so with added ambivalence – a pattern in poems of this period.

7. *scatter*: perhaps an echo of Housman's 'shatter'.

Ms: *B*. **Published text:** *P*.

When first (134)

? October 1916

Apart from *PTP*, there are no ms. or typescript sources for this poem. R. George Thomas dates it to 1 or 2 July 1916: 'From internal evidence I assume it was written after the poet had moved his books from his hill-top study down to his cottage in Steep village during Saturday and Sunday, 30 June and 1 July 1916' (*CP1978*, 344). Yet M_2 contains drafts of all the poems (except *The Cherry Trees*) that Thomas wrote between 4 March (*Celandine*) and 5 July (first draft of *The Dark Forest*) 1916. On 2 October he told Bottomley in terms that parallel the poem: 'I have just seen Steep for the last time. I had 15 hours there' (*LGB*, 271). He was then moving his family to High Beech (near Loughton, Essex), where he had been billeted in October 1915. Since the *PTP* typescript of *When first* looks like Eleanor Farjeon's work, it may be significant that Thomas's letters to her for October 1916 have been lost.

Parallels between *When first* and *The sun used to shine* include rhyme scheme, run-on lines and quatrains, speech-rhythms adapted both to walking and to remembering, and a valedictory tilt though here Thomas is mainly saying goodbye to himself. *When first* is more optimistic about 'the future and the maps' than are most of Thomas's valedictions in Autumn 1916. 'Just hope has gone for ever' signifies not despair, but the end of youthful expectancy. The poem's 'beat' gradually revives 'the heart's dance' in different terms.

12-13. *this year, // The twelfth*. The Thomases moved to Berryfield Cottage, the first of three houses that they rented in the Steep area, in November 1906, but they had been house-hunting there since 1905.

17. *Just hope has gone for ever*: possibly a pun on Hope Webb's name (see notes, 238, 279).

Ms: see above. **Published text:** *P*.

The Child in the Orchard (135)

October 1916

Except for rhyme scheme, Thomas's second poem spoken by a child is formally identical to *The Child on the Cliffs* (see note, 199). If the *LP* editors gave the poem its title, this would explain their choice. Yet formal similarity highlights difference: this child expresses a life wish rather than a death wish. Thomas's spell at firing camp in Wiltshire seems to have reactivated 'Lob' along with 'the Westbury White Horse', prompting another 'will and testament' poem. Given a folksong lilt and nursery-rhyme idiom, the child's voice permits a playful return to the bases of English tradition. What the child, as inheritor, must 'learn' is symbolically encompassed by an actual 'earthy' horse, a horse that spans history and 'rhyme', folk art, and a litany of birds.

5. *hern*: an archaic and dialect form of 'heron'.

7-8. *'Who was the lady...Banbury Cross?* Two answers offered by the *Oxford Dictionary of Nursery Rhymes* are Queen Elizabeth I and Lady Godiva.

14. *the Westbury White Horse.* 'High above me, on my left hand, eastward, was the grandest, cliffiest part of the Plain wall, the bastioned angle where it bends round southward by Westbury and Warminster, bare for the most part, carved with the White Horse and with double tiers of chalk pits' (*IPS*, 176).

20. *At the age of six.* 'I see that "At the age of six" is a rather rough way of explaining who speaks. But he did tell me he was six too and seemed to realise he had a long way to go' (*EF*, 118).

Ms: *B.* **Published text:** *LP.* **Note on title:** *CP1978* brackets the title; *CP2004* drops it. See Note on Text.

Lights Out (135)
November 1916

On 6 November Thomas told Eleanor Farjeon: 'Now I have actually done still another piece [since *The Child in the Orchard*] which I call "Lights Out". It sums up what I have often thought at that call. I wish it were as brief – 2 pairs of long notes. I wonder is it nearly as good as it might be' (*EF*, 218). Coombes warns against one way of reading *Lights Out*: 'we should disregard as far as we are able what it may seem to possess of prophecy; the poignancy doesn't need any adventitious stimulus' (*HC*, 212). Helen Thomas evidently worried that the poem might be received as a suicide note. Myfanwy Thomas writes: 'Though "Lights Out" obviously has undertones of death, Mother was absolutely certain that the poem is initially about going to sleep, that my father would never have used a euphemism for Death or anything else' (letter, quoted *ETFN* 54 [August 2005], 10). By making 'going to sleep' an active principle, *Lights Out* inverts the traditional trope as employed in Sidney's sonnet XXXIX, copied into the Thomases' 'Golden Book' of literary touchstones (Bodleian Library, MS. Don. e. 10): 'Come Sleep, O Sleep, the certain knot of peace, / The baiting place of wit, the balm of woe, /...With shield of proof shield me from out the prease / Of those fierce darts despair at me doth throw'. The poem also transposes the scenario of Thomas's essay 'Insomnia': 'Night after night deliberately we take upon ourselves the utmost possible weakness, because it is the offering most acceptable to sleep... I find that I desire to enter without gradation into perfect helplessness, and I exercise a quiet resolution against the strains even of memory' (*LS*, 39). For Thomas, sleep and dream are usually positive, aligned with the creative process:

> It seems indeed to me that to sleep is owed a portion of the deliberation given to death. If life is an apprenticeship to death, waking may be an education for sleep. We are not thoughtful enough about sleep; yet it is more than half of that great portion of life spent really in solitude... We truly ought to enter upon sleep as into a strange, fair chapel. Fragrant

and melodious antechamber of the unseen, sleep is a novitiate for the beyond... And when the world is too much with me, when the past is a reproach harrying me with dreadful faces, the present a fierce mockery, the future an open grave, it is sweet to sleep. I have closed a well-loved book, ere the candle began to fail, that I might sleep, and let the soul take her pleasure in the deeps of eternity. (*RAP*, 38-40)

I fell into a deep sleep; and in my sleep I had a dream... A great forest hung round about. The might of its infinite silence and repose, indeed, never ceased to weigh upon me in my dream. I could hear sounds: they were leagues away. The trees which I could see were few: I felt that they must be thousands deep on every hand. (*HS*, 71-2)

I had a not unpleasant half-dream seeing myself going far up an infinitely long pillared corridor. It may have been soon after this that I began to have a trivial but strange experience which has been repeated once or twice a year ever since. It happens mostly when I am lying down in bed waiting for sleep, and only on nights when I sleep well. I close my eyes and I find myself very dimly seeing expand before me a vague immense space enclosed with invisible boundaries. Yet it can hardly be called seeing. All is grey, dull, formless, and I am aware chiefly by some other means than sight of vast unshapely towering masses of a colourless subject [?substance] which I feel to be soft. Through these things and the space I grope slowly. They tend to fade away, but I can recover them by an effort perhaps half a dozen times, and do so because it is somehow pleasant or alluring. Then I usually sleep. During the experience I am well awake and am remembering that it is a repetition, wondering what it means and if anything new will occur, and taking care not to disturb the process. (*CET*, 152)

Like all Thomas' forest symbolism, the symbolism of *Lights Out* seems multi-layered: 'shelf above shelf'. A visionary passage in *The South Country* speaks of moments when 'a window is thrown open upon the unfathomable deep...we stand ever at the edge of Eternity and fall in many times before we die' (*SC*, 24). In crossing psychic 'borders', *Lights Out* completes a circuit that began with *The Other* ('The forest ended'). Indeed, *The Other* strangely anticipates the way in which Thomas's inner journey doubles back on itself during the second half of 1916. As for outer journeys (not really distinct): the speaker's balancing of will and fate reflects Thomas's current demeanour towards life and war. He is given sufficient agency to make *Lights Out*, in part, a quest poem: 'losing' and finding oneself seem oddly equivalent. Like *The Trumpet*, its dialectical complement, this poem absorbs war into a larger picture. For Thomas, his (statistically likely) death counted less than the existential test of the trenches. On 9 September he had told Frost: 'I am rather impatient to go out & be shot at. That is all I want, to do something if I am discovered to be any use, but in any case to be made to run risks, to be put through it' (*RFET*, 147). At one level, 'To go into the unknown' accepts this test. Since July 1915, if not since December 1914, Thomas has set out to imagine the future – not just his own

– as fully as possible in the time available. The 'forest brink' is also a dead-line.
7-12. *Many a road... sink.* As in the first stanza, Thomas mimetically plays syntax against line, 'winding' against 'straight'. 'Travellers'/'blurs' aptly 'blurs' a pattern of monosyllabic rhyming on crisp 'k' sounds. The last three lines constitute a diminuendo of six, five and four syllables. As at the end of other stanzas, the final short line reinforces the sense that there is no turning back.
25. *The tall forest towers*: cf. 'the nettle towers' (*The Green Roads*, l.6).

Ms: *B.* **Published text:** *P.* **Differences from** *CP1978*: 3 Forest *Forest,* 4 straight, *straight* 6 cannot *can not* 8 That,...crack, *That...crack* 9 brink, *brink* 10 travellers *travellers,* 13 ends, *ends –* 14 ends, *ends;* 17 ends *ends,* 23 enter and leave *enter, and leave,* 25 towers; *towers:* 27 shelf; *shelf:* **Note:** *CP1978* follows the punctuation of *B* on the grounds that it 'seems to give a clearer indication of how the poem should be read' [366]; this edition follows *P.* **Note on title:** Title is given in *B*.

The long small room (136)

November 1916

Myfanwy Thomas relates this poem to the fact that her father 'liked to work in a stone out-building in [the] very large garden' of Selsfield House, Vivian Locke Ellis's home at East Grinstead (*MT*, 47). In *The Happy-Go-Lucky Morgans* the same building may have contributed to Aunt Rachel's house, which 'was hidden by ivy, which thrust itself through the walls and up between the flag-stones of the floor, flapped in at the windows, and spread itself so densely over the panes that the mice ran up and down it, and you could see their pale, silky bellies through the glass – often they looked in and entered. The ivy was full of sparrows' nests'. The house has 'a large fireplace', and 'you never came down in the morning feeling that you had done the same yesterday and would do the same tomorrow, as if each day was a new, badly written line in a copy-book, with the same senseless words at the head of every page' (*HGLM*, 85-7). After *Lights Out*, *The long small room* seems spoken posthumously: as by a ghost who haunts 'the dark house' of life with unfinished business, a ghost who still pursues memory: 'When I look back' (see note on Thomas's 'ghosts', 202). The moon, 'casement', 'old ivy and older brick' have a Gothic aura, and the detached 'hand' is a disturbing synecdoche.
1. *willows in the west*: changed from 'the distant west' in *B*, presumably owing to Eleanor Farjeon's criticism (see below).
2. *Narrowed up to the end the fireplace filled.* Here the stanza itself 'narrows up' from spaced, open-vowelled monosyllables ('long small room') to the cluttered consonants of 'fireplace filled'. There are hints of a coffin-shape.
12-13. *my right hand // Crawling crab-like.* Thomas's years of literary drudgery make the movement of pen over paper an inevitable image for human bondage. 'Crab-like' implies that his life-writing, including the poem in progress, has always been at an awkward angle to the universe. The sense of agency in *Lights Out* is absent from this slow-motion symbolic journey, lent an Oriental fatalism by the last line.
16. *The hundred last leaves stream upon the willow.* 'I am worried about the impression the willow made on you. As a matter of fact I started with that last

line as what I was working to. I am only fearing it has a sort of Japanesy sudden-
ness of ending. But it is true, whether or not it is a legitimate switch to make'
(*EF*, 221). Thomas may have changed the line (see above and *EF*, 222) because
he 'feared' that he was straying onto the territory of Imagism, with its Japanese
models. But even when referring back to the first line, the effect remains boldly
'sudden'.

Ms: *B*. **Published text:** *P*.

The Sheiling (137)
23 November 1916

Thomas, who would be commissioned 2nd Lieutenant the next day, was on
leave, and saying goodbye in person as well as poems. He wrote *The Sheiling*
when 'travelling back from Gordon Bottomley's (Silverdale)' (*B*). Bottomley lived
at The Sheiling, Silverdale, near Carnforth, on the edge of the Lake District.
Thomas writes of an earlier visit (June 1914) to this northern limestone land-
scape: 'the house... is on a hill top by itself, on all sides approached over slip-
pery tussocky turf and stone mixed with thorn and brier and bracken. The
house is only cut off from this by a stone wall and its trees; hardly any garden:
most of the land inside the wall is the same as outside, stony and grassy' (*LTH*,
72). During Thomas's last stay, Bottomley remembers that they saw 'an epic
turbulence of storm sweeping towards us from the mountains of the Kirkstone
Pass on the northern horizon' (*LGB*, 5).

Bottomley (1874-1948), a chronic invalid threatened by lung haemorrhages,
was a poet and verse-dramatist whose poems or plays appeared in most of the
'Georgian' anthologies. From 1902 Thomas used his correspondence with
Bottomley as a form of psychotherapy (Bottomley's own letters no longer exist).
He called him 'Comforter'; Bottomley called Thomas 'Edward the Confessor'.
Thomas confessed his fluctuating mental state, the exhaustion induced by
reviewing and book-commissions, his dread that he was destroying his talent.
Significantly, he wrote less to Bottomley after the advent of Frost and poetry.
But their literary interchange continued. Bottomley ensured that Thomas's
poems appeared in *AANP*, and tried to get Edward Marsh to publish them in
Georgian Poetry. As regards Bottomley's own work: whether in the letters or a
review, Thomas could be severe. Reviewing *Chambers of Imagery*, he calls
Bottomley's 'new verses...difficult...because they are not always wrought up to
the condition of poetry, but seem to have been left in a raw state that can appeal
to the intelligence only, except in a few places' (*Daily Chronicle*, 5 February
1907). A letter to Frost contains similar but harsher criticism of Bottomley's
verse play *King Lear's Wife*: 'He had to make Goneril run a knife through a
rabbit's eyes. Well, I firmly believe that if he had imagination he would have
kept such a thing dark supposing he could go the length of imagining it. As it
was, it sounded just a thought out cruelty, worse far than cruelty itself with
passion behind it. Of course he pretended there was passion. There wasn't'
(*RFET*, 131-2).

The Sheiling does not celebrate (literary) friendship with the same intensity
as *The sun used to shine*. It is also unusual among Thomas's 'house' poems. In
part, it belongs to the genre of poet addressing patron, as, in grander style,

Yeats salutes Lady Gregory and Coole Park. Like Yeats, Thomas exploits the contrast between extreme landscape and a house that symbolises the architecture of civilisation. The fact that indoors and outdoors interpenetrate ('ancient stairs', 'Painted by the wild air') suggests that art can negotiate the 'wild'. Yet l.13 obliquely sets a limit to the vision of those 'Safe resting there' by implying ('But') that they might be aesthetic spectators (see note on *The Watchers*, 290). That the air is also 'travelling' points in the artistic as well as literal direction that Thomas himself is taking: away from 'peace'. As a psychological parable, the poem associates the house with Bottomley's benign therapy; 'a land of stone' with Thomas's need, his 'cold heart', perhaps his greater strengths. Each stanza has two unrhymed line-endings (apart from the off-rhyme 'house'/'peace') and a single rhyme-sound that includes a same-rhyme. The overall rhythm blends containment with incompletion: a hint of horizons beyond the poem and its subject.

7. *delicate*: a 'delicate' allusion to Bottomley's health and art.

11. *Safe*: 'Soft' is cancelled in *B*.

15. *wild air*: a phrase that also occurs in *The Source* and *Melancholy*.

16. *One maker's mind*. Up to a point, 'oneness' in creativity (starting with Nature's) and mutual 'kindness' reconcile the poem's various tensions. Yet the same-rhyming of 'kind' produces an effect of distance.

Ms: *B*. **Published text:** *P*.

The Lane (138)

December 1916

On 7 December Thomas told Eleanor Farjeon: 'they asked for volunteers to go straight out to Batteries in France and I made sure of it by volunteering. Don't let Helen know' (*EF*, 231). This decision may have conditioned his poetic move from 'a land of stone' to an iconic memory of Steep. Writing to Helen (22 January 1917), Thomas says: 'You never mentioned receiving those verses about Green Lane, Froxfield. Did you get them? They were written in December and suggested by our last walk there in September' (see *CP1978*, 421). The poem also harks back to a lane evoked in *Beautiful Wales*: 'I knew that I took up eternity with both hands, and though I laid it down again, the lane was a most potent, magic thing, when I could thus make time as nothing while I meandered over many centuries' (*BW*, 166). Like other recent poems in which prospect and retrospect converge, *The Lane* has a high self-quotation quota. The poem might be read as an epiphany of Thomas's epiphanies. It presents an abundant timeless moment, collapses the seasons, fuses the senses, and lists flora and fauna. It also combines Thomas's Keatsian mode (*October* etc.) with the 'Steep' poem, unrhymed lines with near sonnet-form. 'Halcyon bells' makes the whole mix strangely magical, as if this oasis in time and war symbolises poetry itself, and a farewell to it.

3. *Green Lane*: a post-Enclosure road, and therefore 'straight'. 'The lane does end suddenly. It is broad because enclosure commissioners always made their new roads to standard widths, with a grass verge on one or both sides' (*WW*, 34).

5. *bracken and blackberry, harebell and dwarf gorse*: cf. 'Harebell and scabious and tormentil, / That blackberry and gorse.../ Bow down to' (*October*).

7. *halcyon bells*: the harebells, blue like the halcyon (a name for the kingfisher). The later allusion to 'waters' may implicate the mythical halcyon: a bird said to breed in a nest that floats on the sea at the Winter solstice, and to calm winds and waves – an image for peace. In l.13 'those bells ring' is a synaesthetic image for the scene becoming sound, for writing the poem.

8. *no vessel ever sailed*: perhaps (together with the dots after the clause) an allusion to Thomas's going overseas.

9-11. *a kind of spring...like summer...winter's quiet*. '[T]he air was vibrant though windless – stirred like water in a full vessel when more is still poured in... It was the most perfect of [February] days. The air had all the sparkling purity of winter. It had, too, something of the mettle and gusto of the spring. The scent of young grass...was sharp though faint, and thus the air was touched with a summer perfume' (*HS*, 130-1).

15. *The lane ends*: cf. the ending of *The Path*: 'sudden, it ends where the wood ends'. The repeated 'same', like the repeated 'ends', is an anti-climactic shock. This historical 'sameness' is not the lane's rich unity.

Ms: *B*. **Published text:** *TP*, *CP1928*. **Note on title:** *The Watchers* and *The Lane* may have been given their titles when they were published together in *TP*. *CP1978* brackets the title; *CP2004* drops it. See Note on Text.

Out in the dark (138)

24 December 1916

This poem was written at High Beech, Essex, where Thomas had rented a cottage for his family: 'It is right alone in the forest among beech trees & fern & deer' (*RFET*, 152). Having been given embarkation leave, Thomas spent Christmas there. Sending *Out in the dark* to Eleanor Farjeon, he remarks: 'It is really Baba who speaks, not I. Something she felt put me on to it' (*EF*, 237). In a letter dated 29 December he asks Baba (Myfanwy) herself: 'Did Mother tell you I wrote a poem about the dark that evening when you did not want to go into the sitting room because it was dark?' (*MT*, 57). But a passage in *The Happy-Go-Lucky Morgans*, possibly based on a childhood memory of his own, seems relevant:

> In the library I found Aurelius reading, with his back to the uncurtained window, by a light that only illuminated his face and page. Running at first to the window, I pressed my face on the pane to see the profound of deepening night, and the lake shining dimly like a window through which the things under the earth might be seen if you were out. The abyss of solitude below and around was swallowing the little white moon and might swallow me also; with terror at this feeling I turned away... Aurelius lighted another lamp. I went over again to the window and looked out. In a flash I saw the outer vast world of solitude, darkness, and silence, waiting eternally for its prey, and felt behind me the little world within that darkness like a lighthouse. (*HGLM*, 54-6)

Out in the Dark probably influenced Hardy's 'The Fallow Deer at the Lonely House'. Having read *P*, Hardy planned to get *LP* 'from the Times Book Club' (Vere H. Collins, *Talks with Thomas Hardy at Max Gate* [London: Duckworth, 1928], 5).

One without looks in tonight
    Through the curtain-chink
From the sheet of glistening white;
One without looks in tonight
      As we sit and think
      By the fender-brink.

We do not discern those eyes
    Watching in the snow;
Lit by lamps of rosy dyes
We do not discern those eyes
      Wondering, aglow,
      Four-footed, tiptoe.

Hardy may have recognised and reclaimed a debt. The diction of *Out in the dark* is unusually Hardyesque: 'haunts', 'sage', drear'. Thomas's poetic dialogues with this key precursor tend to complicate Hardy's metaphysical, psychological and rhythmic structures (see note on *As the team's head-brass*, 301). But sometimes the intertextual traffic flows the other way. In *February Afternoon* and *Out in the dark*, perhaps *in extremis* or *tenebris*, Thomas's vision and cadences approach Hardy's 'most tyrannous obsession of the blindness of fate, the carelessness of Nature, and the insignificance of Man' (*IPS*, 194). In *Out in the dark* Thomas's symbolism of 'outside the house' extends to 'outside the earth'. The speaker, seemingly without agency as in *The long small room*, is exposed to the spaces of the universe. In the second stanza, 'the dark' assumes the agency that the speaker lacks. 'Stealthily', 'haunts' and 'bound' make it an actively sinister force, hunting as well as haunting, and moving fast. At one level, this force embodies the war, as the doe and her fawns represent birth, family, peace. The monotonous rhyme scheme that 'Drums on [the] ear' adds to the poem's fatalistic insinuation that 'the might...of night' is irresistible in all its guises. Thomas may be recalling Keats's self-elegy 'Bright Star, Would I Were Steadfast as Thou Art': 'at the beginning of his "posthumous life"...the sonnet was written. It is the hymn of stillness, equalising the steadfast watching star, and the poet that saw likewise...The snow spreads like winter's grave-cloth over the earth. The star hangs vigilant and regardless' (*K*, 72).

9. *hound*: an image suggested by deer-hunting.

18. *Love and delight*: not deliberately 'turned from', as in *Lights Out*.

20. *If you love it not*. Cf. the end of *Rain*: 'the love of death, / If love it be towards what is perfect'. The ambiguous 'If' leaves open a positive alternative to 'fear', but one that equally surrenders to 'night'.

Ms: *B*. **Published text**: *LP*. **Differences from *CP1978***: 11 star and I *I and star* **Note**: in l.11 this edition [like *CP1928* and *CP1944*] follows *B*, rather than *LP* and a manuscript reproduced by Eleanor Farjeon [*EF*, 238]. The rhythm, including the chiasmus of sounds 'star'/'deer', then 'star'/'deer'/'near'/'far', seems to locate 'I' more effectively in a 'nearness' yet distanced by the repeated 'and'. 'Star' and 'far' also rhyme by being similarly positioned in the line. In l.7 *CP1920*, *CP1928* and *CP1944* print 'the lamp' [*B* has 'a lamp']. **Note on title**: *CP1978* brackets the title; *CP2004* drops it. See Note on Text.

The sorrow of true love (139)

13 January 1917

Thomas wrote this poem at Tin Town, Lydd, Kent, shortly before leaving for mobilisation camp at Codford, Wiltshire. He would embark from Southampton on 29 January. On 11 January he had said goodbye to his family at High Beech, and eaten with his parents and brothers in London. On 13 January he noted in the diary he would take to France, and into which he copied the poem: 'Nothing to do but test compass which never gives same results... Cold drizzle... Even wrote verses' (*CP1978*, 463). Another near-sonnet, these 'verses' (couplets) fit with the fact that Thomas had packed Shakespeare's *Sonnets* into his baggage. As Richard Lowndes points out (*ETFN* 27 [August 1992], 21-2), he echoes the rhymes 'hope' and 'scope' in *Sonnet* XXIX ('When in disgrace with fortune and men's eyes, / I all alone beweep my outcast state'); also *Romeo and Juliet* (II, ii): 'parting is such sweet sorrow'. *The sorrow of true love* glances back over Thomas's 'love poetry', as other valedictory poems have reviewed other genres. He returns to the generic conundrum posed by *Those things that poets said*; to the 'remorse and pity' of *No one so much as you*; perhaps to the contrary ideal of 'true love' in *The Unknown*, which evokes his feelings for Hope Webb (see notes, 238, 279). Like *When first*, but less hopefully, *The sorrow of true love* juxtaposes 'hope' and 'parting'. It also alludes to *Parting*. The condition figured by 'frozen drizzle perpetual' resembles 'the perpetual yesterday / That naught can stir or stain' in that poem, and causes similar grief. There is no happy ending to this 'beweeping', no consolatory Shakespearean final couplet.

Ms: Thomas's 'War Diary' [1 January – 8 April 1917]. **Published text:** *CP1978*. **Differences from** *CP1978*: title: The sorrow of true love *Last Poem* [*The sorrow of true love*] 2 morrow. *morrow:* 8 tempest nor *tempest and* **Note:** *CP1978* follows a transcript of the poem by Edward Cawston Thomas; this edition follows one by Bronwen Simmons and Myfanwy Thomas. **Note on title:** *CP2004* has no title.

BIOGRAPHICAL OUTLINE

1878: Philip Edward Thomas born (3 March) in Lambeth, eldest of six sons. His parents, Philip Henry and Mary Elizabeth Thomas, 'mainly Welsh'. Family later lives in Wandsworth, Clapham and Balham.

1883-95: ET attends various London schools including St Paul's. Spends holidays in Wiltshire. Starts to write about his country walks in manner of Richard Jefferies.

1894-96: ET mentored by writer and critic, James Ashcroft Noble. Meets Noble's daughter Helen (1877-1967).

1896: James Ashcroft Noble dies. Mrs Noble and ET's parents opposed to increasingly intense relationship between ET and Helen.

1897: ET's first book, *The Woodland Life*, published.

1898-1900: ET wins History scholarship and goes to Lincoln College, Oxford. Writes for journals such as *The Academy* and *Literature*.

1899: Helen Noble becomes pregnant. She and ET marry at Fulham Registry Office (20 June).

1900: Philip Merfyn Ashcroft Thomas born. ET gets second-class degree, refuses to enter Civil Service, plans career as freelance writer.

1901-06: ET and family live in Kent, first near Maidstone (Bearsted), then at Elses Farm near Sevenoaks.

1901: ET writes occasional reviews for *Daily Chronicle*.

1902: Rachel Mary Bronwen Thomas born. *Horae Solitariae* published. ET begins correspondence with poet Gordon Bottomley. After Lionel Johnson dies, H.W. Nevinson, literary editor of *Daily Chronicle*, hands on his regular reviewing slot to ET.

1905: ET meets and helps 'tramp-poet' W.H. Davies. Asked to review for *Morning Post*. *Beautiful Wales* published

1906: ET and family move to Hampshire and live in Berryfield Cottage, first of several rented houses around Steep, Petersfield. *The Heart of England* published. ET meets W.H. Hudson and Walter de la Mare.

1907: *The Pocket Book of Poems and Songs for the Open Air* published. ET goes to Minsmere, Sussex, to work on biography of Richard Jefferies (December).

1908: ET at Minsmere (January, February). Has romantic feelings for young girl, Hope Webb, whose father forbids him to write to her. ET and Helen distressed. ET contemplates suicide (November).

1909: ET and family move into house, which they come to dislike, built for them on hilltop at Wick Green. *Richard Jefferies* and *The South Country* published.

1910: Helen Elizabeth Myfanwy Thomas born. *Rest and Unrest* and *Feminine Influence on the Poets* published.

1911: *Light and Twilight*, *Maurice Maeterlinck* and *Celtic Stories* published. ET has severe breakdown (September).

1912: ET undergoes psychotherapy with Godwin Baynes. Writing *Walter Pater*. *Algernon Charles Swinburne*, *George Borrow*, *Lafcadio Hearn* and *Norse Tales* published. While a paying guest at Selsfield House, East Grinstead home of

Vivian Locke Ellis, ET begins autobiographical novel, *The Happy-Go-Lucky Morgans* (November).

1913: ET depressed and suicidal at times. *The Icknield Way* published. ET and family move into small Yew Tree Cottage in Steep village. Meets Robert Frost at St George's Restaurant, London (6 October). Begins autobiography (*The Childhood of Edward Thomas*) while staying at Selsfield House (December).

1914: ET writes three glowing reviews of Frost's *North of Boston*. *In Pursuit of Spring* published. ET and family take holiday near Frosts at Ledington, Gloucestershire (August). ET travels in England, preparing articles for *English Review* about impact of war (September). War dries up book-commissions and reviewing opportunities. ET writes first poems (December).

1915: ET writing poems. *Four-and-Twenty Blackbirds*, *This England* and *The Life of the Duke of Marlborough* published. ET considers joining Frost in US, but enlists in Artists' Rifles (July). Sent to camp at High Beech, near Loughton, Essex (October). Moved to Hare Hall Camp, Gidea Park, Romford, Essex, and promoted to Lance-Corporal (November). Acts as map-reading instructor.

1916: ET writing poems. *Keats* published. ET promoted to Corporal (March). Awarded £300 from Civil List and applies for commission in Royal Artillery (June). Accepted (July). Trains as officer cadet with Artillery in London and moves family from Steep to High Beech (September). Commissioned 2nd Lieutenant (November). Posted to 244 Siege Battery, Royal Garrison Artillery, Lydd, Kent. Volunteers for service overseas (December). *Six Poems* by Edward Eastaway published. Selwyn & Blount accept *Poems*.

1917: ET given embarkation leave, writes last poem and begins 'War Diary' (January). Embarks from Southampton (29 January). Positioned near Arras (11 February). After spell at Group HQ, ET rejoins Battery (9 March). Takes up duty at Observation Post. Killed by shell-blast as Arras 'offensive' begins (9 April). Buried in military cemetery in village of Agny. *Poems* by Edward Eastaway published posthumously.

ABBREVIATIONS

1. Manuscripts, Typescripts & Printings of Poems

AANP: *An Annual of New Poetry* (London: Constable, 1917)

B: Manuscript poems in Bodleian Library, MS. Don. d. 28

BC: Manuscript poems and typescripts (also prose) in Berg Collection, New York Public Library, Berg Coll MSS Thomas, E

BL: Manuscript poems in British Library, Add. MS. 44990

CP1920: Edward Thomas, *Collected Poems* (London: Selwyn & Blount, 1920)

CP1928: Edward Thomas, *Collected Poems* (New Edition), (London: Ingpen & Grant, 1928)

CP1944: Edward Thomas, *Collected Poems* (New Edition), (London: Faber & Faber, 1944)

CP1949: Edward Thomas, *CP1944* (Fifth Impression), (London: Faber & Faber, 1949)

CP1978: (Ed.) R. George Thomas, *The Collected Poems of Edward Thomas* (Oxford: Clarendon Press, 1978)

CP2004: Edward Thomas, *Collected Poems* (London: Faber & Faber, 2004)

*JT: Typescript poems, once owned by Thomas's brother Julian Thomas

LML: Manuscript poems (also prose) in Lockwood Memorial Library, State University of New York at Buffalo

LP: Edward Thomas, *Last Poems* (London: Selwyn & Blount, 1918)

*M₁: Green notebook of manuscript poems, once owned by Thomas's son Merfyn, now in National Library of Wales

*M₂: Blue notebook of manuscript poems, once owned by Thomas's son Merfyn, now in National Library of Wales

*MET: Typescript poems, once owned by Thomas's mother, Mary Elizabeth Thomas

P: Edward Eastaway, *Poems* (London: Selwyn & Blount, 1917; facsimile ed., London: Imperial War Museum, 1997)

PTP: Printer's typescript of *P*, Bodleian Library, MS. Eng. poet. d. 214

RB: *Root and Branch, A Seasonal of the Arts*, edited by James Guthrie 1913-1918

SP: Edward Eastaway, *Six Poems* (Flansham, Sussex: The Pear Tree Press, 1916; facsimile ed., Cheltenham: The Cyder Press, 2005)

TE: (Ed.) Edward Thomas, *This England: An Anthology from her Writers* (Oxford: Oxford University Press, 1915)

TP: Edward Thomas, *Two Poems* ['The Lane' & 'The Watchers'], (London: Ingpen & Grant, 1927)

* Photocopies of these (and other) mss and typescripts are among the archival materials assembled in the Edward Thomas Collection, Cardiff University Library. The abbreviations used for them here are identical with those in *CP1978*.

2. Memoirs, Letters, Diaries, Notebooks

CET: Edward Thomas, *The Childhood of Edward Thomas* (London: Faber & Faber, 1938, 1983); 1983 ed. includes Thomas's 'War Diary', as does *CP1978*

EF: Eleanor Farjeon, *Edward Thomas: The Last Four Years* (Oxford: Oxford University Press, 1958; repr. Stroud: Sutton Publishing, 1997)

FNB: Numbered field notebooks [up to end of 1915] of Edward Thomas, Berg Collection, New York Public Library

HT: Helen Thomas, with Myfanwy Thomas, *Under Storm's Wing* (Manchester: Carcanet Press, 1988), containing Helen Thomas's memoirs, *As It Was* (1926) and *World Without End* (1931)

LA: (Ed.) R. George Thomas, *Edward Thomas: Letters to America 1914-1917* (Edinburgh: The Tregara Press, 1989): cited only for letters to Thomas's aunt, Margaret Townsend (letters to Robert Frost also included)

LEG: Edward Thomas, *A Selection of Letters to Edward Garnett* (Edinburgh: The Tregara Press, 1981)

LGB: (Ed.) R. George Thomas, *Letters from Edward Thomas to Gordon Bottomley* (London: Oxford University Press, 1968)

LJB: (Ed.) Anthony Berridge, *The Letters of Edward Thomas to Jesse Berridge* (London: Enitharmon Press, 1983)

LTH: (Ed.) R. George Thomas, *Edward Thomas: Letters to Helen* (Manchester: Carcanet Press, 2000)

LWD: Letters from Edward Thomas to Walter de la Mare, Bodleian Library, MS. Eng. lett. c. 376

MT: Myfanwy Thomas, *One Of These Fine Days: Memoirs* (Manchester: Carcanet Press, 1982)

NLW: Edward Thomas diaries (1900-1911), NLW MSS 22900-22913; letters from Edward Thomas to Helen Thomas (1896-1917), NLW MSS 22914-22917, National Library of Wales

RFET: (Ed.) Matthew Spencer, *Elected Friends: Robert Frost & Edward Thomas to one another* (New York: Handsel Books, 2003)

SL: (Ed.) R. George Thomas, *Edward Thomas: Selected Letters* (Oxford: Oxford University Press, 1995)

SLRF: (Ed.) Lawrance Thompson, *Selected Letters of Robert Frost* (New York: Henry Holt & Co., 1964; London: Jonathan Cape, 1965)

Note: transcriptions from notebooks, diaries and letters sometimes differ slightly from those in *CP1978*, *SL* and *LTH*. Ampersands and other abbreviations have been translated, except where reproduced from published versions.

3. Prose by Edward Thomas

ACS: *Algernon Charles Swinburne: A Critical Study* (London: Martin Secker, 1912)

BW: *Beautiful Wales* (London: A. & C. Black, 1905)

CC: *Cloud Castle and other Papers* (London: Duckworth, 1922)

COE: *The Chessplayer & other essays* (Manor Farm, Andoversford, Gloucestershire: The Whittington Press, 1981)

CS: *Celtic Stories* (Oxford: Clarendon Press, 1911)

FIP: *Feminine Influence on the Poets* (London: Martin Secker, 1910)

FTB: *Four-and-Twenty Blackbirds* (London: Duckworth, 1915; facsimile ed., Cheltenham: The Cyder Press, 2001)

GB: *George Borrow: The Man and his Books* (London: Chapman & Hall, 1912)

HE: *The Heart of England* (London: J.M. Dent, 1906)

HGLM: *The Happy-Go-Lucky Morgans* (London: Duckworth, 1913)

HS: *Horae Solitariae* (London: Duckworth, 1902)

IOW: *The Isle of Wight* (London: Blackie & Son, 1911)

IPS: *In Pursuit of Spring* (London: Thomas Nelson & Son, 1914)

IW: *The Icknield Way* (London: Constable, 1913)

K: *Keats* (London: T.C. & E.C. Jack, 1916; facsimile ed., Cheltenham: The Cyder Press, 1999)

LAT: *Light and Twilight* (London: Duckworth, 1911)

LDM: *The Life of the Duke of Marlborough* (London: Chapman & Hall, 1915)

LH: *Lafcadio Hearn* (London: Constable, 1912)

LPE: *A Literary Pilgrim in England* (London: Methuen, 1917)

LS: *The Last Sheaf* (London: Jonathan Cape, 1928)

MM: *Maurice Maeterlinck* (London: Methuen, 1911)

NT: *Norse Tales* (Oxford: Clarendon Press, 1912)

O: *Oxford* (London: A. & C. Black, 1903; repr. with Introduction and Notes by Lucy Newlyn, Oxford: Signal Books, 2005)

RAP: *Rose Acre Papers* (London: S.C. Brown, Langham & Co., 1904)

RJ: *Richard Jefferies: His Life and Work* (London: Hutchinson, 1909; repr. London: Faber & Faber, 1978)

RR: Introduction to William Cobbett, *Rural Rides* (London: J.M. Dent, 1912)

RU: *Rest and Unrest* (London: Duckworth, 1910)

SC: *The South Country* (London: J.M. Dent, 1909)

TC: *The Country* (London: B.T. Batsford, 1913; facsimile ed., Cheltenham: The Cyder Press, 1999)

TWL: *The Woodland Life* (Edinburgh & London: William Blackwood, 1897)

WP: *Walter Pater: A Critical Study* (London: Martin Secker, 1913)

Note: Other books edited or introduced by Thomas are cited in the Notes. The most important of these is his anthology *The Pocket Book of Poems and Songs for the Open Air* (London: E. Grant Richards, 1907).

4. Biography, Criticism etc.

AM: Andrew Motion, *The Poetry of Edward Thomas* (London: Routledge & Kegan Paul, 1980)

ETFN: *Edward Thomas Fellowship Newsletter*

GC: Guy Cuthbertson, 'The Literary Geography in Edward Thomas's Work', unpublished thesis, Oxford University, 2004

HC: H. Coombes, *Edward Thomas* (Chatto & Windus, 1956)

JB: (Ed.) Jonathan Barker, *The Art of Edward Thomas* (Bridgend: Poetry Wales Press, 1987)

JK: (Ed.) Judy Kendall, *Edward Thomas's Poets* (Manchester: Carcanet Press, 2007)

JM: John Moore, *The Life and Letters of Edward Thomas* (London: Heinemann, 1939)

JP: John Pikoulis, 'On Editing Edward Thomas', *PN Review* 21, 5 (May-June, 1995)

MK: Michael Kirkham, *The Imagination of Edward Thomas* (Cambridge: Cambridge University Press, 1986)

RGT: R. George Thomas, *Edward Thomas: A Portrait* (Oxford: Clarendon Press, 1985)

SS: Stan Smith, *Edward Thomas* (London: Faber & Faber, 1986)

VS: Vernon Scannell, *Edward Thomas* (London: Longman's, Green & Co., 1963)

WC: William Cooke, *Edward Thomas: A Critical Biography* (London: Faber & Faber, 1970)

WW: W.M. Whiteman, *The Edward Thomas Country* (Southampton: Paul Cave, nd)

FURTHER BIBLIOGRAPHY

Jonathan Bate, *Romantic Ecology* (London: Routledge, 1991); *The Song of the Earth* (London: Picador, 2000)

(Eds) Guy Cuthbertson and Lucy Newlyn, *Branch-Lines: Edward Thomas and Contemporary Poetry* (London: Enitharmon Press, 2007)

(Ed.) Richard Emeny, *Edward Thomas on the Georgians* (Cheltenham: The Cyder Press, 2004)

(Eds) Richard Emeny & Jeff Cooper, *Edward Thomas: A Checklist* (Blackburn: White Sheep Press, 2004)

David Gervais, *Literary Englands* (Cambridge: Cambridge University Press, 1993)

(Ed.) Anne Harvey, *Elected Friends: Poems for and about Edward Thomas* (London: Enitharmon Press, 1991); *Adlestrop Revisited* (Stroud, Gloucestershire: Henry Sutton, 1999)

Peter Howarth, *British Poetry in the Age of Modernism* (Cambridge: Cambridge University Press, 2005)

Alun Howkins, *The Death of Rural England* (London: Routledge, 2003)

(Ed.) Trevor Johnson, *Edward Thomas on Thomas Hardy* (Cheltenham: The Cyder Press, 2002)

Edna Longley, *Poetry & Posterity* (Tarset, Northumberland: Bloodaxe Books, 2000); (ed.) *A Language Not to be Betrayed: Selected prose of Edward Thomas* (Manchester: Carcanet Press, 1981)*

John Lucas, *Starting to Explain: Essays on Twentieth Century British and Irish Poetry* (Nottingham: Trent Books, 2003)

Jay Parini, *Robert Frost: A Life* (New York: Owl Books, 1999)

Robert H. Ross, *The Georgian Revolt* (London: Faber & Faber, 1967)

(Ed.) Vincent Sherry, *The Cambridge Companion to the Literature of the First World War* (Cambridge: Cambridge University Press, 2005)

Stuart Sillars, *Structure and Dissolution in English Writing, 1910-1920* (Basingstoke: Palgrave Macmillan, 1999)

Sean Street, *The Dymock Poets* (Bridgend, Mid Glamorgan: Seren Books, 1994)

Theresa Whistler, *The Life of Walter de la Mare* (London: Duckworth, 1993)

*Note: Most reviews by Thomas, quoted in the Notes, can be found here.

INDEX OF TITLES

EDNA LONGLEY

Poetry & Posterity

Edna Longley's latest collection of critical essays marks a move back from Irish culture and politics to poetry itself as the critic's central concern. She considers how poets are read and received at different times and in different contexts, by academics as well as by a wider readership, and from Irish, English and American viewpoints. But her interest in the reception of poetry is still very much influenced by debates about literature and politics in a Northern Ireland context, and in the book's final essay she relates poetry to the "peace process".

In two of these essays, *The Poetics of Celt and Saxon* and *Pastoral Theologies*, she has some fun with mutual stereotypes (the Hughes or Heaney figure), and with English misreadings of Irish poetry and its cultural and intellectual environment, and Irish poets' frequent complicity in this situation. In other essays she discusses Edward Thomas and eco-centrism, the criticism of Louis MacNeice and Tom Paulin, and the poetry of Larkin and Auden. *Poetry & Posterity* follows Edna Longley's recently reissued *Poetry in the Wars*, her classic work on Ireland, poetry and war, and her much celebrated book, *The Living Stream: Literature & Revisionism in Ireland:*

'Unlike many books on modern poetry, this one has a powerful, disruptive case to make and a genuine *raison d'être*...a fiercely unrelenting and implacable critical intelligence at work'
– NEIL CORCORAN, *TLS*

'Combative, rigorously argued, passionate essays aimed at saving poetry from the politicians' – JOHN BANVILLE, *Sunday Independent*

ISBN 978 1 85224 435 4   £10.95   352 pages

Also available by Edna Longley from Bloodaxe:

Poetry in the Wars: A classic work on Ireland, poetry and war, with essays on Yeats, MacNeice, Frost, Edward Thomas, Keith Douglas, Heaney, Larkin, Mahon and Muldoon.
ISBN 978 0 906427 99 6   272 pages   £9.95

The Living Stream: Literature & Revisionism in Ireland: Longley investigates the links between Irish literature, culture and politics. Questioning the fixed purposes of both nationalism and unionism, she shows in particular where Northern Irish writing fits into this process of change.
ISBN 978 1 85224 217 6   304 pages   £10.95

THE Bloodaxe Book OF
20TH CENTURY POETRY

edited by EDNA LONGLEY

This epoch-marking anthology presents a map of poetry from Britain and Ireland which readers can follow. You will not get lost here as in other anthologies – with their vast lists of poets summoned up to serve a critic's argument or to illustrate a journalistic overview. Instead, Edna Longley shows you the key poets of the century, and through interlinking commentary points up the connections between them as well as their relationship with the continuing poetic traditions of these islands.

Edna Longley draws the poetic line of the century not through culture-defining groups but through the work of the most significant poets of our time. Because her guiding principle is aesthetic precision, the poems themselves answer to their circumstances. Readers will find this book exciting and risk-taking not because her selections are surprising but because of the intensity and critical rigour of her focus, and because the poems themselves are so good.

This is a vital anthology because the selection is so pared down. Edna Longley has omitted showy, noisy, ephemeral writers who drown out their contemporaries but leave later or wiser readers unimpressed. Similarly there is no place here for the poet as entertainer, cultural spokesman, feminist mythmaker or political commentator.

While anthologies survive, the idea of poetic tradition survives. An anthology as rich as Edna Longley's houses intricate conversations between poets and between poems, between the living and the dead, between the present and the future. It is a book which will enrich the reader's experience and understanding of modern poetry.

ISBN 978 1 85224 514 6   368 pages   £10.95